CADOGAN

Richard Lloyd Parry

Tokyo, Kyoto
& ancient Nara

D1007166

Cadogan Guides
West End House, 11 Hills Place,
London W1R 1AH, UK
becky.kendall@morrispub.co.uk

The Globe Pequot Press
6 Business Park Road, PO Box 833, Old Saybrook,
Connecticut 06475–0833

Copyright © Richard Lloyd Parry 1995, 1999
Updated by Edward Morris, 1999
Illustrations © Satoshi Kambayashi
Shrine architecture illustrations © Willaim Schenck

Book and cover design by Animage
Cover photographs (front and back) by Alex Lay
Maps © Cadogan Guides, drawn by Map Creation Ltd
Thanks to the Japan National Tourist Ofice for the Tokyo subway map.

Editorial Director: Vicki Ingle
Series Editor: Linda McQueen

Editing: Mary-Ann Gallagher
Indexing: Isobel McLean
Proofreading: Patrick Anderson
Production: Book Production Services

A catalogue record for this book is available from the British Library
ISBN 1–86011–917–4

Printed and bound in Italy by LEGOPRINT
Reprinted 2000

All rights reserved. No part of this publication may be reproduced, stored in a retrieval system, or transmitted, in any form or by any means, electronic or mechanical, including photocopying and recording, or by any information storage and retrieval system except as may be expressly permitted by the UK 1988 Copyright Design & Patents Act and the USA 1976 Copyright Act or in writing from the publisher. Requests for permission should be addressed to Cadogan Guides, West End House, 11 Hills Place, London W1R IAH, UK.

Please Note

The author and publishers have made every effort to ensure the accuracy of the information in the book at the time of going to press. However, they cannot accept any responsibility for any loss, injury or inconvenience resulting from the use of information contained in this guide.

About the Author

Richard Lloyd Parry first visited Japan in 1986 after winning a holiday on a television quiz show. He has been permanently based there since 1995, covering East Asia as the Tokyo correspondent of *The Independent* newspaper.

Acknowledgements

Like most people who spend time in Japan, I've encountered more kindness than I'll ever be able to repay or acknowledge: my sincere apologies to all those whose names I've missed or whose *meishi* I have mislaid.

This book's been a long time in the pipeline, and would never have come through at all without the generous assistance and help of several organisations. Nippon Travel Agency provided railcards, invaluable introductions and moral support: special thanks must go to Mr Yamaguchi in London, Isao Matsuzawa in Tokyo, Renato Pisa, and Jeremy Hale. Japan Airlines came up with the all important flights, thanks to Joe Brett in London and Geoffrey Tudor in Tokyo. Several generations of employees of the Japan National Tourist Organisation gave tireless answers to factual queries (and more railcards): in London I'm indebted to Simon Halewood, Patrick Wilson, Louise Hooper and Sian Evans; in Tokyo, to Messrs Tsukamoto and Nishikawa. Mr Hiro Takemura arranged a warm welcome courtesy of the Tōkyū Hotel Chain.

For hospitality in Japan, I salute Kathleen Morris and Jonathan Annells in Tokyo, Rupert Naylor in Okawa, Al Ruxton and St Catherine's College in Kōbe, Mark Coutts-Smith and the Kōdo Drummers in Sado, Andrew Allen in Bitchu-Takahashi, and Lesley Parkinson in Nagoya. For friendship, support and advice, thanks to Jim Bennett, Steve Clemons, Jim Davis, Guy Delauney, Dave Jones, Kaori Kawada, Akane and Mrs Kawakami, Terue Kojima and family, Mike and Henrietta Linsell, John Lyon, Yoshiko Magari, Tom McGeehan, Mark Gill, John Lyon, Nick Midgley, Hiroko Ofuchi, Megumi Omori, Andrew Oros, Rod Pryde, Robert Stern, Teruko Takahashi, Professor and Mrs Ryozo Tanaka and Ayako, Sachiko Tamashige, Take Tanioka and the Shinjuku Intellectuals, Tom La Tourette and Seto Inland Sea Lines, Aleks Weiler, Yuka Kunita, and Barry Webb. Steve Kremer and Dylan Tanner of Intermatrix advised me on the Business Section and much else, Robert Whitehouse and Kodansha International supplied books, and Hotei Tomoyasu and the IRC2 Corporation—especially Senji Kasuya, Ken Sugaya, Lennie Zakatek, and Victoria Hodgson—enabled me to see Japan like a rock star. And here's to Bob Holness, for making it all possible.

Thanks to my family for their love and support, and to my friends, particularly Alex, Julia, and Fiona, for living with this book (or the idea of it) over the years, and with the mood swings which it has from time to time provoked.

My greatest debt of thanks in Japan is to Miyoko Hayakawa and her family, especially Shinjiro, who were like a second family. Without their kindness and hospitality I could never have written this book or visited Japan so often and for so long.

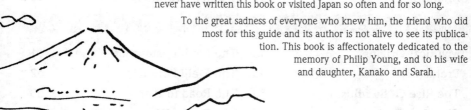

To the great sadness of everyone who knew him, the friend who did most for this guide and its author is not alive to see its publication. This book is affectionately dedicated to the memory of Philip Young, and to his wife and daughter, Kanako and Sarah.

About the Updater

Edward Morris is a writer and academic, currently based in New York.

Contents

It is a peculiarity of conversations about Japan that everyone you meet, no matter how scant their knowledge or experience, knows *exactly* what they think about the place. Japan (you will be told) is a bleeping, sci-fi wonderland of soaring skyscrapers and neon-lit streets, a country where people keep electronic eggs instead of pets, and where even the lavatories have control panels. Others will cherish images of misty mountains, *geisha* in kimono and rice paddies tended by old men in pointy hats. Each one of these observations is true, but none reflects more than a fraction of the whole picture. One of the best reasons for visiting Japan is simply to see what it's really like—one of the richest, most varied, and most underestimated of Asia's travel destinations. Japan combines the comfort, safety and convenience of Western Europe with

Introduction

the excitement and exoticism of Asia. In Japan you can mountain climb, whale-watch and island-hop. A few hours' travel will take you from world-class skiing to volcanic zones where you can be buried up to your neck in thermally heated sand. But the heart of the country is its cities, and particularly the three historic capitals which are the subject of this

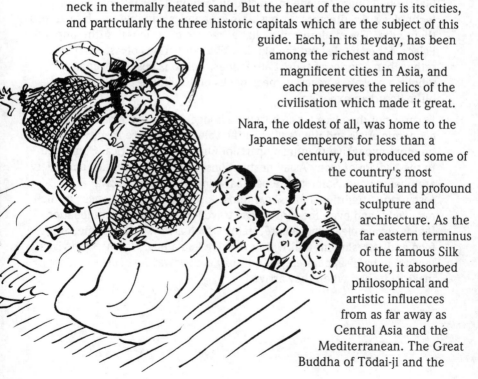

guide. Each, in its heyday, has been among the richest and most magnificent cities in Asia, and each preserves the relics of the civilisation which made it great.

Nara, the oldest of all, was home to the Japanese emperors for less than a century, but produced some of the country's most beautiful and profound sculpture and architecture. As the far eastern terminus of the famous Silk Route, it absorbed philosophical and artistic influences from as far away as Central Asia and the Mediterranean. The Great Buddha of Tōdai-ji and the

Gold Hall of Horyū-ji are, respectively, the largest bronze statue and the oldest wooden building in the world. Today, Nara's deer parks, gardens, clean air and small town atmosphere make it a refreshing escape from the tumult of the larger cities.

Kyoto, by contrast, was the imperial capital for eight centuries; during this period, the history of Kyoto was the history of Japan. The city's worship halls, palaces, villas, castles, treasure houses, and gardens are the finest of their kind anywhere. Some—like the Golden Pavilion and the famous Zen rock garden in Ryōan-ji—are emblems of Japan recognised all over the world, but the city also contains countless small, local shrines and temples off the tourist trail. Kyoto is one of the best places to experience the traditional aspects of Japanese culture, including *kabuki* and *noh* drama, *kaiseki* haute cuisine and the *ryokan* or traditional Japanese inn.

If its predecessors Nara and Kyoto are repositories of the ancient, then the present emperor's home, Tokyo, is a city of the future. The modern capital has the world's busiest railway station, most expensive property prices, most exquisite department stores, and the boldest and most bizarre buildings. Anyone interested in fashion, international cuisine, technology, architecture, or business economics will find much to absorb them here. The modern capital has attractive historic relics (the Imperial Palace, for example, and the old 'low city' attractions of Asakusa) but, rather than a series of tourist attractions, Tokyo is best enjoyed as a whole; a ceaseless, feverish megalopolis of 30 million people, the ultimate urban experience.

Japan is not the place for a shoestring budget holiday, but since the Asian economic crisis and the decline in the value of the once mighty yen, it is no more expensive than many parts of Europe and America. Compared to the bedlam of many Asian destinations, standards of service and safety are unsurpassed. Some of the best bargains—the cosy *izakaya* restaurants, traditional *minshuku* inns—are cultural experiences in their own right, and even the most frugal traveller will find accommodation that is always clean and secure, trains which always run on time, and food and refreshment that will never give you a bug. No one who visits Japan will be disappointed, even if they come away less sure what to make of it than when they arrived.

Travel

By Air

Japan is comprehensively connected by air to most of the major cities of Europe, Asia, Oceania and North America, almost all of which have direct non-stop flights. The days of the 18-hour haul over the North Pole from London to Tokyo, with the obligatory stop at Anchorage Airport, are past; nowadays, with favourable weather, it takes little more than 11 hours from London and a little less than 14 hours from New York.

Remember that if you plan to conduct most of your sightseeing or business in the Kansai area (Ōsaka, Kyoto, Nara), you will save time and money by flying to the **Kansai International Airport** in Ōsaka rather than to Tokyo's inconvenient **Narita**. If Tokyo is your destination, investigate the possibility of flying in by **China Airlines**, especially if you're coming from Asia. They remain the only carrier still flying into the old (and much handier) Tokyo airport, **Haneda**, a mere taxi or monorail ride from the centre of Tokyo.

From the UK

British Airways, Virgin, Japan Airlines and All Nippon Airways fly non-stop from Heathrow to Narita. Japan Airlines and All Nippon Airways also fly non-stop from Heathrow to Kansai airport. The advanced purchase PEX fare (from two weeks to three months; no option to change your flight) is about £1,000 off peak, but this is considerably reduced when bought through an agent.

It's cheaper—but more time-consuming—to take an indirect flight. Numerous national carriers will fly you from London to the home capital, and from there to Japan. Among the more respectable carriers are KLM (via Amsterdam), Finnair (via Helsinki), and Scandinavia Airlines, all quoted at a little more than £600. Cheaper still are Airlanka, and the budget traveller's favourite, recently tarnished by a poor safety record, Aeroflot. Bucket shops (look in the classified ads of a Sunday newspaper or a magazine like *Time Out*) are cheapest of all: several quote return fares for under £600.

From the USA

Most American airlines now serve both Narita and Kansai, as does Japan Airlines, All Nippon, and many other international airlines. Prices vary according to season, but generally the advanced purchase PEX fares range from about $1300 in the winter to over $2000 in the summer. However, it is always a good idea to shop around. You can often find surprisingly great deals through 'consolidators', which specialize in selling blocks of unsold tickets from airlines. Among the several firms that specialize in tickets to Japan are Pacifico Creative Service (℃ 213 239 2424 in Los Angeles, ℃ 202 833 3531 in Washington DC, ℃ 713 65 1933 in Houston), Creative Marketing Management (℃ 212 557 1530 in New York), Overseas Tours (℃ 800 631 2824) and Chisholm Travel (℃ 800 631 2824). Prices as low $630 are not unheard of, but expect something closer to $800 or $900.

From Canada

From Toronto and Vancouver you can fly to Narita and Kansai; Calgary connects with Narita only.

From Europe

The following cities connect directly with Narita only: Athens, Brussels, Geneva, Madrid, Munich, Rome and Stockholm.

From Paris, Frankfurt, Helsinki, Milan, Moscow and Vienna, you can fly to Narita, Kansai and Nagoya.

From Australia and New Zealand

Darwin, Melbourne and Perth connect directly with Narita only; Sydney, Auckland Cairns, Brisbane and Christchurch connect with Narita and Kansai.

From Asia

Most Asian capitals, apart from obvious political mavericks like Pyongyang in North Korea, have direct flights to Narita and Kansai, and often the regional airports too.

airlines in Japan

British Airways, ✆ 03 3593 8811.

Virgin Atlantic Airways, ✆ 03 3499 8835.

Japan Airlines, ✆ 0120 25 5971 (toll free).

All Nippon Airways, ✆ 0120 029 222 (toll free).

Northwest Airlines, ✆ 06 6228 0747.

United Airlines, ✆ 03 3817 4411.

By Sea

A few cruise companies offer fly and sail packages: jet out from Europe or North America and begin your cruise in Asia.

Orient Lines runs a 22-day China and Japan holiday, including a 14-day cruise, from £2950. They can be contacted at 38 Park Street, London W1Y 3PF, ✆ 020 7409 7500/2500; or, in the USA, 1510 SE 17th Street, Fort Lauderdale, FL 33316, ✆ 305 527 6660.

For other cruises inquire at your nearest Japanese National Tourist Office (JNTO). In New York they can be contacted at One Rockefeller Plaza, Suite 1250, New York, NY 10020, ✆ 212 757 5640; in London, at Heathcoat House, 20 Saville Row, London, W1X 1AE, ✆ 020 7734 9638.

ferries

Various ferry services connect Japan with mainland Asia and Russia. Among the more useful are: the Vladivostok to Niigata service (one way fares begin at ¥43,780); and the ferry (¥8500) and jetfoil (¥12,400) which connect Fukuoka (Hakata) and Pusan in Korea.

Other possibilities include: Tianjin to Kōbe, Shanghai to Kōbe, Ōsaka or Yokohama, Pusan to Shimonoseki, Kōbe or Ōsaka, and Naha (in Okinawa) to Kaohsiung or Keelung. Again, contact your nearest Japanese National Tourist Office (JNTO) *see* p.6.

You can't go all the way of course, but from Moscow it's possible to take the Trans-Siberian railway as far as Vladivostok and then take a ferry. Agencies which specialize in the Trans-Siberian include:

In the UK
Intourist Travel, Intourist House, 219 Marsh Wall, London, E14 9FJ, ✆ 020 7538 8600.

In Japan
Japan-Russia Tourist Bureau, Head Office, Kamiyachō Bldg, 3F, 12–12 Toranomon 5-chome, Minato-ku, Tokyo, ✆ 03 3432 6161.

STA Travel, Head Office, 4F Nukariya Bldg, 1–16 Minami Ikebukuro, Toshima-ku, Tokyo, ✆ 03 5391 2889.

In Australia
Gateway Travel Pty. Ltd., 48 The Boulevard, Strathfield NSW 2135, ✆ 02 9745 3333, ✉ 02 9745 3237; get an agent or member of the sales staff at *agent@russian-gateway.com.au*, or information at *info@russian-gateway.com.au*.

In the USA
White Nights, 610 La Sierra Drive, Sacramento, CA 95864, ✆/✉ 916 979 9381, *wnights@concourse.net.*

Package and Specialist Holidays

Package holidays to Japan are proliferating and, for those with limited time, or anxieties about getting by in a non-English speaking country, they offer convenience and good value. But weigh up the pros and cons. Package tours are still in their relative infancy, and operators tend to turn their customers over to English-speaking Japanese guides who may offer a rather bland interpretation of their own country: unimaginative itineraries, characterless Western-style hotels and inane non-stop commentary. Tours offered one year may not always be repeated the next, so you should check details. Among the most interesting are the following:

in the UK

Nippon Travel Agency, ✆ 020 7437 2424, Academy House, 161–167 Oxford Street, (entrance on Poland Street), London,W1R 1TA, offers a number of imaginative deals and individual itineraries. For independent travellers there's a Discover Japan package which includes a return flight from London to Narita on ANA, a 7-day Japan Rail Pass, and your first night's accommodation in Tokyo, Kyoto or Ōsaka. In the USA they can be contacted at Suite 901, 120 W. 45th Street, New York, NY 10036, ✆ 212 944 8660.

The Japan Experience is the only British operator to publish a brochure dedicated to Japan. Packages include the main cities, and two-country tours which take in Bali, Hong Kong, Singapore or Bangkok. Individual itineraries are also arranged. Kingfisher House, Rownhams Lane, North Baddesley, Hampshire, SO52 9LP, ✆ 01703 730830.

Creative Tours Ltd (run by Japan Airlines) runs specialist tours. Recent brochures have included a bonsai tour and a cycling tour, visiting out of the way places and staying in simple *minshuku (see p..* 2nd Floor, 1 Tenterden Street, London W1R 9AH, ✆ 020 7495 1775.

British Museum Tours, ✆ 020 7323 8895, organize occasional cultural holidays.

Other companies offering tours including (or based exclusively in) Japan include:

Airwaves, 10 Bective Place, London SW15 2PZ, ✆ 020 8875 1188.

The Asia Experience, 83 Mortimer Street, London N1 7TB, ✆ 020 7636 4343.

Asia World, 230 Station Road, Addlestone, Surrey KT15 2PH, ✆ 01932 820050.

Finlandia, Regent Street, London W1R 8PD, ✆ 020 7409 7334.

Jasmin Tours, High Street, Cookham, Maidenhead, Berkshire SL6 9SQ, ✆ 01628 531121.

Kuoni Travel, Kuoni House, Dorking, Surrey RH5 4AZ, ✆ 01306 740719.

Premier Holidays, Westbrook, Milton Road, Cambridge CB4 1YQ, ✆ 01223 311103.

Silverbird, 4 Northfield Prospect, Putney Bridge Road, London SW18, ✆ 020 8875 9090.

Speedbird Worldwide (British Airways), Pacific House, Hazelwick Avenue, Three Bridges, Sussex RH10 1NP, ✆ 020 8741 3369.

Virgin Holidays, Ground Floor, The Galleria, Station Road, Crawley, West Sussex RH10 1WW, ✆ 01293 617181.

in the USA

Pacifico Creative Service, Inc., ✆ 800 221 1081 in Los Angeles and ✆ 888 727 8785 in New York, offers a range of relatively inexpensive airfare and tour packages in Tokyo and Kyoto. Prices for a seven-day itinerary start at $860.

Pacific Bestour, ✆ 800 688 3288, *www.bestour.com*, also offers airfare and tour packages at bargain rates. Many of their plans include Hakone, a hot spring resort town in the shadow of Mt. Fuji.

TBI Tours/General Tours, ✆ 800 233 0266, *www.generaltours.com*, features China-Japan combination tours and also has Tokyo and Kyoto packages at modest rates.

Espirit Travel, ✆ 800 377 7481, *www.espirittravel.com*, offers an in-depth tour walking tour of Kyoto and an interesting 'Art Tour of Japan: Two Great Cities' package featuring art highlights in Tokyo and Kyoto.

At Last the Best! Custom Travel, ✆ 800 445 8857, *http://atlastthebest.com*, offers a tour of Kyoto and Nara called 'Ancient Kyoto, the Artisans Way'.

Other companies providing tours of Tokyo, Kyoto and Nara include:

Absolute Asia, 180 Varick Street, New York, NY 10014, ✆ 800 736 8187, *info@absoluteasia.com*.

FultonEX, 106 Fulton Street, 3rd Floor, New York, NY 10038, ℂ 800 345 1888, *www.1888online.com*, *travel@fultonex.com*.

Japan & Orient, 4025 Camino Del Rio South, Suite 3200, San Diego, CA 92108, ℂ 800 377 1080.

Kirby Tours, 2451 S. Telegraph, Dearborn, MI 48124, ℂ 800 521 0711, *kirby@kirbytours.com*.

Northwest World Vactaions/MLT Vacations, 5130 County Road 101, Minnetonka, MN 55435, ℂ 507 281 3490.

Orient Flexi-Pax Tours, 630 Third Avenue, New York, NY 10017, ℂ 800 545 5540, *www.isram/ofpt.com*.

Pacific Protour, 139 Kinderamack Rd., Park Ridge, NJ 07656, ℂ 800 PRO 8882 or ℂ 201 768 8896, *www.pacificprotour.com*.

Visits Plus Inc, 27 William Street, Suite 728, New York, NY 10005, ℂ 800 321 3235, *www.visitplus.com*.

Travel Agents

Two of the biggest Japanese agents are **Nippon Travel Agency** (NTA) and **Japan Travel Bureau** (JTB). They have thousands of branches throughout Japan, with English-speaking staff in the big cities. The foreign branches listed below are all authorized sales outlets for the Japan Rail Pass.

Nippon Travel Agency (known in Japan as *Nihon Ryōko*)

Japan: Foreign Tourist Department, 3rd Floor, Shimbashi Ekimae Building 1, 2–20–15 Shimbashi, Minato-ku, Tokyo 105, ℂ 03 3572 8743, ✆ 03 3572 8766.

UK: Academy House, 161–167 Oxford Street, London W1R 1TA, ℂ 020 7437 2424, ✆ 020 7437 2954.

USA: 120 W. 45th Street, New York, NY 10036, ℂ 212 944 8660, ✆ 212 944 8973; 3 Twin Dolphin Drive, Suite 100, Redwood City, CA 94065, ℂ 415 508 2077, ✆ 415 591 7634.

Canada: 1075 W. Georgia Street, Suite 2600, Vancouver, BC V6E 3C9, ℂ 604 662 8002, ✆ 604 688 4767.

Australia: Level 9, 135 King Street, Sydney, 2000 NSW, ℂ 02 221 8433, ✆ 02 223 8907.

Japan Travel Bureau

Japan: International Travel Division, 1–13–1 Nihonbashi, Chūō-ku, Tokyo 103–0027, ℂ 03 3276 7803, ✆ 03 3271 4134.

UK: 3rd Floor, 10 Maltravers Street, London WC2R 3EE, ℂ 0171 836 9367, ✆ 020 7240 8147.

USA: 11th Floor, Equitable Tower, 787 7th Avenue, New York, NY 10019, ℂ 212 246 8030, ✆ 212 246 5607.

Canada: Suite 2300, Four Bentall Centre, PO Box 49317, 1055 Dunsmuir Street, Vancouver, BC V7X 1L3, ℂ 604 688 0166, ✆ 604 669 5849.

Australia: 46th Level, Nauru House, 80 Collins Street, Melbourne, Victoria, 3000, ℂ 03 9650 6088, ✆ 03 9650 6450.

Entry Formalities

You must have a passport valid for the duration of your stay and you must have a visa. If you're going to earn Japanese currency during your stay you're required to have a working visa. There are various different types and the process of applying for them can be complicated and time-consuming. Consult your nearest Japanese embassy or consulate as far in advance as possible.

Tourists and anyone studying or doing business in the short term (usually less than three months) only need a temporary visitor's visa. Almost everyone can get one of these stamped in their passports as they pass Immigration in Japan.

Citizens of Austria, Germany, Ireland, Liechtenstein, Mexico, Switzerland and the UK will get a 90-day stamp which they can later extend for another three months. To get an extension you'll need to fill out a form, supply photographs, pay a fee, and satisfy the immigration office that you're not illicitly working.

Travellers of many other nationalities, including those from Belgium, Canada, Denmark, Finland, France, Greece, Italy, Luxembourg, the Netherlands, New Zealand, Norway, Portugal, Spain, Sweden and the USA, will get a three-month stamp which can't be extended (you must leave the country and then re-enter).

Everyone else must obtain a visa before entering Japan. A temporary visitor's visa usually takes only a few days. Australia is the most notable country to lack a visa exemption agreement. However, Australian, New Zealand and Canadian nationals aged 18 to 25 are eligible for working holiday visas, extendable up to 18 months (the age limits and duration may change from time to time). Contact your local consulate or the **Japan Association for Working Holiday Makers,** ℂ 03 3389 0181, *www.mmjp.or.jp/jawhm.*

Getting Around

By Air

All Japan's significant cities have airports, well served by several domestic carriers. The fares are close to those of the *shinkansen* (bullet train), so if you need to get round fast and haven't got a railcard, it's almost as cheap to fly as to go by bullet train. This is especially true when travelling outside Honshū. Note, however, that on short to medium length journeys the time taken up by travelling out to the airport, and travelling back into town at the other end, may tip the balance back in the *shinkansen's* favour.

By Sea

Ferry services connect all the inhabited islands of Japan and can be a reasonable alternative to train travel. However, there is no service that connects Tokyo to a port on the main island in the Kansai area.

The quickest, most comfortable and most convenient means of getting from one place to another will usually be the train. Since 1872, when British engineers laid the 27km stretch between Tokyo and Yokohama, 26,500km of track have been constructed, from Wakkanai in northern Hokkaidō to Yamagawa in southern Kyūshū. Of these, 13,000km belong to Japan Railways, the former nationalized corporation, privatized in 1987 into seven regional networks. The rest are operated by 14 smaller private companies, like Kintetsu, who tend to operate in busy commuter and resort areas; their trains are often cheaper and faster than the loss-making JR which dutifully serves the unprofitable, outlying regions. You could spend weeks travelling in Japan, using nothing but the trains. They are unfailingly clean, spacious, punctual and safe and, in the shape of the Japan Rail Pass (*see* p.9), they represent one of Japan's few authentic travel bargains.

timetables

JNTO publishes an abridged railway timetable in English, adequate for most purposes: it includes JR *shinkansen* and limited express times, a few of the major private lines, along with fare and mileage tables. If you need more up-to-date detail, look out for the bilingual *JTB Speed Jikokuhyō* (¥330), sold in big stations, bookshops and travel agencies. Any tourist information centre will supply you with fare and timetable information, or call JNTO's Japan Travel Phone, ✆ 03 3201 3331.

tickets and reservations

Even in out of the way places, all station employees can be coaxed into a few words of English. The facts you need to convey are: where you are travelling from and to, and what kind of train you wish to travel on. If you are making a seat reservation, state the date and time of your journey and whether you want a smoking or non-smoking compartment. If simple spoken English fails, then write the details out in capitals on a piece of paper. Ideally, have someone write your ticket request out in Japanese.

Most tickets are sold through automatic dispensing machines. Insert coins, notes or a pre-paid card, press the button corresponding to your destination, and tickets and change are dispensed automatically. Diagrams of the network, indicating the fare to each station, are generally displayed above the ticket machines; however, these seldom include much English. Ask station staff or passers-by for help.

Travel agents like NTA and JTB sell tickets for express trains, and big stations have travel centres where you can also pay by credit card. Otherwise expect to pay in cash. Unused tickets which are still valid can be refunded, minus a handling charge.

Guriin-sha (Green Cars) are first-class coaches, correspondingly more expensive: more leg room, comfier seats and a better class of punter. Second class is *futsū-sha* (Ordinary Car).

Certain trains become very crowded on weekends and holidays, even the *shinkansen*. Sitting on your luggage for hours at a time is no fun so, if in doubt, make a reservation (*yoyaku*) which only adds a few hundred yen to the fare. Useful vocabulary: reserved seat is *shiteiseki* (pronounced 'shtay-secky'); unreserved seat, *jiyūseki* ('gee-you-secky'); non-smoking car, *kin-en-sha*.

Trains of different speeds often depart from the same platform; you can waste time by getting on the wrong one, so be prepared to ask station staff and fellow passengers. **Futsū** is a local train, stopping at every station. **Kaisoku**, usually translated as rapid train, is a bit faster, stopping at fewer stations. These are aimed at commuters and rarely have reserved carriages. **Kyūkō** is an express, **tokkyū** is the faster limited express. The quicker the train, the more expensive and comfortable the journey.

The famous bullet train (no one in Japan calls it that; get used to saying **shinkansen**, 'new trunk line') is no longer the fastest super express in the world, but it's certainly the oldest, the most famous and the most comprehensive. The Tōkaidō line between Tokyo and Ōsaka opened for the Tokyo Olympics in 1964. Since then the network has been extended to Fukuoka in the southwest, Niigata in the north, and Yamagata and Morioka in the northeast. The *shinkansen* is one of the reasons why Japan sometimes seems a small country. On the fastest *nozomi* service, the 1700km journey from Kyūshū to northern Tōhoku takes about nine hours.

In 30 years of high-speed travel there hasn't been a single fatality. The trains run so smoothly in fact that, once the novelty of moving at up to 220km/h has worn off, it can actually be rather a dull experience, with more of the blandness of the international flight than the romance of the railway. Bowing hostesses dispense snacks and drinks, chimes and taped voices politely announce each station as it approaches. Stations and scenery belt by, but so silently and frictionlessly that they could almost be on video: aficionados of smoke and grime and clanking points will be disappointed. But for ease, speed and security, it's unmatched: everyone, especially holders of the Japan Rail Pass, should use the *shinkansen* as much as possible.

If you haven't got a pass, it's expensive, almost as much as a domestic flight. Fares are based on the standard price, with a fat surcharge on top of that—there's a price list in the JNTO railway timetable. Not all *shinkansen* stop at every station: check with the conductor that you're getting on the right one. The *nozomi*, which began in 1993, is the fastest and most expensive of all: all seats are reserved, and the Japan Rail Pass can't be used.

If you're getting on at the first station, the chances are that you'll find an unreserved seat. Otherwise, reservations cost ¥500, free to rail pass holders.

Japan Rail Pass

This is essential for almost anyone planning to travel extensively around Japan. It allows unlimited travel on most JR services, including ferries and buses, for a fixed period of time.

	Ordinary	Green
7 days	¥28,300	¥37,800
14 days	¥45,100	¥61,200
21 days	¥57,700	¥79,600

Children aged 6 to 11 pay half the adult price.

At first glance this may not look cheap at all, and a little arithmetic may be necessary to work out whether the pass will save you money. On local and ordinary express trains you would have to travel a very long way in a short time to make it worthwhile. In general, visitors staying in a single region or city of Japan will be better off buying individual tickets—in areas like Kansai, for instance, the non-JR lines (on which you can't use the pass) are quick and cheap.

The pass comes into its own, however, on the *shinkansen*. A return from Tokyo to Kyoto, with reservations, costs ¥25,940—only ¥1,860 less than a rail pass for the whole week. Add to these the cost of ordinary trains, the convenience of not having to buy tickets in advance (and being able to break your journey at any point), and the advantages become clear. Rail pass holders can also make reservations for nothing, although you must do this in person and in advance.

The Japan Rail Pass can only be obtained outside Japan.

Buy one *before* you go. You can do this only at authorized agencies, like Nippon Travel Agency and Japan Travel Bureau (your nearest branch of JNTO will have a list). Pay in your own currency; in return you receive an exchange order which is valid for three months from the date of issue. This is exchanged for the pass itself at any JR Travel Service Centre. These are found only in the following stations:

In Tokyo: Narita Airport, Ueno, Ikebukuro, Shinjuku, Shibuya and Tokyo Station.

In Kansai: Kansai Airport, Kyoto, Ōsaka and Shin-Ōsaka.

You must state the day you want the pass to begin, and show your passport. It is possible to exchange it when you arrive at the airport—it can be used immediately to take you into Tokyo or Osaka proper. The Japan Rail Pass is available *only* to those with temporary visitor visas.

other discount passes and tickets

Those just travelling in the Kansai area (Ōsaka, Kyoto, Nara) should look into the JR West Rail Pass. Although you can not use the shinkansen with this pass, you can get a JR train from Kansai Airport, use JR's train lines within Osaka, including the handy Osaka Loop Line and travel to Kyoto and Nara. Notable sights outside the cities such as Hōryūji and Uji are also in reach. A four day pass is ¥6,000, a one day pass is ¥2,000 (children are half price), and unlike the nationwide Japan Rail Pass it can be purchased in Japan.

The *sei-shun jū-hachi kippu* (Youth 18 Ticket) is probably the cheapest way of getting round Japan, but very, very slow. They're designed for vacationing students and other impecunious types, and can only be used during the following periods: 1 Mar–10 April, 20 July–10 Sept, 10 Dec–20 Jan. The tickets are sold in booklets of five; each booklet costs ¥11,500, and they can be split up and used by different people (tickets are often sold individually on student campuses).

On the day of travel, the date is marked on the ticket. For the rest of the day, until midnight, you can travel anywhere in Japan—but only on local (*futsū*) or rapid (*kaisoku*) trains. Thus, if you started early enough, it would theoretically be possible to travel from Tokyo to Hiroshima for ¥2,300—but you would have to stop at virtually every station in between. Journeys can be broken at any time. Unused tickets can be refunded, minus a ¥210 handling charge.

By Bus

City buses take a little getting used to: timetables, destination panels and on-board announcements are almost never in English, and drivers speak only Japanese. Where relevant, specific bus routes are mentioned in the text; otherwise, seek local guidance from the nearest tourist information centre.

Inter-city buses are economical. They often depart at night, so you save not only on the fare (generally a third cheaper than the *shinkansen*), but also one night's accommodation. A few examples, all one-way fares from Tokyo:

Kyoto	8 hrs	¥8,030
Ōsaka	8 hrs	¥8,180
Nara	9½ hrs	¥8,400

There are many different bus companies; again, ask a tourist information centre for details.

By Car

With such a choice of superlative trains, few short-term visitors to Japan will ever need to drive. Outside the urban tangle, driving is fairly straightforward. Japanese motorists are generally cautious and polite, signposts on main roads are widely labelled in the Roman alphabet (*rōmaji*), and petrol costs about the same as in Europe.

The Japanese, like the British and Australians, drive on the left. Standard international rules of the road and signposting conventions apply. To drive in Japan you must have an International Driving Permit *and* your own national driving licence, but this arrangement only holds for six months—after that you must apply for a Japanese licence. Ask your national automobile asociation whether they have a reciprocal arrangement with an equivalent Japanese body—the chances are they'll be affiliated with the **Japan Automobile Federation** which issues an English-language booklet called *Rules of the Road* for ¥1860. English speaking staff can answer questions at © 03 5926 9755. Various English road atlases are available in book shops: try to get a bilingual one so that you have a chance of recognizing the *kanji* characters even when the signposts are not Romanized.

Most roads have a **speed limit** of 50 km/h, although whether the traffic will permit you to go that fast is another matter. Expressways, which traverse all of the main islands, have a legal limit of 80 km/h. These are toll roads, and the tolls mount up: to drive from Tokyo to Ōsaka costs ¥10,000—not much less than a single ticket on the *shinkansen*.

The **police** are a discreet presence on the roads. Speed traps are mounted from time to time—the only sure way to avoid them is not to break the limit. If you're stopped for a minor offence, then profuse apologies and an inability to speak Japanese will often forestall anything stronger than a ticking off. Remember that, as well as your driving documents, you must carry your passport with you at all times.

car hire

For regional excursions, the most sensible thing is to take a train to the nearest town and hire a car there. 250 JR stations have their own **Eki Rent-a-car** offices. For English-speaking rental offices in Tokyo *see* p.119.

By Bicycle

This is a very pleasant and popular way of exploring both the countryside and the smaller cities. In bicycle-friendly towns, hire shops can usually be found near the railway station. Youth hostels often rent out their own. These bikes are basic, usually gearless, and rather small, but adequate for a few hours of sightseeing.

The small size of Japanese frames is more of a problem when you're planning to cycle long distances or over steep country. Multi-gear touring and mountain bikes in large sizes are hard to get hold of in Japan. If possible, bring your own: most airlines will carry them for you if you remove the pedals. The cheap and comprehensive delivery services (*see* 'Post', p.37) make it very easy to send your bike around Japan. Bikes are allowed on trains for a few hundred yen, but must be transported in carrying cases—invest in one of these. Get hold of a bilingual road atlas, too, and plan your routes in advance. The secret of happy cycling is to keep clear of the main routes, with their snarl-ups and tunnels: even if the traffic doesn't bring you to a stop, the gathering fumes are very unpleasant.

Repair and maintenance shops can be found all over the country, although spare parts for unfamiliar models (like mountain bikes) may be hard to get hold of outside the cities: bring a spare tyre if your wheels are large.

Despite Japan's enviably low crime rate, bike theft is common: carry a good padlock and use it. Cyclists should be doubly careful to carry their passports with them at all times, and some kind of proof that the bike isn't stolen.

The **Bridgestone Cycle Co Ltd** sells big frames and has an English-speaking overseas department in Tokyo, ℂ 03 3274 3411.

Hitch-hiking

Japanese people almost never hitch-hike, but for foreigners it's a nice way of travelling for nothing, and meeting the natives. Hitchers tend to fall victim to heartbreaking acts of kindness: stories abound of travellers being entertained and put up for the night by their lifts, or disembarking to find gifts of money tucked into little envelopes in their luggage. You'll feel less sheepish about this if you carry round a stock of token gifts—sweets, cigarettes, postcards from home.

Lifts aren't hard to come by, but you'll increase your chances by looking respectable and cheerful, and by holding out a card bearing the name of your destination in Japanese or, failing that, clear Roman capitals. Wave and smile rather than sticking out a thumb. Japan is a safe country, but it is never advisable for a woman to hitch-hike on her own.

Practical A–Z

Addresses and Directions

With the exception of major thoroughfares, and a handful of cities built on a grid, like Kyoto and Sapporo, streets in Japan do not have names, and houses and buildings do not have individual or consecutive numbers. Postal addresses identify two-dimensional plots of land, like British post codes; with one of these, and a detailed map, you can narrow your search down to an area of a few hundred metres. But, unless you know the location of every individual building and household, you could spend hours plodding fruitlessly round the neighbourhood checking each name-plate and building name.

Everyone gets flummoxed once in a while by this Byzantine system, not just foreigners, and coping with it has become a way of life. Try to phone ahead for clear directions in Japanese as well as English, so you can show them to passers-by if you get lost (if necessary, have your hotel phone and do this on your behalf). Many establishments have a printed map of how to reach them, which they will post or fax. Often this will be found on the back of their business card: if you might want to find a place again, pick up one of these before you leave.

Get into the habit of noticing landmarks (police boxes, convenience stores, unusual buildings) as you walk around: these will enable you to retrace your steps on a return visit. Stop passers-by or ask in police boxes, local shops or hotels. Pronounce your destination clearly, write it down (point to the Japanese words in this book if necessary, and remember that everyone can read the Roman alphabet).

Don't be embarrassed to keep phoning until you have reached your destination. Call before you leave, call from the station, and call again if you are still lost. This will not raise eyebrows. Even the smallest restaurant or inn will often send someone out to meet you.

Allow time for getting lost.

Baths and Hot Springs

From Shinto ceremonies to the white gloves worn by subway drivers and shop assistants, rituals of purification and symbolic cleansing pervade Japanese society. Not surprisingly, bathing is about much more than simply removing the day's grime. Springs of geothermally heated water (*onsen*) occur naturally all over Japan's volcanic archipelago: for centuries people have bathed in them—on mountains, in caves, in the snow—for their medicinal, erotic and relaxing properties.

The biggest difference between the Western and Japanese idea of a bath is that, in the latter, you don't do any washing at all. Soaping, scrubbing and rinsing of limbs and hair is performed outside the bath. Only when you are thoroughly clean do you enter the water to soak and relax and, as a result, the water is fit to be used by several people.

Baths, bathrooms and bath houses come in all shapes and sizes, but the standard arrangement consists of an outer room where you undress completely, leaving clothes and possessions in a basket or locker. Beyond here is the bath room itself (toilets are almost always housed separately), consisting of the tub, and a tiled and sluiced washing area.

There will be shower taps on the wall, low set mirrors and low stools on which you sit to douse yourself with water, and wash with soap, before rinsing off thoroughly. Buckets can be used to scoop up water from the tub to pour over yourself. You must be squeaky clean, and suds free, before moving onto the next stage.

The worst thing you can do is to get into the bath still dirty or soapy—in bath tubs made of cypress (the most expensive and desirable kind) the soap can stain and mar the wood. Individual tubs are deep, and you immerse yourself up to your neck. The temperature is often high, but don't cool it unless you are the last person in the tub. Soak for as long as you like, or until someone knocks on the door. In public baths (*sentō* and *onsen*), patrons often lounge around for hours, dipping in and out of baths of different temperatures and mineral contents, gossiping, preening and dozing.

It's common to make use of a little hand-towel for scrubbing and scouring. In public facilities, bathers who are uncomfortable about nudity can hold or dangle this above their private parts. These towels should never be taken into the bath itself, although bathers often sit with them folded on their heads, which is said to allay the wooziness induced by the high temperature. It can be very hot indeed, and feels wonderful afterwards. Move as little as possible once you are in, and you will feel the heat less.

Books and Media

Since the 'rediscovery' of Japan in the 19th century, libraries of **books** have been written on almost every aspect of Japanese culture, although high street book shops usually have only a small selection. Try the following specialists:

In the UK:

Japan Centre, 221 Piccadilly, London W1V 9LD, ✆ 020 7439 8035.

Fine Books Oriental, 38 Museum Street, London WC1B 3PA, ✆ 020 7242 5288, 🖷 020 7242 5344.

In the USA:

Kinokuniya, 10 W. 49th Street, New York, NY 10020, ✆ 212 765 1461.

Kinokuniya, Japan Center, 1581 Webster Street, San Francisco, CA 94115, ✆ 415 567 7625.

Kinokuniya, New Ōtani Store, 110 S. Onizuka Street, Los Angeles, CA 90012, ✆ 213 687 4480.

In Japan most big book shops stock at least a shelf of English-language books, although these may consist largely of dictionaries and abridgements of classics for Japanese students. The nationwide chains Maruzen and Kinokuniya are big importers of books with whole floors of foreign titles in their major stores, but their mark-ups are enormous: for everyday holiday reading, bring your own. Languages other than English are poorly represented.

In Tokyo, the Kanda-Jimbochō area is famous for its second-hand book shops, some of which specialize in foreign material.

The Japanese are voracious devourers of **newspapers** (*shimbun*), and the national dailies have the highest circulations of any in the world. Several of them also publish English-language editions, a digest of translated reports, syndicated news, and writing by foreign residents. Look out for the *Mainichi Daily News*, the *Daily Yomiuri*, the *Asahi Evening News* and, biggest and oldest of them all, the independent *Japan Times*. Like their parent organs, they tend towards the bland and colourless, although the *Mainichi* and the *Yomiuri* have some lively columnists. The *Nikkei Weekly* is a digest of translated financial news from the respected *Nikkei Shimbun*. The *International Herald Tribune*, *Asian Wall Street Journal* and *Financial Times* also publish in Japan, and can be found in Tokyo and Ōsaka, and in big book shops. In the big cities you might track down airmail copies of imported papers, at a big mark-up. *Time* and *Newsweek* are the most widely available English language **magazines**. Of the many domestic publications produced by foreigners *Tokyo Classified* and *Kansai Time Out* are the liveliest and best, with features, comment and useful listings of events for their respective regions.

NHK **television** has a nightly bilingual news, available on special sets in some hotels; certain international films can also be listened to in their original undubbed version—consult the English language press for details of these. The bigger hotels often carry CNN.

Bilingual (part-Japanese, part-English) commentary is fashionable on FM **radio** stations, like Tokyo's J-Wave. The only exclusively English channel is the American military's moronic Far Eastern Network (FEN).

Budgeting

Fear of the expense, more than anything else, puts people off visiting Japan. It's never going to be a bargain place to go on holiday. Principally because of the cost of permanent accommodation, Tokyo and Ōsaka consistently come out as number one and number two on a businessperson's index of the most expensive cities in the world. By the standards of the rest of southeast Asia, Japan is pricey: you could live for several days in India or Thailand for the cost of a half-hour taxi ride in Tokyo.

But this is the wrong standard to apply. Japan is the second richest country in the world, and it offers comforts and standards undreamed of in developing nations. Top hotels in Tokyo are no more expensive than their counterparts in London or New York, and, in terms of quality for cost, day-to-day eating is cheaper than in many European cities. Scandinavia and Switzerland are expensive countries, too, but travellers happily visit them. Japan does not deserve its unique reputation as a financial black hole. You will not save money by coming here; but there is no reason why, with a little cunning and fore-thought, you should haemorrhage it either.

Tips for Saving Money

Japan's problem is that it lacks obvious bargains to offset the stories of staggering excess that everyone's heard about (£100 melons, £6 cups of coffee, etc.). Things are either a regular price, or they are expensive. Here are a few suggestions for saving yen.

Japan has one authentic bargain: the Japan Rail Pass. If you're going to do any substantial travelling then you must buy one—*before* you leave your own country (see p.9).

If you don't have a pass, or on private lines where it cannot be used, be aware of the difference between various classes of train. For every express which gets you there in no time and costs a fortune, there will probably be a number of slower, cheaper services, from the *tokkyū* (limited express) down to the self-explanatory *kaku eki teisha* (every station stopping train).

On long inter-city journeys, travellers without rail passes should investigate the possibilities of overnight buses. Not only are these cheaper than the equivalent *shinkansen* fare, but they save you a night's accommodation (*see* p.11).

If you plan to do a lot of travelling in a limited geographical area, ask JNTO about regional excursion tickets. The **Sei-shun Ju-hachi Kippu** is a very cheap but slow way of covering long distances (*see* 'Getting Around', p.10).

food and drink

Think twice about patronizing anywhere that immediately looks Japanese. Moss gardens, stone lanterns, waitresses in kimono, acres of *tatami* and private rooms with sliding screens are nice once in a while, but they come at a premium. Equally good, but unostentatiously presented food can be had at a lower price. The same goes for accommodation.

Certain everyday foods and drinks are especially expensive. Japanese sandwiches are always a big disappointment: tasteless cubes of cotton wool bread with soggy and inappropriate fillings. For a snack buy rice balls (*onigiri*) instead. Coffee in coffee shops is notorious: seldom less than ¥400 a cup and sometimes ¥1,000 or more, with no free refills. Again, it's the atmosphere and the chance to sit down and relax which you are paying for. If you must have a regular caffeine fix, consider the following: cheap chain coffee shops, like Doutor, which charge as little as ¥180 a cup; hot can coffee from vending machines for ¥120 (it's always milky and sickly sweet); buying a jar of instant from a convenience store and making it in your room (all lodgings provide their guests with a thermos jug of hot water).

Go for lunchtime set menus (*teishoku*) which include a bowl of rice, salad, soup and a delicacy like *tempura* or *katsu* (cutlets). Treat lunch as the main meal of the day, and make do with a snack of noodles in the evening. Take advantage of the inclusive dinner and breakfast offered by *ryokan* and *minshuku*. (see pp. 4–48)

Sample Daily Budget

The following is based on an actual budget for one person in Kyoto—a very full day, with a lot of walking, and no extras like souvenirs. Costs of meals and accommodation include 3% consumption tax. This probably represents a realistic minimum for an active day of travelling. If you stayed in a good Western-style hotel and went by taxi instead of tram and foot, the total would be double.

Breakfast (at inexpensive *ryokan*)	¥500
Bus and subway pass (half of two-day pass):	¥1,000
Kiyomizu-dera (temple)	¥300
Kyoto National Museum (admission)	¥420
Lunch (tempura set)	¥1200
Nanzen-ji (temple)	¥400
Philosopher's Walk	Free
Drink (canned)	¥120
Ginkaku-ji (temple and garden)	¥500
Dinner (noodles)	¥800
Beer (one can)	¥320
Minshuku (inexpensive)	¥4800
Total:	**¥10,360**

Climate and \When to Go

Japan's climate is broadly temperate, but, because the country is so long and thin, conditions at any one time vary enormously between Siberian Hokkaidō and sub-tropical Kyūshū and Okinawa. The four seasons, and the melancholy feelings associated with their passing, have been a theme of art and literature from the earliest times. Japanese people are very proud of them: you may even be told that Japan is the only country in the world that has four distinct seasons. Actually, it has five, including the rainy season.

Winter is cold, but dry. In Hokkaidō, the mountains of Tōhoku, and the Japan Alps, there is heavy snow, but Tokyo, Kyoto and Nara seldom freeze.

Spring is mild, and often rainy. In March the first cherry blossoms appear in Okinawa and southern Kyūshū, and pass in a wave across the country, reaching Kansai and Tokyo in April, the final flowers falling from the trees of northern Hokkaidō in May.

Summer months are the most difficult and enervating in Japan. The **rainy season** afflicts the whole country south of Tokyo: a wet blanket of warm rain and humidity from mid-June to mid-July. Summer itself is hot and humid: mean August temperatures are around 18–27° but can go much higher. Kansai (Ōsaka and Kyoto) is slightly hotter than Tokyo. In late August and September typhoons bring more rain, and a handful of fatalities; for tourists, the greatest risk is that flights will be disrupted and vulnerable railway lines closed.

Autumn is the loveliest time of the year, and the best time to visit, especially in October and November, with clear mild days and cool nights, and stunning red autumn foliage on mountainsides and in parks and temples.

Apart from nasty weather, the most important thing to avoid when timing a visit is **public holidays** (*see* p.35) when offices close, and hotels, roads, airports and public transport become clogged with Japanese holidaymakers. At New Year in particular, the whole country shuts up shop and goes home.

Crime and Emergencies

Compared to other first world economic superpowers, crime rates are enviably low, but it would be wrong to describe Japan as crime-free. Take all the usual precautions: don't flash quantities of cash around; keep an eye on your belongings, especially in a crowd; keep purses and wallets in inside pockets.

Every neighbourhood has a *kōban*, a police box manned 24 hours, often indicated by a red lamp outside. **The national police emergency number is ✆ 110. For ambulances, or in case of fire, ✆ 119.**

With close to zero crime, the job of the neighbourhood policeman (*o-mawari-san*, literally 'Honourable Mr Walkabout') is not arduous. Never hesitate to ask for directions or assistance, but don't expect much English.

It is still an offence for a non-Japanese to venture out in public without a passport or (for longer term residents) alien registration card. Technically, you can be arrested for this, without the option of returning to your hotel to retrieve the necessary document. *Gaijin* are very unlikely to be stopped without good reason, although foreigners in cars or on bicycles are said to be particularly at risk—bike theft being one of the few growth areas of Japanese crime. Don't be caught out.

If you do ever find yourself on the wrong side of the law, the best strategy is to adopt an expression of crestfallen stupidity and apologise profusely. Charging a non-Japanese-speaking foreigner with a minor offence is a headache every policeman can do without.

drugs

Possession of even small amounts of soft drugs is viewed harshly in Japan, as Paul McCartney found to his cost. At best, you will be deported and barred from re-entry; at worst, you will spend a long time in one of Japan's notoriously inhumane and disciplinarian jails. There are one or two spots in Tokyo where young foreigners might be offered illegal substances, almost always by other *gaijin*. The risks, as well as the prices, are high.

Earthquakes

Early in the morning of 17 January 1995 a huge earthquake, 7.2 on the Richter scale, struck the northern tip of Awaji island in the Inland Sea, and devastated the nearby city of Kōbe. It was the most powerful tremor to hit a heavily built-up Japanese city since 1923. In the days after the quake, television pictures and photographs of the stricken city were circulated all over the world. They seemed to show total devastation. Whole neighbourhoods burned; landfill islands were inundated and shaken to a sodden jelly; entire buildings toppled face down into the street; a lengthy section of the Hanshin overhead expressway fell sideways on its supports, which had snapped at their bases like concrete mushrooms. For a week the death toll steadily rose, as more and more bodies were extracted from the rubble. By the end of the rescue operation 5,000 were confirmed dead, with many more injured and more than 50,000 buildings destroyed. Commentators made much of the apparent failure of Japanese earthquake precautions. How, they asked, could the world's most advanced technological society be so unprepared for the inevitable?

In fact, Japan was, and is, about as well prepared as it could possibly be. The aftermath of the disaster, with government relief agencies hesitating and fretting and failing to talk to one another, was an embarrassing shambles. But the 20 seconds of the quake itself showed how far construction technology has come in 70 years. It is impossible to know exactly how much worse the damage could have been, but strict building regulations introduced in the early 1980s undoubtedly saved many, many lives. When the initial period of shock and mourning had passed, plenty of people in Japan were able to find much reassurance in the Kōbe catastrophe, strange though that may sound.

Earthquakes have always been a part of daily life in Japan. The islands owe their existence to the interlocking tectonic plates which centuries ago thrust up the spiny archipelago of volcanic mountains from the bed of the ocean. Four of these plates join one another in the sea close to the centre of the main island of Honshū. As they press into one another, massive pressure builds up. When the contending plates shift or slip over one another, the pressure is released in the form of earth tremors.

There are thousands of these every week, most of them so weak as to be undetectable except on the most sensitive seismic instruments. Every few weeks come tremors which are strong enough to be felt, but which cause little or no damage. But every now and then, a large shift occurs. The damage caused depends on the depth of the tremor, the kind of rock in which it occurs, and its proximity to human habitation. At worst, a strong tremor causes landslides, tidal waves (*tsunami*), liquefaction of soft soil and coastal land, and shaking sufficient to destroy buildings and elevated roads, fracture gas mains and chemical storage tanks, and bring down live electric cables.

Although the theory of earthquakes is well understood, predicting them early enough to save lives is almost impossible. Some earthquakes seem to occur at regular intervals— since the 17th century, Tokyo, for instance, has been struck by devastating earthquakes at what seem to be 70-year intervals. The last one was in 1923, so the next 'Big One' would appear to be due any day. It's actually not that simple: the picture is immensely complicated by different types of quake, on different, overlapping cycles, which have at various times coincided and even triggered one another. The nature, scale and even existence of an imminent 'Big One' is hotly debated. But earthquakes in general remain a constant and unpredictable hazard.

What is known beyond doubt is that certain kinds of building stand up better to tremors than others, a fact that has profoundly influenced native architecture. Traditional Japanese buildings are wooden—plainly, stone or brick buildings would be suicidal. Timber, by contrast, yields to the strain of earth tremors, is cheaper to reconstruct and is far less deadly when it falls. The difficulty comes in cities, where large numbers of wooden houses are built side by side. In all the worst Japanese earthquakes, it has been fire, ripping through the tinder-wood of collapsed buildings, that has claimed more lives than any other single cause. In Kōbe, it was the older, poorer wooden neighbourhoods where the worst devastation occurred and where the greater number of lives were lost.

Modern engineers have devised ever more cunning ways of compensating for the shaking of the earth, and all new construction above a certain height is required to incorporate earthquake defence measures. High-rises can be built with heavy weights attached to moving belts on their exteriors: when a shock is detected, they move automatically up or down the building, counter-balancing and neutralizing the shocks. Buildings are mounted on cushioning mattresses of springs, with skeletons of flexible girders which move with the building, absorbing and dissipating the stresses on it. During storms, the upper stories of such skyscrapers sway gently in the wind, a disconcerting effect for which one might be very grateful if the worst came to the worst.

In Kōbe, the new techniques and building codes underwent their first non-laboratory test and, by and large, they achieved what they were intended to achieve. The worst damage, as everyone had expected, was in old wooden neighbourhoods. Modern structures built more than 15 years ago, under the old building codes, suffered heavy, but lesser damage; most stayed up. The photographers and TV crews reporting on the disaster ignored the newest blocks: many of these suffered no significant damage whatsoever.

The life-saving effects of these measures are reflected in the death tolls of successive Japanese tremors. The 1923 Tokyo earthquake killed 143,000 out of a population of two million. A 1948 tremor killed 3900 in Fukui, a small city on the Japan Sea coast. In Kōbe, 5,000 died, but out of a population of 1.5 million, in one of the most densely populated areas in the world. The most darkly apocalyptic projections of Tokyo's next Big One predict 60,000 dead—out of an affected population of 12 million.

It may seem a perverse conclusion to draw, but in modern Japan, in the most powerful kind of earthquake, victims have at least a 99.5% chance of surviving. In that, there is much cause for comfort.

Earthquake Safety

In seismically active zones like Tokyo, small earthquakes rattle the windows every few weeks. Almost all pass after a few seconds. If an earthquake appears to be serious, observe the following drill:

⚠ Turn off all gas taps and extinguish naked flames.

⚠ Take shelter in a safe spot. Best of all is in a ground floor doorway where you run the least chance of either becoming trapped or being struck by falling objects in the street outside. Next best is under a table. Keep clear of heavy pieces of furniture like bookshelves which could topple over and cause injury.

⚠ Evacuate as soon as it is safe to the designated spot, usually an open space like a park or playing field. In serious earthquakes, the majority of fatalities are caused not by the shaking itself but by the fires which follow.

⚠ If you are in a car, stop it immediately, trying if at all possible not to block the centre of the road. Switch off the engine, get out and take shelter.

⚠ If you are by the sea or on low-lying coastal land, evacuate to high ground to avoid the *tsunami* or seismic tidal wave which often follows a marine earthquake.

⚠ If you're planning to spend some time in Japan, be aware of dangers inherent in certain buildings. Wooden structures are the most vulnerable, especially those with heavy tile roofs (which could collapse and crush the occupants) in wooden neighbourhoods (unfortunately these include the most interesting parts of many Japanese towns). Concrete buildings over 20 years old may look solid, but are often less structurally sound than those built since 1980.

⚠ Wherever you are, make sure you know the route to be taken in an emergency (inns and hotels display maps indicating these) and have access to a torch (again these are obligatory in hotels).

Electricity

The standard current is 100 volts AC. Eastern Japan (including Tokyo) operates on 50 cycles, western Japan (including Nagoya) is 60 cycles. Plugs consist of two flat parallel prongs, identical to those in the USA and Canada, and most American devices (including lap-tops) designed for 117 volts will work well enough. British 240 volt devices, however, require a transformer. Adapters, transformers and conversion plugs for most foreign gizmos can be found in the Akihabara area of Tokyo.

Embassies and Consulates

Australia: 2–1–14 Mita, Minato-ku, Tokyo 108–0073, ✆ 03 5232 4111.

Canada: 7–3–38 Akasaka, Minato-ku, Tokyo 107–0052, ✆ 03 3408 2101.

China: 3–4–33 Moto-Azabu, Minato-ku, Tokyo 106–0046, ✆ 03 3403 3380.

France: 4–11–44 Minami-Azabu, Minato-ku, Tokyo 106–0047, ✆ 03 5420 8800.

Germany: 4–5–10 Minami-Azabu, Minato-ku, Tokyo 106, ✆ 03 3473 0151/7.

Ireland: Ireland House, 2–10–7 Koji–machi, Chiyoda-ku, Tokyo 102–0075, ✆ 03 3263 0695.

New Zealand: 20–40 Kamiyamachō, Shibuya-ku, Tokyo 150–0047, ✆ 03 3467 2271.

Russia: 2–1–1 Azabudai, Minato-ku, Tokyo 106–0041, ✆ 03 3583 4224.

United Kingdom: 1 Ichibanchō, Chiyoda-ku, Tokyo 102–0082, ✆ 03 3265 5511.

Consulate, Chūō-ku, Hakurō-cho, 3–5–12, Seikō Ōsaka biru 19F, Ōsaka, ✆ 06 231 3355.

United States: 1–10–5 Akasaka, Minato-ku, Tokyo 107–0052, ✆ 03 3224 5000.

Consulate, 2–11–5 Nishi-tenma, Kita-ku, Ōsaka, ✆ 06 6315 5900.

Japanese society is a dense, invisible network of favour and obligation, exclusion and inclusion, to which there is no fixed set of rules or responses. An individual's relations with other members of the society depend not just on circumstances, but on the age, rank and sex of the parties and their relative place within the system. Foreigners (the literal meaning of the Japanese word *gaijin* is 'outside person') are largely exempt from all this. Good manners are the same all over the world, and for every sociological generalization there is an exception. Japan is a society based on reserve, fastidiousness and personal modesty—but walk down any city street on a weekend evening and you will see crowds of jolly drunks, singing, vomiting and urinating in the gutters. If there is a general rule, it is: don't stand out. Follow the lead of those around you, and you will never cause embarrassment.

There are, however, situations where knowledge of a few simple rules is necessary. Some of these are dealt with elsewhere in this chapter: Japanese baths (pp.14–15), table manners (p.32). For business etiquette *see* '**Business Culture**' (pp.97–108).

greetings

Japanese bow to one another when greeting, thanking and parting from one another. The depth of the bow depends on the relative status of the individuals. 'Greeters', the young women who welcome customers at the doors of department stores, are trained to calibrate their bows with special bowing machines: one angle for peers, another for senior staff members, a deep bow for members of the public. Foreigners tend to look (and feel) awkward attempting a full bow: a deep nod does just as well. Modern Japanese shake hands too, but the friendly continental-style peck on the cheek to acquaintances of the opposite sex may cause embarrassment: a kiss is still a largely sexual gesture.

shoes and slippers

In private homes, some offices, and anywhere containing *tatami* mats, outdoor shoes are removed. A transitional entrance area, called the *genkan*, just inside the front door, is the place for this: you'll recognize it by the rows of other shoes lined neatly up at one side. Slip out of your shoes and, without touching the floor of the *genkan* with your unsheathed feet, step inside and into the slippers which will be provided for your use.

These can be worn in all areas apart from two: on *tatami* mats which you should step onto only in stockinged feet; and the toilet, for which special toilet slippers are provided. Step out of your indoor slippers and into the toilet slippers; when you've finished, don't forget to change back into the indoor slippers. There's a powerful cleanliness/uncleanness, inside/outside taboo at work here; breaking the rules is very bad manners.

To summarize:

> **Outside**: outdoor shoes only to be worn. Never pop out in indoor slippers and then come back inside.
>
> **Genkan**: take off outdoor shoes, and step into indoor slippers.
>
> **Tatami**: stockinged feet only.
>
> **Toilet**: toilet slippers only.

All this stepping in and out of shoes raises practical points. Slip-ons, for a start, are much easier to get in and out of than lace-ups. Holes in socks, and smelly or unwashed feet, are obvious and embarrassing.

sitting

All offices and many restaurants have Western furniture, but on *tatami* one sits at low tables on the floor. Women should always (even on upright furniture) sit with their legs folded to one side, or on their heels. Crossed legs are for men only, but can be agonizing for those unaccustomed to it: nobody will mind if you sprawl a little bit.

tipping

Tipping is unnecessary anywhere. Good service is understood: to insist on a gratuity will cause embarrassment and is rude. In exceptional circumstances (if a taxi driver has tracked you all over town to return a lost wallet, say) you may want to slip notes into a plain envelope and present it discreetly. Even then don't press too hard. The gesture in itself will be appreciated. It is better to offer a gift.

gifts

Japanese people present one another with gifts at every opportunity although the gesture is often more important than the present itself. During the two great gift-giving seasons, summer and New Year, Japanese houses are piled high with identical bottles of whisky, melons, preserved local delicacies and golf accessories—many of them destined to be passed on unopened the next time around. If you are likely to enjoy hospitality in Japan (and everyone can arrange this, through the Home Visit system), then it is a good idea to buy a few simple souvenirs of home before you go. Picture books of your country or region, non-perishable foods like biscuits or sweets, small trinkets or mementoes will all go down well. Wrapping is all important: ribbons and glossy paper, preferably bearing the name of a famous shop or brand, can elevate even the humblest gift.

Food and Drink

 For a picture of the range and weirdness of Japanese food, visit the basement food hall of a big department store or—harder to find these days—an old-fashioned local market. There you will see frothing gastropods, writhing octopi and bags of seaweed, alongside beef raised on beer, £100 melons, sweet potatoes and sour plums. The most surprising thing about Japanese cuisine is its variety—and the variety of prices. A *kaiseki* banquet can cost as much as a return air ticket to Korea. On the other hand, you can eat a new, strange and delicious dish every day for a week, and not spend more than ¥1000 a head. Whatever your other money worries, eating out need not be one of them.

Restaurants and eating places are classified in three categories, based on the approximate cost of dinner for one, including tax and service, but excluding drinks. These should be treated as rough guidelines; remember also that many restaurants offer lunchtime *teishoku* or sets which are much cheaper than the evening *à la carte* prices.

Restaurant price classifications in this guide	
expensive	Above ¥5,500
moderate	¥3,000–¥5,500
inexpensive	Under ¥3,000

meals

The traditional Japanese **breakfast** is the only meal that many foreigners find they cannot become accustomed to, even after repeated exposure. Typically it will consist of a piece of broiled fish, pickles, a raw egg, green tea and rice, which the diner rolls up into little parcels between pieces of dried green seaweed. Somehow it's the rice that is the most unpalatable element: that dense volume makes you want to go straight back to bed, or leaves you feeling as if you're recovering from a heavy lunch at 8.30 in the morning. Many will prefer to eat in a *kissaten* (coffee shop) which can be found in most Western-style hotels and on every other street corner. Here you can get a *mōningu sābisu* (morning service) of coffee, toast and boiled egg for around ¥700.

Lunch is eaten early in Japan: 12 to 1 is the hour when restaurants are most crowded, rather than 1 to 2. Many restaurants, including the most expensive, do cheap lunch sets which can be an extremely reasonable way of sampling otherwise unaffordable food.

For businesspeople and young people out on the town, the **evening meal** is often little more than an accompaniment to alcohol. Set menus are fuller and much more expensive than at lunchtime.

rice dishes

Sticky white short-grained rice is the staple of every meal, even more so than bread or potatoes in the West. The Japanese words for breakfast, lunch and dinner (*asagohan, hiru-gohan* and *bangohan*) mean literally 'morning rice', 'afternoon rice' and 'evening rice'. Like many staple foods, the eating of rice has over the centuries acquired sacramental associations. Many of the Shinto legends and ceremonies are concerned with appeasement of the gods in order to secure a successful rice crop; bowls of boiled rice are offered in temples and shrines, and at household ancestral altars. Its polished whiteness and purity are essential, and the foreign taste for brown rice is considered very peculiar indeed.

For a bowl of plain boiled rice, ask for *gohan*. *Chahan* is Chinese-style egg fried rice, served in cheap restaurants as a meal in itself, but never eaten with other Japanese food.

Donburi is a kind of cheap snack, popular as a quick lunchtime filler. A large bowl (the literal meaning of *donburi*) is filled with hot boiled rice and various toppings: *ten-don* is rice with pieces of *tempura*, *unagi-don* is rice with strips of eel. Other common varieties are *tonkatsu-don* (deep-fried battered pork), *oyako-don* (literally 'parent and child', hence chicken and egg) and *gyū-don* (beef).

Onigiri is even more informal, the equivalent of a rice sandwich, eaten with the fingers, and the staple of picnics and packed lunches. A ball of rice, often shaped into a rough triangle, is wrapped in dried seaweed or rolled in sesame seeds, with a small piece of fish or pickle in the middle. Convenience stores sell 'instant onigiri', cleverly packaged so that the dry seaweed and damp rice come into contact only when they are unwrapped. *Umeboshi* (pickled plum) is the most common filling; they can also contain tuna, seaweed and fish eggs.

Kamameshi is a rice casserole, not unlike a simple paella: clams, chicken, vegetables or meat, cooked and served in an old-fashioned iron dish with a wooden lid.

noodle dishes

Noodles are the pasta of Japan—cheap, simple and versatile, and (like spaghetti) introduced originally from China. Every region of Japan has its own version of the main varieties, which inspire intense connoisseurship and local loyalty. Noodle partisans can debate for hours the relative merits of, say, Izumo and Tokyo *soba*.

As you will quickly gather on your first visit to a noodle restaurant, noodles are slurped. Hold the bowl in one hand and raise it towards your face before lifting a clump of noodles to your mouth with chopsticks; then suck, and don't worry about the noise. It's perfectly proper to raise the bowl to your mouth with both hands to finish off the tasty soup in which they are served.

Ramen are Japanized Chinese egg noodles, served in a variety of broths and garnished with morsels of pork, seafood, fish sausage and vegetables. In the smallest Japanese town, you will never be more than half a mile from a *ramen-ya*, sometimes a simple restaurant with a counter bar and a few tables, often a portable cart on wheels parked opposite the station, with a couple of stools and a canopy to keep off the rain. *Ramen* are served in a variety of broths. *Miso ramen* comes in a delicious salty, cloudy soup of fermented soy bean. *Shōyu* is thinner, based on soy sauce.

Soba and **udon** were also imported from China, but so long ago as to be considered thoroughly Japanized. The former are made from buckwheat flour and can vary in colour from off-white through brown to dark grey. *Udon* are made from wheat flour, and are plump and white, with a blander, more floury taste. Both are served in a broth which varies subtly over different regions, with or without a garnish. Popular *soba* and *udon* dishes include *tempura* (with a few pieces of battered fish), *sansai* (nutty mountain vegetables), *tsukimi* (with a raw egg) and *zaru soba/udon*, a summer dish, served cold with a separate sauce to which leeks and horseradish are added before dipping.

Other noodle dishes include *sōmen*, a thin form of *udon*, like vermicelli, and *champon*, a rich jumble of egg noodles, seafood and vegetables introduced from China via Nagasaki.

grilled dishes

Okonomiyaki (pronounced, almost, 'Economy-yacky') is a cheap, filling, fun food, something like a cross between a pizza and a pancake. Many *okonomiyaki-ya* feature DIY cooking. You sit down at a table with a hot griddle in the centre, and the ingredients— cabbage and vegetables, egg batter, plus your choice of prawns, squid or meat—are brought to your table in a bowl which you mix up and pour onto the iron. Tamp it down with the spatula, and turn it over when one side is done. Then top with sweet sauce and writhing flakes of dried bonito fish. Someone will give a hand until you get the hang of it.

Yakitori (literally 'grilled bird') is another informal dish, very palatable to foreign tastes. Portions of dismembered chicken (they seem to have a use for every last giblet), plus vegetables and nuts, are pierced with wooden skewers, rubbed with salt or a sweet, soy-based sauce and cooked over a smoky barbecue. Two skewers generally constitute one portion, which costs a few hundred yen. In itself, a round of *yakitori* is insubstantial, so unless you stoke up with something heavier (try *yaki-onigiri*, grilled rice balls), you can find yourself spending a surprising amount of money before you're full. It's often less messy to prize the morsels off with chopsticks and eat them off the plate, than to gnaw them straight off the skewer. The following is a typical *yakitori* menu:

tsukune	chicken meatballs
tebasaki	chicken wings
rebā	liver
sasaki	breast
motsu	giblets
momoyaki	thighs
negi	leeks
asupara	asparagus
piiman	green pepper
shiitake	mushroom

Tonkatsu are cutlets of lean pork, deep fried, and served either on rice (*tonkatsu-don*) or in a set (*teishoku*) with rice, soup and pickles.

tempura

The word *tempura* is said, implausibly, to come from the Latin *tempora*, meaning Lent, and to have been introduced by Portuguese traders during the 16th century. When asked why they were eating fried fish instead of their usual meat, they replied that it was because of *tempora*, and the name stuck. Nowadays, the big pink prawns in their golden overcoats of spiky batter are a quintessentially Japanese food, but still one which foreigners find very easy to eat. A humble version of *tempura* crops up as a garnish on noodles and rice, but there are restaurants dedicated to it, some very expensive, with their own secret formulae for batter, oil and cooking time.

Tempura doesn't have to be fish: vegetables, nuts and leaves can also be dipped in the fine batter, deep fried in oil, and plopped on the table on white paper. A plate of tempura comes with a thin, light brown sauce into which you tip a pile of grated ginger and radish. Dip each piece in momentarily, and eat at once. It's often ordered in a set (*teishoku*). Common ingredients are *ebi* (prawn), *ika* (squid), *kakiage* (chopped shrimps and vegetables), *nasu* (aubergine), *shiitake* (mushroom) and *shiso* (a refreshing, aromatic leaf).

fish

The waters of the Japanese archipelago range from the iceberg-encrusted Sea of Okhotsk to the sub-tropical South China Sea; Tokyo-based factory ships range as far as the Antarctic and the deep Pacific. As a result, Japan is an icthyophagist's paradise, with the finest, freshest, and most hygienically prepared seafood in the world.

Sushi and **sashimi,** the famous Japanese 'raw fish', are not always raw and may not even be fish. *Sashimi* are mouth-sized morsels of seafood dipped into a mixture of soy sauce (*shōyu*) and grated green horseradish (*wasabi*); most are uncooked, but octopus (*tako*) *sashimi* is always boiled first, and prawns (*ebi*) usually are too. *Sushi* consists of balls of vinegared rice with pieces of raw or cooked fish or omelette pressed onto the top. *Maki* (wrapped) *zushi* are made by rolling up chopped vegetables and fish in a tube of rice, wrapped in dried seaweed, and chopping the long cylinder into small round pieces.

Foreigners are often revolted by the idea of eating raw fish, but the reality is seldom what they expect. Forget those images of fishmongers' shops, with limp carcasses lying on the slab all day, and flies buzzing round—Western restaurants *have* to cook their fish because it is allowed to sit around for so long. In Japan, only the finest and freshest cuts are used (so it's not cheap), and Japanese hygiene standards are the best in the world. The fishy tastes and smells which first-timers dread are entirely absent. *Sushi* and *sashimi* are odourless and surprisingly mild in flavour—it is the texture of the different species, and the beautiful presentation of the ingredients on the plate (red tuna, pink prawns, yellow omelette, white rice) which excite and satisfy the appetite.

A few pieces of *sashimi* form a part of many traditional Japanese meals; some restaurants also offer a set menu including soup, rice and pickles for a reasonable price. *Sushi*, because it includes rice, is more of a meal in itself. At the top end, you can spend as much as you want, but an entertaining and inexpensive introduction to the dish can be found in *kuru-kuru-zushi* restaurants (literally, '*sushi* that keeps coming'). Here customers sit on the outside of a circular conveyor belt, onto which chefs place the *sushi* on little plates which are colour-coded according to the price of the dish. You sit down, watch the dishes coming round and, when you see one you fancy, lift it off. Eat as much or as little as you like and, at the end of your meal, present your stack of empty plates to be totted up.

At other establishments your *sushi* will be served on a board or placed on the counter directly in front of you. Put a little soy sauce (*shōyu*) into the separate dish and dip each piece, fish side down so the rice doesn't crumble. You can lift them with chopsticks, but it is perfectly acceptable to use your fingers.

Sashimi is served with a little pyramid of grated *wasabi* (horseradish) at the side. Using chopsticks, transfer a little of this into a saucer of *shōyu*. It's very strong: go easy until you know how much you like.

It's cheaper to order *nigiri moriawase*, a selection of eight or so different pieces. For *à la carte* orders, try the following:

maguro	tuna
toro	fatty tuna
ebi	boiled prawn
amaebi	raw sweet prawn
ika	squid
tako	octopus
anago	broiled sea eel

tai	sea bream
awabi	abalone
torigai	cockle
aji	herring
hamachi	yellowtail
ikura	salmon roe (*sushi* only)
tamago	sweet omelette (*sushi* only)

Unagi is broiled eel, barbecued over charcoal and steeped in a sweet sauce of *shōyu*, *sake* and sugar. Served on a bed of rice (*unagi-don*), or on its own, it's the opposite of austere, minimalist *sashimi*—rich, sweet, and indulgent.

Fugu is another dish which has achieved sensational fame outside Japan. The puffer fish (aka blowfish, globefish or swell fish) is an uncharismatic creature caught off the western coast of Honshū, with three unpleasant properties: it is extremely ugly, it can inflate itself into a spiny ball when threatened, and its liver and ovaries contain deadly toxins which can paralyse the respiratory and motor-nervous system within 20 minutes of ingestion. *Fugu* can only be served by chefs who are rigorously trained and licensed by the Ministry of Health and Welfare. The Imperial Family are forbidden by law from touching the stuff, but since the system was introduced there has been only one fatality: Bandō Mitsugorō, a *kabuki* actor, who was determined to sample the liver and suffered the consequences.

A *fugu* banquet consists of several stages. First warm *sake* is poured over the toasted fins of the fish, to produce a fishy aperitif. Then *fugu-sashi*, transparently thin slices of the flesh are eaten raw, dipped in a sauce containing *shōyu*, radish, pepper and bitter orange. Next comes *fuguchiri*, a hot-pot of *fugu* flesh boiled with vegetables. Finally, the soupy residue is boiled into a rice porridge. The flesh is white, mild, and—to the non-connoisseur—really nothing very special at all. It rarely comes cheaper than ¥4,500.

stews and hot pots

Nabemono (things in a pot) are steaming casseroles, heated up on a flame at the table, and filled by the diners from plates of vegetables, leaves, *tōfu* and, sometimes, meat. *Chanko-nabe* is a high-protein version made famous by sumo wrestlers, who eat quantities of it to achieve and augment their distinctive waistlines. *Sukiyaki* and *shabu-shabu* are meat-based *nabe* dishes, both invented since the foreign popularization of beef in the late 19th century. The former is a rich, meaty dish of onions, mushrooms, *tōfu*, bamboo shoots and *konnyaku* (devil's root jelly), simmered in a suet broth with strips of thin, often fatty beef. *Shabu-shabu* can be made with pork as well: thin slices are dropped into boiling water with vegetables, allowed to cook for a few seconds, then dipped in a sesame seed sauce. 'Genghis Khan' is a novelty version served in Hokkaidō with lamb as the staple meat; it was allegedly invented by the notorious Mongolian warlord.

Oden is a basic, working man's food, an unglamorous but tasty brown stew of fish sausages, *tōfu*, cabbage, radish and vegetable jelly, dolloped out and eaten with mustard.

Japan produces delicious mandarin oranges (*mikan*), apples (*ringō*), watermelons (*suika*), peaches (*momo*), strawberries (*ichigō*), and grapes (*budō*), as well as two delicious fruit not familiar in Europe: the *kaki* or persimmon, a crisp, sweet, smoky fruit, the shape of a big tomato; and the *nashi*, a crisp, succulent autumn fruit, between an apple and a pear.

vegetarian cuisine

Vegetarianism has never caught on in Japan and it's notoriously difficult to explain to well-meaning hosts and puzzled waiters. The exception is in Buddhist, and especially Zen, temples where the injunction against taking the life of living creatures has led to the development of an ancient, delicate and sophisticated cuisine. A few city restaurants specialize in *shōjin ryōri*, as it's called, but the best place to sample it is in the restaurants adjacent to a big temple complex like Daitoku-ji or Nanzen-ji in Kyoto, or on Mt Kōya, in Wakayama prefecture. The strictest Buddhist canons forbid even the use of garlic or onions, two of the 'Five Fragrant Vegetables' which are held to provoke an unhealthy lust for the food. Instead, wise and varied use is made of *tōfu*, *miso*, beans, vegetables, and plant extracts.

kaiseki ryōri

Kaiseki ryōri is the epitome of what many people think of as typical Japanese cuisine— fresh, natural ingredients, minimally cooked and flavoured, and exquisitely presented in tiny ceramic dishes arranged on lacquer trays. It began as a simple accompaniment to tea, and developed into a kind of culinary theatre in which the room, the hanging scrolls, the serving vessels, the view from the window, the demeanour and dress of the waitresses, the appearance and order of the dishes and their appropriateness to the season are as important to the connoisseur as the taste of the food which he finally digests. The food itself is elegantly simple—a series of short courses, including *sashimi*, cooked fish, vegetables, meat and rice. The ingredients are chosen for their seasonal freshness and, in Kyoto, are served with the minimum of seasonings. Kyoto chefs traditionally look down their noses at slobs from Tokyo—and abroad—who drown their delicately balanced meals in streams of soy sauce.

As you'd expect, this kind of experience doesn't come cheap. Having made your reservation (this must be done at least a day or two in advance), you'll be lucky to spend less than ¥10,000 per person for an authentic *kaiseki* meal in the evening. The alternative is to visit between 11am and 1pm when many restaurants serve lunchtime *bentō*—those lacquered lunch boxes with a morsel of food in each of their compartments—for under ¥5,000; the experience is less elaborate, the portions smaller, but the food is exactly the same. Best of all, dine in a good Kyoto *ryokan*. The evening meal is included in the price, and the best *ryokan* are superb restaurants in their own right.

foreign and hybrid food

The influence of Chinese cooking has already been made clear, but every kind of national cuisine—from Balinese to Nigerian—seems to have a restaurant somewhere in Japan, most of them in Tokyo. International convenience foods like sandwiches (*sandoitchi* or *sando*), burgers (*hambāgā*), spaghetti (*supagetti*), pizza (*piza*), and curry (*karii raisu*) are as much a part of the everyday diet as in the West. Even if you don't find any native dishes to your liking, there's no need to go hungry, or to resort to the ubiquitous *Makudonarudo* (McDonald's). Japanese chefs have always been adept at tailoring foreign dishes to domestic tastes to produce often delicious half-breeds. *Mukokuseki ryōri* (no-nationality cooking) is the fashionable expression used to describe trendy hybrid restaurants, serving such delights as *gyōza* (Chinese dumplings) stuffed with mozzarella.

Restaurants

For Japanese food, the top-of-the-range restaurants are the **ryōtei**, purveyors of *kaiseki* haute cuisine, and often beautiful examples of traditional tea-house style architecture in their own right. Dining at a *ryōtei*, in the evening anyway, isn't a casual experience. They tend to tuck themselves away behind gardens and fencing shrubs; reservations must be made more than a day in advance so that the ingredients can be freshly ordered and prepared. The most exclusive *ryōtei* are like informal clubs, and may expect an introduction from an established customer.

Other establishments are classified according to the particular type of cuisine in which they specialize. It would be unusual to find a restaurant that served both *tempura* and *okonomiyaki*, for instance, so it's necessary to have some idea of what you want to eat as well as how much you want to pay. The suffix *-ya* means roughly 'business'—thus a **sushi-ya** is a raw fish restaurant, a **ramen-ya** is a noodle shop. Among the most congenial places for general relaxation and decent, non-gourmet eating are the thousands of little establishments classified as **nomi-ya** (drinking shops). These include **aka chōchin** (red lantern bars), humble working men's places with a few tables, a television and a trade-mark paper lantern hanging outside the door, and **izaka-ya**, which are a bit more up-market, but just as noisy and informal. Groups of diners usually order a number of individual dishes (and much alcohol) which are shared. **Robata-yaki** is hearty country-style grill cooking, performed in front of the diners, amid much smoke and sizzling. *Yatai* are outdoor carts, serving similar sorts of food, where customers sit on stools beneath an awning. Some *yatai* serve superb food at very reasonable prices.

One of the best places to get your culinary bearings is on the restaurant floor of a **department store**, usually near the top of the building. Big city stores may have half a dozen different restaurants, each serving a different kind of cuisine at very reasonable prices. Styles of foreign restaurant are as varied as styles of foreign cuisine.

Kissaten are the ubiquitous coffee shops. The coffee is expensive; the simple snacks of pasta, pilaff and curry are cheap.

ordering

The chances of encountering English-speaking waiters decrease as you descend the price scale. Restaurants in the cities often have bilingual menus, and even in the smallest towns you will see window displays with plastic models of the various dishes, along with the prices. Simply lead the waiter outside, and point.

The most important skill you can master before coming to Japan is the use of chopsticks. If your chopstick skills are a little rusty, practise by picking up small objects with a couple of long pencils. Japanese chopsticks (*hashi*) are made of wood, sometimes lacquered, with pointed ends. Impaling food is a little indelicate, but friendly indulgence is extended to foreigners. Never transfer food from one set of chopsticks to another: the only time this happens is after a Buddhist cremation when relatives do this with the ashes of the deceased. Don't stick them upright in a bowl of food—again, this is reserved for offerings to the dead.

Apart from that, Japanese table manners are reassuringly relaxed and practical. Slurping food or rice is fine, indeed encouraged (it's said to improve the flavour), and it's quite all right to lift up your own bowl or plate of food to your chin and shovel the food in from there. Neighbours at table pour one another's drinks. When a bottle is proffered, place your hand on your glass to acknowledge the courtesy, and reciprocate afterwards. An empty glass is an invitation for a refill: if you want to stop drinking, leave it full.

Drinking

Lager (*biiru*) and **whisky** (*uisukii*) are popular. Domestic beer brands (Kirin, Sapporo, Asahi, Yebisu) are famously good; Japanese whisky (Suntory and Nikka) is notoriously rough. *Mizu-wari* is whisky, ice and water. Imported brands of both drinks are widely available, but more expensive.

Sake isn't one of the world's great drinks, but it's a pleasant accompaniment to a lot of Japanese food. Drunk hot, it's a delicious winter warmer. *Shōchū* is a white spirit, made from rice, potatoes, barley and whatever else was to hand at the time. It's cheap, rough and very intoxicating. Mixed with soda water and fruit cordial, it makes a refreshing, and deceptively mild-tasting, cocktail called *sawā*—*raimu sawā* (lime), *remon sawā* (lemon), and *ume sawā* (Japanese plum) are popular.

Health

You don't need any immunizations or certificates to enter Japan. Health and life expectancy in Japan are high, and medical treatment is good, if expensive. Tap water is safe to drink in all areas.

You may find yourself suffering from **stomach upset** but this is likely to be the result of a long flight, unfamiliar air, water and food, rather than specific germs. It should pass in a few days and can be relieved by a standard preparation like Kaolin and Morphine.

If you need **prescription drugs**, carry an adequate supply and a separate copy of your prescription, in case of loss. Make sure you know the full name of the drug rather than just its brand name which may not be the same in Japan.

Mosquitoes are not dangerous, but they can be a painful nuisance in the warm months: bring repellent. The most effective measure is the electronic mosquito repeller which is plugged into the mains and fuelled with small solid tablets. These are inexpensive and are widely available.

The **sun** can be surprisingly strong, so cover your head and wear a good sunblock. Remember that ultra-violet rays do damage even on overcast days—during the summer rainy season, for example.

Food, including raw sea fish, is safe to eat, but you should always refuse raw river fish, raw wild boar, raw bear, and raw chicken which can carry parasites. Avoid walking barefoot in **rice paddies** and drinking from **mountain streams** for the same reason.

Healthcare in Japan is good, and English-speaking doctors are not hard to find, but a serious accident or illness could quickly become ruinously expensive. Adequate **insurance** is essential, and you should arrange it before you go.

contraceptives

Bring your own supply of the **pill**: as a contraceptive it is dispensed only reluctantly in Japan. **Condoms** with names like 'Love Me Jelly' and 'Yes, Satisfaction!' are widely available, even from vending machines on the street. Foreign users often complain that differences in scale between the Western and Oriental anatomy make them uncomfortable and unreliable. You might want to bring your home brand of these as well.

Meeting the Japanese

Japanese people are compulsively, touchingly, almost painfully kind and welcoming to foreigners, but they can also be rather shy in their presence and, especially outside the internationalized cities, breaking through the diffident eye contact and embarrassed smiles can be a struggle. The best way round this is to take advantage of the many formal schemes established to promote contact between Japanese and foreigners. For anyone wanting to live for a while with a Japanese family, there are numerous **Home Stay** programmes in different parts of Japan. You should arrange this before you arrive: enquire at your nearest branch of JNTO for an up-to-date list of organizations.

More suitable for short-term visitors are the **Home Visit** schemes run in dozens of cities and towns. Via a tourist information centre, you make an appointment to spend a few hours with an English-speaking Japanese family (other languages are sometimes available). Usually there is no charge: your hosts' only motive is to practise their English and learn about the West. Arrive on time, take along some small gifts and photographs of your home and family, if you have them. Loyal and long-lasting friendships can begin in this way.

Volunteer Guides, often local university students keen to practise English, operate in several of the big tourist cities, including Kyoto and Nara. You pay for their entrance fees, transport, and lunch, if they are with you for the whole day; they guide and interpret for you as you tour the sights. Again, a small gift and a postcard when you get home are all that is expected.

Money

Notes come in denominations of ¥1,000, ¥5,000, and ¥10,000. Coins are ¥1, ¥5, ¥10, ¥50, ¥100 and ¥500. All display their value in Arabic as well as Japanese numerals, apart from the ¥5 coin, which is brass and has a hole in the middle.

Cash is still the most common medium of payment in most shops, restaurants and on public transport. Street robbery is very rare, so the only risk of carrying large amounts of cash is that you will lose them.

International **credit cards** like MasterCard (Access), DC, Visa and American Express are increasingly accepted in city hotels, department stores, big restaurants and travel agents, but it is unwise to assume this unless you have checked in advance. Only the biggest railway stations accept cards in payment for tickets. They can also be used to withdraw cash directly from automatic teller machines in certain banks and department stores in big cities and international airports. Enquire at the nearest tourist information centre.

Traveller's cheques and **foreign currencies** like dollars and sterling can be cashed in major banks (which offer the best rates), *bureaux de change* and big hotels, but are almost never accepted in shops and restaurants. In smaller towns, not all the banks perform foreign exchange; stock up on yen before heading out to the sticks.

Banks open between 9am and 3pm, and close at weekends and on national holidays. Transactions can be time-consuming. If there is a queue, you may have to take a number from an automatic dispenser, wait for your number to be called, hand over your passport and cash or cheques, then wait for them to be processed. When this has been done behind the scenes, your name will be called and your currency handed over.

Museums

Museums and art galleries generally close over New Year and on Mondays, unless Monday is a national holiday, in which case they close on Tuesday.

Admission prices given in this book are for adults only. High school students (18 and under) almost always pay a cheaper rate, around half or two-thirds of the full ticket price.

Names

Japanese uses given names (what we call 'Christian' names) more reluctantly than English. It is quite usual for someone to introduce themselves by their family name alone (Mori or Watanabe, rather than Keiko or Noboru) even in an informal setting. In formal and business contexts, the form is to precede even the family name with the name of the company or institution: 'Toyota's Mr Nakamoto' or 'Tokyo University's Miss Higuchi'. Names are first and foremost a means of identifying the group to which the person is affiliated, not an individual handle. Among the young and Westernized, Western practice is very common, however. When introducing yourself, do what feels most natural in English.

Names are usually combined with some kind of honorific suffix. *-San* is the most common and neutral, being equivalent to Mr, Mrs, Miss or Ms. *-Sama* is formal and refers to the very honoured, including Shinto deities. *-Chan* is a pet, familiar form, used for young children, family members, very close friends and cute animals. Just as with English Mr and Mrs, one never employs a suffix in referring to oneself or one's own family or close circle.

Throughout this book names are given according to the Japanese practice: family name first, given name second. When one name is given, it is usually the family (i.e. the first) name. A few historical figures, however, are conventionally (and arbitrarily) referred to by their given names. Thus the wartime Prime Minister Tōjō Hideki, and the novelist Mishima Yukio, are always Tōjō and Mishima. But the Meiji-period writer Natsume Sōseki and the 16th-century warlord Oda Nobunaga are often Sōseki and Nobunaga.

Confusingly, emperors are often referred to by more than one name. During his lifetime, the father of the present sovereign was known, outside Japan, as Hirohito; posthumously, he is referred to as Shōwa, after the era name for the period of his rule.

National Holidays

On national holidays, banks and offices close, trains and hotels are booked up weeks in advance, and tourist spots become clogged with Japanese making the most of their free time. There are thirteen such days.

Note that three national holidays cluster at the end of April and beginning of May, a period known as **Golden Week** when most of the country takes a holiday and bookings are most difficult to obtain.

1 Jan	**New Year.**
15 Jan	**Coming of Age Day** honours those who will turn 20 in the next year.
11 Feb	**National Foundation Day** commemorates the date of accession of the legendary first emperor, Jimmu.
21 Mar	**Spring Equinox Day.**
29 April	**Green Day.** The birthday of the late Emperor Shōwa (Hirohito).
3 May	**Constitution Day.**
5 May	**Boys' Day.** Families fly colourful carp banners for their sons.
15 Sept	**Respect for the Aged Day.**
23 Sept	**Autumn Equinox Day.**
10 Oct	**Physical Fitness Day** in commemoration of the 1964 Tokyo Olympics.
3 Nov	**Culture Day.**
23 Nov	**Labour Day.**
23 Dec	**The Emperor's Birthday.**

National Treasures

The Japanese passion for classification ('Three Finest Scenic Views', 'Three Most Beautiful Gardens', etc.) is seen nowhere so clearly as in its museums. Every year, after vigorous vetting, a few more favoured statues, paintings and buildings are singled out for the cultural equivalent of the Oscars: as Important Cultural Properties or, for *la crème de la crème*, National Treasures.

The system has its roots in the 19th-century Meiji period when political victimization of Buddhist temples made it difficult for them to care for many of their finest art properties.

Large numbers of temple treasures were taken into custody by the government, and laws were passed concerning their care and preservation. Countless priceless works were destroyed in air raids during the Second World War, and in 1950 a revised law was passed which introduced the term Important Cultural Properties. Nowadays there are some 12,000 of these. One thousand of them are further designated National Treasures, including many of the finest Oriental art treasures in the world. The classifications are made carefully by experts: if you hear of a National Treasure, it's almost always worth going out of your way to see it.

As well as honouring physical objects, the 1950 law created another category: Intangible Cultural Assets, such as weaving, pottery or traditional performance arts. Human 'Bearers of Intangible Cultural Assets', better known as Living National Treasures, are also named. There can be no more than 70 of them at any one time. Living National Treasures receive an annual stipend and, importantly, massive commercial interest in their work. Holders of the honour are almost always eminent, very elderly craftsmen, artists and performers; for the rest of their lives they can charge for their work virtually what they want.

Nuisances and Dangers

There are more of the former than the latter: Japan is still one of the safest countries in the world.

earthquakes

These are potentially the greatest danger. Small quakes which rattle the windows alarmingly are common; severe, life-threatening ones are rare but, as the Kōbe disaster of January 1995 showed, their consequences can be frightening. In the end, though, the number of tourists to have been killed or injured in Japanese earthquakes is so small as to be negligible. And, if the chances of natural disaster are higher than at home, the chances of robbery, assault or murder are much lower. It would be an exceptionally cautious person who avoided Japan solely because of the earthquake danger. For a full discussion of earthquakes and earthquake safety, *see* pp.19–22.

dangerous animals

These are not something to worry about in Japan, particularly in the three cities covered in this book. However, there are a couple of poisonous snakes with a nasty bite, so if you find yourself in a more rural area, avoid walking barefoot through long grass. If anyone is bitten, keep them still and seek immediate medical help.

height

The Japanese are getting taller but their doorways and beams are not. In older homes and offices, castles and temples, and even some trains, anyone approaching the six foot mark will have to duck constantly to avoid cracking their head. After a while, the protective stoop becomes second nature; until you're used to it, beware.

lost property

Never give up on an item of lost property. Mislaid goods do get handed in, unplundered, and the systems for recovering them are straightforward and well-organized. Transport companies generally hold on to lost property for a few days, after which it is transferred to a local police station for one month, and finally to a central police station. In the first instance contact the taxi firm or bus or train station of the company which you travelled with; then go to the police. You might want to hand over a few thousand yen (depending on the value of the recovered item) as a reward for the finder.

In Tokyo, the following are useful numbers:

JR East Infoline, ✆ 03 3423 0111.

Tokyo Taxi Kindaika Centre, ✆ 03 3648 0300.

Metropolitan Police Department Lost and Found Office, ✆ 03 3581 4321.

You may need to ask your hotel to make some of these calls for you in Japanese.

Packing

Suits and ties are the rule for offices but, outside work, Japanese people dress casually (but smartly) even in grand restaurants and hotels, although obviously dirty or worn-out garments may be frowned on. Unless you have business to do, or very formal functions to attend, you can leave dressy clothes at home. There are few religious sensibilities to offend: Japanese tourists happily tramp round temples and shrines clad in shorts and mini-skirts and nobody minds.

Between Tokyo and the Kansai cities of Kyoto, Nara and Ōsaka, you will not find a terrific difference in temperature. Summers are hot and humid and you should bring the lightest, most comfortable clothing possible. Warm weather lasts until October, by which time the nights are getting chilly. Autumn and spring are the best times to visit, but even then you should bring plenty of versatile clothing as temperatures vary. Winters are cold but you will see plenty of sunshine. In the humid summers, and particularly in the rainy season (approximately June 10 until July 20), the most important garment is a lightweight water-proof, although you might prefer to make do with an umbrella, which you don't need to bring with you. They are cheaply available in every convenience store and souvenir shop.

Slip-ons make the complicated business of taking off and putting on footwear much easier. Bring strong comfortable shoes for all the walking you will inevitably be doing. Bear in mind that large foreign sizes of all clothes and shoes are expensive and difficult to get hold of in Japan.

Remember adapters and transformers if you're bringing over mains electrical equipment. A pocket torch can make all the difference in ill-lit temple halls and treasure houses.

Perhaps the most useful purchase which you can make before departure is the Japan Rail Pass. This can save you hundreds of pounds, but you must buy it before departure (*see* 'Getting Around', pp.9).

Post

The word for **post office** is *yūbin kyoku*. Its symbol is a red capital letter 'T' with a horizontal line over the top (〒), which also features in Japanese addresses to indicate the post code number.

Airmail letters under 10g cost ¥100 to North America and Oceania, ¥120 to Europe. Postcards are ¥70 worldwide, but there is a standard size; anything bigger is charged as a letter. Aerogrammes are the best value at ¥80. For parcels, pack printed matter separately and leave the envelope unsealed; it is charged at a lower rate. Post offices also send **faxes**, although it's usually quicker to do it from the reception desk of a big hotel.

Most post offices are open between 9 and 5, and closed at weekends and on holidays. **Tokyo International Post Office**, next door to Tokyo Station, is open for domestic and international mail 24 hours a day, 365 days a year.

For parcel deliveries in Japan, the cheapest and most efficient means of dispatch is one of the **courier delivery services** which operate out of convenience stores, rice and liquor shops. You can recognize these by their logos, all of which depict some kind of animal: **Perican-bin** (a pelican) and **Kuro-neko** (a black cat) are the most popular. From Tokyo you can send up to 20kg anywhere in Japan for less than ¥2,000. This is an excellent way of dealing with bulky souvenirs, luggage, etc. which you don't want to lug around: send it c/o your hotel and pick it up just before your departure.

Shopping

Shopping is the Japanese national pastime. For bustle, choice, affluence and expense, Knightsbridge and Manhattan have got nothing on the department stores of Tokyo's Ginza on a Saturday morning. During the economic bubble of the 1980s, when Japan had more money than it could flush into the Pacific, Tokyo became the consumer fetishist's dream. You could buy anything you wanted, and many, many things you never wanted at all— from mink lavatory seats and gold leaf noodles, to evening dress for dogs. All this cost a lot of money, naturally, but then that was all part of the fun. Compared to their counterparts in other first-world countries, Japanese consumers command little power in terms of choice and price, and all kinds of iniquitous monopolies and mark-ups flourish in the Byzantine distribution and retail networks. Since the bubble burst, matters have improved a little, with the spread of discount stores and the popularity of plain, workaday, non-designer goods. In general though, apart from uniquely Japanese items like crafts, you will find few bargains here, certainly when compared to other Asian cities. Instead, shop as the Japanese do—for the human drama, the attentive service, or the sheer pleasure of spending grotesque amounts of money.

Shopping etiquette is similar to that in the West, in other words, haggling is not expected (and may cause embarrassment) if the price is marked. A friendly shopkeeper may volunteer a discount, or throw in a free gift, but this is up to him. The biggest difference you'll notice is the attention paid to wrapping even the humblest items. The time this takes can add significantly to the length of your shopping trip—bear this in mind if you're in a hurry.

In general you get what you pay for: bargains are few, but so are obvious rip-offs, apart from those produced by the exchange rate and the genuine cost of living. As with restaurants, however, the more obviously Japanese a shop looks (sliding screens, assistants in kimono) and the more geared towards tourists, the more you are likely to pay.

Art and Antiques

Japanese art is prized all over the world—long gone are the days when you could pick up priceless statues for a few yen in a market because the stall-keeper didn't know what they were. Woodblock prints (*ukiyo-e*) were first shipped to the West as wrapping paper; now good impressions by famous artists cost millions of yen. Nonetheless, prints produced in editions are a good buy compared to 'original' works of art. Cheap but attractive versions of famous prints can be bought in tourist shops for a few thousand yen.

In Tokyo and Kyoto there are many shops specializing in one kind of art or another, often found in the vicinity of big Buddhist temples. Remember that whatever the art you are interested in, there is bound to be a museum somewhere specializing in it, where you can acquaint yourself with styles and techniques and train your eye.

Ceramics

Yakimono (literally 'baked things') are made all over Japan, in dozens of different local styles, some of them centuries old. They range from priceless and ancient tea bowls, to simple pots and cups produced by anonymous craftsmen for sale in local shops. Whatever you choose to spend, ceramics are among the most worthwhile souvenirs you can bring back from Japan.

There are over 100 pottery villages in Japan where traditional local ceramics are still made by hand. The most famous of these are Arita in Kyūshū, the home of Imari porcelain; the Bizen area, near Okayama, which produces an austere earthenware, much prized in the tea ceremony; the city of Kanazawa, for its gorgeous Kutani porcelain; Hagi, in Chūgoku, where a pinkish ware used in the tea ceremony is produced; and Kagoshima, in southern Kyūshū, where the white, porcelain-like Satsuma-yaki is made. Unfortunately, the demands of commercial production have turned some of these pottery towns into rather grimy and unattractive places. Mashiko, for instance, north of Tokyo, where the 20th-century folk potter, Hamada Shoji, had his workshop, has nothing worth seeing apart from its kilns and ceramic museums. Kilns are often rather inconveniently situated, away from the tourist sights on the outskirts of the towns. Most are happy to show visitors round but may prefer you to make an appointment. For serious pottery lovers, it's often a good idea to contact the local tourist office in advance, and set up a few meetings. Ask the tourist information centre in Tokyo or Kyoto for advice about this.

The most expensive of the handmade wares are works of art, prized by museums and collectors and priced accordingly. But even big name potters sell smaller items or kiln seconds at very affordable prices. Several pottery towns have a craft gallery, run by the potters, where a wide selection of items will be displayed, without big mark-ups. The best places to start shopping are often the craft floors of local department stores; the Maruzen chain of book shops also has a few of these. Even humble city supermarkets carry a range of teapots, plates and bowls for a few hundred yen each: they may not be collectors' items, but are designed according to the same ideals of elegance, dignity and simplicity.

Popular ceramics include teapots and bowls, *sake* sets (a flask and cups), dishes and serving bowls, vases and ashtrays.

Kimono: Visitors sometimes come to Japan with the idea of buying a kimono, only to come away disappointed. There are many different types of kimono (the word means simply 'thing worn') but the kind familiar in the West from woodblock prints and photographs is more than just a silk dressing gown. Properly worn, it's a complicated item of formal attire with strict rules governing the choice of patterns, the co-ordination of the colours, the length of the sleeves and the cut of the gown. Japanese women often attend classes in the art of wearing kimono; mastery of it can take years, and a hand-tailored garment costs as much as any evening dress.

It's also peculiarly unsuited to the Western figure. Even young Japanese women, taller and fuller-figured than their mothers, find strapping themselves into one rather a struggle; then there's the problem of walking and breathing at the same time. Of course the image of the kimono-clad woman as a gorgeous parcel, waiting to be unwrapped, is all part of the allure, but perhaps this is easier to appreciate when you're not wearing one. The traditional kimono, at least nowadays, is also rather a formal garment. Opportunities to wear one are rare enough in Japan, let alone back home in the West.

Of course, there's no reason why a kimono gown shouldn't be worn casually, and there are all kinds of places where these can be picked up cheaply enough. Department stores are worth investigating. Tourist shops always have a selection, but marked up and not always of the best quality. The best value of all are second-hand kimono. There are a handful of shops in Kyoto and Tokyo which specialize in these—for the price of a nasty nylon job from a souvenir shop, you'll be able to pick up the genuine silk article. The monthly fairs held at many shrines and temples are another good place to look: check local press for details.

Far more practical are *yukata*: light, cotton kimono with simple patterns in blue or black, worn by both men and women. They are usually provided in inn and hotel rooms. In traditional *ryokan* and *minshuku* you can wear them around the inn and in bed, instead of pyjamas. During the summer, especially in hot spring resorts, you will see people wearing them outside, with *geta*, clumpy wooden clogs. They are inexpensive, cool, comfortable, excellent for drying off in after a bath or *onsen*, and make fine souvenirs. Your inn may be willing to sell the *yukata* from your room; otherwise try department stores.

Other clothes: Japanese people are astonishingly neat and elegant, and many beautiful clothes, including the world's best designer goods, are on sale. For foreigners the problems are size and price. The above average *gaijin* counts as outsize in Japan. There is no equivalent of the discount 24-hour tailors in other Asian cities. Unless you simply can't live without it, wait to pay less back home.

Crafts

Along with pottery, hand-made crafts are the best Japanese souvenirs. When buying them, the same advice applies: visit a Folk Art Gallery (*Mingei-kan*) to get an idea of quality and design; try craft galleries and department store craft floors, and expect to pay more in obviously tourist-oriented shops.

wood

For centuries, wood has been the principal medium of Japanese sculpture, architecture, and many of its finest crafts. The best forests were once as valuable and closely guarded as gold mines, with ferocious penalties for timber smugglers. These days there are almost as many styles of wood craft as there are of ceramics.

Northern Japan has some particularly interesting wood crafts. The Ainu people of Hokkaidō carve blocks of soft wood into long, streamer-like wood shavings. In Yamagata prefecture, the *itto-bori* ('one-knife carving') technique is used to produce the tails and wings of wooden cockerels and owls. In Tōhoku, *kokeshi*, limbless wooden dolls, the shape of giant pegs, are produced on a spinning lathe, their features painted in with simple brush strokes. Kakunodate in Akita prefecture is famous for *sakura-kawa-zaiku*, a method of covering boxes and tea caddies with flexible cherry bark in rich dark colours. Nearer to Tokyo, Kamakura is the home of *Kamakura-bori*—plates, trays and boxes with cloud and flower designs carved into the surface in low relief, then burnished with a deep red lacquer and charcoal. In the *Hakone-zaiku* style, from the hot spring area under the shadow of Mt Fuji, the flat surfaces of trays and boxes are covered with a mosaic pattern of tiny squares of different coloured wood, in geometric patterns.

When purchasing wood crafts, check that they are solid. Cheaper wares are often produced by affixing an outer veneer to lower quality wood, metal or plastic (of course, these hybrids often look just the same as the real thing). The small objects described above usually cost no more than a few thousand yen each. Antique Japanese furniture—low tables for *tatami*, the big hardwood chests called *tansu*, and ingenious items like steps with space-saving drawers underneath—are much more expensive and hard to get hold of.

paper

Japanese paper, called *washi* to distinguish it from Western *yōshi*, is more than just a material for writing. It's a building and craft material in its own right, as delicate as tissue paper or as tough as canvas and used, in its various different textures and strengths, for sliding screens, windows, umbrellas and lampshades, as well as for writing and painting. The manufacturing process is laborious. Mulberry branches are steamed and stripped to expose the softened pith within, which is heated, rinsed, purified and pounded with mallets into a fine pulp. The sheets are formed on fine screens of bamboo mesh, then dried and individually trimmed and coloured. Some shops specialize in *washi* products— envelopes, cards, notepaper, lampshades, fans and waxed paper umbrellas all make inexpensive, lightweight souvenirs.

lacquer

Much Japanese architecture and craft emphasizes the natural grain and unpainted beauty of the wood. Lacquering does the opposite. The wood is sealed forever beneath a thin but impenetrable glaze of hardened sap. It's an acquired taste: to the uneducated eye, an opaque lacquer might just as well be a highly polished piece of plastic. The weight, texture and heft of the lacquered object in the hand all contribute to the connoisseur's appreciation. Like certain porcelains, the finest lacquer suggests unfathomable depth and mystery beneath the opaque exterior.

The raw lacquer—a brown, smelly, poisonous gum—is tapped from the *urushi* tree, and coloured and thickened before being applied in thin, even layers to a prepared surface of wood, paper, leather, or even metal. Each layer is dried for up to a week in a warm, humid, dust-free atmosphere, then polished with charcoal before the next layer is applied. This process might be repeated as many as 90 times. Finally, a sealing layer is applied and polished with powder made from deer's horns. The famous *maki-e* lacquerware has powdered gold and silver sprinkled onto the wet lacquer to produce iridescent patterns. Mother-of-pearl and semi-precious stones can also be incorporated. When a certain thickness has been achieved, the lacquer itself can be carved into three-dimensional designs.

Gizmos

Surprisingly, given its status as a world centre of technological innovation, Japan is not a particularly cheap place to buy cameras, computers, electronics and hi-fi. Hong Kong is much better, and you can haggle there too. Even with the present exchange rates, it may be cheaper to buy Japanese technology in Europe or America. If there's a special piece of equipment you're looking for, investigate prices before you leave home, and then compare them with those in an electronics district like Tokyo's Akihabara. Don't assume you'll save anything, especially for bigger objects which require shipping fees and insurance.

Where Tokyo does lead the way is in innovation: the latest Japanese models are on sale here first, and if novelty is more important to you than price, you have come to the right place. State-of-the-art gizmos may not be available in export models, however, which means that anything running off the mains will require adaptors and transformers. Satisfy yourself that you understand the operation of your gadget before walking away with an instruction book written only in Japanese, and bear in mind that guarantees, spare parts and service warranties may be difficult to invoke once you have taken your toy home.

Sport

In Japan, if you look hard enough, you can find almost any sport on the planet, plus several you've probably never heard of, from Ultimate Frisbee to Gateball, a curious croquet-clone played by very old people in white hats. Sumo is the *kokugi* or 'national accomplishment', though it's rivalled in popularity by baseball, and recently by the J-League, a professional soccer tournament launched, to tremendous public enthusiasm, in 1993.

The same rules apply to spectator sport as to all leisure activities in Japan: book early and try to avoid weekends and public holidays. One of the easiest ways to get hold of tickets (although you pay for the convenience) is through one of the nationwide booking agencies. **Ticket Pia** has an English language line, but it is almost always busy (© 03 5237 9999). If possible, ask a Japanese-speaking person to try the regular line (© 03 5237 9977). **Ticket Saison**, © 03 3250 9999, offers only Japanese—but you might get lucky and get an English-speaking operator. If all else fails you may want to go in person to one of the many Pia locations, a list of which you can find in Pia magazine. This magazine also provides comprehensive listings of concerts and events, but is entirely written in Japanese. Local media in English such as *Tokyo Classified*, *Kansai Time Out* and the English language newspapers will provide dates and times of all major sporting events.

sumo

There are six tournaments (*basho*) a year: Tokyo in January, May and September; Ōsaka in March; Nagoya in July; and Fukuoka in November. They begin around the 10th of the month and last for 15 days. The excitement (and most intense demand for tickets) mounts in the last few days of the tournaments, when the junior wrestlers have been filtered out and the big stars compete with one another for the highest honours.

It can be very difficult to get a seat, as tickets tend to be block-booked by companies who disburse them as corporate freebies. If you have connections, use them. Failing that, ask the local tourist information centre for advice. A few tickets are reserved for sale on the day but you will often have to queue very early in the morning to be sure of these. A heavy sumo habit can be expensive: seats vary from a few thousand yen to a few tens of thousands for the most expensive boxes. During the course of a tournament every TV and radio in Japan seems to be tuned in to the sumo. You will certainly have plenty of chances to see the excitement, even if you don't make it in person.

In Tokyo, the **National Sumo Stadium** (Kokugikan) is close by Ryōgoku, on the JR Sōbu line, ✆ 03 3623 5111. In Ōsaka, the **Prefectural Sumo Stadium** (Furitsu Taiikukaikan) is 10 minutes on foot from Namba subway station, ✆ 06 6631 0121.

baseball

Baseball was introduced in 1872 by Horace Wilson, an American teacher at the forerunner of Tokyo University. By the turn of the century most schools and colleges had baseball teams, and a professional league began in 1934. During the nationalistic war years, when Western influences and foreign words were undesirable, English loan words in the sport were banned. Baseball itself was, and sometimes still is, known as *yakyū*.

There are two leagues with six teams each. Teams are sponsored by corporations. The Pacific League, for instance, includes the Seibu Lions, owned by the department store chain, and the Nippon Ham Fighters (proprietor: Nippon Ham). The Central League contains the Chūnichi Dragons, Hanshin Tigers, Hiroshima Toyo Carp, Taiyō Whales, Yakult Swallows and—everyone's favourites—the Yomiuri Giants. The **Giants** play at the vast Tokyo Dome stadium (nearest stations Suidōbashi on the JR Sōbu line, and Kōrakuen on the Marunouchi subway line). Tickets cost between ¥1,000 and ¥5,600. In the Kansai area, the **Hanshin Tigers** play at Nishinomiya, between Ōsaka and Kōbe.

soccer

Whatever the quality of the football, the launch of the J-League in 1993 was one of the most successful marketing exercises in history. In its first year it generated ¥140 million revenue in advertising, sponsorship and—above all—merchandising. Attendance at a Japanese football match has none of the tribal elements of the European sport, in fact which team you support hardly seems to matter. Having the right J-League bag, J-League mascot and J-League anorak is much more important.

Verdi Kawasaki (owned by the giant Yomiuri newspaper corporation) is based near Musashikōsugi Station on the JR Nambū line or private Tōkyū Toyoko line. Take a bus from outside the station (on match days there will be plenty of people going in the same direction) to Shiei Todoroki Guraundo-mae.

In Kansai **Gamba Ōsaka** are your team. Take the Midōsuji subway line to Senri Chūō station, and change to the Ōsaka monorail for Bampaku Kinen Kōen station. The ground is a 20-minute walk away.

martial arts

Judō, aikidō and karate aren't the only ones—there are more than 20, including *kendō* (fencing with wooden staves), *kyūdō* (archery, using the traditional bamboo bow) and *naginata* (the art of the Japanese halberd). For long-term visitors there are many local clubs and associations offering classes. Many *dōjō* (martial arts halls) admit visitors to watch practice and competitions. The most famous in Japan is the Nippon Budōkan in Tokyo's Kitanomaru Park, north of the Imperial Palace. For information about tournaments, of which there are dozens each year, ring ✆ 03 3216 5139; for details of classes call ✆ 03 3216 5143, preferably in Japanese (or try the tourist information centre which keeps English language information on both).

Telephones

Public phones come in several types and colours. **Red, pink** and **yellow phones**, often located on the street and inside small shops, are the most basic. They take ¥100 or sometimes just ¥10 coins, and are good only for domestic calls. **Green phones** accept telephone cards but only work within Japan. **Green phones with gold plates** and **grey phones** (the Rolls Royce of phones) can make direct-dialled international calls. Buy **telephone cards** from shops, hotels or vending machines in the phone booths. For English language assistance with overseas calls, or to reverse the charges, insert a coin or card and dial 0051 for the KDD International Operator. To call overseas direct, dial 001, followed by the country code, followed by your full phone number, minus the initial zero. Home Country Direct is a free service which puts you in direct contact with an operator in your home country: UK, ✆ 0039 441, USA, ✆ 0039 111, Canada, ✆ 0039 161, Australia, ✆ 0039 611, New Zealand, ✆ 0039 641, Hong Kong, ✆ 0039 852.

Time

Japan is 9 hours ahead of Greenwich Mean Time (London), and 14 hours ahead of American Eastern Standard Time (New York). It has no daylight saving time, so during British Summer Time the difference is 8 hours.

Toilets

Japanese toilet technology is the most advanced in the world. Self-flushing lavatories with heated seats, built in bidets, hot air 'dryers' and recordings of light music or running water (to mask embarrassing noises) are commonplace. The littlest room in the Japanese house frequently has a button control plan reminiscent of the bridge of the Star Ship *Enterprise*, and there are even plans for a new generation of 'intelligent toilets' which will automatically process waste and warn the householder in advance of any worrying medical problems. At the same time, an amazing proportion of Japanese homes, even in the cities, are not on a mains sewer: at regular intervals a man driving a big tanker calls round, switches on his suction pump, and slurps. The lesson is to be prepared for anything.

In tourist facilities, Western-style sit-down toilets are the rule these days, but you will come across the traditional Asian squat models, especially in small rail and bus stations. These usually consist of an oval hole with a ceramic hood nearest the wall. Squat over the hole, facing the hood (gents can also stand and aim), steadying yourself if necessary on the pipes on the wall. This can be a uncomfortable position for the unsupple: skiing exercises are the best practice. The biggest hazard, for those wearing trousers, is that keys, change, etc. will tumble out of your pockets and into the abyss below. The consequences of this could be unspeakable. Loos of the Asian type can be unreliably stocked with paper: as always when travelling, a miniature packet of tissues is invaluable. Smaller establishments sometimes don't have both a ladies and gents, so don't be surprised if a member of the opposite sex barges in while you are washing your hands.

The character for ladies is 女 ; for gentlemen 男 . Toilet can be rendered お 手 洗 , *o-tearai*, literally 'honourable hand wash'. In extremis, ask for *toire* (pronounced 'toy-ray'). *Benjo* is a bit vulgar, but will get you where you need to be.

Tourist Offices

The best of these are run by the estimable **Japan National Tourist Organisation** (JNTO) which has 16 overseas offices, including the following:

United Kingdom::   Heathcoat House, 20 Saville Row, London W1X 1AE, ✆ 020 7734 9638.

United States: Rockefeller Plaza, 630 Fifth Avenue, Suite 2101, New York, NY 10111, ✆ 212 757 5640.

401 N. Michigan Avenue, Suite 770, Chicago, IL 60611, ✆ 312 222 0874.

360 Post Street, Suite 601, San Francisco, CA 94108, ✆ 415 989 7140.

624 S. Grand Avenue, Suite 1611, Los Angeles, CA90017, ✆ 213 623 1952.

Canada: 165 University Avenue, Toronto, Ontario M5H 3B8, ✆ 416 366 7140.

Hong Kong: Suite 3704–5 37/F, Dorset House, Taikou Place, Quarry Bay, ✆ 2968 5688.

Australia: Lv 33, The Chifley Tower, 2 Chifley Square, Sydney, NSW 2000, ✆ 02 9232 4522.

In Japan JNTO runs four **tourist information centres** where you can find out anything you need to know about travelling in Japan. Maps, pamphlets, brochures, bulletins, lists and magazines are available, as well as personal advice from multilingual assistants. The centres also take bookings for the Welcome Inn group of hotels. They can get crowded, and for personal assistance you may be required to take a number and wait in a queue.

Tokyo: Near Yūrakuchō JR station, Tokyo International Forum, 6–6 Yūrakuchō 1-chome, Chiyoda-ku, Tokyo 100–0005, ✆ 03 3201 3331.

Kyoto: Under Kyoto Tower, opposite the main JR station, Kyoto Tower Building, Higashi Shiokōji-chō, Shimogyō-ku, Kyoto 600–8212, ✆ 075 371 5649.

Narita Airport: 1st Floor, New Tokyo International Airport, Passenger Terminal Building, Narita, Chiba 282–0023. Terminal 1, ✆ 0476 32 8711; Terminal 2, ✆ 0476 34 6251.

Kansai Airport: 1st Floor, Kansai International Airport, Passenger Terminal Building, Sennan-gun, Ōsaka 549–0011, ✆ 0724 56 6025.

Tourist information centres also operate the **Japan Travel Phone**, a nationwide service for those in need of English-language information and assistance. In Tokyo, dial ✆ 03 3201 3331. You will be charged as if for a local call. If outside Tokyo or Kyoto you can dial ✆ 0088 22 4800 or ✆ 0120 44 4800 (both toll free). The service operates from 9am to 5pm daily.

Many prefectures, cities and towns operate their own tourist offices. These are principally aimed at Japanese tourists, but usually have some English-language information as well. They go under various names—tourist information office (*kankō annaijō*) or tourist association (*kankō kyōkai*). Almost all of them are located in or opposite JR railway stations.

Where to Stay

Japan's inns and hotels are among its biggest attractions. Top Tokyo hotels such as the Imperial and the Ōkura, and Kyoto *ryokan* like the Tawaraya, are as luxurious as any in the world, but even in modest family-run inns, standards of service and courtesy are uniformly high, and rip-offs are almost unheard of.

The most important consideration, after price, is whether you want to stay in Western-style or Japanese-style accommodation. Even within these categories there are distinctions, but Japanese-style establishments will generally be in low-rise buildings (sometimes, but not always, made of wood), furnished with *tatami*, with shared Japanese baths. Guests take off their shoes, sleep on futon mattresses laid on the floor and eat Japanese food in their rooms. Western-style means you keep your shoes and sleep on a bed in a room which usually has a private bathroom. Some Western-style hotels have Japanese-style rooms or wings and vice versa. Nobody who visits Japan should miss the chance to stay at least once in a Japanese-style inn. The cheaper *minshuku* are not expensive: consider it as crucial a part of your holiday as travelling on the bullet train or tasting raw fish.

Western-style

International hotels range from one-offs like the Imperial and Ōkura in Tokyo, to nationwide networks like the Tōkyū, Ōtani, Prince, ANA and Hilton. All have English-speaking staff, multiple restaurants and business facilities; many have pools, gardens, shopping arcades and gymnasia. **Resort hotels** are found in mountain and seaside locations, and are aimed at holidaymakers rather than businesspeople, with hot springs, golf links and often a floor of Japanese-style rooms. Prices generally begin at a minimum of ¥12,000 for a single, more in the big cities.

Business hotels are designed for convenience, compactness and low price. The basics of the standard hotel room—lavatory, bath, shower, sink, bed, TV, cupboard—are concentrated into an ingeniously small space. They seldom have much character, but are usually in good positions, close to stations and downtown. Nationwide business hotels, like the Tōkyū Inn, Washington and Sunroute chains, often rival the city hotels in terms of restaurants and facilities, with smaller rooms and lower prices (from about ¥6,000).

Pensions are hardly Western-style at all, though they may think they are. They are found in ski, hot spring and resort areas and provide Western-style rooms (beds and carpets), home cooking and friendly family service. Many are purpose-built in an allegedly Alpine 'chalet-style'; interiors are often 'cute' (i.e. kitsch). From ¥8,000 or so, including meals.

Japanese-style

A night in a traditional Japanese inn is a unique experience, a combination of theatre, architecture and gastronomy that may well be the high point of your holiday. Inns vary widely but fall into three principal categories.

Ryokan and **minshuku** overlap and the designation is often an arbitrary one. The biggest distinction is price: top *ryokan* are world-class restaurants housed in miniature palaces, and can cost ¥50,000 upwards per person. More modest ones, in regional towns, are as cheap as ¥8,000. *Minshuku* are a bit like bed-and-breakfasts, run by families with whom you eat your breakfast and evening meal. Service is more informal—you may have to lay out your own bedding for instance, although someone will always be on hand if you're not sure what layer goes where. **Shukubō** are temples which provide *ryokan*-style accommodation. They are generally found near big Buddhist complexes and are principally intended for pilgrims, although non-believers are usually welcome.

a night in a Japanese inn

You'll be asked, when you make your reservation, what time you expect to arrive—try to keep to this, and phone ahead if you are likely to be significantly late or early. You'll be greeted in the *genkan* or entrance porch, and, after removing outdoor shoes and donning slippers, escorted to your room by a maid. The Japanese guest expects to be fussed over, almost mothered, and, compared to the invisible discreetness cultivated in grand Western hotels, *ryokan* service is hands-on. This can be off-putting if you're not used to it, but don't be surprised if your maid hovers around and pops repeatedly in and out, enquiring after your every need in incomprehensibly polite and formal Japanese—a nod and a smile are all that's needed to reassure her. No matter how solicitous she is, a tip is never necessary.

Slippers are removed before you step on to the *tatami* matting which covers the floors of your room. Before you unpack, your maid will serve green tea and sweet bean cakes at the low table in the middle of the room. After this, you will be asked when you wish to eat, though in a smaller inn or *minshuku*, the time may be fixed. *Ryokan* usually have a preferred period when they serve meals, often surprisingly early—from 6 to 8. It may be a bit of a liberty to expect food after this time and, once again, you must keep to schedule. It may be assumed that, as a foreigner, you're unable to eat anything but pork chops and scrambled eggs—if this isn't the case, make a point of saying that you want Japanese food. You'll also be asked to fill in a form with your name, nationality and passport number. Next you'll be shown the facilities of the inn, including the toilet and bath. Japanese generally take a bath before eating, and dine in their rooms, wearing the *yukata*, a blue and white patterned cotton kimono, provided in each room. (You may be able to buy one of these before leaving.) Consult the sections on 'Baths and Hot Springs' (p.14) and 'Toilets' (p.45) for the etiquette appropriate to each of these rooms.

At the agreed time your food will be brought to you on trays, along with any drinks you have ordered. When the meal has been cleared away, your futon will be laid out on the *tatami*, and you will be left to your own devices. Posh *ryokan* would never be so presumptuous as to impose a curfew (smaller places might), but if you do intend to be out late, notify them of this, or request a late key.

Other types of accommodation

Youth hostels, both official and unofficial, are found all over the country, and are always the cheapest places to stay in the short term. They vary in quality. The best ones, often in mountain areas and national parks, can be beautiful buildings in their own right, run by enthusiastic volunteers who will have up-to-date and expert information on local hiking, cycling and skiing. The worst are grim detention centres run by embittered despots. JNTO publishes a guide map listing about 300 reliable hostels. Rates vary between ¥2,000 and ¥4,000, with or without meals.

Gaijin (foreigner) **houses** are cheap, urban lodgings for back-packers who are spending a few weeks in one place. They have a reputation for being rowdy and squalid, but are good places for gathering information about travelling and jobs.

The famous Japanese **capsule hotels** aren't nearly as ubiquitous as everyone seems to expect. Found near big urban transport termini, they offer a coffin-like bedroom with built-in TV and alarm clock, and a lounge area with machines vending noodles and drinks. Their clientele seems to consist entirely of single men: unaccompanied women might feel distinctly odd in one of these, or even be refused entry.

Love hotels are another Japanese phenomenon: rooms, rented by the hour or by the night, for amorous purposes. In a country of thin-walled houses and limited privacy, they're a blessing for married as well as illicit couples. There's nothing necessarily seedy about them, although theme love hotels may feature gaudy décor, whips, manacles and electric accessories. Bizarre though it may sound, they can be a very economical form of accommodation. Rates (higher at weekends) are generally no more than a business hotel, with the advantage that you pay by the room, not the person. In theory the whole family could bed down for as little as ¥10,000, as long as you don't mind a late check-in (nightly bookings begin after 10pm) and early check-out.

Reservations are advisable in most situations, especially for non-Japanese speakers. Japanese tourists book every night of their holidays months in advance, and at busy times (public holidays, during big festivals and the entrance exam season) your choice will be restricted if you don't think at least a few weeks ahead.

Arriving off a thirteen-hour flight into the bedlam of Tokyo or Ōsaka, it's certainly reassuring to know where you are going to lay your head. You can book from home through **travel agents** (*see* pp.6–7) like NTA or JTB, or through the foreign offices of big chains like Tōkyū and Prince Hotels. Overseas offices of the Japan National Tourist Organization (JNTO) provide leaflets and brochures, including information on the reasonable Japanese Inn Group and Directory of Welcome Inns (*see* below). Most lodgings in Japan have faxes.

In Japan itself, there are many options. Your hotel will often phone on your behalf to make reservations for the next night's accommodation. Agents often charge a commission. For cheaper accommodation use the free service provided by the **Welcome Inn Reservation Centre**, ✆ 03 3211 4201, ✉ 03 3211 9009, or its satellite desks in the Tokyo, Kyoto and Narita Airport tourist information centres. Hundreds of small hotels, *ryokan* and *minshuku* are classified as Welcome Inns; all charge less than ¥8,000 a night and are used to foreign guests. A similar service (for Japanese-style accommodation only) is provided by the members of the excellent **Japanese Inn Group** (book your room in English; pick up a brochure from a tourist information centre or JNTO office).

If you find yourself getting off the train with nowhere to stay, go straight to the local tourist information centre, usually called the *kankō annaijo* or *kankō kyōkai*. Even the smallest towns have these, often located in the railway station. The chances are that someone there will have at least a few words of English. Explain how much you want to spend, how long you'll stay, and whether you want meals or not: they will phone round for you and point you in the right direction.

Alternatively, phone yourself. The chances of finding an English speaker increase proportionately to the cost of the establishment and its proximity to a big city. Small town *minshuku* owners are likely to get flustered by a foreign voice gabbling incomprehensibly on the end of a phone: if you have Japanese, use it; if not, don't be surprised if phones are hung up on you. Off the beaten track you may notice a reluctance on the part of proprietors to accommodate foreigners. Infuriating though this can be, it's based on a fear of misunderstanding rather than xenophobia, and a pervasive image of foreigners as gallumphing disaster areas liable to wear their shoes on the *tatami*, use soap inside the bath, and vomit at the merest sight of something uncooked. The onus is on you to be reassuring: smile and nod a lot, never lose your temper, and season your speech with phrases like *Nihongo o wakarimasu* (I understand Japanese), *Ofuro o wakarimasu* (I know how to use the Japanese bath), and *Ofuton/washoku ga ii desu yo* (Sleeping on a futon/Japanese food is absolutely fine). *See* **Language**, pp.299–302, for other useful phrases.

Depending on the vicissitudes of the exchange rate, deluxe accommodation costs about the same in Japan as anywhere in the world. It is at the bottom end of the scale that choices become more limited. There simply is no equivalent of the £12 bed-and-breakfast. Even youth hostels rarely come cheaper than ¥2,000 a night. There are bargains here and there but, on the whole, you get what you pay for. If a place seems unrealistically cheap there is probably be a reason (small rooms, poor transport links, inconvenient position, etc.). The good news is that accommodation, certainly in the medium price bracket, seems to be getting cheaper. A combination of recession and stiff competition is causing hotels to drop their prices and good deals (big discounts, a double room for the price of a single) can be had. They're usually available only for limited periods, and aren't prominently advertised outside Japan; non-specialist agents may not know about them. Ask your nearest JNTO office and try phoning around the overseas offices of a few of the big chains.

In this book, prices for accommodation are banded according to the following categories:

luxury	above ¥30,000
expensive	¥15,000 – ¥30,000
moderate	¥ 8,000 – ¥15,000
inexpensive	¥ 4,500 – ¥ 8,000
cheap	¥ 4,500 and under

These categories are based on a single room (in Western-style accommodation) or a single night for one person (Japanese-style). Double rooms in hotels usually cost a bit less than two singles; in a *ryokan* or *minshuku*, however, even if several people share a room, they will generally all pay the full per person rate. Note, though, that Japanese-style accommodation almost always includes breakfast and dinner. Thus a moderate *ryokan* charging ¥8,000 a head is actually a better bargain than an inexpensive single hotel room at ¥7,000—as long as you are prepared to stay in for your Japanese meal and breakfast. If you don't want these, you can sometimes negotiate a lower rate at the less formal places. Note that the prices categorized above exclude service and a 3% consumption tax. In resorts and big cities, seasonal rates may apply.

Women Travellers

For a Japanese woman to travel extensively alone is considered unusual. Foreigners who do this can expect curious enquiries, but no unpleasant attention. The biggest cities have astonishingly low crime rates; even in a self-consciously seedy area like Tokyo's Kabukichō, it would be possible to walk around alone all night and suffer nothing worse than a few cat-calls. Foreign women occasionally report being groped on crowded commuter trains. The perpetrator of this intrusion relies on the Japanese reluctance to draw public attention to oneself; a Japanese girl would blush and get off at the next station. Foreigners should feel no such compunction. Grabbing the offending hand, and announcing out loud that you have caught a *chikan* (pervert) should bring the incident to a swift conclusion.

History

Until the tragedies of the twentieth century, Japanese history reads like a fantastic comic book, dense with grotesque heroes, baroque battles and gaudy detail—gripping for as long as you are immersed in it, but easy to forget once you've cast it to one side. Minamoto no Yoritomo, Oda Nobunaga, Tokugawa Ieyasu—the names are as exotic and meaningless to first-time visitors as Lex Luther and the Incredible Hulk. Who are these people? What have they to do with us?

The answer, a lot of the time, is nothing. In the late 1630s, less than a century after Japan's first, tentative contacts with the European world, the ruling shogun instituted a policy later known as *sakoku*—'closed country'. All Europeans, bar a handful of Dutch sailors in Nagasaki, were expelled within the space of a few years. Japanese nationals were forbidden any contact with the outside world; anyone who left the country was promised execution if they ever returned. The policy remained in force until 1853. In the rest of the world, kingdoms, empires and republics rose and fell, colonies were founded and lost, trade networks were established, industrialization spread across Europe and America, and unprecedented advances were made in the fields of science, philosophy, warfare and the arts. To all of this great intermingling of ideas and people and influences, Japan was oblivious.

For 250 years, the country was a sealed cabinet, a fable commemorated only in sailors' stories and on the edge of old maps. History (along with art, theatre, music, literature, science, religion and politics) was turned in on itself. Japan was (and still is, in many ways) like one of those freakish Oceanic islands, isolated from the continental mainstream by acres of sea, where nature is left to do its own thing, nurturing weird blooms and bizarre wildlife, a country of cultural platypuses and eucalyptus trees.

Periods of Japanese History

c. 10,000–c. 300 BC	**Jōmon period**	1333–1573	**Muromachi period**
c. 300 BC–c. AD 300	**Yayoi period**	1573–1600	**Momoyama period**
c. 300–c. 700	**Kofun period**	1600–1868	**Edo period**
538–645	**Asuka period**	1868–1912	**Meiji period**
645–710	**Hakuhō period**	1912–1926	**Taishō period**
710–794	**Nara period**	1926–1989	**Shōwa period**
794–1185	**Heian period**	1989–	**Heisei period**
1192–1333	**Kamakura period**		

Mythical Origins

The earliest account of Japanese history is the *Kojiki* (Records of Ancient Matters), an extraordinary chronicle compiled from traditional legends in the 8th century, which describes the sensational origins of the Japanese islands. They were formed by the incestuous union of **Izanagi** and **Izanami**, a brother and sister who came down from the Plain of High Heaven 'when the earth, young and like unto floating oil, drifted about medusalike'. Unsure of where to make a landing, they dipped a jewelled spear into this primeval soup, and the brine which dripped off it coalesced into land. Having established this first base, Izanami and her brother set about procreating first the other islands, and then the gods and goddesses of Japan. Not all of these were conceived in the conventional way. In fact, the divine couple could hardly scratch an itch without some new god or other springing into spontaneous life. The chroniclers gave them elaborate polysyllabic names, like the deity Heavenly-Water-Drawing-Gourd-Possessor, and the brother and sister team, Foam-Calm and Bubble-Calm.

During one particularly gruelling bout of child-bearing, Izanami had the misfortune to give birth to the fire god, an experience from which she never recovered. Even this tragedy brought forth new life, however, as new deities burst forth from her vomit and bodily fluids and her brother/lover's tears. Izanagi made the mistake of seeking out his loved one, by now rotting and infested with maggots, in the underworld. Fleeing from this horrible vision, he purified himself, and as he washed his eye, a new deity came into life. This was the sun goddess, **Amaterasu**, the most famous and revered of the ancient gods of Japan, whose shrine at Ise, near Kyoto, is the holy of holies of the Shinto religion.

Several generations of feuding, fighting and frantic copulation later, the descendants of the divine duo had spread throughout Japan. In 660 BC (on 11 February according to the legend, even today a national holiday), **Jimmu Tennō**, great-great-great-grandson of Amaterasu, celebrated his subjugation of central Japan by building a palace, and became the country's first emperor. Until 1946, when the late Emperor Hirohito formally renounced his divinity, all incumbents of the Chrysanthemum Throne claimed direct descent from Amaterasu Ōmikami, the Heaven-Shining-Great-August Deity.

Prehistory

Jōmon (10,000 BC–300 BC), Yayoi (300 BC–AD 300) and Kofun (AD 300–c. 700) periods

Splendid though they are, the *Kojiki* stories are not, of course, history; they are not even mythology. Their original function was political—propaganda designed to reinforce the authority and prestige of the imperial house, and to give form to the Japanese people's centuries-old conviction of their own uniqueness.

The inhabitants of Japan did not jump down from the clouds, and nor did their home. Until the end of the last ice age, around 11,000 BC, it was not even an island. Two great land bridges (later submerged by the rising sea) stretched to Siberia in the north and Korea to the west, and across these came waves of immigrants from China and Korea. The nature of these proto-Japanese is obscure; scholars make the best of an impenetrably murky prehistory by dividing it up into periods, based on archaeological finds.

The earliest known inhabitants were the Neolithic **Jōmon** (10,000 BC–300 BC), primitive hunter-gatherers who take their name from a style of pottery—striking, thick-rimmed earthenware decorated by pressing rope against the wet clay. Jōmon culture was concentrated in the north of the country; traces of it seem to have survived with the **Ainu**, a mysterious race of Siberian or even Caucasian origin, who underwent forced assimilation in the 19th century, but who still live in small numbers in present-day Hokkaidō.

Jōmon culture was supplanted by the **Yayoi** (300 BC–AD 300), a rice-growing people who imitated the bronze and iron instruments of their Chinese forebears, and spread into central Japan from their settlements in Kyūshū. It is during this period (perhaps the 1st century AD) that the historical prototype of Emperor Jimmu may have lived—one theory holds that he was a pirate-adventurer from Malaysia who united the bickering tribes, and imposed a form of central government based in the Yamato Plain, the site of present-day Nara. A Chinese chronicle of the late 2nd century describes the 'Land of Wa' (probably Kyūshū), ruled over by a shamaness-queen called Himiko or Pimiko, and details the habits of the people. 'They are much given to strong drink. They are a long-lived race, and persons who have reached 100 are very common. All men of high rank have four or five wives; others two or three. The women are faithful and not jealous. There is no robbery or theft, and litigation is infrequent.' Some of these generalizations hold true even today.

Large earth burial mounds, many containing elaborate bronze, glass and clay ornaments, give their name to the **Kofun** (tumulus) period (AD 300–c. 700)—in remote and unconquered parts of northern and eastern Japan, these tombs were being built as late as the beginning of the 8th century. By this time, the clans of the Yamato region were loosely united under the leadership of a dominant family, whose chieftain called himself emperor, and claimed divine descent. There was large-scale immigration from Korea and China, and much trade, mercantile and intellectual, was carried on with the Asian mainland, including two of the imports which have done most to shape the country as it exists today. The first was the adoption of Chinese ideograms in the writing of the (linguistically quite distinct) Japanese language. The second, also from China via Korea, was Buddhism.

The Rise of Buddhism

Asuka (538–645) and Hakuhō (645–710) periods

In the mid-6th century, a friendly Korean prince, angling for the loan of troops from his Japanese allies, sent to the emperor a Buddhist image, a collection of sutras and a letter commending the new religion, 'of all doctrines the most excellent'. The present provoked a rift in the Yamato aristocracy, between the powerful **Soga** and **Nakatomi** clans—the former champions of Buddhism, the latter hereditary high priests of Shinto. Successive emperors inclined first one way and then the other, but, by the end of the 6th century, temples had been built, more priests, statues and scriptures shipped over from Korea, and the new faith was firmly established—alongside Shinto which, despite the political rivalry between the different clans, it never sought to displace.

In 607 the great temple of Hōryū-ji, near Nara, was founded by the Prince Regent **Shōtoku Taishi** (572–621), an outstanding figure of Japanese cultural history, who—as a sculptor, artist, moralist, philosopher, teacher and scriptural commentator—did much to promote

Buddhism, at least among the ruling classes. A coup headed by the rival Nakatomi family broke the power of the Soga clan. The emperor was deposed, a compliant rival crowned in his place, and in 646 the **Taika** (Great Reform) was promulgated, an ambitious new constitution which sought to abolish the clan system, replacing local chieftains with imperially appointed governors who would administer law and order and dispatch taxes to the central coffers. This ambitious and minutely bureaucratic centralized government, based on the Chinese model, was the work of the chief rebel, **Fujiwara Kamatari** (614–669). The imperial throne continued to pass smoothly from one emperor to the next, but in reality, for about 400 years, the Fujiwara family were the true rulers of Japan.

The Nara Period 710–794

The Taika reforms also made provision for the construction of a new permanent capital (until now the residence of the emperor had been moved after the death of the previous incumbent), but it wasn't until 710 that this was finally achieved. **Nara**, built on a geometric grid in imitation of the Chinese capital, Chang-an, was Japan's first real city, and the stability which it afforded to the imperial household fostered a vigorous artistic culture, much of it self-consciously emulating the glorious Tang dynasty. This was the time of the *Kojiki* (712), and a later volume of chronicles, the *Nihon-shoki* (720), both of them imitating Chinese histories. As well as the new palace (now an archaeological site), the great temples of Yakushi-ji, Tōshōdai-ji, Kōfuku-ji and, above all, Tōdai-ji (752), were built in Nara. Their halls were filled with statues and paintings from the workshops of the continental artisans who had been settling in the area for several generations; for the first time Japanese art began to take on a recognizably Japanese character. Gifts from visiting dignitaries, as well as touchingly personal everyday objects like toys and dolls, were stored in the Shōsō-in imperial repository where they can still be seen today.

The Heian Period 794–1185

·The Nara temples were centres of education and art, but they were also crucial administrative bases, the collection points for the regional taxes levied by the Fujiwaras. The power and wealth of the bonzes eventually put them at odds with the aristocratic government. Some of the more worldly abbots even kept their own militias, and by 784 their threatening presence was causing unease among the Fujiwaras who moved the capital briefly to Nagaoka and then, in 794, to **Heian-kyō**, which remained the capital of Japan— later as Miyako, finally as Kyoto—until 1868. The Heian period was one of the peaks of Japanese civilization although, even in Kyoto, pitifully few of its relics have survived to the present day. It began with a long and eventually victorious campaign against the Ainu 'barbarians' in the north, and ended in civil war, but for the greater part of nearly 400 years there was peace, under the firm stewardship of the **Fujiwara clan**.

They ruled by an ingenious system of 'marriage politics'. A young emperor, often no more than a child, would be married off to an older (i.e. teenage) Fujiwara daughter, of which there were many. He would remain on the throne for just long enough to father an heir, and then abdicate in favour of the child, who had a Fujiwara mother, a Fujiwara grandmother and, as often as not, a Fujiwara regent ruling in his name. There the cycle began again. The family trees of the time are dense circuit diagrams of criss-crossing relationships. The greatest of the chancellors, **Fujiwara Michinaga** (966–1027), managed to become father-in-law of two emperors, grandfather of a third, grandfather and great-grandfather of a fourth, and grandfather and father-in-law of a fifth.

This incestuous, inward-looking world bred one of the most delicate and appealing civilizations in history. With political power securely in the grasp of a single family, the emperor and his court were able to concentrate on the finer things in life: state ceremonial, contemplation of the beauties of nature, literature and art, and love affairs—which became a kind of art form in themselves, the subject of strict etiquette and forms of behaviour. In literature, the courtly poets perfected the delicate, gnomic 31-syllable *tanka*. More accessible to modern readers are the prose works of the period, many of them by women: tragic dewy-eyed stories of doomed lovers and selfless servants, gossipy diaries and feverish love letters—all of which are combined in Lady Murasaki's unique, and thoroughly readable, *Tale of Genji* (*Genji Monogatari*) written around AD 1000. Equally brilliant, but often anonymous, achievements in the visual and plastic arts—architecture (both secular and religious), painting (on silk, screen and scroll), lacquered boxes and furniture, calligraphy and sculpture—as well as the architecture and landscape gardening of the temples, shrines and palaces—made Kyoto one of the cultural treasures of Asia, a city as rich and multi-textured as Venice, Byzantium or Oxford.

After centuries of enthusiastic apprenticeship, Japan was outgrowing the influence of the Tang dynasty which, in any case, had internal problems of its own. Concepts and institutions, originally imported from China generations ago, were given unique, home-grown inflections—the familiar process of 'Japanization'. So, although Chinese characters to this day form the basis of the written language, scribes during this period developed the two *kana* syllabaries for spelling out Japanese pronunciations and indicating the grammatical function of individual words. Two monks, Saichō and Kūkai, returned from study in China to establish radically new schools of Buddhism—the **Tendai** and **Shingon** sects—which fused traditional teaching with the native gods and goddesses of Shinto. In 894 the official missions to Chang-an were terminated. For the next few centuries, Japanese culture stood aloof from the rest of the world, stewing confidently in its own rich juice.

But great changes were also in the offing. The Fujiwaras began running out of marriageable daughters and the emperors began to assert themselves. After centuries of successfully playing one regional clan leader off against another, the Fujiwara family, in the 12th century, became factionalized. The court had no military resources of its own, so the competing branches enlisted the support of certain regional clans among whom two arch enemies—the **Minamoto** and the **Taira**—were paramount. For a while the Taira, under their ruthless leader **Taira no Kiyomori** (1118–81), were victorious, and began the task of insinuating themselves into the royal dynasty as the Fujiwara had before them. But the sons of the defeated Minamoto renewed the struggle a generation later in an epic civil war, dramatized in plays, paintings and poems like *Tales of the Heike*, as central to Japan's culture as the Trojan war is to Europe's. In 1185, the last of the defeated Taira threw themselves into the sea at the battle of **Dan no Ura** in the straits of Shimonoseki between

Honshū and Kyūshū. The emperor was allowed to remain in Kyoto, in powerless but untroubled luxury. But the true seat of power moved to the coastal town of Kamakura with the victorious general **Minamoto no Yoritomo** (1147–99).

The Kamakura Period 1185–1333

In 1192 Yoritomo was granted the title 'great barbarian subduing general', *sei-i tai-shōgun*, or *shōgun* for short. It was a profound change: for the next 800 years, military men, rather than civilian courtiers, wielded true power in Japan. They were the first samurai ('those who serve'), and it was during this time that the warrior code of service, obedience, and loyalty-to-the-death first found widespread expression. It was also a period of great artistic achievement: the large-scale rebuilding of the war-damaged temples of Nara and Kyoto fostered vigorous new schools of sculpture, and the austere **Zen sect**, which found particular favour with the samurai, brought with it from China fresh architectural techniques.

Yoritomo died in a riding accident in 1199 and within a few years his heirs had been usurped, in all but name, by another warrior family, the Hōjō. A bizarre system of government now existed, suggestive of those Russian dolls, each containing a smaller and still smaller replica. Japan's nominal ruler, the emperor, delegated authority to a Minamoto shogun, who was in turn a puppet of the **Hōjō regent**. All three titles were hereditary, and the picture was often complicated by the existence of a retired monk-emperor who effectively dictated the actions of his successor, after his formal abdication. Amazingly, thanks to the efficiency of the Hōjō, this system ran fairly smoothly for a hundred years.

The great crisis came in 1268 when the Kamakura government received a haughty letter from the great Mongol conqueror **Khubla Khan**. Addressed to 'the King of Japan', from 'the Emperor of Great Mongolia', it demanded tribute from the Japanese, and threatened war if none was forthcoming. When the demand was repeated a few years later, the envoys who carried it to Kamakura were beheaded. In 1274, therefore, 60,000 of the Khan's men sailed to Kyūshū in 450 ships. They made a great impression on the defending Japanese with their powerful long bows and rock-throwing artillery, but, after inconclusive fighting, storms arose and the fleet was dispersed with the loss of nearly a quarter of its men. Seven years later, Khubla Khan tried again, this time with a force of 150,000. In Japan there had been frantic preparations, including a defensive wall along the north coast of Kyūshū. Prayers for national deliverance were held in every temple and shrine across the country, and the Hōjō regent copied out sutras in his own blood.

Two separate armadas began to arrive in waves from the end of June 1281, and fighting continued for more than 50 days. Then another mighty storm arose and blew furiously for two days. It uprooted entire trees, and blew the Mongol boats far out to sea, or dashed them aground on the rocks. Less than half the original force limped back to the continent.

Yet again a 'divine wind', the original *kamikaze*, had been sent by the gods to save Japan. Actually the country remained on war alert for another 20 years and the cost of the crisis brought about the downfall of the Hōjō regency. After successful civil wars, the victor could reward his allies and supporters with enemy territory. The repulsion of the Mongols brought reprieve from slavery, but no material gain. Regional lords raised militias out of their own coffers, and peasants were conscripted to the detriment of the rice crop. In 1333 there was a serious dispute about the imperial succession. One of the candidates, **Emperor Go-Daigo**, mustered enough support to send an army to Kamakura. A number of the town's defenders defected to the other side and when the city fell, the last Hōjō regent, with 800 of his family and retainers, committed suicide in a mountain cave.

The Muromachi Period 1333–1573

For 60 years, two imperial factions—the **Northern and Southern Dynasties**—maintained bickering claims to the throne. In the end, the southern court, rivals of the late Go-Daigo, were victorious, but the real winners were another military family, the Ashikaga, who had themselves proclaimed hereditary shoguns from 1336. Kyoto was once again the administrative, as well as cultural, capital of Japan, but the emperors were no closer to real power than they had been a century before.

The rule of the **Ashikaga shoguns** was characterized by extremes of artistic distinction and political disaster. Culturally, it was one of the richest periods in Japan's history. Under Ashikaga patronage, many of the forms and genres considered today as quintessentially Japanese achieved their greatest expression. Zen Buddhism flourished, and Zen masters built superb meditation gardens, like the moss garden at Saihō-ji by the priest-artist, **Musō Kokushi**. New architectural forms also emerged, from the simple but artful huts built for the tea ceremony, to the exquisite villas built by the Ashikagas for their retirement, the **Golden** and the **Silver Pavilions**. Here the shoguns drank tea, watched performances of *nō* drama, and amassed priceless collections of ink paintings and ceramics, especially those of the Chinese Sung dynasty with whom relations had been resumed. The canons of taste established by the Ashikaga rulers—quietness, understatement, a taste for natural subjects and rustic simplicity—underpin Japanese aesthetics even today.

They were bitterly ironic ideals. Outside the temples and pleasure palaces, often in the streets of Kyoto itself, Japan was in a state of almost continuous civil war. Even after the succession dispute was resolved, battles between regional feudal lords, fanned by epidemics and famine, smouldered on in different parts of the country. From 1467 to 1477 the **Ōnin Wars** made a battleground of the capital itself. Shogunal authority was at an all-time low; the imperial court moved helplessly from place to place, as one palace after another was burned down. One emperor was even reduced to selling examples of his own calligraphy to buy food and fuel. The period from 1500 is known as *Sengoku jidai*, the Era of the Country at War.

The most interesting development of the 16th century came in 1542 when a crew of Portuguese sailors were shipwrecked on Tanegashima island, off southeast Kyūshū. Portuguese merchants and missionaries from China and Malaysia followed, and in 1549 the Spaniard **Francis Xavier** (later St Francis) was given permission to preach in Kyūshū and Yamaguchi where he gained many Christian converts. Even more significant, perhaps, was the other Western invention which the Portuguese brought with them: gunpowder and arquebuses, which were enthusiastically copied by local craftsmen. For centuries afterwards muskets were known in Japan as *tanegashima*.

The Momoyama Period 1573–1600

In the late 16th century, three great generals emerged from the mass of feuding samurai and between them brought order to the country. The first was **Oda Nobunaga** (1534–82), heir to a minor barony south of Kyoto, who attracted the attention of the emperor after a series of victories over technically superior armies. The Kyoto government was at its lowest ebb with the Ashikaga shogun a virtual refugee. Within a few years Nobunaga had supplanted him in all but name, and became the emperor's protector, rebuilding the Imperial Palace, as well as a personal stronghold, Azuchi-jō, the first of Japan's modern castles. He was extremely tolerant of the Jesuits ('These are the men I like,' he said, 'upright, sincere, and who tell me solid things.'), largely because he saw them as a means of breaking the power of the Buddhist orders which, with their large estates and private armies, contributed much to the bloodiness of the era. His most famous display of ruthlessness came in 1571 when he burned down the 3000 temples of Mt Hiei, northeast of Kyoto, and butchered their inhabitants. Two years later he imprisoned the last of the Ashikagas, and became *de facto* shogun. On his death, at the hands of a disaffected lord, he was master of half of the provinces of Japan, and all the most central and strategically important ones.

Nobunaga was succeeded by **Toyotomi Hideyoshi** (1536–98), one of his most brilliant lieutenants, who saw off the Oda heirs and cemented his authority with the construction of a massive castle at Ōsaka. Hideyoshi, a small, exceedingly ugly man, was born the son of a foot soldier and rose by sheer intelligence; he was a skilled diplomat as well as a warrior, and throughout his life showed a love of extravagance and display verging on megalomania. Hideyoshi's two palaces (one of them, at Momoyama, south of Kyoto, lent its name to the period) were as rich and gaudy as the Ashikagas' were austere and restrained, with profuse carvings of flowers, Chinese legends and mythical monsters on gates, pillars and transoms; visionary screen paintings of mountain sides, peopled by sages and tigers, in bright colours and gold leaf; curving eaves and heavy tile roofs. Hideyoshi loved public spectacle: on one fabled occasion in 1597, he held at his palace a huge open-air tea ceremony to which everyone in the country, from peasants to lords, was invited. The festivities went on for ten days. After his death the palaces were dismantled and distributed hall by hall among Kyoto temples like Nishi Hongan-ji, where they were reconstructed and preserved; many survive to the present day.

By 1590, after the siege of Odawara, the remaining provinces yielded to Hideyoshi's control, but even this didn't quench his ambitions. Rather than consolidating his remarkable achievement—national peace, for the first time in 260 years—Hideyoshi set about the astonishing project of invading and subduing Korea and China. Two separate armies set sail, in 1592 and 1597. The first got as far as the Korean-Chinese border; the second was making slower progress when, in 1598, news came through of Hideyoshi's death, and the campaign was abandoned.

Tokugawa Ieyasu (1542–1616) was one of the trustees appointed by Hideyoshi to guarantee the succession of his son, he was a trusted ally who had previously given loyal service to Nobunaga. A famous tale illustrates the differences in character between the three men. Nobunaga, Hideyoshi and Ieyasu, it is imagined, are presented with a nightingale, but nothing anyone can do will make it sing its famous song. Nobunaga approaches the bird. 'If you won't sing, little bird,' he says, 'I will kill you.' Hideyoshi tries next: 'If you won't sing, little bird, I will make you sing.' Last comes Ieyasu. 'If you won't sing, little bird,' he promises, 'I will wait.' This is how history remembers him. After the hot-blooded cruelty and unpredictability of his predecessors, he was a different kind of leader: cold, shrewd, with a reptilian patience which ultimately brought him the greatest prize.

Rather than jostling for position in central Japan, Ieyasu secured himself a base in the Kantō plain, and built an impressive castle at the small village of Edo. He managed to wriggle out of the Korean adventure, so that when his moment arrived, he was in a better position than many of his fellow lords to take advantage of Hideyoshi's death. Predictably, his master's will was not executed according to his wishes, and Ieyasu was soon at war with his fellow trustees. At the **Battle of Sekigahara** on 21 October 1600, they were decisively defeated. Enemy lords were stripped of their domains; Ieyasu's allies were richly rewarded, and in 1603 he himself was confirmed by the emperor as shogun. Ieyasu's headquarters, by now a booming city, became the administrative capital of Japan, and has remained so ever since, as Edo and, eventually, Tokyo.

The Edo Period 1600–1868

The defeat and death of Hideyoshi's son at the siege of Ōsaka in 1615 brought an end to nearly three centuries of civil war. The following year Ieyasu died, although, as shogun, he had already been succeeded by his son, Hidetada, in 1605. Although much of the ground-work had been laid by others, he had succeeded in the feat which eluded both of his predecessors: passing on his victory to the next generation. The dynasty he established was to rule unchallenged in Japan for 15 generations.

Shoguns came and went. Some were interesting and forceful characters; many wielded little more personal power than the emperors, mere puppets of their advisers. It is more accurate, in speaking of these men, to talk of the work of the shogunate, rather than the shogun. Peace and stability were maintained by an autocratic government which sought, above all, to stifle change and prevent any alteration to the status quo. Hierarchy was all-important: society was divided into four classes—from samurai, through farmers and artisans, to the lowest rung, merchants—and strict rules governed the dress, duties and conduct of each rank. Freedom of movement was strictly curtailed, and contacts with the outside world were reduced almost to nothing. Even in the time of Hideyoshi, anti-Christian edicts had been promulgated and the Tokugawas, wary of the rivalry between different branches of the church, and fearful of their interference in Japanese internal politics, enforced these brutally, expelling or martyring many missionaries and their converts. Western books were banned, and by 1641 the only Europeans allowed in Japan were a group of Dutch merchants confined to an artificial island in Nagasaki harbour (although trade with China and other parts of southeast Asia was sustained intermittently throughout these years).

The cultural achievements of the period were largely associated with the city of Edo, and the 'Floating World' of teahouses, geisha houses and brothels which sprang up there. Woodblock prints (*ukiyo-e*) by artists like Hokusai and Hiroshige, *kabuki* drama and the

Ōsaka *bunraku* puppet theatre, and the *haiku* and travelogues of the poet Bashō, were all products of these years. In the latter part of the period, the strains of the unbending Tokugawa system began to show in the economy. There were epidemics and famines, and discontent spread among the increasingly impoverished samurai whose military function was by now completely redundant. Nationalist intellectuals began to study the *Kojiki* and other Shinto-inspired histories, and to re-examine the role of the emperors who, throughout this time, lived on in Kyoto in powerless seclusion.

The Meiji Restoration 1854–1868

In the mid-19th century, while trains, factories and telegraph wires were appearing all over Europe, Japan was still effectively in its middle ages. Travel, on foot, horse or palanquin, over rough mountain roads, was slow and dangerous; medicine and science were crude and unenlightened; and the feudal hierarchy was strained near to breaking point by the rise of the merchant class and the switch from a rice to a cash economy. The shogunate was also harried by foreign worries: Russian and American vessels had been sniffing around Japan's territorial waters. Japan possessed no navy; if these incursions were to escalate to the point of an armed stand-off, there was no question who would be the loser.

Then, in 1853, **Commodore Matthew Perry** of the United States Navy steamed into Edo Bay at the head of four warships. He carried letters from President Fillmore requesting the opening of trade relations. After delivering them, he did a turn round the bay, much to the astonishment of spectators on the shore, and sailed away, with the promise of a return visit, with a bigger fleet of 'Black Ships', next year. A few months later a Russian admiral turned up in Nagasaki with similar demands.

The shogunate blustered and hesitated, even consulting the emperor who insisted that the barbarians be repulsed. Sea defences were erected but, on Perry's return, the Japanese had little choice but to accede to his demands and to open up the ports of Hakodate and Shimoda to American sailors. More comprehensive treaties followed, with Russia, Britain, France and Holland as well as America, and in Japan the presence of the foreign diplomats and traders caused great unrest. An anti-shogunal faction emerged, led by samurai clans in western Honshū and Kyūshū, under the slogan, 'Revere the Emperor, expel the Barbarians!' This the shoguns seemed about to do, but the threat proved an empty one, and when a few zealots fired on foreign ships from shore batteries, they were quickly blasted into submission. At this point the anti-shogunal forces changed tactics. A number of young samurai from the rebel clans of Chōshū and Satsuma, including future prime ministers, were secretly sent abroad to Europe to study. Their samurai armed and organized themselves along Western lines.

By 1867, the shogun's hold on power was increasingly wobbly. Rebel forces entered Kyoto to 'free' the emperor, and defeated the shogunal army in a battle south of the city. Further skirmishes occurred in Tokyo, northern Honshū and Hokkaidō, but the shogun himself quickly abdicated and surrendered. In 1868 the 16-year-old Emperor, Mutsuhito, posthumously known as Meiji, entered Edo, and the following year he took up full-time residence there. The city was renamed Tokyo, 'Eastern Capital'.

The Meiji Period 1868–1912

The period of Meiji's rule was one of the most extraordinary in any country's history. Japan was weak when it began, divided and fearful of colonial incursion by the Western powers. By its end, she was an industrialized power, the victor of wars against both China and the mighty Russian Empire. Not only a military and industrial but also a social revolution had taken place. Foreign inventions (steam trains, Western dress, umbrellas, watches, gas lamps, horse carriages, bicycles, cameras, brick buildings and newspapers), foreign institutions (a Western-style educational system, parliament and armed forces), and foreigners themselves (teachers, missionaries, engineers, military attachés and advisers) were a fashionable part of everyday life. In less than half a century, Japan had bounded from the middle ages to the forefront of the 20th century.

The early years of Meiji were the time of greatest enthusiasm for things foreign, but by 1889 when the first Diet was inaugurated (the country had until then been ruled by an oligarchy made up of leaders of the Meiji Restoration) a certain insularity had taken hold. The **Meiji Constitution** was a conservative document, hedged around with vague qualifications of the limited freedoms which it guaranteed. Little more than one per cent of the population was entitled to vote for the Lower House of the Diet, which could be dissolved at any time: Japan was effectively still ruled by an oligarchy. The Imperial Rescript on Education of 1890 consolidated this authoritarian set-up by enjoining the Confucian virtues of loyalty to emperor, family and state. Buddhism, tainted by association with the shoguns, was disestablished and many of the great temples suffered confiscation of their assets and privileges. In its place, Shinto was encouraged, particularly the aspects of it associated with emperor worship. The ancient and honourable tradition of syncretic worship was outlawed; hybrid shrine-temples were purged of their Buddhist elements.

Industrialization gathered pace in the 1890s and the great family combines, the *zaibatsu*, were formed (*see* **Business Culture**, pp.98–100). The Meiji forces' victory in the **Sino-Japanese War** (1894) was scuppered by Russia, France and Germany who forced Japan to restore many of the territorial gains it had made on the Asian mainland. Tensions with Russia over control of Korea led to the Anglo-Japanese Treaty of 1902 which survived in various forms until 1921 and did much to boost Japanese self-confidence. In 1905 it was sent to dizzy heights by the **defeat of Russia**, especially the Battle of Tsushima, when the Japanese navy (equipped and trained by the British) sank or captured all but two of Russia's Baltic Fleet. By 1910 **Korea** had been fully annexed; it remained a Japanese colony until 1945. These victories created a tremendous prestige for the military and a growing mood of ultra-patriotism. At the same time a vocal socialist and anarchist movement emerged. In 1911, the year before his death from illness, a murder plot was uncovered against the Emperor, and this was taken as a pretext for a crack-down on all forms of left-wing dissent.

The Road to War 1912–1941

The short reign of the mentally ill **Emperor Taishō** (1912–26) was a breezy and optimistic period when the efforts of a few liberal-minded statesmen seemed to have stifled the authoritarianism of the Meiji Constitution. During the First World War, Japan, as the ally of Great Britain, mopped up a few of Germany's possessions in China, and there was an inconclusive intervention in Siberia in the Russian Civil War of 1918. But on the whole, Japanese relations with the rest of the world were cordial. In the cities, students with bobbed hair or Oxford bags danced to jazz and discussed Marxist ideas in the new beer halls and cafés. In 1921, the Crown Prince Hirohito, by now regent for his enfeebled father, made a famous visit to Britain. He was photographed wearing a tweed cap and plus fours, playing golf with the Prince of Wales. Tokyo was all but destroyed by the 1923 **Great Kantō Earthquake,** but it was quickly rebuilt, and the reign of **Emperor Hirohito** (1901–89) began in 1926 in a spirit of confidence and hope. It was given the official name *Shōwa,* 'Enlightened Peace'.

Depression, endemic throughout the world in the 1930s, struck Japan early, with a banking collapse in 1927. The suffering this caused among poor farmers provoked widespread anger, particularly in the army which was becoming increasingly powerful and independent. Young army officers, contemptuous of corrupt politicians and the self-seeking capitalists of the *zaibatsu,* toyed with the idea of a military coup, and several politicians were assassinated by fascist 'patriots'. In China, where Chiang Kai-shek's nationalist Kuomintang army was threatening Japanese interests, army officers took unilateral action, attacking and occupying the city of Mukden. Because the army had a veto over the appointment of army and naval ministers, it could effectively bring down the Cabinet whenever it chose. While Japanese politicians helplessly assured the League of Nations that their withdrawal was imminent, the army itself surged deeper into Manchuria to set up an 'independent' state under a Chinese puppet emperor.

At home, plots and coup attempts rumbled on. In February 1936, several members of the Cabinet were wounded or assassinated at their homes and two infantry regiments mutinied. The coup was quashed by the army itself but the incident stood as a grim warning to politicians who were now virtually dictated to by the military. In the same year Japan signed the Anti-Comintern Pact with Germany. The country began to arm for a full-scale invasion of China. In December 1937, in one of the most notorious incidents in Japanese history, thousands of civilians were massacred in the Chinese nationalist capital Nanking by the rampaging army. But Chiang Kai-shek escaped, and the war lingered on.

When war began in Europe, Germany urged her Asian ally to attack the Allied colonies in the Far East. Japan held back, and Ribbentrop's Non-Aggression Pact between Germany and the USSR made it seem all the more likely that Japan would avoid involvement in the European war. But it was clear that, if fighting did spread to Asia, it could cripple the Japanese economy which relied so heavily on imported oil. War was developing its own momentum, and many in Japan had a lot to gain from it: the demand for munitions and the raw materials obtained from the conquered Chinese territories had already created a booming war economy. When Japanese forces in Indo-China threatened Malaya and the East Indies, economic sanctions were imposed by Britain, America and Holland. Japan was faced with a choice between economic disaster, a humiliating climb-down, or war.

Talks with the United States proceeded inconclusively. On 8 December 1941 Japanese planes made a devastating surprise attack on the US naval base in Hawaii's Pearl Harbour, and simultaneous assaults on Hong Kong, Malaya, Singapore and the Philippines.

The Pacific War 1941–1945

For four months Japan didn't put a foot wrong as, one after another, the colonial outposts of East Asia toppled before the imperial forces: Penang, Hong Kong, Manila, Singapore, Batavia, Rangoon and Mandalay. Massive new sources of raw materials were opened up; full-scale invasions of India and Australia seemed to be only a matter of time. But Japanese forces were repelled from New Guinea, and in June 1942 the US navy won a crucial victory at the Battle of the Midway. Thereafter, the whirlwind of early victories began to look more and more like beginners' luck, as the Japanese gains were first slowed, then halted, and finally, in battles of agonizing duration and ferocity, reversed. By mid-1943, Japan was losing the war. Any public articulation of this state of affairs was regarded as defeatist, and the activities of the military police, as well as domestic shortages, made life in Japan increasingly uncomfortable.

The country was far from defeated though; if Prime Minister Tōjō had been prepared to seek a peace at this point, he might have come away with treaty recognition for large portions of the conquered territories. Fanatical confidence in its invincibility was the greatest failing of the Japanese leadership, coupled with an arrogance and brutality in its treatment of prisoners of war which is a source of bitterness even today. Japan's pretext for the invasion of the European colonies—that it was liberating them from Western domination, in pursuit of an independent, self-determining Greater Asian Co-Prosperity Sphere—was taken seriously by nationalist groups in many parts of the continent. But the racism and cruelty of the occupying armies turned many potential allies into enemies, and contributed to Japan's eventual defeat. The decisive loss came in June 1944 when American forces gained the Pacific island of Saipan, which put the Japanese mainland within reach of their heavy bombers. By the end of 1944, the imperial navy had been effectively destroyed at the Battle of Leyte Gulf, and General MacArthur was well on his way to winning back the Philippines. To anyone in a position to know, it was clear that Japan's decline was irreversible. But it was glacially slow. In February 1945 the tiny island of Iwo-jima was taken after nine weeks and 20,000 American casualties; the Japanese garrison of 23,000 fought to the last man. The capture of Okinawa in June was similarly agonizing, and by now the airforce had started to employ the famous *kamikaze* pilots— young volunteers who dived onto Allied ships in planes loaded with explosives. Incendiary air raids on the mainland were burning out the wooden hearts of the Japanese cities, and supplies of food and raw materials, including oil, were perilously low.

From the outside, the Tokyo leadership seemed as far away as ever from a statement of surrender. However, from their deciphering of Japanese diplomatic codes, the Americans knew that Stalin was being asked to mediate a settlement on Japan's behalf. The Cabinet recognized that defeat was unavoidable; their one, insistent demand was that the emperor system should remain untouched. But in July 1945 Churchill, Truman and Chiang Kai-shek (Stalin was deliberately excluded) issued the Potsdam Declaration, demanding immediate and unconditional surrender. 'The alternative,' they asserted in an ominous phrase, 'is prompt and utter destruction.' Publicly, the Declaration was haughtily rejected; privately, the diplomatic wires revealed the anxiety of the Japanese high command.

On 6 August, an atomic bomb was exploded above Hiroshima. Communications between Tokyo and the west of the country were so bad that the full extent of damage was not immediately known by the leadership. Perhaps more significant than the second atomic attack on Nagasaki on the 9th, was the news of the day before—that Stalin's Red Army was invading Japan from the north. At noon on 15 August, the entire country gathered around wireless sets to hear a remarkable broadcast. It was the Emperor, addressing his people for the first time in their history. Urging his people to 'endure the unendurable and suffer what is insufferable', he announced the government's acceptance of the Potsdam Declaration. At no point were the words 'defeat' or 'surrender' used. 'The war situation,' the Emperor nonetheless noted, 'has developed not necessarily to Japan's advantage.'

The Occupation 1945–1952

In contrast to the savagery, fanaticism and stupidity of the war itself, its aftermath was a model of calm and order, in Richard Storry's words, 'the most peaceful and, to outward appearance, most harmonious occupation of one great country by another that has ever been known'. A few responded to defeat in the traditional way, by committing ritual suicide, but the mass of the population, once the initial shock was over, welcomed the American forces, and the relief from suffering which they symbolized.

The Americans set about a comprehensive programme of political and social reform. In charge was the 'American Shogun', **General Douglas MacArthur**, the Supreme Commander for the Allied Powers and hero of the battle for the Philippines. Pre-war institutions held responsible for the war, such as the army and bureaucracy, were comprehensively purged. The *zaibatsu* were abolished, and a number of senior politicians, including the wartime Prime Minister, Tōjō, were hanged as war criminals. Right-wing organizations were banned, labour unions were established, and the old education system, with its emphasis on loyalty to the emperor, was liberalized. A **new constitution** was drafted, including a clause which renounced forever the use of force in resolving international disputes. Perhaps the most important decision related to the Emperor. His personal role in the build-up to war is still a matter of scholarly dispute, but at the time many people would have been quite happy to see him put on trial alongside his ministers. MacArthur wisely let him stay. The peerage was abolished, and Hirohito's role was reduced to that of symbolic head of state. He issued a rescript explicitly refuting 'the false conception that the emperor is divine'. With the outbreak of war in Korea and growing American fears of communism, a number of these reforms were reversed, or at least watered down. A large number of businessmen and bureaucrats were de-purged, and the *zaibatsu* re-emerged, in looser form, as the *keiretsu* collectives (*see* p.98). The pacifist clause in the constitution which renounced Japan's right to air, sea and land forces became a particular embarrassment, and was overcome by a form of words. In the shape of the 'Self-Defence Forces', Japan today has one of the biggest and best equipped military machines in the world.

The Economic Miracle 1952–1980

The Occupation brought large amounts of aid to devastated Japanese industry, but what kick-started the economy was the Korean War, and Japan's role as victualler and manufacturer to the anti-communist forces. With large numbers of American troops stationed in Japanese territory, it was, for a few years, as if the Occupation had never ended. Communist supporters organized noisy anti-American demonstrations and, in 1955, in reaction to the left-wing revival, the two principal right-of-centre parties amalgamated into the Liberal Democratic Party (LDP). Compared to the European or American idea of a political party, the LDP has always been a divided institution, a flag of convenience for a number of fiercely competitive individual factions. Nonetheless, for the next 38 years, it held on to power. Its politically stagnant, but stable, period of rule saw one of the most remarkable economic recoveries in history—perhaps the greatest since the reconstruction of the country during the Meiji period. In the 1950s the phrase 'Made in Japan' was synonymous with cut-price shoddiness. By the 1980s it signified reliability, value for money and innovation; few homes in the industrialized world are today without their Japanese car, TV, video, stereo or computer.

After a brief slump at the end of the Korean War, the economy—under the firm stewardship of the Ministry of International Trade and Industry (MITI)—achieved astonishing levels of unbroken growth, based on generous tax breaks, government subsidy of key industries and relentless encouragement of exports. Year after year, growth targets were exceeded: from 9 per cent in 1955 to 14.4 per cent in 1961. In 1960, Prime Minister Ikeda promised to double salaries before the end of the decade; the target was reached by 1967. As wages and the standard of living rose, Japanese families strove to acquire the 'three sacred treasures': car, refrigerator and colour television.

With the blossoming economy came a new mood of national self-confidence. The Tokyo Olympics in 1964, the first to be held in Asia, seemed to mark the symbolic end of Japan's period as an ailing, defeated, underdog nation. Hotels, roads, stadia and railways were built, including the first of the famous *shinkansen* bullet train lines. A cultural landmark of a different kind came two years later, when thousands of screaming fans turned out to see the Beatles at the Budōkan stadium. But there were social tensions, too, as a younger generation of Japanese grew up, with no direct memory of the war and less tolerance of the austere lives led by their parents. The construction of Tokyo's new international airport at Narita and the renewal of the US Treaty in 1970 became the focus for rioting among students and left-wingers, and for a few febrile months, change was in the air. The climax came in November 1970 when the novelist Mishima Yukio committed ritual suicide after a spectacularly bungled coup attempt.

In retrospect the incident marked the end of an era, as the restless students of the late 1960s became the obedient 'salarymen' of the 1970s. It was a less spectacular decade than those which had gone before it, but remarkable in its own way. In 1974, the Lockheed bribery scandal brought down Prime Minister Tanaka Kakuei, and exposed publicly the institutional corruption of Japan's political system. The oil crisis of the same year cast a nasty cloud over a country almost entirely dependent on foreign fuel imports, but, miraculously, even this potential catastrophe was turned to Japan's advantage. With unerring discipline, the government and the country embarked on a systematic programme of energy conservation which minimized the recession, and allowed Japan to emerge from it even further ahead of her floundering international competitors.

The 1980s

At the end of the 1970s, Japan had the lowest inflation, lowest unemployment, lowest interest rates, and highest growth of any developed country—in other words, the strongest economy on the planet. By the middle of the next decade, Japan was not just beating the rest of the world in industries like steel, ship-building, cars, electronics and microchips, it was also bank-rolling its competitors. The seven biggest banks in the world were Japanese—in 1985, as the United States became the world's biggest debtor nation, Japan became its biggest creditor, largely through its purchase of US government bonds. This extraordinary reversal had several consequences. Japan had long exported far more of its own goods than it ever imported from abroad, and the resulting balance of payments surplus rapidly began to infuriate its trading partners. Trade friction frequently threatened to flare into trade war; the danger has only recently begun to recede.

Increasingly, Japan's corrupt political head looked absurdly unsuited to its powerful economic body. The 1980s saw only one prime minister of any substance—Nakasone Yasuhiro, a statesmanlike and internationally-minded character who nonetheless caused unease with his nationalist sentiments and attempts to increase defence spending. Otherwise, party leaders were the usual LDP drones, the puppets of powerful, behind-the-scenes factions, embarrassingly prone to scandal and disgrace. In 1989 a prime minister was forced to resign after being implicated in a bribery scam. Two months later his successor followed him after saucy revelations about after-hours activities with a *geisha*.

But Japan looked and felt like a rich country. As the yen grew stronger, imported goods became cheaper, and luxury foreign labels flooded into the shops. Companies ploughed their profits into tax-free expense accounts and bonuses, and consumer industries boomed as their employees found ever more costly ways of entertaining themselves. All over the country, gleaming new offices and public buildings went up. Japanese corporations acquired a reputation abroad as voracious snappers-up of cultural icons, at prices that Western capitalism could no longer afford—from Impressionist paintings to Columbia Film Studios and New York's Rockefeller Centre.

The Heisei Era 1989 onwards

In January 1989, Emperor Hirohito died at the age of 88, and the Shōwa ('Enlightened Peace') period came to an end, having disgraced and lived up to its name in equal measure. Public grief was muted; the Emperor had been ill for months, and Japan soon had other things to think about. The new Emperor Akihito christened his ruling era Heisei, 'Accomplished Peace', but the first big issue to confront his country was the Gulf War. As a member of the United Nations (with hopes for a permanent place on the Security Council), Japan was under pressure to contribute troops to the international force being assembled for the liberation of Kuwait. On the other hand, the 1945 constitution expressly forbade the active employment of Japanese forces overseas. The issue paralysed the Japanese Diet; eventually a compromise was reached whereby Japan provided £4 billion in financial aid, and a token force of non-combat units.

In 1993, the LDP, wormy with corruption and riven by in-fighting, splintered. An important faction, grouped around the sinister and intelligent Ozawa Ichirō, quit the government and brought it down in a vote of confidence. By now the 'bubble' economy of the 1980s had burst. Unnaturally inflated asset growth had finally reached its ceiling and, although the recession caused few of the ugly consequences felt in other industrialized countries, growth was reduced and bankruptcies and unemployment rose. In the election that followed, the LDP's vote was split between several new parties founded by its former members; despite winning the largest number of seats, the Liberal Democrats lost control to a seven-party coalition which included these turncoat politicians and the old Socialist (renamed the Social Democratic) Party. Psychologically, this was a mighty coup: after 38 years of one-party rule, the LDP appeared to be out on its ear.

At the end of the millennium, however, it is still in power. The newly reformist government of Morihiro Hosokawa announced ambitious reforms to eliminate political corruption—but a financial scandal of his own brought down the new prime minister in April 1994. A bizarre eighteen months followed in which the LDP returned to government in an ill-co-ordinated coalition led by its old adversaries in the Socialist Party.

1995 was a truly dreadful year for Japan although politics, as it turned out, was the least of the country's worries. A series of disasters, natural and man-made, shattered the sense that Japan was a country insulated from crime and social discord. In January, a massive earthquake killed 5,000 people in Kobe. In March, 12 people died and 6,000 became sick after the religious cult Aum Shinrikyo released sarin nerve gas on the Tokyo subway. At the end of the year, the defence treaty between Japan and the United States came under strain after a 12-year-old girl was raped by American marines on the island of Okinawa.

The greatest disaster of all, however, was taking place in the economy. For fifty years, Japan had been governed by the so-called 'iron triangle'—a tacit alliance between politicians, big business and the bureaucracy. The big government ministries acted as unofficial directors of the country's biggest firms, which in return were protected from domestic and international competition by government regulation. During the period of recovery the system worked well, but in the age of globalization it created companies which were lazy, inefficient and bloated. Nowhere was this sclerosis more dangerous than in the country's banks. The bursting of the bubble had left them with unrecoverable debts running to the hundreds of billions of dollars, but the banks and their bureaucratic patrons reacted to the impending crash like rabbits caught in headlights. Murayama's successor as prime minister, the LDP leader Hashimoto Ryutaro, inaugurated financial and economic reforms but their full-blooded implementation was eschewed in favour of short-term public spending. By the end of 1997, the Asian economic crisis and the collapse of currencies in Thailand, Indonesia, and South Korea had brought matters to a head. Unemployment rose drastically and, for the first time since the 1950s, increasing numbers of homeless people were seen on the streets of Tokyo and Ōsaka. After years teetering on the brink, the Japanese economy slipped into outright recession. By 1999, another LDP prime minister, Obuchi Keizo, had halted the decline, but recovery was still a long way off.

After a dizzying 20th century, of glory, followed by shame, followed by astonishing prosperity, Japanese enter the new millennium with the queasy suspicion that history may be beginning to turn upon them once again.

Culture

Art and Architecture

Beyond a vague familiarity with pagodas and woodblock prints, most first-time visitors arrive knowing very little of Japanese art and architecture, and many leave none the wiser. Everyone who has ever been on a guided tour of Kyoto is familiar with the condition known as 'temple fatigue'—after four hours and half a dozen different Buddha halls, you totter back to your lodgings with a roll of photographs but no cogent idea of what you have seen or what it means. This is nobody's fault: until the 20th century, the influence of Japanese art on the West was negligible, and its origins, history and conventions are as alien as can be.

One of the unswerving characteristics of Japanese art (with a few spectacular exceptions) is its simplicity. Plain, unpainted wood and simple use of lines form the basis of much architecture and painting. Differences in style are frequently ornamental, and can appear trifling to the non-connoisseur: the depth of the eaves on a shrine, or the glaze on a tea bowl, may be all that distinguishes entirely separate schools of architecture or ceramics. Obviously, this isn't something that can be picked up overnight—still, a little knowledge makes a big difference, and with preparation and reading you can greatly reduce your chances of culture-overload.

Don't try to do too much and, unless your time is limited, avoid guided group tours. Plan your temple and shrine visits and ascertain in advance the basic characteristics of the sites you will be visiting—age, historical significance, style and sect. In the Kyoto and Kansai region, for instance, it would be possible to spend a few days visiting the great architectural treasures of Japan, in chronological order, tracing their evolution from the Nara to the Edo period. Only specialists would want to follow such an itinerary strictly, but even casual tourists can add a lot to their appreciation by a little intelligent planning.

Detailed commentaries on individual buildings and collections are given in the regional chapters. The following descriptions are not comprehensive, but attempt to join the dots between various historical periods and genres.

Art

Prehistoric (*c.* 10,000 BC–*c.* AD 700)

The earliest inhabitants of Japan of whom traces survive are the **Jōmon** ('cord pattern') people (*c.* 10,000–300 BC), named after the pottery they produced. Damp clay, shaped by hand into pots and cooking vessels, was wrapped with ropes which left a distinctive imprint on the surface. Carbon dating shows the earliest fragments to be more than 12,000 years old. The most impressive items were made during the Middle Jōmon period (*c.* 3500–*c.* 2500 BC): the 'Flaming Jōmon' ware, so called because of the elaborate, rippling loops of inlaid clay which swirl and writhe over the surface and above the rim of the flat-bottomed vessels.

The size and ornateness of these jars suggests they were used for ritual offerings. Further tantalizing glimpses into the spiritual life of the proto-Japanese are provided by the *dogū*, clay figures with distorted bodies and stylized features. There's something simultaneously appealing and creepy about these mannequins. The writer Erich Von Daniken insisted that some of the later and more bizarre *dogū* provided proof that extra-terrestrials had visited and communicated with Jōmon man, and they do indeed look like astronauts, with little arms emerging from some kind of bulky suit or armour, round head-dress and slit eyes peering through goggle-like lenses.

Yayoi was the next artistic and cultural era (*c.* 300 BC–*c.* AD 300), the consequence of large-scale immigration from the Asian continent. The invaders brought with them bronze, iron, wet rice agriculture, and an understanding of the potter's wheel. The new ceramics were smoother, more regular and symmetrical, and more varied in form: goblets, narrow-necked bottles, ewers and handled cups, as well as jars. Bronze was used to make striking bells called *dōtaku*, incised with meandering S-patterns. Comma-shaped jewels called *magatama* as well as polished mirrors and ornamental swords also survive from this time; mirror, jewel and sword are the three sacred objects of the imperial regalia.

The next distinct period, **Kofun** (AD 300–*c.* AD 700) takes its name from the huge burial mounds in the shape of bells or keyholes which dot the Kansai area. From these, many beautiful objects have been excavated, including crowns and helmets of bronze and gold, and *haniwa*, clay renderings of the creatures and objects which the deceased prince might find useful in the afterlife. There are clay houses, clay horses, deer, dogs and cattle, and many clay people—these seem to have been a humane replacement for living servants and warriors who would at one time have been sacrificed and buried alongside their dead lord. Many of them have great charm: simple, cheery faces, with elaborately detailed renderings of costume, jewellery and armour.

The best collection of prehistoric art is in the **Tokyo National Museum**.

Early (552–794)

From the introduction of Buddhism in the mid-6th up until the mid-8th century, Japanese art was heavily influenced by—and often copied from—foreign models. Religious treasures were imported from the continent, along with Chinese and Korean sculptors, painters and temple-builders who settled and established studios. Nonetheless, the **Asuka** (552–710) and early **Nara** (710–794) periods are among the richest eras of Japanese art. War and disaster have erased many of the Chinese and Korean originals; the Japanese works, tucked away in a few Nara monasteries, are some of the finest of their type in the world.

Statues and altars have fared better than paintings, and surviving examples of each show a freshness and grace, combined, in the earlier and more formal statues, with an archaic flatness and symmetry—the bronzes of the Korean master, Tori Busshi, for instance, in the magnificent collection of **Hōryū-ji** temple. Following the Taika (Great Reform) of 645, contact with Tang China became even more intense. Under the influence of Tang art, statues and painted figures became fuller and more three-dimensional, expressive of rhythm and motion.

In 710 the emperor and several of the early temples moved to a new capital—Heijō-kyō, today called Nara. Full-time workshops of artists and artisans were maintained by the state, and construction reached its peak in 752 with the consecration of the Daibutsu (Great Buddha), a 15m-high colossus of bronze in the great **Tōdai-ji** temple. Unsurprisingly, not much metal was left over for other purposes. In the statues created for the sub-temples of the Tōdai-ji complex, the sculptors were forced to turn to wood, clay and a technique known as dry lacquer which allowed for greater versatility and realism. In these beautiful portraits of deities and famous abbots (many of them preserved in the treasure house of Nara's **Kōfuku-ji** temple), Japanese art began to escape the influence of China, and assert a confident individuality of its own. As well as Tōdai-ji and its sub-temples, Nara period art is displayed in **Yakushi-ji**, **Tōshōdai-ji**, and the **Nara National Museum**.

Heian (794–1185)

The arrival from China of two new Esoteric Buddhist sects, Tendai and Shingon, introduced a whole new army of deities and religious iconography into the Japanese capital of Heian-kyō (Kyoto). Among the most popular were benevolent bogeymen like Fudō Myō-ō, a fearsome chastiser of evil, depicted with fangs, sword, lasso and a halo of flames, who appeared in statues and paintings, as well as in mandalas—concentric pictorial diagrams of hundreds of buddhas, bodhisattvas, demons and saints. These were intellectual and meditational tools as much as decorative works of art, a visual *Who's Who* of the complex hierarchy of Esoteric Buddhist icons.

Early Heian sculptures were rather heavy and brooding. Then, in the 11th century, popular worship came to focus on Amida, Buddha of the Western Paradise, a merciful being who offers salvation to all who invoke his name in a simple prayer. Amida halls enshrined seated statues of the saviour, surrounded by carvings and paintings of his heavenly attendants. A famous sculptor called Jōchō brought great finesse and variety to these figures by the perfection of a new technique. Instead of a clumsy single piece of solid wood, statues were composed out of several smaller blocks, hollowed out and joined together by apprentices, before being finished off by the master. The resulting carvings were lighter and less liable to warp and crack, permitting much greater detail and versatility than the old techniques. The **Byōdō-in** in Uji, outside Kyoto, contains the masterpieces of this style.

One of the most popular painted scenes was the *raigō*, the moment when Amida and his retinue descend from the clouds to welcome the dying soul into Paradise. It became fashionable for ailing aristocrats to lie on their deathbeds alongside a *raigō* picture. The dying man would chant Amida's name and hold a piece of cord, joined at the other end to the painted image, on which his soul would be tugged into Paradise.

But some of the most appealing remnants of Heian-kyō are secular, the products of the tiny, idle, introverted circle of courtiers and royalty. By the 10th century, contacts with the declining China of the Tang Dynasty had been cut off. Isolated from the rest of the world, Japanese artists began to respond to the landscape, language and emotions of their own country. In painting, the gentle, rolling hills of Yamato (the Japanese heartland containing Nara and Kyoto) replaced the beetling mountain tops and precipices of Chinese art. Exquisite narrative handscrolls (*emakimono*) depicting scenes from the *Tale of Genji* showed life in the *shinden* villas of the aristocracy, and reflected the preoccupations of the day—nature (especially in its transient and melancholy aspects), style (the subtle colours and contrasts of court kimono), and poetry (Heian-kyō was the birthplace of Japanese calligraphy, and the text of the narrative scrolls is often just as delicate and artistic as the images).

In the late 12th century, a very different style of narrative scroll was produced, depicting court intrigues, miracles from the lives of saints, and satires featuring anthropomorphic animals and cartoon-like demons and ghosts. The wars between the Taira and Minamoto clans inspired epic renderings of battles and armies.

The temples of **Kyoto** are the best place to view Heian art, especially **Tō-ji** for its Esoteric Buddhist statues, the **Byōdō-in** for its Amida Hall, and the **Kyoto National Museum**. The temples and treasure houses of **Mt Kōya** (in Wakayama prefecture) possess a huge collection of the art of the Esoteric Shingon sect.

Medieval (1185–1573)

Much of Nara was destroyed during the 12th-century wars. When the country had settled down, its new military rulers set about reconstructing its buildings and filling them with new statues, inspired by the old masterpieces. The shoguns of the **Kamakura period** (1185–1333) consciously dissociated themselves from the effete aestheticism of the court, encouraging an art that expressed their own ideals of spiritual alertness and martial virtue. Close study of the originals, plus the advantages of the multi-block technique, created a new style of unmatched energy and realism.

They were the first true portraits. Paintings and statues of Minamoto Yoritomo, victorious leader of the Genji clan, combine an almost abstract treatment of his billowing formal robes with a shrewdly realistic rendering of his cruel, haughty features. Even when portraits—of famous sages and monks, for instance—were posthumous, they looked and stood like living men, not sacred idealizations. Lumps of crystal were used for the eyes, and it was in the statues of Buddhist gods, particularly those of a fierce or grotesque character, that the Kamakura style found its most entertaining expression. Rippling, muscular torsos, flailing arms, flaring nostrils, manic grins and knotted brows expressed the divine anger of deities such as Emma-ō, King of Hell, who sit in judgement on mortal souls. The finest of these were created by a single studio of sculptors, a family descended from Jōchō of the Byōdō-in: Kōkei, Unkei, and Tankei, father, son and grandson. In the mid-13th century an unknown artist created another great Daibutsu in the town of Kamakura—

smaller than Nara's, but artistically superior and far better preserved. Japanese sculpture would never reach such heights again.

Zen Buddhism, which took root in Japan during the Kamakura period, became the conduit of renewed contact with China, especially in the arts. In the **Muromachi period** (1333–1573), most of the great developments in the arts—in painting, gardening, architecture, the tea ceremony, *nō* drama—took place under the auspices of Zen monks. More than other sects, Zen emphasized the transmission of knowledge between master and pupil, so it was only natural that some of the finest portraits should be created by its followers—highly personal, realistic and often grim and unflattering pictures of ageing masters. Just as its practice was based on strict discipline and epiphanic flashes of irrational insight, Zen pictures were austere and elliptical, painted in a few simple strokes of black ink (*sumi*), with rare use of colour. The subjects of Zen painting—landscapes half lost in wreaths of blank mist, tiny human figures dwarfed by looming trees and mountains—suggested ideas of timelessness and human insignificance in keeping with Zen thought. They were heavily influenced by Chinese models which were objects of enthusiastic connoisseurship during the Muromachi period—the master painter, Sōami (d. 1525), was curator of the collection of the Ashikaga shoguns, and the great shogun Yoshimitsu patronized an official painting academy in a Kyoto temple. Sesshū (1420–1506) created more solid, less ethereal compositions of flinty mountains, while a monk from remote Tōhoku, Sesson, created memorably turbulent images of storm-wracked seas and cruel birds of prey which seem to reflect the troubled character of the times.

The Pre-modern Period (1573–1868)

The **Momoyama period** (1573–1600) was dominated by a succession of military leaders who finally brought an end to the civil wars which had wracked the country for a century and a half. They raised castles at strategic locations, and asserted their personal authority by building themselves great fortified palaces, lavishly decorated with the finest and most expensive materials. Rooms were wide and high, and required big, bold designs to fill and animate them. The windows were small, to aid defence, and the dimness of the light they admitted encouraged the use of reflective gold leaf on screens and ceilings. Practical considerations apart, the artistic ebullience of the age matched the hubris and megalomania of its great leaders, Oda Nobunaga and Hideyoshi Toyotomi, low-born men who rose to the height of wealth and power. After centuries of spirituality, nuance and restraint, Japanese art exploded in a blaze of colour and ornament, 'a procession as with torches against the sober grey mist that lay behind' in the words of one historian.

Momoyama motifs, even where they were used in temples, were generally secular: flowers, landscapes, birds, animals (lions, tigers, dragons) and human figures of sages and children, painted in thick, bright pigments on gold foil. The greatest works were produced by a hereditary school of painters headed by Kanō Eitoku (1543–90) who decorated the *shoin* style rooms of Nobunaga's (long-gone) Azuchi castle, and whose work survives in several Kyoto temples. During the **Edo period** (1600–1868), the Kanō school flourished as official painters to the great Tokugawa Ieyasu and the succeeding shoguns. Kanō Tanyū, Eitoku's greatest heir, supervized the painting of the pines in Kyoto's Nijō castle.

By the mid-17th century, contact with foreign countries was effectively outlawed; the Momoyama and early Edo years were the last time for two centuries when foreign styles and subjects could work their influence on Japanese art. In the 1590s, Hideyoshi's brutal campaigns in Korea produced much continental loot, and the simple, rustic work of Korean potters was prized for use in the tea ceremony. Until the banning of Christianity, European goods and learning were extremely fashionable. The huge galleons, flouncing costumes, bright hair and big noses of Westerners (called *nanban* or 'southern barbarians') became popular subjects. Japanese artists were exposed to perspective painting and began, for the first time, to experiment with oils, although it was centuries before these techniques were widely adopted.

The most dazzling figure of the early 17th century, Hon'ami Kōetsu (1558–1637), established his own artistic colony outside Kyoto, where painters, potters, paper-makers and lacquerers lived and worked communally. Kōetsu was a superb craftsman and tea master, as well as an artist. Everyday objects, such as a case for writing instruments, were turned into works of art, by treating the curving exterior as a single plane surface and wrapping the design around it. During the same period, men like Tawaraya Sōtatsu (d.1643) of the Rimpa school created evocative landscapes by dropping ink onto wet paper to create blurred, cloudy, watery outlines. Unlike the aristocratic Kanō artists, both men came from the rising urban merchant class, which became increasingly important as a source of patronage and which had its heyday during the exuberant period known as **Genroku** (1688–1704). Ōgata Kōrin (1658–1716) is the great name from this time, an outrageous extrovert whose bold, vigorous compositions of waves and flowers are strikingly modern. Kōrin was also a great perpetrator of artistic 'happenings'. Once he presented a friend with a giant rice dumpling. When it was sliced open, hundreds of tiny live crabs scuttled out, each one decorated on its back with a minute gold-lacquered landscape.

By the Genroku period, the art of the Kyoto aristocrats and the Edo samurai had become stagnant and mannered. All the most interesting art (as well as drama and literature) was being produced in the 'floating world' of the cities of Edo (Tokyo) and Ōsaka, dominated by merchants and an increasingly literate population of craftsmen and shopkeepers. Improved woodblock techniques allowed artist-printers to produce large cheap editions of illustrated prints, often combining text and pictures. The subjects of these *ukiyo-e* ('floating world pictures') reflected the urban, earthy, often frankly erotic concerns of the Edo townsman: street scenes of local festivals and bustling crowds; and portraits of *kabuki* actors and famous courtesans, the pop stars of the age. Earlier print-makers like Suzuki Harunobu (flourished 1765–70) and Kitagawa Utamaro (1754–1806) produced elegant, gently humorous renderings of *geisha* and their patrons. During the 18th century *ukiyo-e* became increasingly grotesque and satirical. Even the world famous Katsushika Hokusai (1760–1849) created several albums of *manga* (cartoons) and euphemistically entitled *shunga* or 'spring pictures'—rollicking albums of pornography featuring grimacing couples with gargantuan genitalia. His delicate, visionary landscapes of Mt Fuji, like *The Great Wave,* are the most famous Japanese pictures in the world. Andō Hiroshige (1797–1858) explored the Edo townsman's fascination with travel in the series *Fifty-three Stations of the Tōkaidō,* showing famous spots on the road between Kyoto and Edo.

The Modern Period 1868–

With the opening up of the country after the Meiji Restoration of 1868, Japan was swamped by a wave of Western influences which threatened for a while to extinguish native traditions altogether. Woodblock artists produced charming impressions of the new brick quarters of Tokyo and the foreigners who were increasingly to be seen in and around them, and during the Sino-Japanese (1894) and Russo-Japanese (1904) wars they served as war correspondents dispatching vivid, if nationalistic, depictions of Japanese valour back to the public at home. Bright Western dyes replaced the delicate shades of the early masters, and perspective was employed, sometimes uneasily. Young artists studied abroad in Europe. The best of them, like Kuroda Seiki (1866–1924) achieved an intelligent synthesis of Western technique and Japanese subject matter and sensibility; many more produced only lifeless pastiches, and *yōga*, as Western-style painting was called, yielded few masterpieces. A new genre, contrastingly called *nihonga* (Japanese pictures), emerged in the early 20th century. Despite Western pigments and perspective, the work of painters like Kobayashi Kōkei (1883–1967) and Higashiyama Kaii (born 1908) retains a distinctively oriental feel, in plangent, misty landscapes of pine, snow and mountain. But it's a minor genre and attracts little attention outside Japan.

20th-century Japanese art still seems to be uneasily poised between native and Western traditions, neither fully assimilated or at ease with the other. There are several great names: Noguchi Isamu (1904–88), the half-American sculptor; and the woodblock artist Munakata Shikō (1905–77), whose unique, primitive black and white images might have come from any age. The successes of the Folk Arts Movement, lead by the potters Hamada Shōji (1894–1978) and the Englishman Bernard Leach (1887–1979), gave crafts (particularly ceramics) an impetus and popularity which they retain to this day. In recent years, Japanese designers like Ishioka Eiko, Issey Miyake, Kawakubo Rei and Yamamoto Yōji have brought Japanese simplicity to international cat-walks and advertising. But culturally, Japan is at a stage it has been through many times before: a transitional period in which powerful foreign influences are being digested and assimilated and where fully fledged movements of any significance are difficult to identify.

Architecture

Shrine Architecture

The earliest Shinto shrines were not buildings, but natural features: boulders, ancient trees, even the mountains themselves. At festival times, the deities would be summoned from their natural abode to temporary, probably portable, structures where prayers and offerings could be presented directly. These developed into permanent shrine buildings.

Buddhism brought with it an ancient architectural tradition that greatly influenced Shinto; no shrine which still stands today can have been untouched by it. The oldest, and probably the purest, shrine styles are Sumiyoshi (named after the Sumiyoshi shrine in downtown Ōsaka), and Shimmei and Taisha, exemplified by Ise Jingū in Kansai, and Izumo Taisha on the Japan Sea coast, respectively. Principal features of the different styles are as follows:

Shimmei

Crisp, straight lines, with almost no use of paint, inlay, carving or other decoration. Steps lead under an entrance which is beneath the eaves, on the long side of the 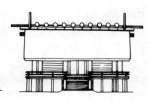 building, parallel to the roof ridge. The floor is raised on posts which are driven directly into the earth; the roof is often thatched. Cylindrical billets of wood (*katsuogi*) lie along the roof ridge, and forked finials (*chigi*) project upwards. Shimmei shrines are thought to have been based on ancient storehouses.

Taisha

With its curving roof and metal orna- 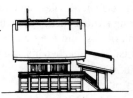 ments, Izumo Taisha shows more of the Buddhist influence. The entrance, up steps and via a covered porch, is through the gable end. The posts rest on stone foundations. Roof billets are smaller and fewer than the Shimmei style; the finials do not project up from the bargeboards, but are attached to the roof as separate structures. The Taisha style was based on early palace buildings.

Sumiyoshi

Similar to the Taisha style, but with  straight eaves, and without the covered entrance porch. While Ise and Izumo are plain, Sumiyoshi Jinja is painted in white and red.

The influence of Buddhism produced over the years the following styles:

Nagare

This is the most common of all shrine types,  and examples can be seen all over the country. It resembles the Shimmei style, minus billets and finials, and with the eave on one side sweeping outwards over the entrance and steps to provide a sheltered area for worshippers.

Kasuga

The second most popular style is named after the  ancient Kasuga Shrine in Nara. It resembles the Sumiyoshi shrine (painted, entrance under gable, billets and finials), but on a smaller scale and with the addition of a wide protective roof over the gable entrance.

Hachiman

In some shrines, a sheltered oratory (*haiden*) where worshippers could offer prayers was built separately from the main hall (*honden*), the residence of the deity. In shrines dedicated to the god of war, Hachiman, a Kasuga-style *honden* and *haiden* were built so close together that their front and back eaves touched, and they effectively became one structure. In the **Gongen style**, a second roof ridge was built at a right angle to the two roofs of a Hachiman structure. The area beneath it is a corridor linking the main hall and oratory.

In the Momoyama and Edo periods (late 16th to late 19th century), shrines became increasingly ornate and elaborate. Tiles came to replace the traditional thatch and cypress shingles, the supporting struts beneath the curved hip and gable roofs were carved into shapes of humans and beasts, and the outer surfaces were painted, gilded and studded with metal ornaments. This reached its gaudy climax in the Tōshō-gū Shrine to the Tokugawa shoguns, in Nikkō.

Visiting a Shrine

Shinto worship is a casual and ill-defined business with no distinction between the faithful and the infidel. The chances are that you will be invited to pay your respects at one sometime during your visit to Japan.

Shrine architecture, like Japanese society, is much concerned with the division between inner and outer, and the delimitation of areas of greater and lesser sanctity. The entrance to every shrine is marked by a *torii*, a symbolic gateway consisting, at its simplest, of a pair of uprights topped with a single horizontal bar. These can be made of wood, stone, concrete or metal, painted or unpainted. There may be a series of *torii* one after another, each marking a deeper level of sanctity. These are sometimes flanked by **guardians**, frequently a pair of *koma inu* (Korean dogs), dragons, archers, or—in the case of an Inari shrine—foxes. *Shimenawa*, twisted ropes of straw, often very thick, are another sacred marker. They're hung around sacred trees or boulders, or from the beams of *torii*. *Gohei* are zig-zags of paper, a bit like stylized thunderbolts, which adorn shrines and signify the presence of the *kami* (deities). Often these, and the round mirrors seen inside the shrine buildings, are the closest thing to a representation of the deity. Unlike Buddhism, the gods of Shinto are very seldom pictured in statues or paintings.

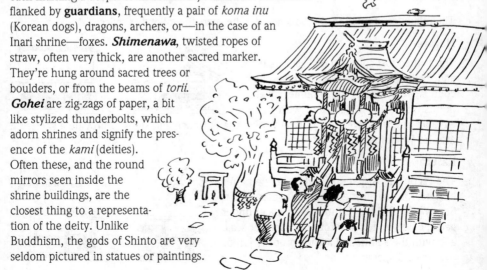

Inside the shrine, perhaps at the end of a wooded path, will be a courtyard of blank **white gravel**, another symbol of purity. Here is found a *chōzuya* (ablution basin) where worshippers cleanse themselves before proceeding. Rinse each hand with water poured from one of the ladles provided. Then ladle water into your hand and rinse it around your mouth, before spitting it out. Finally fill the scoop for the last time, and tip it backwards so that purifying water runs back over the long handle which you have been holding. Water—from hands, ladle or mouth—mustn't be allowed to fall back into the basin, but only onto the surrounding gravel. Don't worry if you get this wrong—many Japanese don't know the proper way to do it either.

At the edges of the courtyard there are likely to be **shrine shops** selling information booklets (ask for one in English), and dedicated to bringing various kinds of good luck (safe childbirth, success in exams, safety from traffic accidents). At the edges of this area may also be wide racks hung with *ema* or votive plaques: tablets of wood bearing a picture on one side (usually of an animal or legendary scene), and with a blank reverse on which worshippers write their prayers and requests. You can buy these from the shop for about ¥500. Even if you don't want to leave a prayer, they make attractive souvenirs. Other lesser shrine buildings may include a **stage** for the performance of sacred dances, and a **storehouse** for the *mikoshi* (portable shrine).

At the far side of the courtyard will be the entrance to the shrine proper. Generally no one but the priests is allowed into the inner sanctum where the *kami* lurk. What visitors see is an outer **oratory** where prayers and offerings are made. The usual way of paying respects is as follows. Stand in front of the large slatted cashbox and throw in a small coin. Ring the bell by shaking the thick rope—this attracts the attention of the deity. Make two deep bows and two claps, then stand with eyes closed and hands clasped muttering your prayer. Conclude with two more bows. For an account of Shinto and its deities, *see* pp.90–94).

Temple Architecture

Buddhism came to Japan with a long-established architectural tradition which distinguished itself from native styles by the use of tile on roofs and floors, painted surfaces, and clay wattle and daub walls, rather than planks. Central to the earliest temples was a reliquary where fragments of the Buddha's body were stored. In India, this was a stupa, a dome of earth and stone with a spire on top; in China and Japan, it developed into the **pagoda** (*tō*), a roofed tower of three or five storeys, built around a huge central pillar beneath which relics were buried in a sacred vessel.

As the historical Buddha yielded in importance to other deities, the focus of worship moved from the pagoda to the **golden hall** (*kondō*), where statues were displayed. In Hōryū-ji, near Nara, the country's oldest pagoda and *kondō* (c. 710) stand side-by-side, on an equal footing. Forty years later, when Tōdai-ji temple was built, two pagodas (neither of which survives) were raised in front of the main precinct, but by now they were marginal, supporting structures, rather than centres of sanctity and worship. The halls of this period, like Tōshōdai-ji and Yakushi-ji in western Nara, are Chinese in inspiration: big, stately buildings with massive hipped roofs of tile, arranged symmetrically on a north–south axis.

During the **Heian period** (794–1185), new currents in Buddhist thought produced new temple styles. In particular, the cult of Amida, the Buddha of the Western Paradise, gave rise to the **Paradise hall**, the finest of which is the Phoenix Hall of the Byōdō-in in Uji, near Kyoto. The deity was enshrined in a hall representing the 'Pure Land' where all devout souls hope to travel when they die. The interior walls were painted with murals of thronging heavenly scenes, and the halls were often surrounded by ponds; worshippers sat on the far side, or even on a floating raft, and adored Amida across the 'Western Ocean'. Two other sects, Tendai and Shingon, built their headquarters at the top of mountains (Hiei and Kōya), which necessarily broke up the symmetry of the compounds. Being remote from centres of craftsmanship and manufacture, the architects of these halls depended more on natural materials: thus, shingles of cypress wood and wooden boards replaced ceramic tiles on the roofs and floors.

The sect that gave architectural impetus to the **Kamakura period** (1185–1333) was **Zen**, introduced from China in the 12th and 13th centuries. Zen emphasized discipline and regimentation, in the design of the monks' environment as much as in their daily routine. Seven principal halls were prescribed, the most important of them arranged in a straight line from south to north: main gate (*san-mon*), Buddha hall (*butsu-den*), lecture hall (*hattō*). Also within the compound, at points to either side, were the dormitory (*sōdō*), kitchen (*kuin*), latrine (*tōsu*) and bath house (*yokushitsu*)—Zen discipline encompassed everyday activities like sleeping, eating and bathing. In the bigger temples, like Daitoku-ji and Nanzen-ji in Kyoto, small sub-temples grew up around the edges of the formal main compound. These were often strikingly informal in character, converted villas or houses with rambling and irregular paths and gardens.

The new sect brought with it from Sung China a number of new architectural details: even today Zen temples look distinctively foreign and exotic. Each of the main halls is set on a raised stone base, and has a stone floor, often made up of diagonally arranged flags. The posts are set into the floor on stone plinths, and the doors swing open (rather than slide) on wooden hinges. Light is admitted to the interior through open-work transoms above the doors, and through the distinctive arched or cusped windows.

In the **Muromachi period** (1333–1573), these ornamental details were combined in the pleasure pavilions, later converted into temples, which two of the Ashikaga shoguns built for themselves on the margins of Kyoto. The Golden Pavilion (Kinkaku-ji, 1398) has the ground floor of an aristocratic villa (veranda and removable shutters), the middle floor of a Japanese-style Buddha hall (sliding wooden doors), and the top floor of a Zen chapel (cusped windows and swinging doors). The Silver Pavilion (Ginkaku-ji, 1484) does the same with two storeys.

The warlords who brought peace to the country during the **Momoyama period** (1573–1600) were great patrons of the arts, especially Toyotomi Hideyoshi, who built two lavish castles in Kyoto. After his death they were dismantled and distributed among the temples: the Chinese Gate in Daitoku-ji and the *shoin* villa of Nishi Hongan-ji are examples. The best of the Momoyama style had passed by the mid-17th century, but the rich detailing which characterized it—curved eaves, brightly painted woodwork, elaborate carving— was employed in diluted form throughout the Edo period (1600–1868). Registration at a

Buddhist temple became compulsory for all the shogun's subjects, and pilgrimages became popular as a means of circumventing the restrictions on travel. As a result, temple halls became very large, capable of holding huge congregations, with bright, attention-grabbing paintings and big, exaggerated statues. Kyoto's Kiyomizu-dera and Zenkō-ji in Nagano were ancient temples rebuilt in this manner.

Secular Architecture

The life of the Heian aristocracy, intimately chronicled in Lady Murasaki's *Tale of Genji*, revolved around the sprawling residential pleasure complexes where they lived, entertained and conducted their wistful love affairs. The *shinden* style, as it's known, survives only in bastardized reconstructions, like the Kyoto Imperial Palace and Heian Shrine, as well as in numerous narrative picture scrolls (*emakimono*) illustrating the writings of women like Murasaki. A 'sleeping hall' (*shinden*) faced, to the south, a large pond with bridges, islands and piers where dragon-shaped pleasure boats were moored. The master of the house lived in the *shinden*; covered corridors extended on either side, linking it with satellite halls and pavilions where wives, children and mistresses resided with their own retinues of servants and guards. Walls were flimsy and removable; the wooden-floored interior was partitioned off by hanging curtains, bamboo blinds and painted screens. The entire complex was surrounded by tile-roofed earthen walls.

By the late 16th century, the *shinden* had developed into a distinctive new style called *shoin*, literally 'writing hall'. The elements of the *shoin* room developed out of the study rooms of abbots in Zen monasteries, and were later adopted by secular scholars and leaders as a mark of their learning, wealth and piety. The classic *shoin* room, like those from Toyotomi Hideyoshi's palace (now reassembled in Kyoto's Nishi Hongan-ji temple) contains certain recurring elements. It is carpeted entirely with *tatami* mats, which had by now become the standard floor covering, and has a coffered ceiling. *Fusuma* (sliding screens, often elaborately painted) divide rooms from one another; on the outside of the building are thinner paper screens (*shōji*), protected from the elements by heavier sliding panels. Parts of the room may be raised a few centimetres above the rest, and at the back lies an alcove called a *tokonoma* where a hanging scroll, an incense burner and a flower arrangement are often set. In the same wall are staggered shelves (*chigaidana*) for books or ornaments, and on the adjacent wall is a long, narrow desk (*tsukeshoin*), built into the wall, perhaps below a window overlooking a garden or view. Opposite this are a set of double doors (*chōdaigamae*), ornamented with brightly coloured tassles. These last four—alcove, shelves, desk and doors—are the defining elements of the *shoin* style, used in the most elegant inns and restaurants even today.

The finest examples of *shoin* architecture—in Kyoto's Nishi Hongan-ji temple and Nijō Castle—are prodigies of ornamental excess, with screens, ceilings and even nail covers lavishly painted and gilded for the glorification of the generals who commissioned them. Around the same time, though, the *sukiya* style, altogether quieter and more refined, was being developed by the much older families of the Kyoto aristocracy. *Sukiya* means 'abode of refinement' and was influenced by the austere aesthetics of the tea ceremony. An intimate, rustic atmosphere was cultivated, by the use of irregularity and gentle understatement. Posts were left unplaned, with some of their bark still adhering, paintings (on gentle, natural themes) were simple and unpretentious, and the few adornments were unobtrusive and witty—symmetrical openwork carving on the transoms between rooms, door handles in the shape of plants or musical instruments. Katsura Detached Villa near Kyoto is the finest example of the style.

With the rise of the military class from the 12th century onward, a distinctive style of warrior architecture began to emerge. **Castles** are the most obvious manifestation of this, but during peacetime the feudal lords and their samurai lived in stout dwellings outside the inner citadel. The **buke yashiki** (samurai houses) of the Edo period (1600–1868) often had defensive features (massive gates, thick walls and secret rooms for bodyguards or eavesdroppers), but above all they embodied the minute social distinctions on which the shogunate was based. Certain rooms were reserved only for those of a given rank or above; strict sumptuary laws forbade the use of lavish decoration by merchants and other members of the lower classes.

Traditional Japanese Arts

The Floating World

Ukiyo, 'floating world', is one of those unique terms which seems to provide the key to an entire culture, but which remains tantalizingly resistant to translation or straightforward definition. Even in Japanese the word is ambiguous. In the Heian period, *ukiyo* meant 'sorrowful world'—the human vale of tears and impermanence for which faith in the Buddha was the only escape and remedy. During the decadent Genroku era, the first element, *uki*, came to be written with the character that means 'floating'. The floating world of the brilliant cities of Edo (later Tokyo) and Ōsaka seemed as different as could be from the sorrowful one of the ancient Buddhist monks. Money, sex and style were its currency; at its heart were the licensed pleasure quarters where samurai, merchants, craftsmen, artists, poets and apprentices could escape the stifling social codes of the feudal state to eat, drink, dress up, watch plays and street shows, and enjoy the attentions of *geisha*, courtesans and prostitutes.

But something of the old Buddhist melancholy remained: for all the gaiety and life of the theatres and brothels, the floating world was haunted by a consciousness of its own artifice and evanescence. The cherry blossoms in a woodblock print (*ukiyo-e*, 'floating world picture') of a famous *geisha* are celebrated for their beauty but serve also as a *memento mori*: like them, her beauty will wither and die. The love affairs between courtesans and their admirers, celebrated in novels and poems, and in the plays of the *kabuki* and *bunraku* (puppet) theatres, cannot survive outside the boundaries of the pleasure quarters and inevitably end in suicide or tragedy. The prints and plays are still admired and performed, but much of the art of the floating world—its literature, for instance—has dated less well. The essence of the era lay in fashions of dress and behaviour. Books, plays and pictures might record but could never capture it. 'Edo culture', wrote Edward Seidensticker, 'was better than anything it left to posterity.'

The cities which fostered the floating world have changed beyond recognition, but the aesthetic which developed there is still in evidence. There are *geisha* in Tokyo's Ginza, Kyoto's Gion, and old cities like Kanazawa, but they are fewer, older and more expensive than ever. Their place has been taken by bar hostesses who—instead of playing the *koto* or performing classical dances—pour drinks, squeeze knees and sing karaoke. Prostitution was outlawed in 1957, but survives in the 'bath houses' and 'massage parlours' where an extraordinary menu of activities, from the conventional to the bizarre, are purveyed under a range of ingenious euphemisms. Above all, there's a contradictory innocence about it all, and a poignant sense of escapism. The same salaryman who pays hundreds of pounds to manacle teenage girls in an S&M parlour might be seen, an hour later, weeping sentimental tears as he wails folk songs in a karaoke bar. The next morning, he will cram himself into the early train, spend the day bowing to his superiors, and dine with his wife and family with no sense of incongruity whatsoever.

Geisha

Geisha—true *geisha* anyway—are not prostitutes. A man might have an affair with his *geisha* just as he might with his piano teacher, but it would be many expensive evenings and presents before that stage was reached, and even then the relationship would be closer to that of patron and protégé than client and call girl. The word means 'art person': *geisha* are highly-trained performers whose principal function is to create a lively, civilized atmosphere at the kind of male gatherings which, these days, can only be afforded by the very rich or well-connected.

The numbers of practising *geisha* are on the decline, as much thanks to the demands of modern compulsory education as to cheap alternatives like bar hostesses. The apprentice *geisha* is called a *maiko*. Traditional training begins as young as seven, when the trainee becomes attached to a *geisha* house where she may also live. Over the years, she studies classical dancing, the playing of traditional instruments like the *shamisen*, and the arts of the kimono, the tea ceremony, flower arranging and calligraphy. *Geisha* are also expert conversationalists: jokes, teasing banter, and the performance of little skits are as much a part of the job as more formal accomplishments and the serving of food and drink.

Hiring *geisha* is a costly business, and several intermediaries take their cut of the fee paid by the client. The entertainment itself generally takes place in a high class Japanese restaurant or 'tea house'. Even money is not enough in itself; indeed, without an introduction, and usually some knowledge of Japanese, the casual visitor is unlikely ever to encounter *geisha*, except as fleeting presences in the early evening streets of Ginza or Gion. Travel companies sometimes advertise night-time tours including an hour or two at a 'geisha party'. Be assured: if it's that easy, then it can't be the real thing.

Sumo

With its colossal wrestlers, medieval costumes and barking ritual, sumo, at first glance, looks impenetrably alien and remote, but turns out to be one of the most appealing and accessible of Japanese spectator events. The fights themselves are intense bursts of energy

seldom more than a couple of minutes long—
so it's impossible to become bored with any
one bout. The stamping, glaring stand-offs
which precede each one are bravura
dramas of bluff and psychological
warfare. Anyone can enjoy sumo,
and, even if baseball wins bigger
audiences these days, it is still
very much the *Kokugi*—
National Accomplishment.

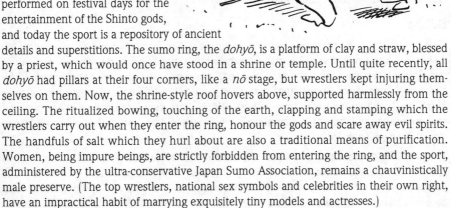

Like *nō* drama, its origins are religious. Wrestling matches were
performed on festival days for the
entertainment of the Shinto gods,
and today the sport is a repository of ancient
details and superstitions. The sumo ring, the *dohyō*, is a platform of clay and straw, blessed
by a priest, which would once have stood in a shrine or temple. Until quite recently, all
dohyō had pillars at their four corners, like a *nō* stage, but wrestlers kept injuring themselves on them. Now, the shrine-style roof hovers above, supported harmlessly from the
ceiling. The ritualized bowing, touching of the earth, clapping and stamping which the
wrestlers carry out when they enter the ring, honour the gods and scare away evil spirits.
The handfuls of salt which they hurl about are also a traditional means of purification.
Women, being impure beings, are strictly forbidden from entering the ring, and the sport,
administered by the ultra-conservative Japan Sumo Association, remains a chauvinistically
male preserve. (The top wrestlers, national sex symbols and celebrities in their own right,
have an impractical habit of marrying exquisitely tiny models and actresses.)

The wrestlers (*rikishi*) live and train in hierarchically organized 'stables', administered by
retired champions. Like *geisha* and *kabuki* actors, they begin their apprenticeships young,
cooking, cleaning and skivvying for their seniors (the apprentice's duties are rumoured to
include wiping the buttocks of colleagues too bulky to perform their own ablutions), and
bulking themselves out on high-protein foods, including a famous stew called *chanko
nabe*. Mature *rikishi* look extraordinary, like members of an entirely different race. The
average weight is around 300 pounds, and the mightiest are half as big again. But not all of
them are gross: victory requires agility and strength as well as bulk, and a relatively slim-
line *rikishi* can often overcome a much larger adversary. The fighting names they adopt on
entering the profession contain delicate references to flowers, trees and mountains.

The tournaments, called *basho*, last 15 days, and are held six times a year. If your visit
coincides with one, you will know about it: every TV, radio and newspaper is seemingly
tuned to the comprehensive coverage which continues late into the night with post-match
highlights and analysis. The day's bouts are preceded by a great deal of ritual, as the
contenders parade around the ring in their ceremonial aprons. The rules themselves are
very simple. On the clay floor of the *dohyō* is a ring of thick rope, similar to the *shimenawa* sacred ropes seen in Shinto shrines. The wrestlers face one another across it, glaring

and stamping through several false starts designed to disconcert their opponent and demonstrate their 'fighting spirit'. Finally, in an atmosphere of rising tension, the kimono-clad referee gives the signal, and the *rikishi* hurl themselves at one another. The wrestler who forces his opponent out of the rope ring, or causes him to touch the ground with any part of his body other than the soles of his feet, is the winner. There are dozens of different techniques for achieving this, from sheer bulldozing force to picking up the opponent by his waist band and hurling him bodily out of the ring.

At the end of each day, the complicated rankings are revised. Excitement gathers towards the end of the *basho* as the leading fighters struggle to move up the ranks to qualify as champions: *ozeki* or, highest of all, *yokozuna*—grand champions, who wear sacred white ropes around their waists. For information on tournaments and tickets *see* 'Sport', p.42.

Tea

Unlike the Chinese and Indian varieties drunk in the West (called *kocha* in Japan), the leaves of Japanese tea are not fermented, and remain their natural colour: a rich green. Infused with hot water, green tea comes out yellow, and foreigners sometimes find the pale, urinous colour off-putting. But the delicate taste is easy to acquire, and the sharing of tea is one of the basics of Japanese hospitality. Every *ryokan* room, corporate conference table and Japanese home has its small ceramic teapot and handleless cups (always in sets of three or five—the number four, *shi*, is homonymous with the taboo word for death). The hot water is added and the tea brewed for a few moments before pouring. It is drunk without any milk, lemon or sweetener. There are many different grades and varieties; the general word for green tea is habitually prefixed with the honorific: *o-cha*, 'esteemed tea'.

It was introduced from China and popularized in the 12th century by Zen monks who used it as a medicine and a stimulant during long periods of meditation (a few cups can deliver a surprisingly strong caffeine kick; insomniacs should avoid it before bedtime). From these religious beginnings developed a unique rite, called in Japanese *chadō*, 'The Way of Tea', and commonly referred to in English as the tea ceremony. In the 15th and 16th centuries, it became formalized under the patronage of the Ashikaga shoguns, great connoisseurs of *nō* drama, Chinese Sung pottery, Zen Buddhism, pavilion architecture and gardens. *Chadō* combines elements of all these in a secular act of communion very hard to describe. Like much Japanese art, it is about the cultivation of mood and tranquil emotion. The preparation and serving of the tea, according to a strict sequence of prescribed actions, fosters an atmosphere of harmony and heightened aesthetic appreciation—of the tea, the company, the setting and the ineffable order of things.

Famous tea masters, like the 16th-century samurai Sen-no-Rikyū, commanded the respect and reverence accorded to the greatest painters and poets. Even today, there are schools of tea run by the descendants of great practitioners where students can spend years studying the practice and philosophy of the Way. There are varying degrees of formality—the most authentic tea ceremonies are inaccessible to casual visitors since they are, by definition, private gatherings of a few hand-picked initiates. Hotels, tourist shops and temples, as well as the big schools of tea, like Ura Senke in Kyoto, sometimes put on tea ceremony demonstrations open to the public which capture the outer form of the ritual, even if the inner resonances are lost.

A full-blown tea ceremony lasts several hours and includes a formal *kaiseki* meal followed by sweets and 'thick' tea. This is followed by a break during which the guests enjoy the garden, then a drink of informal 'thin' tea, and a light dry sweet or biscuit. It takes place in a purpose-built tea house, often part of a villa or garden complex, expressing through its architecture the tea ceremony's ideals of simplicity and rustic beauty.

Less rigorous versions can be held in any *tatami*-matted room. The guests kneel in front of the host, and eat a small sticky sweet while he or she attends to the cooking implements: an iron kettle (ideally heated over a charcoal fire), a bamboo water ladle, a wooden or ceramic tea caddy, a bamboo scoop for measuring out the tea, a large tea bowl and a bamboo whisk. All of these objects are handmade; the finest tea bowls are priceless artworks handed down from one generation of tea masters to the next. Even the simple bamboo objects are made and treated with great care and respect—every year there are special ceremonies, when piles of exhausted tea whisks are burned in front of altars and ritually 'thanked' for the service they have provided.

The tea used in the tea ceremony is powdered; when a small amount of water is added and whisked, it bubbles up into a thick, dark green froth. The host places the bowl in front of the guest who carefully picks it up, and rotates it clockwise a few inches. This is to avoid drinking out of the 'front' of the bowl, a gesture of modesty. The tea has a refreshing, slightly bitter taste; it is drunk by raising the bowl up to the face, in two or three slow sips. When the bowl is empty, the guest cradles it for a few moments, admiring its beauty and perhaps offering a few learned words of appreciation, before replacing it in front of the host. Host and guest bow deeply to one another, the bowl is retrieved, and the same routine is performed for the next guest.

Performing Arts

Nō and Kyōgen

Nō has been performed continuously since the 14th century, making it the world's oldest theatrical form. Little has been added to the repertory in the last 450 years, and the stage, masks, costumes and acting conventions were established in their present form before the time of Shakespeare. Of all the Japanese forms, *nō* (pronounced more like English 'nor' than 'no'; frequently written as 'noh') retains the most obvious links to the religious rituals from which most world drama originally sprang. It's performed on a special cypress stage, polished to a slippery shine using only the natural oils of the wood. The stage is 5.8m square; at each corner is a pillar. The use of plain wood, white gravel which surrounds the stage, and the shrine-style roof, all suggest the Shinto architecture from which it is derived. The stage is undecorated, apart from the painting of a gnarled pine tree on the back wall. Earthenware jars, carefully placed beneath the stage, amplify the noise of the actors' dancing feet.

A covered corridor lined with three real pine trees leads off from rear stage right, along which the actors and musicians enter and exit. First to appear, in formal, undecorated kimono, are the chorus and musicians. The latter sit at the back and consist of a flautist and two or three percussionists playing drums of various sizes and tones. The music serves as an emotional and atmospheric accompaniment to the songs and dances, its pace and volume increasing at climactic moments. The musicians are also responsible for the yelping cries ('Hyioow!') which contribute so much to the strangeness of a *nō* performance. The chorus usually numbers six and sits at stage left. They comment on the action and, as in the Greek theatre, relate events which take place offstage, or before the opening of the play.

Nō performers are all male, and are categorized according to the kind of part each actor plays. The first character to appear on stage is generally a type called the *waki*. *Waki* never wear masks and play the supporting, passive role—the priest, warrior or traveller to whom the central mystery of the story will eventually be revealed. The principal character is called the *shite* (pronounced 'sh'teh'). He (or she, although female roles are always taken by men) may not be what he first appears—a peasant who turns out to be a ghost, for instance, or a demon in the shape of a court lady. If the *shite* is a woman, an elderly person, a court noble, or a non-human ghost or monster, he will wear one of the beautiful masks for which *nō* has become famous. The third main group comprises the *kyōgen* actors. Not every *nō* play features *kyōgen*, but they sometimes take supporting roles as peasants or retainers. Their most important function is to summarize, in simple language, the events of a play during its interval. *Kyōgen* is also the name of a separate dramatic genre: homely, satirical comedies about venal priests, drunken lords, dim-witted samurai and their rascally retainers, originally performed as light relief during a lengthy *nō* programme. *Kyōgen* is as light and accessible as *nō* is profound and demanding, and these days it is increasingly performed in its own right.

All the actors wear elaborate formal costumes of the finest brocade. The sumptuousness of the kimono usually indicates the importance of the character, although costume, like everything else, is stylized—even peasants and fishermen wear clothes of beauty and quality. *Kyōgen* actors are identifiable by their yellow *tabi*—cotton slippers with a separate compartment for the big toe, like mittens for feet. Especially striking are the trousers worn by samurai characters, with extra long legs which trail behind them as they walk.

Nō plays are simple in the extreme, and their stories, such as they are, can be summarized in a few lines. There are various different types of play, but the typical 'plot' goes like this: a traveller (the *waki*—often a priest, warrior or imperial envoy) encounters the *shite*, who may be young or old, male or female, great or humble. The *shite*, however, is disguising his true form. In the second act of the play, this will be revealed in a climactic dance. Then, after pious concluding remarks, the actors, chorus and musicians slowly process off stage. There are five different types of play, labelled according to the nature of the *shite* character: 'god plays' which are generally upbeat and celebratory, 'warrior plays', in which the *shite* is often a member of the warring Taira or Minamoto clans, 'woman plays', 'madman plays' and 'devil plays'.

The language is highly poetic and allusive—even a Japanese spectator will often use an annotated script to follow the densest speeches. Without some knowledge of the plot (or good Japanese), it would be very difficult to work out, from simply watching the actors, what is going on. Realistic portrayal of action is irrelevant to a *nō* actor. In fact, it is considered vulgar and a distraction from the real purpose of the form—the cultivation of *yūgen*, an untranslatable concept meaning something like 'mysterious profundity'.

Restraint is everything. *Nō* solves the central question of the theatre—how to portray real lives and emotions in an essentially non-realistic environment—by withdrawing utterly from any attempt at naturalism. Movement is slow and stately; the passage of an actor across the stage might indicate a journey of thousands of miles. Props are simple and few—chief among them is the actor's fan which can stand for anything from a sword to chopsticks. (In one play, a dying lady is represented by a folded robe at the front of the stage.) In such an austere, understated atmosphere, tiny gestures can stand for deep and powerful emotions—a mother's delight at finding her long-lost son might be suggested by nothing more than the tilt of a mask; a hand brushing the face represents tears of grief.

Getting the Most out of *Nō*

A fine *nō* performance can be a hauntingly transcendent experience, a piece of living history, mysterious far beyond the sum of its parts. To first timers with unrealistic expectations, however, it can also be gibberish—a fiasco of atonal wailing and tuneless twanging, like a two-hour-long Monty Python sketch. Certainly, it's the least accessible of the traditional performing arts, and you have to approach it in the right frame of mind. Don't come expecting anything as mundane as action, plot or character. Leave the children at home.

Try to get hold of an English version of the play. Several of these are available, including classic translations by Arthur Waley and Donald Keene, but the most comprehensive is probably *Japanese Nō Dramas*, translated by Royall Tyler (Penguin Classics). If the play you're planning to see isn't in one of these, consult *A Guide to Nō* by P.G. O'Neill (Hinoki Shoten) which contains character lists and plot summaries of all the plays still in the repertoire. *Nō* theatres often hand out photocopies of these to foreign members of the audience.

Kabuki

Kabuki is the exact opposite of *nō*. Where one form whispers, the other yodels. If a grieving father in a *nō* play laments the murder of his son by brushing a sleeve against his downward tilted mask, his *kabuki* counterpart will wail, sing and perform a stamping dance, before metamorphosing into a dragon to avenge his child's death. *Kabuki* is noisy, camp and over-the-top, and, for newcomers to Japanese drama, it's the ideal place to start.

Kabuki's louche beginnings were in the early 1600s, when a woman named Okuni led a troupe of female dancers in performances of *kabuki odori* (frolicsome dances) on the banks of Kyoto's Kamo River. The shows were associated with lewdness and prostitution, and the authorities intervened to ban women from taking part. They were replaced by handsome young boys, but the problem of prostitution did not go away. Eventually the rules were changed again—today *kabuki* parts are played by adult men.

The plays became popular as part of the merchant's culture which grew up in 17th- and 18th-century Edo (Tokyo), and incorporated all the elements closest to the Edo townsman's heart: lavish and stylish costumes, beautiful women (even if they were men), and epic tales of love, betrayal, gallantry, war, ghosts and death, set in the feudal present as well as the heroic past. It was very much an actors' theatre—the big *kabuki* players were the pop and movie stars of their day, portrayed in their famous roles by woodblock print artists, and famously fond of improvization and banter with the audience. Even today, actors wink effortlessly in and out of character, and plays written centuries ago are spiced up with sly references to contemporary politics, scandals, sport, TV and pop music.

The *kabuki* stage is big, and closer to the Western proscenium style than the platform employed by *nō*. Its most striking feature is the *hanamichi* (flower path), a long catwalk linking the front of the stage with the back of the auditorium; along it, principal characters make important entrances and exits. The stage floor conceals complicated apparatus for the stunts and *coups de theatre* in which *kabuki* revels: trap doors through which characters leap or vanish; revolving panels for quick changes of scenery; ropes and pulleys for flying a character across the stage. Music is played live, but the players are usually semi-concealed behind wooden slats. The music is more exuberant and noisy than *nō*, but still far from melodic, with much use of drums and clackers to point up spectacular moments.

Kabuki actors serve long apprenticeships, being born or adopted into long-standing acting families which have dominated the art since the Edo period. As in *nō*, actors specialize in certain kinds of role, the most specialized of all being the *onnagata*, female impersonators, whose exquisite dress, movement and high-pitched voices render them more feminine than any real woman ever was. They wear thick white make-up, like *geisha*; other actors are painted to indicate their character, with red suggesting evil. *Aragoto* is the rough, gruff, bombastic style of acting used to portray heroes and warriors. These actors sometimes have stripy make-up, a bit like that in the Peking Opera; at key moments they freeze in dramatic grimaces, and turn their faces to the lights. Aficionados demonstrate their connoisseurship at these moments by shouting aloud the name of the actor's family.

Bunraku

The traditional puppet theatre of Japan (also called *ningyō jōruri*) is as far as could be from the Punch and Judy shows and twitchy marionettes of the West. Wandering puppeteers were known in Japan in the 11th century, but it was during the 17th century that *bunraku* achieved huge popularity, largely thanks to a playwright named Chikamatsu Monzaemon whose 130 plays are the core of the modern repertoire. The subjects and style of *bunraku* are quite different from those of *nō*: Chikamatsu developed the genre known as *sewa-mono*, 'talk of the town plays' about recognizable Edo-era types (*geisha*, apprentices, merchants, samurai) and the tragic conflicts that arose between feudal duty (*giri*) and human feeling (*ninjō*). The archetypal *bunraku* plot traces the course of an ill-fated love affair, and its pathetic, and usually fatal, consequences. Chikamatsu's most famous play, *Sonezaki Shinjū*, was one of 20 he wrote on the subject of love suicides, often based on contemporary real-life tragedies. *Bunraku* became a forum for propagation of the latest gossip and scandal, often thinly fictionalized with Chinese or historical settings.

The *bunraku* stage is wide, and on two levels. On the lower, rear stage stand the puppeteers, three for each puppet. All are plainly visible throughout the performance—the great thrill of the best *bunraku* is the way in which one's attention is tugged away from the work of the puppeteers by the delicate and realistic movement of the puppets. One assistant operates the left arm and hand, another controls the legs and feet. Both are masked and dressed in black. The master puppeteer moves the face, eyes, mouth and right arm; he wears a plain formal kimono, and is unmasked.

The puppets are works of art in themselves, hand-made by a dwindling number of specialist craftsmen. They are about two-thirds life size, realistically clothed in miniature Edo-period costumes, similar to those used in *kabuki*. The narration and the voices for all the different characters, including women, are performed by a chanter (*tayū*), who sits at stage right alongside a *shamisen* player. His is the most important and exhausting role of all; a long play might involve several different narrators, substituted through a revolving door in the side of the stage.

Religion

Visitors often find the subject of religion in Japan difficult to get to grips with. By Western standards, it is riven with contradictions and surprises. Few countries, on the face of it, appear so committed to the secular virtues of technological progress and materialism; yet every new bank or factory building is blessed by a priest, and frequently has a miniature shrine on its roof. The typical young Japanese professes no strong religious beliefs; but he or she would never dream of visiting a temple or shrine without faithfully going through the rituals of cleansing, clapping, bowing and making offerings. In the early 1990s, for example, a survey showed that 107 million Japanese claim affiliation to a Shinto organization, 96 million to a Buddhist one; yet the total population is only 124 million. Plainly, religious life in Japan is organized along very different lines from those of the Christian West.

The most important religions of Japan are Shinto, indigenous and unique to Japan, and Buddhism, the great religion of Asia, founded in India in the 5th century BC. Shinto deities are worshipped at buildings called *jinja* or *jingū* (*-gū* or *-sha* at the end of a word); this book follows the standard practice of translating these words as 'shrine', in contrast to the Buddhist *tera* (*-dera* or *-ji* or *-in*) which is always given as 'temple'.

Perhaps the greatest historical difference between Japanese and European religion is the tolerance with which Shinto and Buddhism have always regarded one another. For centuries, rival groups of Japanese carved one another up in ruinous civil wars, but these were almost never fought for sectarian reasons, and it is still common to find shrines and temples standing side by side within the same precincts. As statistics show, most Japanese regard themselves as both Shinto and Buddhist, at different times and places. In general, Buddhist ritual is used to mark the solemn, transcendent occasions such as funerals, Shinto for auspicious events like weddings or festivals.

Shinto

The survival of Shinto as a living faith is remarkable; it's rather as if the Classical or Celtic deities were still being revered in modern Greece and Britain, alongside the Christian God and his saints. Historically, in fact, there have been many kinds of Shinto; one of the reasons for its survival is undoubtedly its adaptable, multi-valenced nature. 'A person is Shinto in the same way that he is born Japanese', wrote Ian Buruma in *A Japanese Mirror.* 'It is a collection of forms and ceremonies that give form to a way of life. It is a celebration, not a belief. There is no such thing as a Shintoist, for there is no such thing as Shintoism.' Over the years, Shinto has been many different things to different Japanese, and it is unfortunate that it is known in the West almost exclusively for its last incarnation: State Shinto, a sentimental, nationalistic brand of emperor worship invented in the Meiji period and exploited during the 1930s by the fascists and totalitarians of the Pacific War.

Early Shinto was vague and inchoate; the word itself didn't exist until after the 6th century when the introduction of Buddhism made it necessary to distinguish between the traditional 'Way of the Gods' (*Shintō*) and the imported 'Way of Buddha' (*Butsudō*). It began as the religion of a nation of rice farmers. Fertility rites, both human and agricultural, have always been important elements in Shinto worship, and many of the most important *matsuri* (festivals) are essentially prayers for the success of the crop offered at crucial moments of the rice-growing cycle. The earliest deities were thus the sun, which nourishes the crop, the storm, which can ruin it, and natural features like mountains, rivers and lakes, which collect and supply the water essential for irrigation. Worship seems also to have been offered to natural features which were not necessarily useful or fearful, but simply impressive. The earliest shrines were not buildings at all, but natural objects like rocks or trees, which were marked with sacred symbols. Even today it's common in the older shrines to see particularly ancient cedars or boulders girt with a rope or paper streamers indicating the presence of a *kami*, a Shinto deity. This delicate appreciation of natural beauty for its own sake is a constant thread in Japanese art and aesthetics of all periods.

If a fertility cult based on nature worship is the first element in Shinto, then reverence for ancestors, a common strand in much Asian religion, is the second. The two fused naturally enough in Shinto's most controversial aspect, the cult surrounding the emperor and his family. The imperial family, after all, started out as one of a number of clans whose wealth and power depended on their success as rice farmers. As the most successful of the bunch, they were able to dominate and rule over their peers; and it was only natural that they should legitimize their power by setting up their forebears, not just as honoured conquerors and administrators, but as children of the gods. The earliest surviving Japanese book, the *Kojiki*, was compiled in 712 with this very purpose in mind: the genealogy of the 8th-century emperors is traced back to the sun goddess and beyond, to the legendary founders and begetters of the islands of Japan.

These three kinds of worship—of nature, ancestors and the emperor—have formed the basis of Shinto. Beyond this, it's difficult to make definite statements about Shinto belief. It possesses no scripture (the *Kojiki* and similar collections are legends, not dogma) and no commandments, code of ethics, or system of philosophical speculation, and answers none of the abstract questions posed by great world faiths. It's difficult to call it a religion at all.

Instead, Shinto asserts the existence of many thousands of *kami*, a word usually translated as 'god' which literally means 'superior'—those removed from or above humanity, but not necessarily transcending it. *Kami* range from Amaterasu Ōmikami, the sun goddess, ancestor of the imperial family, and principal deity of the pantheon, down to the nameless spirits who inhabit rocks, trees and wayside shrines. These *kami* possess power over different areas of life, and can be propitiated or angered by the practice, or omission, of certain ritual acts. It is in the observance of these rituals, rather than in any abstract beliefs about the nature of the deities or of existence, that Shinto endures.

Outstanding among these rituals are those concerned with purification: the contrast between clean and unclean is as strong in Shinto as the dualism of good and evil, innocence and guilt, in other religions. Certain states of impurity are offensive to the gods, and much ritual concerns itself with the elimination or avoidance of pollution. Physical grubbiness was only part of the story: among the things that made the original *kami* squeamish were sex, menstruation and childbirth—in early times, separate buildings were constructed away from human habitation where affected individuals (principally women, of course) would confine themselves for the period of their pollution. Illness, injury and death were also great taboos. One of the reasons why the imperial capitals shifted around so much before the 8th century was that entire palaces had to be moved and rebuilt after the death of an old emperor. In Heian times, even the death of a cat within the precincts of the imperial enclosure was the cause of much troublesome purifying and exorcizing.

Vestigial traces of this urge to cleanliness can be seen throughout modern Japanese society. Every shrine and temple contains in its courtyard a font where worshippers wash their hands and rinse out their mouths, and at some Shinto services the (white-clad) priest will wave a wand of paper streamers over worshippers—an act of cleansing, rather than blessing. When sumo wrestlers toss salt over their shoulders before a bout, they are performing a purification ritual; piles of salt can often be seen on household altars and shrines. Even the white gloves worn by taxi drivers, and the Japanese love of hot baths and spas undoubtedly owes something to this deep-rooted preoccupation.

Actual historical figures can become *kami*—Heian-period statesman and scholar Sugawara Michizane is worshipped in shrines across Japan as Tenjin-sama, god of learning, principally by high school students hoping for success in their university entrance exams. With more recently deceased figures, it can be difficult to distinguish between worship and reverence. The great 19th-century Emperor Meiji is enshrined as a *kami* in Tokyo's Meiji Shrine, but how much this has in common with the ancient shrine to the sun goddess at Ise, for instance, is open to question. The traditional belief in the ruling emperor as a living god was renounced by Emperor Hirohito in 1945; nonetheless, some Japanese still regard him as a *kami* in the literal sense—one symbolically 'above' his subjects and nation.

Shinto worship is loose and open ended. Its most obvious and enjoyable manifestations are in *matsuri* (festivals) which vary from a small fair at a village shrine to spectacular three-day extravaganzas of dance, music and drunkenness which dominate an entire city, and attract visitors from all over the country. *Matsuri* are big tourist attractions, but the entertainment they offer—parades of floats, dances, traditional drama, stunts involving fire, contests of strength, feasts and boozing—were originally intended for the entertainment of the *kami*. At a typical *matsuri*, the priests, after carefully purifying themselves, use prayers, offerings and sacred music to summon the *kami*, who is then paraded around the neighbourhood in an ornate portable shrine called a *mikoshi*, carried on the back of chanting, and often extremely drunk, local men. *Matsuri* vary in scale and spectacle, but they are always joyful, earthy, raucous occasions which the gods are intended to enjoy as much as the participants. Having fêted and entertained the *kami*, it is hoped that they will bring luck and prosperity to the people and their crops over the next year.

There are no mandatory services, fasts, or days of Shinto obligation. On request, after payment of a fixed 'donation', shrines will perform rituals of blessing or purification, often accompanied by sacred dances, for worshippers with a particular prayer or wish (good luck in education, child-bearing, marriage, etc.). Most babies are still presented, a few weeks after their birth, at their parents' shrine; and the *shichi-go-san* ('seven-five-three') festival is a popular event held in November when children of those ages dress up and accompany their families to the shrine. Other than that, Shinto observation is simply a matter of purification and prayer at individual shrines, as often or as seldom as an individual wishes.

Notable Deities

Amaterasu Ōmikami

The prime deity of the Shinto pantheon, she is the goddess of the sun and light, born out of the left eye of her father, Izanagi. She taught her earthly subjects to plant rice and weave but was so incensed by the unruly behaviour of her brother, the storm god Susano-o, that she hid herself away in a cave, and plunged the earth into darkness. The other gods gathered to discuss the problem, which they solved with a trick. A female *kami* performed an obscene dance which caused great amusement, and tempted Amaterasu to peep out of her cave to see what all the fuss was about. She was pulled out into the open, the cave blocked off, and light returned to the world. Her grandson's great-grandson was Jimmu, the legendary first ruler of Japan; all subsequent emperors have claimed descent from her. Amaterasu is worshipped in different shrines all over Japan. The great shrine of Ise is the oldest Shinto site in the country.

Hachiman

The Emperor Ōjin (legendary dates 201–312), deified as the god of war, and worshipped alongside his mother, the Empress Jingū.

Inari

The most widely worshipped god in Japan, a popular name for the rice or food deity, and the patron of wealth and commercial enterprises. Inari shrines vary from the huge Fushimi Taisha in south Kyoto to countless local shrines in gardens, temples and at roadsides. They're recognizable from their tunnels of closely built red *torii* gates, and the sinister-looking statues of foxes, the messengers of the god.

The Seven Lucky Gods

The *Shichi Fuku-nin* are a popular, but obscure, collection of folk deities apparently derived from Hindu, Chinese and native traditions, representing the blessings of longevity, wealth, virtue, contentment, popularity and wisdom. The father and son team, Ebisu and

Daikoku, are the most commonly represented. The former carries a fishing rod and a fat *tai* (sea bream), the latter a mallet and a pair of bulging rice bags. The others are the goddess Benten and the gods Fukurokuju, Bishamon, Jurōjin, and Hotei.

Tenjin-sama

Sugawara no Michizane was a 9th-century scholar and statesman unjustly framed by jealous enemies and exiled to Kyūshū. After his death, evil portents were witnessed in the capital. In order to appease his angry spirit he was posthumously awarded high office, and a cult developed around his memory. As the patron of intellectual endeavours, he's fervently worshipped by students and schoolchildren facing examinations who throng his many temples, including Kitanōtemaru-gū in Kyoto. The plum blossom is his flower, and the ox his messenger.

Tōshō-gū

Tōshō-gū is the deification of Tokugawa Ieyasu, first and greatest of the Tokugawa shoguns who united Japan in the early 17th century. His main shrine is the gaudily magnificent Nikkō Tōshō-gū, north of Tokyo. Others are found in castle towns, where the Tokugawa family wielded influence.

Buddhism

The religion founded by the Indian Prince, Siddhartha Gautama, posthumously known as the Buddha or Enlightened One, is the greatest of the many outside influences that have worked on Japan, and few areas of Japanese culture remain untouched by it. Japan's most magnificent buildings, its finest statues, its greatest philosophy and its most plangent poems have been created by men who were either Buddhist priests themselves, or whose view of the world was shaped profoundly by its gentle and melancholy tenets. It is difficult to come to an understanding of Japanese culture without some knowledge of Buddhist history and iconography.

After its genesis in the 5th century BC, Buddhism spread outwards from India and divided into two branches. Hinayana ('Lesser Vehicle') Buddhism is the faith still practised in South and Southeast Asia, emphasizing monasticism and an individual quest for personal salvation according to the teachings of the historical Buddha. The Buddhism practised in Japan is known as Mahayana ('Greater Vehicle'). It was a thousand years old by the time the first Buddhist images were shipped over from Korea in the 6th century AD, and on its long journey through Central Asia, China and Korea, it had acquired doctrines, superstitions and iconography undreamed of by its Indian founders. Over the centuries, and during the long periods of isolation from the rest of the world, the sects took on native Japanese characteristics, incorporating traditional Shinto beliefs and deities; new sects broke away and developed their own teachings to form a panoply of faiths and deities quite as varied as the denominations of European Christianity.

Deities

The Buddhist hierarchy is a complicated one, as a glance at a mandala—a beautiful picture diagram of the heavenly pantheon, with buddhas in the middle, human saints at the edges—will demonstrate. Local variations, inconsistent use of Sanskrit and Japanese terms, and the countless exceptions to every rule, make the task of deciphering Buddhist art a baffling one. The following should help enlighten you as to which of the Enlightened Ones you are looking at. The first term given is Japanese; it is followed by the phrase most commonly used in English, often a transliteration of the Sanskrit. The use of the male or female pronoun, by the way, is a misleading convention; apart from Shaka, heavenly beings are effectively sexless.

Nyōrai (Buddhas)

Originally there was only one Buddha—**Shaka** (or Sakyamuni in Sanskrit), also known as the Historical Buddha, or Prince Gautama Siddhartha, the name he bore during his earthly life between about 563 and 483 BC. Shaka was an Indian prince who abandoned his powers and privileges for the life of a wandering holy man. After years of fruitless austerities, he achieved enlightenment while meditating under a linden tree. In a flash, he grasped that the cause of suffering is ignorant desire, and that it can be eliminated only by adherence to the Eightfold Path: right understanding, right thought, right speech, right conduct, right livelihood, right effort, right mindfulness, and right concentration. By following the Path, an individual hopes to achieve freedom from the endless cycle of rebirth—the state known as Nirvana. The stupas and pagodas associated with Buddhist temples were originally reliquaries enshrining ashes, a tooth, or a fragment of bone of the Historical Buddha.

Dainichi Nyōrai ('Great Light'; also known as the Cosmic or Universal Buddha; in Sanskrit, Mahavairocana or Roshana) is the supreme Buddhist deity, the Nyōrai of ultimate reality, who embraces, and is manifested in, all things. The Shinto sun goddess, Amaterasu Ōmikami, is identified with Dainichi; even Shaka is but an aspect of him.

Amida (Amitabha) is one of the most popular Nyōrai, and in the Heian period (794–1185) a number of sects emerged based on his worship. He is a merciful and accessible being, ruler of a western paradise called the Pure Land, into which he welcomes all souls who sincerely call on him with the simple formula *Namu Amida Butsu* ('Save me, Amida Buddha').

Yakushi Nyōrai (Bhaisajyaguru) is the Buddha of Healing, recognizable in sculpture for the jar of medicine which he often holds out in his left hand.

Bosatsu (Bodhisattvas)

The Bosatsu are beings of great spiritual merit who have attained the self-knowledge necessary for enlightenment, but who choose to defer it in order to save other beings. They're widely worshipped and represented in art, and are often depicted flanking the Nyōrai in triptychs.

Kannon Bosatsu (Avalokitesvara) is one of the most popular of all Buddhist deities, honoured all over the country as the Goddess of Mercy. Tokyo's Sensō-ji (Asakusa Kannon) and Kyoto's Sanjūsangen-dō temples are dedicated to her, and there is a famous pilgrimage of the 33 Kannon temples in the Kansai area. With her gentle, feminine nature, Kannon has often been likened to the Virgin Mary. During the religious persecutions of the early 17th century, Japanese Christians used to worship images of 'Maria Kannon', with a cross concealed underneath or on the back. Other manifestations of the deity include *Jūichimen* (Eleven-faced) Kannon (the supernumerary faces are on the top of the main head), *Senju* (Thousand-armed) Kannon whose limbs grasp and save floundering souls, and *Bato* (Horse) Kannon whose miniature steed peeps out from the deity's crown. Kannon is an aspect of Amida Nyōrai, whom she often accompanies.

Jizō Bosatsu (Ksitigarbha) is another profoundly merciful being, usually represented as a wandering monk with tonsure and staff. He is the patron of travellers and children. As the former, his image is often found along roadsides; as the latter, statues of him are often adorned with red bibs and childish toys, like windmills. These are offerings left by the parents of *mizu-ko*, miscarried or aborted children whom Jizō guides and protects from demons in the grim Buddhist limbo.

Miroku Bosatsu (Maitreya) is the 'Buddha of the Future'. Five thousand years after the enlightenment of Shaka, he will descend from heaven and bring all beings to enlightenment. Miroku has several manifestations. Two of the most beautiful are the early, probably Korean, statues in Nara's Hōryū-ji and Kyoto's Kōryū-ji, showing a young, slim youth seated in meditation.

Other Deities

Fudō Myō-ō was one of a group of deities (the Myō-ō or Vidyaraja in Sanskrit) absorbed into the Buddhist pantheon from Indian Hindu mythology. He is depicted as a ferocious demon, seated amid flickering flames, with a long pony-tail, snarling fangs and skin of red or blue. In his right hand is a sword, in his left a lasso. With these he ensnares and punishes evil, and terrifies the good into renewed discipline.

Ni-ō (Guardian Kings) are the half-naked musclemen often found in pairs in the main gate of a Buddhist temple. They wear fierce expressions, and serve to protect the sacred precincts from evil influence. One has his mouth open, the other closed. They are said to be pronouncing the letters ah and un, the alpha and omega of the Sanskrit alphabet.

Emma-ō is the King of Hell, the fearful judge who weighs the souls of the departed and dispatches them to paradise or damnation. He sits cross legged, wearing a crown bearing the character for king; the style of his robes indicates his Chinese origins. He is sometimes accompanied by lesser scribes of hell who record the deeds of the living with scrolls and ink brushes.

The Shi-Tennō (Four Heavenly Kings) guard the four cardinal points. They're usually sculpted in the armour of central Asian warriors, with fierce expressions, stomping comically grotesque demons beneath their feet. Bishamonten, one of the most popular, is also one of the Seven Lucky Gods of Shinto folk religion. He guards the north, and is depicted with a pagoda in his hand.

Business Culture

In Nagasaki, I was pleased to see that business was at a low ebb.
The Japanese should stay away from business.

Rudyard Kipling

Of all the activities which bring foreigners to Japan, none is as fraught with prejudice and disinformation as the world of business. The subject unites a range of foreign anxieties about Japan: an alien language, impenetrable rules of politeness and etiquette and, above all, dazzling and world-beating success, equalling or outstripping that of the West. You only have to glance at the shelves of an English-language book shop in Tokyo for one symptom of this confusion: the countless advice books and 'How to...' guides to business with the Japanese, new ones published every month, as indistinguishable and repetitive as sex manuals. They're like sex manuals in other ways too: they contradict one another; they make something natural appear fraught and complicated; and they're dedicated to creating problems to which, suspiciously, they are also the solution.

There is no magic formula for doing successful business in Japan, any more than for Britain, America or Europe, and the search for one is a wild goose chase. Markets and consumers differ, management styles and work habits vary, but business anywhere is about adaptability, and what is good practice in London and New York will never be unacceptable in Tokyo. The recipe may alter, but the basic ingredients are the same.

What follows is a general introduction to ways of thinking about business in Japan. Ninety per cent of good advice is a statement of the obvious. One of the 'How to...' guides recommends staying in as smart a hotel as you can afford, since this will inspire respect and confidence in your Japanese clients and customers—although it's hard to think of any country in the world where this wouldn't be the case. Another warns against the dangers of blowing your nose in business meetings (excuse yourself and go to the toilet, or make do with a series of sniffs). But, come to think of it, noisily relieving oneself of nasal mucus would be an uncool move in formal settings all over the world. The lesson is: trust in your instincts. Care, patience and sincerity are the secret of doing successful business in Japan—and they are no secret, because they apply to successful business all over the world. Demonstrate these qualities, and it really won't matter how you hold your chopsticks.

Zaibatsu and Keiretsu

The Japanese economic 'miracle', which transformed a defeated country into the second largest economy in the world, was, of course, not miraculous at all. Industrial power was nothing new to Japan, and the foundations of many of the country's most distinctive institutions were laid long before the US Occupation and the huge injections of American aid which got the economy back on its feet in the 1950s. Japan was becoming an industrial power as early as 1905 when the Imperial Navy destroyed the Russian Baltic Fleet in the Straits of Tsushima. By 1915, almost half of the Japanese workforce was employed in industry, which organized itself into the notorious *zaibatsu* collectives whose successor corporations, the *keiretsu*, remain such a distinctive feature of Japanese business today.

The *zaibatsu* developed from the policies of the 19th-century Meiji government which, having established key industries, passed them on, at ridiculously cheap prices, to a small group of privately owned family companies. After the war, they re-emerged as the *keiretsu*, looser but increasingly massive agglomerations of financial, commercial and manufacturing power, each grouped around a major bank. Between them the six groups—Mitsubishi, Mitsui, Sumitomo, Fuyo, Sanwa and Gai-ichi Kangyo embrace a total of 650 companies, employing 5 per cent of the Japanese workforce, and netting 17 per cent of the nation's profits.

The strength and influence of these institutions on all aspects of life is enormous, and Japan's economic history would have been utterly different without them. Structurally, they function not through outright ownership of one company by another, but through a dense web of cross-shareholdings. About a fifth of any one company's equity will typically be distributed among fellow members of the combine, while it in turn owns a proportion of their shares; their presidents may well be on its board of directors, and vice versa. This produces an elaborate and irregular structure resembling (in Peter Tasker's words) 'complex molecules, each component binding with several others'.

The arrangement is based firmly on the values of loyalty and group consciousness visible throughout Japanese society. The *keiretsu* function as giant industrial department stores, providing member companies with all the services they require, and conveniently reducing the need to shop elsewhere. Thus, having secured loans from the Mitsubishi Bank and purchased land through Mitsubishi Real Estate, the Mitsubishi *keiretsu* member will hire Mitsubishi Construction to build its new factory with materials from Mitsubishi Metal and Asahi Glass (a Mitsubishi company). Machinery, lifts and air-conditioning will come from Mitsubishi Heavy Industries and Mitsubishi Electric, and trucks from Mitsubishi Motors. The whole lot will be covered by Tokyo Fire and Marine Insurance, the finished products will be sold through the Mitsubishi Corporation trading company and, at the factory's launch party, guests will drink Kirin beer, and soft drinks bottled by Chukyo Coca Cola Bottling—all of them companies under the Mitsubishi umbrella.

The members of a *keiretsu* are under few formal obligations to one another, but transactions like those described above usually make sense for all concerned. Fellow companies can share resources in finance, research, marketing and personnel. It's not a completely closed shop, of course, but it is common for *keiretsu* members to favour one another, even though outside companies can offer better terms. Cost, in other words, isn't always the bottom line when a company has the future of its relationships within the *keiretsu* to take into account. To the Japanese mind, this is loyalty, but also common sense. To foreign critics, it's an NTB, a Non-Tariff Barrier to free trade. Several analysts have predicted the gradual dissolution of the combines under the eroding forces of international competition. The recent economic crisis and subsequent reforms may bear this prediction out. But for the time being, at least, they are a fact of business life.

The character of the collectives is probably the single most important difference between Japanese and foreign markets. An inclination to operate in mutually supportive groups permeates all levels of Japanese business. Even if you're not dealing with one of the big six combines, the chances are that you'll encounter elements of this arrangement, which may affect the way you do business. Does the company you are pitching to already have a relationship with an existing supplier in a *keiretsu* or similar association? If so, this must be taken into account when presenting new proposals. Even if the answer is no, the principles behind the *keiretsu* are the principles by which Japanese customers will judge you and your business: loyalty, a preference for long-term relationships over quick and easy profits, sensitivity about the effects of any action on others (on a personal, as well as company, level). Awareness of these values will add greatly to your prospects for success.

Getting Started in Japan

Clichés and misconceptions work both ways; however mistaken the Western view of Japan, the Japanese have some clunking prejudices of their own. A European or American stereotype of the Tokyo businessman might include the following impressions: hard-working, devoted to the company, protocol-bound, sexist, soulless and inscrutable, tends to copy the ideas of others. The equivalent Japanese picture of the Westerner might go like this: creative and energetic, but impatient, opportunistic and concerned only with the short-term; incapable of understanding Japan and its unique culture; enviably 'free' from social constraint, but correspondingly irresponsible, unreliable and, potentially, untrustworthy. Not every Japanese will hold these individual opinions but they may underpin dealings, and it is in your interests to counteract them as early as possible.

Your biggest initial disadvantage is very simple. Japanese society is structured around membership of (often fiercely competing) groups which exist at all levels—from the family, through the individual's school and university, to the company, the *keiretsu*, and finally the Japanese nation itself. As a foreigner, you exist outside the outermost of these concentric and overlapping rings, and you are different from those inside. This, to the Japanese mind, is not a value judgement, but a statement of immutable fact. Outsiders *can* be allowed to enter into relationships with those on the inside. But this is a slow and gradual process, not to be undertaken without long reflection and consultation. The trick in dealing with a Japanese company, therefore, is to minimize your 'outsideness'. This doesn't mean trying to act like a Japanese; it means observing the Japanese business virtues, and offering as little disruption as possible to the established way of doing things.

Preparation

Thorough preparation before you go to Japan isn't just an optional extra, it's the basis of any successful visit. The cost of travel alone makes it essential that as much as possible of your itinerary is organized before you get on the plane.

The most valuable commodity you can take with you from home is a good set of **intro-ductions**. Japan is absolutely not the sort of country where you can breeze into town, make a few calls and watch the meetings materialize in your diary. How you secure these contacts will depend on the nature of your business: for some it will be necessary to hire an agent in Tokyo. Others should contact the organizations listed below, especially JETRO and (in Britain) the Department of Trade and Industry. Your first meetings in Tokyo should be with your country's Chamber of Commerce, and the commercial department of its embassy. Don't forget that many Japanese companies have European and American offices: acquaintance with a member of staff at one of these may stand you in good stead when you get to Japan. Try to remember the names and titles of Japanese acquaintances when you encounter their colleagues in Japan. Don't be shy of a little name-dropping, or underestimate its power to break the ice.

Equally important is mental preparation. Some people take to Japan better than others, and a few, it must be admitted, react negatively. More than in Europe or America, selecting **appropriate personnel** to send to Japan is an important decision which will bear directly on the success of your mission.

It's difficult to generalize usefully about the type of person who will respond well to Japan, except to say that the most valuable quality is adaptability. In the age of multinational corporations and international business schools, styles are becoming homogenized—for every Japanese manager who speaks through an interpreter and says no when he means yes, you'll come across a fluent English-speaker educated in Europe or America. Half the trick (as in all communication) is to judge who you are talking to, and engage them in the appropriate tone. If in doubt, err on the side of caution. Japan is a conservative country where the quieter virtues of patience, deference to seniors and attention to detail are still primary. What in the West passes for grit and determination can easily seem in Japan like American insensitivity or European arrogance. No one ever won a contract in Japan by bullying; no one ever lost one by being over formal or courteous.

Business is war in Tokyo as much as anywhere else, but campaigns are fought slowly and strategically, and a combative, gung-ho approach to negotiation will not bring success. Patience, coupled with persistence, is the most important abstract quality a Japan-bound businessperson can possess. In practice this means a willingness to sit out a decision-making process much longer and more drawn out than is common in the West, through seemingly endless meetings whose only function may be to repeat what has already been stated and give the participants an opportunity to get to know one another better. Straightforwardness is always a good thing but 'straight-talking', as the expression is commonly understood, is inappropriate.

Harmony, an appearance of outward concord and good feeling, is to be preserved at all times. This doesn't mean that dissatisfaction and disagreement can never be expressed, only that they must be phrased indirectly in such a way as to preclude personal blame and ignominy. Thus 'I am surprised' comes to mean 'I'm disappointed'; 'that's interesting' all too often means 'that's difficult'; and 'that's difficult' means 'it's absolutely impossible'. Indirectness of this sort is used by everyone from time to time, but in Japan it is a way of life. Some people find it exasperating and hypocritical; to others, it's a challenge. On your team you want the second sort, not the first.

Also desirable in your salespeople or negotiators is good standing within the company, and thorough grounding in the field of business under discussion. Loyalty to the organization is still an esteemed Japanese virtue. One of the first questions new arrivals are asked is how long they have been with the company, and a seasoned and long-serving manager will fare better than a recent recruit.

The Language Barrier

You'll hear contradictory things about the usefulness of Japanese in international business. Some claim it's essential: so many of the codes and distinctions of Japanese society are embodied in its language that it's impossible to penetrate the culture without it. Others complain that confident use of Japanese can be a barrier to communication, that it provokes mistrust in Japanese clients who enjoy the opaque cloak of their language.

Neither view is adequate. Unquestionably, a command of spoken and written Japanese is a tremendous advantage to anyone doing business in Japan. But it is not the most important skill, and the considerations discussed above (personality, standing within the company, experience in the field) should take precedence. A good firm can succeed in Japan with no Japanese speakers at all, and fluency in the language will never bring success to an inherently undesirable business proposition.

Still, it is dangerous (and discourteous) to assume that the other side will automatically speak good English. All Japanese have studied some English, but many are more comfortable with the written than the spoken word and, for this reason, faxes are often a safer way of communicating than phones. Even if the Japanese contact speaks good English, important details (prices and orders, dates and times of meetings) should be confirmed in simple language by fax.

In conversation, speak clearly and evenly (which doesn't mean loudly and slowly). Avoid baby-talk and never omit particles, conjunctions or auxiliaries in the interests of supposed clarity ('You, me—we go meeting?'). Be literal-minded. In many ways, Japanese is a very logical language compared to English; usages likely to get you into trouble include colourful metaphors and idioms ('If you go out on a limb, it'll raise the stakes—but it's your funeral'), double negatives ('I don't dislike what you're saying') and negative questions. In answer to the question, 'Don't you want to buy my marmalade?', a Japanese will answer 'Yes', meaning, 'Yes, you're right, I don't want your marmalade,' or 'No', meaning 'No, you're wrong. I want your marmalade'.

If interpreters are required, it is the responsibility of the sellers to provide them. Japanese companies will often detail one of their own staff to interpret for you in situations like this, but it's wiser and politer to hire your own, despite the expense. When it gets to the stage of drawing up contracts and product specifications, professional translators and lawyers should be engaged.

Mastering a few simple phrases of Japanese (*see* p.299) and using them at the beginning of a meeting is a gesture that will be appreciated, however awkward it makes you feel.

Sex and Race

Women are active in all areas of Japanese business—but not at all levels. In some fields—the leisure industries, for instance, especially areas like fashion and design—the differentials are less obvious, but surveys routinely show that female employees start lower down the company than their male contemporaries, have poorer prospects for promotion, earn less for the same work and occupy only a tiny fraction of the top posts. In the long term, international competition will bring about change, for the simple reason that sex discrimination halves the number of talented employees which a company has to draw upon. By the standards of Europe and America, though, the Japanese businesswoman's situation is dismal.

Most Japanese understand that the situation is different abroad, and it would be a remarkably old-fashioned and unworldly busimessman who received more than a superficial surprise at encountering an opposite number in a skirt. If the best person for the job is a woman, then that is that. Part of her suitability, however, will be a discreet awareness of what her gender means to those she's dealing with. All over the world there are men who feel uncomfortable with confident and powerful women; Japan contains more than most. For the foreign businesswoman who ends up facing one, the challenge is to understand his behaviour, and act in such a way as to command his respect, as well as putting him at ease. This can be difficult and ultimately depends on making snap judgements about the people you find yourself with. There may be occasions when it would appear more seemly for a woman to decline an invitation (to a hostess bar, for instance), and leave it to her male colleagues. On the other hand, a bit of noisy carousing with the lads may be just what's needed to break the ice. Either way, there is no point in becoming paranoid; an alert set of antennae is necessary, nothing more.

Race, however, is a different matter. Non-white foreign workers are well-established in Japan, including Iranians, South Americans, Afro-Caribbeans and other Asians. Certainly, they face prejudice in work, education and social situations; life is harder for them than for white-skinned *gaijin*. But in many ways business transcends these prejudices. In China, for instance, despite a history of war and enmity, Japan is the biggest foreign investor, a major export market for many of its former enemies in the Asia Pacific region. The broad picture proves that whatever the superficial state of relations between the Japanese and other races, if the product price, service and quality are good enough, money will flow. Racism exists in Japan as elsewhere, but it should not be seen as a barrier to successful business.

Meetings in Japan

Like face-to-face meetings everywhere, your formal dealings with Japanese businesses have two functions: to communicate clearly and pointedly the message you are trying to get across; and to cultivate the personal bond, to build up ease, trust and intimacy between the participants. All meetings will contain an element of both, but in Japan—and especially in the early stages—expect the emphasis to be firmly on the latter. However innovative your product, however incisive your presentation, there's little hope of a quick decision after the first meeting. You should go into it with this in mind: you are not expecting a deal, you are building up a relationship.

Relationships are based on trust, respect and—a key word—harmony: a sense that the parties understand and empathize with one another and, despite cultural differences and communication difficulties, are making efforts to move in the same direction. This is the intangible, magical quality which you are trying to achieve, but it depends on much more than a few points of etiquette. Meeting Japanese clients is not like taking a driving test (one mistake, and you fail). If you suspect you have made a gaffe, apologize, make a joke of it, and carry on (apology is a way of life in Japan; your hosts will do it incessantly, and on the flimsiest of pretexts).

For every meeting (as well as supporting documents, texts and summaries of presentations, etc.) you will need a good supply of **business cards** (*meishi*), with English on one side and a Japanese translation on the other. They should indicate clearly your rank within the company. You can order them from a specialist printer before you go, through big hotels in Japan, and sometimes even from your airline. Keep a supply of them in a pocket.

Arrive on time, and be confident that you have spaced your meetings so that you will not need to leave early, or hurry your presentation, in order to make it to your next appointment. Allow more time than you expect: Japanese meetings can be interminable, with lots of recapitulations and ruminative silences. Use of a translator will add dramatically to the time it takes to deliver your pitch.

Introductions are important and not to be skipped over. Once you have been led to the meeting room, address yourself to the most senior person. Don't try to bow—foreigners never really get it right, and a deep nod does just as well. Instead shake hands (your host may find this a little uncomfortable, so no bone-crunchers), give your name and say 'How d'you do?', 'Nice to meet you', or *Hajime mashite* (Ha-jee-meh mash-teh). Present your business card (held in both hands if they are free, and with the writing facing your host), and receive his. The general rule, not worth worrying about too much, is that you should offer your card first if you are the seller, or junior in rank or age.

Don't put the card away. Scrutinize it politely, repeat the name, and then place it on the table. When you take your leave, put the collected cards away in a briefcase or wallet. Never fold them up or stick them casually into a back pocket. Once you're outside, it's a good idea to jot notes and aides-memoires on the back (Mr Fuji likes golf, Miss Watanabe studied in LA, etc.) to facilitate small talk at the next meeting, but don't do this in the meeting. A business card is the proxy of its owner: treat them with respect.

Follow your hosts' lead on what to do next. Sometimes everyone in the room will swap cards with everyone else (this takes ages); sometimes one side will each present their cards once to the senior member of the other side. It's common to line up the cards on the table to correspond with the seating order of the team facing you—that way you can see at a glance who is sitting where, and whom you are addressing. The most important thing you should have gathered by now is who is senior to whom. This can be a tricky one because, if the boss doesn't speak good English or is the strong and silent type, then the person doing most of the talking may be quite junior. If anyone present does not proffer a card then they are probably a secretarial, non-executive type. Be polite, but don't devote them too much of your attention. Cards, of course, are only exchanged at a first meeting, but bring a person's card along every time you think you're likely to meet him or her.

Next comes coffee or tea (if it's Japanese green tea, don't add sugar or milk), and small talk. Don't feel that you have to do any selling at this point. Small talk can be very small indeed and, after a few first-time meetings, you will be thoroughly acquainted with the standard questions: when did you arrive, how is your hotel, is this your first time in Japan, do you like Japanese food, what is your impression of Japan? Insight and profundity is not expected here, but if you have just visited an interesting temple or eaten an interesting meal, then do say so. Japanese often assume complete ignorance on the part of foreigners; being able to discourse knowledgeably on the temple you've just visited will surprise and impress.

Gift-giving generally marks a significant stage in the relationship between two companies and isn't usually necessary at a first meeting—but a corporate memento, or a picture book about your country or region would be a nice token.

When the time comes to deliver your presentation and talk business, speak clearly and steadily (which doesn't mean slowing to half speed). Remember that low price in itself will not be enough to win over your potential customers: you must offer them strong additional incentives to overcome their reluctance to switch from an existing supplier and to engage an outside, foreign company. Quality must be emphasized and re-emphasized; so must reliability, and the capacity to meet delivery times unfailingly. Talk also about service, the ability to support your product with spare parts, overhaul, even accessories like Japanese-language manuals. Demonstrate to your audience that you are aware of these issues and have thought about them. Many sales of good products have been lost because the service and back-up details have been neglected.

Visual aids like overhead projections are helpful in breaching the language barrier. Remember that you will be judged by your efficiency and organization, and that general information is as important as the hard sell. Remember also, especially in the early stages, that your Japanese opposite numbers are trying to build up a general impression of the feel of your organization, and its compatibility with their own. Make your sales pitch forcefully, but don't omit background remarks on the nature of your operation, its history, subsidiaries, etc. Always begin a presentation by introducing yourself, describing your role in the company, and emphasizing your years of service or experience within your field.

Try to make all claims modestly. Japanese respect pride in the company, but displays of personal arrogance or over-confidence will go down badly. In the same way, you should always receive a professional compliment by passing the credit on to your team or company.

Don't be rattled if your audience fails to react, avoids eye contact or sits in silence during or after your presentation. Nods and smiles of encouragement are not the Japanese style, and you shouldn't play it for laughs, as you might back home. The time for amusement will come later; be sober, restrained and politely direct.

After Hours

After hours socializing is a crucial part of any business relationship and, if your initial contact is successful, you are certain to be entertained by your Japanese associates sooner or later. Where you are taken will depend on the nature of the business and the state of the relationship: if you are invited out in the evening, then you can expect eating and drinking, possibly in at least two different venues which could be Japanese, Western, or anything in between. Anything involving golf, hostesses or *geisha* is an especially profound honour, simply because of the gargantuan sums of money involved.

This is the time to relax, and to cultivate getting on well with everyone. The contrast between your hosts' office and after-hours demeanour may amaze you. Singing, teasing, tearful declarations of affection and loyalty, and extreme drunkenness are routine. Go with the flow, and take every chance to show what a good egg you are: if the party ends up at a *karaoke* bar, and if it has songs in English, then (horrible though it is) you must stand up and warble. Tipsiness, at the very least, is routine: if you don't drink alcohol, accept one glass for the toast and nurse it all night. This kind of drinking can be particularly debilitating when combined with jet lag: if you want to stop drinking then leave a full glass. An empty or half-empty one is an invitation to your neighbour to refill it (you should perform this service for him or her too).

The only rules are to enjoy yourself and to think *harmony*. Beware of the temptation to talk only about yourself. Trenchant debates on controversial topics don't generally go down well in Japan so, unless you have something anodyne to say, avoid subjects like the Imperial Family, trade disputes, Japanese politics, the war, sexism or racism, at least until you know your hosts better.

The Decision-making Process

With any important proposal, it is rare for a decision to materialize quickly after the initial meeting. The famous Japanese method of consensus decision-making is called *nemawashi*, a horticultural term meaning 'digging around the roots'. Briefly, a decision is established from the middle up, not imposed from the top down. All parties who might be affected by dealings with your company are required to add their seal and comments to a consultation document which is then submitted to senior management. Several drafts may travel up and down before the executive with the final say feels in a position to make a decision, a process which may take weeks or months.

In the meantime, you may be left completely in the dark. If you find yourself faxed or telephoned with tough questions or requests for further information, then the signs are good: this means that the man with responsibility for compiling the consultation document is doing his job, and responding to queries from his own colleagues. Expedite the process by responding promptly, however tiresome or pointless these requests may seem.

If you hear nothing, then it may mean that the answer is no. Alternatively, the consensus-building process may be simply ticking along quietly behind the scenes, based on the comprehensive information which you have already furnished. Make a habit of keeping in touch with your contacts even if you have to invent pretexts to do so: fax them to thank them for their time and invite them to contact you for more information; dispatch 'updates' and news of 'new developments' relating to your products or services; send greetings cards at Christmas or New Year.

The advantage of the *nemawashi* process is that by the time a decision is made and a final agreement reached, all the parties are so familiar with the proposal that they are already moving at full speed. This can catch foreign companies out: late delivery is one of the worst sins of Japanese business, so you need to remain alert and capable of delivering the basis of your proposal long after it was originally made. A Japanese customer may test a new supplier's efficiency and 'sincerity' with a small order as a preliminary to large-scale business; it would be a mistake to be dismissive of a disappointing order, or to give it a low priority.

Negotiation

The most important quality in dealing with Japanese companies, it must be emphasized again and again, is patience. Few successful deals materialize on the basis of introductory meetings and a few faxes, and the blow-by-blow negotiations towards the conclusion of an agreement are certainly the most challenging and difficult part of any business deal.

The biggest hurdle may be divining whether your Japanese counterparts are, in fact, interested in a deal at all. The word for 'yes' (*hai*), famously, does not always mean yes but something more like 'I understand'. The word for 'no' (*iie*) is used reluctantly (in everyday conversation, dissent is more usually expressed by the word *chigaimasu*, literally 'it is otherwise'). It would be almost inconceivable for a Japanese businessman facing a potential client to inform him, even in the most polite terms, that his proposition was of no interest. For those unused to the signs, this can be very frustrating indeed.

The most obvious sign may be silence. Persistent evasiveness, late or non-existent replies to queries, or vague promises to get in touch in the future may all be ways of saying no. Don't assume that further meetings are necessarily a positive sign; if you find yourself facing junior employees with no power or inclination to commit one way or another, this, too, may be a way of letting you down gently. The best way to pose a direct question is to reverse it so that your interlocutor is able to disappoint you by answering 'yes'. If the query 'Is this arrangement "difficult" for you?' provokes the response *hai*, then *hai*, you can be pretty sure, means *hai*.

Even if it is simply details which are being quibbled over, you must be conscious of the importance of face. Solutions to differences must be resolved in a way that lets both sides appear—at least superficially—to have come out on top. Typically, this might involve offering a discount as a gesture of 'sincerity' during final negotiations. The best business deals, like the best Japanese baseball games, are those that end in a draw.

Help and Further Reading

The best approach to dealing with Japan depends, of course, on the nature and scale of your business; the best advice will always be individual. Luckily, there are several sources of generous information and aid, much of it free.

The **Japan External Trade Organization (JETRO)** was originally established by the Ministry of International Trade and Industry (MITI) to promote Japanese trade overseas. By the 1980s, however, Japan's trade surplus had become so embarrassingly large that its function was virtually reversed. JETRO now has 80 international offices dedicated principally to helping foreign companies export their own products into Japan, and establishing links between Japanese and foreign businesses.

Approaches to JETRO should be made in writing, explaining the nature of the business and the information being sought, as far in advance as possible of the planned trip to Japan. JETRO libraries contain information and reports on different market sectors. One of its most valuable resources is its Business Support Centres, in Tokyo, Nagoya, Ōsaka and Kōbe, containing specialist advisers, libraries, and free office space. Not everyone is considered eligible for these; applications must be made well in advance.

JETRO London, Japan Trade Centre, 6th Floor, Leconfield House, Curzon Street, London W1Y 7FB, UK, ✆ 020 7493 7226.

JETRO New York, 44th Floor, McGraw-Hill Building, 1221 Avenue of the Americas, New York, NY 10020–1079, USA, ✆ 212 997 0400.

JETRO Los Angeles, 725 S. Figueroa Street, Suite 1890, Los Angeles, CA 90017, USA,✆ 213 624 8855.

JETRO Toronto, Suite 700, Britannica House, 151 Bloor Street West, Toronto, Ontario M55 1T7, Canada, ✆ 416 962 5055.

JETRO Sydney, Level 19, Gateway 1, Macquarie Place, Sydney, New South Wales 2000, Australia, ✆ 02 241 1181.

The British Government's **Department of Trade and Industry (DTI)** has a full-time Japan Desk. General information about markets, the economy and useful contacts in Japan is available free. Individual businesses can get advice from desk officials or from several export promoters on secondment to the DTI from the private sector. More detailed or specific reports on markets and companies can be commissioned from embassy staff at less than commercial rates.

DTI Japan Desk, Kingsgate House, 66–74 Victoria Street, London SW1, ✆ 020 7215 4269.

Further Reading

Dodwell Market Research Consultants publish *Industrial Groupings in Japan* annually, providing comprehensive listings and statistics on the cross-holdings of Japanese companies, invaluable in navigating the *keiretsu* conglomerates.

Doing Business in Japan by Jonathan Rice (BBC Books) is a calm, sensible and readable overview by an experienced consultant, with chapters on the work ethic, joint ventures and negotiation.

Tokyo

There's no point apologizing for Tokyo: it's teeming, ugly, expensive but also, in Edward Seidensticker's words, 'the world's most consistently interesting city'. The 23 wards of the city proper are home to 7,976,000 people; add on the satellite cities and commuter towns of the contingent urban sprawl and the total for Greater Tokyo comes to 30 million, almost a quarter of the entire population. Tokyo has the world's biggest station, the most expensive property prices and the kitschest and most bizarre architecture. If crowds and excess and 24-hour city fever excite you, then it's the ultimate urban experience.

If they don't, then it's still not to be written off. There's another side to Tokyo, seldom discovered by tourists, but much appreciated by those who live here. Underlying the superficial chaos, there's a deep calm, almost an innocence to Tokyo. Trains and subways run like clockwork. Neighbourhoods are tidy. Street crime is negligible. Visually an urban hell, Tokyo, by any international standard, is law-abiding, harmonious and safe. The novelist Angela Carter lived here in the 1970s. 'Tokyo ought not to be a happy city,' she wrote, 'no pavements; noise; few public places to sit down; occasional malodorous belches from sewage vents even in the best areas.' But it 'somehow contrives to be an exceedingly pleasant place in which to live.' The title of Carter's essay is *Tokyo Pastoral*.

If it still gives you a headache, there's no point grinning and bearing it. You might as well accept the city on its own terms, and try to pack as much as possible into a short time before escaping to the more relaxing areas a train ride away. Of these, there's no shortage: from Nikkō, opulent burial place of the great shogun, Tokugawa Ieyasu, to the hot springs and lakes of Hakone and the Mt Fuji region, and the medieval town of Kamakura, a mini-Kyoto of temples, shrines and rural walks.

History

Few cities are so blindly and wilfully committed to the present (present profit, present convenience); but few are so earnestly and sentimentally attached to their own past.

Edward Seidensticker, *Low City, High City*

Tokyo's past is a struggle to get to grips with, even for long-term residents. The obvious historic sights are fragmentary and so frequently recycled (gardens on the grounds of old temples, palaces on the sites of castles, ancient shrines rebuilt in ferro-concrete) that it's hard to put them into a chronological perspective, to develop a clear picture of what led to what. The obvious reason—Tokyo's notorious accident proneness—isn't the only one. It's difficult to find a period of 50 years (the present post-war era may be the longest) when Tokyo hasn't been wiped clean by one calamity or another—fire, earthquake, flood, plague or war. But even allowing for acts of God, it's always been a restless and protean city. If the B-29s had stayed away, and the Great Earthquake had never struck, Tokyo, one suspects, would be nonetheless jumbled and chaotic.

The Founding of Edo

For seven of its eight centuries Tokyo has been called Edo, 'River Mouth', the name given by a junior member of the Taira clan to the spot where he built a fortified house in the 12th century. It was little more than a marshy fishing village until 1457 when a junior lord named Ōta Dōkan established a military presence here, training conscripts in a walled fortress. By 1486 Ōta's success had become a cause of anxiety to his masters; after taking sides in a factional dispute he was assassinated, and for the next century Edo was overshadowed by the castle at Odawara to the south.

In 1590 Odawara fell to Toyotomi Hideyoshi, the second of the three great warlords who between them brought about the unification of modern Japan. Hideyoshi offered the newly pacified eastern domain to his general, Tokugawa Ieyasu, who, to the surprise and dismay of his advisers, accepted it. Hideyoshi feared his cunning ally; at the time, this seemed like a transparent attempt to shunt him sideways, out of the Japanese heartland and out of harm's way.

But patience was Ieyasu's great virtue, and the distance and isolation worked in his favour. While Hideyoshi embarked on his ruinous invasions of Korea, Ieyasu stayed quietly put, draining and fortifying little Edo, and strategically doling out land to his supporters. When Hideyoshi died, the Tokugawa forces swooped, and in 1600 decisively defeated their rival lords at the Battle of Sekigahara. The mopping up operations lasted another 15 years, by which time Edo was firmly established as the *de facto* capital of the new Japan.

The High City

Personal conquest was not enough for Ieyasu; the great challenge was to pass on the fruits of victory to his heirs. This he achieved by a radical reorganization of the social structure, based on Confucian theory, which remained theoretically in place until 1868.

The Tokugawa state was essentially a military dictatorship: at the top of the social scale were the samurai, presided over by the shogun and his 270 regional *daimyō* (feudal lords) who divided up administration of the country between them. *En masse* the *daimyō* were more than a match for any individual shogun, and Ieyasu quickly instituted a complicated set of protocols designed to neutralize their power and freedom of action. He needed his lords to be kept busy and broke, and this he achieved by a system known as *sankin kōtai*, 'alternate attendance'. For roughly six months of the year, *daimyō* resided in their home fiefs, gathering taxes and keeping an eye on things; for the rest of the time they were required to live in Edo where their wives and children remained all year round, as pampered hostages.

The effect of these rules was dramatic, as the roads to and from the capital became crowded with *daimyō* and their retainers processing backwards and forwards on their annual pilgrimages to the shogun. Each one had to maintain an expensive Edo household, commensurate with his wealth and status. All lords were not equal; Ieyasu distinguished carefully between the *fudai daimyō* (dependent lords), whose families had fought along-side him at Sekigahara, and the *tozama daimyō* (outer lords) whom he had defeated. The innermost parts of the castle compound, clustered around the shogun's own citadel, were reserved for the *fudai daimyō*; the outer lords dwelt outside, between the next ring of moats and fortifications. Pitched against one another in their struggle for the shogun's favour, the *daimyō*—as Ieyasu intended—strove to create ever more opulent and expensive mansions in the extravagant Momoyama style (which survives today in Kyoto temples like Nishi Hongan-ji). Surrounded by gleaming moats, with the towers of Edo Castle at the centre of the fortress hill, the *Yamanote* (High City) was a marvel, an architectural embodiment of the tough new order which Ieyasu and his heirs had brought to Japan.

The Great Fire of 1657

The first great disaster came in January 1657. It became known as the *Furisode* (Long Sleeves) Fire, and ghostly tales and portents were associated with it. On 16 January 1655, a young woman named Okiku had died of a broken heart after falling in love with a mysterious young man. She was buried in her long-sleeved kimono at the Honmyō-ji temple in Hongō. A year later—to the day—another girl named Ohana died in mysterious circumstances shortly after receiving the gift of a purple long-sleeved kimono. When the priests of the temple found themselves conducting a third funeral—another young woman, another strange illness, another purple *furisode*—on the same day in 1657, they realized that something was very wrong. Solemn services were held two days later to placate the souls of the young women and whatever evil force was cutting them down.

Tokyo winters are dry; for 80 days there had been no rain and the wooden city was as parched as tinder. Every night the bells were rung as a warning against fire. The ceremonies began at Honmyō-ji on the afternoon of 18 January. Priests chanted the Lotus Sutra and, at the climax of the recitation, cast a long-sleeved purple kimono onto the sacred fire. The wind caught it and blew it up onto the temple roof, igniting the thatch, and the houses all around.

Fire tore uncontrollably through the crowded city; by the time it had burned itself out three-quarters of Edo—including 500 *daimyō* mansions, 800 samurai residences, and 350 temples and shrines—was reduced to cinders. Over 108,000 people died, a quarter of the population, including 20,000 who perished in a single spot when a city gate was locked against their flight. After three days the flames died down; the next morning it snowed.

The Low City

Less lavish and minus its central keep, the High City was rebuilt within a few years. Individual Tokugawas came and went, but, ensconced in its mansions and citadels, protected from intrigue by formidable networks of spies and informers, the institution of the shogunate ruled unchallenged for the next 200 years. It was an arid and paranoid regime, paralysed by hierarchy and conservatism, committed only to the perpetuation of its own power. The interesting and lively things in Edo culture were happening on the other side of the moats, among the teeming wooden dwellings between the castle and the Sumida River. This was *shitamachi*, the 'Low City'—low in the social as well as the geographical sense. *Shitamachi* occupied the flat, marshy reclaimed land in the east of the city, and it sprung up as the home of the *chōnin*, the townspeople who moved to Edo from the commercial cities of the west. Artisans and merchants stood on the lowest rungs of the Tokugawa social ladder, but they made up half the Edo population: 600,000 people crammed into 16 per cent of the city's area, more than three times as crowded as the most densely inhabited area of modern Tokyo. In this atmosphere, the stuffy hierarchies and minuscule social distinctions of the High City plainly could not hold. From about 1700, the Low City developed its own unique urban culture—as much an attitude to life and a sense of style as a formal aesthetic instinct of the kind expressed in literature and pictures.

The main streets of the Low City were lively and rather grand. Here were the homes of the merchants who, although socially despised, were among the wealthiest men in the city. They also functioned as shops, with open frontages where customers could step up to inspect and purchase goods, and warehouses, with fireproof earthen walls painted in black and white, and tile roofs. Most of the population lived in wooden dwellings, some elegant, but many—the *nagaya*, or 'long houses', which filled the alleys behind the main streets—comfortless slums, with a single bare room, and shared sanitation. 'Fires and fights are the flowers of Edo,' went the saying: in such teeming conditions, both must have flourished. As the city got back on its feet after the Long Sleeves Fire, new rules about the width of avenues and compulsory fire breaks in the centre of each block were quickly forgotten. Between 1603 and 1868 there were 100 major blazes. Firemen, organized into fiercely competitive local brigades, each with its own banners and livery, were the heroes of the city. The life expectancy of the average *shitamachi* building was no more than 20 years.

The other defining feature of the city in its early days was its gender ratio. Edo was an immigrant city and the immigrants, by and large, were men who left their families behind in their home towns. For several generations there was no more than one female Edoite for every three males. This imbalance accentuated the importance of what were, in any case, key areas in every Japanese city: the 'streets of flower and willow' (as the brothel areas were called), and above all Yoshiwara, the biggest and most celebrated of them all.

The Yoshiwara, the Nightless City, has been romanticized beyond all reason. It was, in many ways, a disgusting institution based upon child prostitution, sexual slavery and government-sponsored exploitation. During its heyday though, the area just north of Asakusa's Sensō-ji temple was the most exciting and creative in the city, much more than just a place for bought sex. The most famous *oiran* (courtesans) and *geisha* of Yoshiwara were paragons of fashion and sophistication, skilled dancers, story-tellers and players of the *shamisen*. Poets and print-makers idolized them as passionately as any *kabuki* actors; indeed the most popular Edo plays were often love stories about doomed affairs between *oiran* and their merchant or samurai suitors. It was a place subject to different rules from those that governed everyday life, where style rather than rank was the mark of status, and townsmen and soldiers could mingle if not on equal, then at least on intimate terms.

The Shogunate Goes to the Dogs

By the 1720s the population had grown to 1.3 million. Until London got ahead in the mid-19th century, Edo was the largest city in the world. It was a phenomenal place: a seething, expanding—frequently burning—urban sprawl pinned forcibly in place by the still, oppressive force of the shogunate at its centre. Ieyasu's system of ministers, bureaucrats and spies worked so well that within a few generations it ran itself. Like the emperors before them, the ruling shoguns became largely symbolic figures, dependent on the advice and consent of the inner cabinet: a fortunate arrangement, since individually the Tokugawas were weak and ineffectual and, in at least one case, barking mad.

Tokugawa Tsunayoshi, the fifth in his line, was a cultured and gifted ruler who took an active part in government, but he is known irrevocably to history as *Inu Kubō*, the Dog Shogun. Unable to father an heir, he was convinced by his overbearing mother that he was being punished for crimes committed in a previous life. By way of atonement, Tsunayoshi instituted a national policy of kindness to animals, with ferocious penalties for those who ignored it. He had been born in the Year of the Dog, and canine welfare was given the highest priority. Shogunal kennels were erected on Tsunayoshi's estates; their occupants were conveyed in covered palanquins with guards of honour. All canine deaths had to be reported to the authorities who were obliged to investigate them thoroughly for any evidence of foul play. Numerous dog-killers were executed or exiled, and in 1686 an Akita man was put to death for the murder of a swallow. The policy failed to achieve its objective. Tsunayoshi had no heir, and was succeeded on his death in 1609 by a nephew whose first act was to repeal all pro-animal legislation.

By the 19th century, worsening economic conditions were undermining the shogunate and breaking up the old feudal distinctions. Merchants grew richer, samurai poorer. The latter frequently adopted the sons of the former in return for money or liberation from debts. The arrival off Edo Bay of the American Commodore Perry in 1853 was only the catalyst for a reaction that had been slowly taking place for more than half a century.

The Birth of Tokyo

In 1868 the last of the shoguns abdicated and Emperor Meiji moved his court from the Kyoto Imperial Palace to the site of the vacated Tokugawa castle. In the brief civil war that accompanied the Meiji Restoration, the city—renamed Tokyo, 'Eastern Capital'—had been largely undamaged, but the social, intellectual and industrial revolution which took place over the next 50 years was to leave it profoundly altered, if not unrecognizable.

Tokyo did not just modernize, it Westernized: foreign clothes, foreign-style buildings and a few foreigners themselves transformed the superficial look of the streets and people. Most significant of all, perhaps, were the new forms of transportation which the new age brought. Palanquins gave way to *jinrikisha*, then horse carriages, then automobiles. The construction of railway termini brought new life to old areas and marginalized others. The canals, arteries of the old city, were gradually filled in or built over. 'Venice would not be Venice if its canals were filled in', wrote Edward Seidensticker. 'Tokyo, with so many of its canals turned into freeways, is not Edo.'

The Great Kantō Earthquake

By 1923 Japan was a military empire with lands stretching from Taiwan, through Korea and Manchuria, to the southern part of Sakhalin Island. Tokyo, with a population of just under two million, was still largely built of wood, but had all the trappings of a bustling modern city: multi-storey buildings, asphalted roads, oil-powered industrial centres. The First World War in Europe had stimulated Japan's growing industrial production. In Hibiya, the ultra-modern Imperial Hotel had just been built by the American architect, Frank Lloyd Wright.

On 1 September 1923, one minute from noon, a huge earthquake struck Yokohama, and 45 seconds later the tremors reached Tokyo. All over town braziers were cooking lunch for the occupants of the wooden houses. When the multiple shocks had subsided, thousands of fires erupted spontaneously. There was no time for rescue work to get underway; anyone trapped beneath the rubble was done for. But even those who scrambled out of the wreckage were not safe as the flames joined hands across the city. The fires in Nihonbashi burned so fiercely that buildings on the far side of the Sumida River ignited spontaneously from the heat. In Hongō, to the north, 40,000 people took shelter on a vacant 20 acre plot of waste ground. Fire devoured all the buildings up to its edge, and the vacuum of air between these walls of heat sucked the flames in burning cyclones which incinerated all but a few hundred refugees. Elsewhere the fires turned the roads into giant fly-papers: fleeing crowds became mired in the sticky asphalt and asphyxiated where they lay. At Yokosuka, an oil tank ruptured and vomited burning oil into the sea where hundreds had taken refuge. Those who jumped into ponds and lakes were boiled alive. In the hysterical aftermath of the disaster, there were vile atrocities. Four thousand innocent victims—left-wingers, 'unpatriotic' elements and, above all, Koreans—were lynched by rampaging groups of zealots. The death toll from the earthquake and fire was 140,000.

Recovery and War

Once the initial shock had worn off, the city quickly recovered. By 1930 there were few traces of the destruction of less than a decade before, but at least one vital change had taken place. The Low City which had borne, as usual, the worst sufferings of the earthquake became depopulated as thousands of its inhabitants, weary of *shitamachi*'s constant misfortunes, relocated in the new suburbs that were mushrooming in the west of the city.

The inter-war years were lively ones when the districts of the capital took on much of the shape and relative importance which they have today. Tokyo had its jazz age, and it had its financial collapse as well, in 1927. Old-style drinking places yielded in popularity to cafés and dance halls. For the first time, baseball began to rival sumo as the national sport. But as nationalism tightened its grip, a mood of dour solemnity and growing xenophobia gathered in the city. Cigarette brands and popular performers who had adopted foreign names were constrained to change them to Japanese, and even architecture, like the *kabuki* theatre in Ginza, took on an oppressive, totalitarian character. In the months after Pearl Harbour, parks and gardens were converted into anti-aircraft gun emplacements. By the end of 1944 American forces had got close enough to the Japanese mainland to mount sustained raids on Tokyo. The worst of these were on the night of 9–10 March when as many as 80,000 people died in the space of a few hours, three-quarters of the city's entire civilian casualties. Winds fanned the incendiary bombs and two-fifths of the city was destroyed, with most damage, naturally, in the Low City.

The Post-War Period

By winter 1945, Tokyo was an occupied city: flattened, starving and brimming with American and Allied servicemen and administrators. The black market flourished; so did prostitution. In 1950, salvation came in the form of the Korean War. As off-shore supplier and victualler to the anti-Communist forces, Japan started to become prosperous again. In 1964 the Tokyo Olympics unleashed a frenzy of optimistic construction and national self-awareness: streets were widened, subways and monorails opened, and Shibuya was transformed by the athletes' village and the bold gymnasia designed by Tange Kenzō. In the late seventies and early eighties, opposition to the Japanese-American Security Treaty and the new Narita Airport fused in a noisy student protest movement: there were violent demonstrations, battles with police and a handful of deaths.

Within a few years, though, settled conformity had returned to Japan. The streets of Tokyo reflected the swelling economy as taller, grander and more expensive buildings rose in the booming sub-centres. For a few years, at the height of the bubble economy in the late 1980s, Tokyo might just have been the richest city in the history of the world. Its land area was said, in real estate terms, to be worth as much as the whole of the United States. With billions of yen of excess capital, company expense accounts swelled, employees' bonuses multiplied and Tokyoites found new and ever more absurd ways of spending money: £1,000 a head hostess bars, gold-leaf *sushi*, mink lavatory covers. The bursting of the bubble in the early 1990s gave corporations and politicians a nasty shock, but it was only with the severe banking crisis in the late 90's that Tokyo began to recoil from its high-flying days. The city still bristles with neon and the train stations at midnight are still hysterical, but any Tokyoite will tell you that a cautious mood has settled on the city. One concrete sign of hard times is the massive vacant edifice in Nihonbashi, formerly a branch of the Tōkyū department stores. Tōkyū has had problems selling off the real estate, but perhaps by the time you read this, new occupants will have moved in and it will be business as usual.

Getting to Tokyo from the Airports

Tokyo, as you'd expect, is accessible by plane, coach or train from almost every-where in Japan. Just one place, seemingly, lacks decent connections with the capital: its international airport.

Haneda, Tokyo's old airport, is close to the city, but only domestic airlines and a handful of international carriers still use it. Simply take the **monorail** to Hamamatsuchō station to the south of central Tokyo, and then pick up a subway, overland train or taxi.

Narita, where almost all international travellers find themselves arriving, is a different story. Your mode of transport will depend on where you are travelling to/from within Tokyo, and on the amount of time and money you have available. The **arrival lobby** of Narita Airport has ticket counters for the various buses and trains.

by taxi

You can forget this, unless someone else is paying. It takes about 1½ to 2hrs depending on traffic, and during the day costs around ¥25,000.

by rail

Tokyo station is the main station on the west side of the city.

The JR **Narita Express** (N'EX) travels non-stop between Narita Airport station and Tokyo station in an hour, and costs about ¥2,940 depending on the season. The N'EX also goes to **Shinjuku** and (infrequently) **Ikebukuro** stations, 79 and 94mins respectively, for ¥3,110. Airport-bound expresses get booked up, especially in peak season. You should buy an advance reservation at a JR ticketing counter (found in most stations) or a travel agent. The N'EX is covered by the JR Rail Pass.

The **Airport Narita** rapid train is a slower JR service which stops at Shinbashi station in Tokyo and various others along the way. It takes 1hr 20mins between Tokyo station and the airport and costs ¥1,260.

The **Keisei** line is a private service between the airport and Keisei Ueno station, just south of Ueno Park. The **Skyliner Express** takes about an hour and costs ¥1,740; the **limited express** (*tokkyū*) takes only 10mins longer, but at ¥940 is the cheapest form of public transport to and from Narita. For information, call ✆ 03 3831 0131.

by bus

The most convenient means of transport, especially if you have heavy luggage to heave around, is the **Limousine Bus** service which shuttles between the airport and a number of key locations and big downtown hotels. Even if you're not booked in at one of these, you can have yourself dropped off at the one nearest to where you're staying and take a short taxi or subway ride from there. On the return journey out to the airport, a useful trick is to make your way to the **Tokyo City Air Terminal** (TCAT; Suitengūmae subway station on the Hanzōmon line) where the Japanese airlines (and a few foreign carriers) have check-in counters. From here you can take a bus direct to the airport, unencumbered by your luggage.

The bus to and from TCAT takes between 60 and 90mins, depending on traffic, and costs ¥2,900. Tokyo station is another 10mins or so, and an extra ¥200. The bus also runs to Haneda, costs ¥1,200 and takes 30mins. For information, call ✆ 03 3665 7232.

Getting Around

Tokyo is a vast city, but it has one of the cheapest, safest, cleanest and most reliable urban transportation networks in the world. Compared to the grimy urinals which pass for subways in some countries, it is a joy to use; the speed and efficiency of the system makes Tokyo seem smaller than London or New York.

Get an idea of Tokyo's general layout from our **orientation map** on the *inside back cover*. The **Tourist Map of Tokyo**, provided free by the tourist information centre, is also good.

on foot

The usual rules about finding your way around in a city without addresses apply (*see* 'Practical A–Z', p.14).

by bus

The Tokyo bus network is complicated, vulnerable to traffic jams, and, unlike the JR lines and subways, little help is available in English. It's a matter of trial and error; visitors with limited time who are interested in just the main sights will be better off using the trains.

Various private companies operate buses in Tokyo but the most comprehensive system is the **Tōei** service. Most of these charge a flat rate fare of about ¥180, regardless of the length of journey. Drop coins or insert a ¥1,000 bill into the fare box by the driver as you enter; change is dispensed automatically. Books of multiple tickets, called *kaisū ken*, can be purchased from the driver or from bus terminals at a slight saving over individual tickets.

A recorded voice announces destinations in advance. Tell your destination to the driver or a passenger, and someone will see you off at the right place.

The following is a small selection of useful routes.

Tō [都] 01 runs between the south exit (*minami guchi*) of Shibuya station (i.e. not the Hachikō exit) and Shinbashi station, along Roppongi-dōri—an area poorly served by trains.

Tō [都] 03 runs between Shinjuku station east exit (*higashi guchi*), along the south moat of the Imperial Palace, through Hibiya and Yūrakuchō, to wind up finally in Harumi Wharf on Tokyo Bay.

Higashi [東] 42 goes from the Yaesu exit (to the east) of Tokyo station up along the Sumida River, near to Asakusa.

by subway

Tokyo's first subway opened between Ueno and Asakusa in 1927. Today there are ten lines forming a dense interconnecting grid penetrating far into the suburbs. A map of the subway system is printed on the *inside front cover* of this book.

Fares start at ¥160. Exact fares are shown on the wall maps above the ticket machines in each station, but these have very little English on them. Ask a passer-by or pay at the manned window. Failing that, it's acceptable to buy the minimum ticket and pay the difference at the other end. Just present the ticket at your destination, offer the inspector a handful of change, and let him fish out the excess.

Several subway stations, especially those which unite a number of lines, are labyrinths of underground pedestrian tunnels. There are good bilingual maps every few yards, but allow time for getting lost if your journey includes a change in one of these stations.

by train

The Yamanote line is the most useful for tourists, girding the city in an irregular oval loop, intersected by ten criss-crossing subways lines. (*See map on inside back cover.*). It is only one of dozens of JR and private lines which connect central Tokyo with its dormitory suburbs. Buy tickets in the same way as on the subway.

After the Yamanote, the most useful service is the **Chūō line**, which cuts through the centre of Tokyo north of the Imperial Palace, joining Shinjuku (and the suburbs to the west), Ochanomizu and Tokyo. For information, call ✆ 03 3423 0111.

car hire

With such good trains, you'd be mad to attempt driving within Tokyo. However, the following agencies have branches all over the city, and English-speaking staff. Prices start at around ¥6,000 a day.

Nippon Rent-A-Car: ✆ 03 3485 7196.

Nissan Rent-A-Car: ✆ 03 5424 4123.

Orix Rent-A-Car: ✆ 03 3779 0543.

For motorcycle hire, try:

S.C.S.: ✆ 03 3815 6221. Most of the staff don't speak English; ask for Mr Sato who will soon put you right.

tours

Several package companies offer morning, afternoon, evening or all day **coach tours** in English to spots in Tokyo, as well as day trips outside the city—pick up their ubiquitous brochures at the tourist information centre or your hotel. They're a superficial and expensive way of doing what, with a little more time and for much less money, you could easily organize yourself. Tours promising 'geisha parties' and the like are tacky fakes.

Japan Gray Line: ✆ 03 3433 5745.

Japan Travel Bureau: ✆ 03 3276 7777.

Hato Bus: ✆ 03 5620 9500.

Mr Oka Nobuō conducts highly-praised personal guided tours of the *shitamachi* area. Contact him directly on ✆ 0422 51 7673.

Tourist Information

The Japan National Tourist Organization's **tourist information centre** (*open Mon–Fri 9–5, Sat 9–12 noon*, ✆ 03 3201 3331) is on the west side of the railway tracks, 100m south of Yūrakuchō station.

Here you can pick up endless English pamphlets, maps, fact sheets, timetables, price lists and events calendars for Tokyo and the rest of the country, make reservations at establishments in the Economical Inn Group and arrange a **Home Visit**. From outside the city you can call them free on the **Japan Travel Phone** number, ✆ 0120 222800.

There's another information centre in Terminal Two of **Narita Airport** (*open daily 9–8*, ✆ 0476 30 3383).

Teletourist Service is a recording of current events in and around Tokyo, ✆ 03 3201 2911.

travel agents

Nippon Travel Agency (Nihon Ryokō)
Foreign Tourist Department, 3rd Floor, Shinbashi Ekimae Building No.1, 2–20–15 Shinbashi, Minato-ku, Tokyo 105–8606, ✆ 03 3572 8744, 🖷 03 3572 8766.

Japan Travel Bureau (Nihon Kōtsu Kōsha)
1–6–4 Marunouchi, Chiyoda-ku, Tokyo 100–0005, ✆ 03 5620 9500.

maps and media

The tourist information centre's free **Tourist Map of Tokyo** is perfectly adequate for sightseeing purposes, with an overall view of the city, area close-ups, a subway map and a transit diagram on the back. It wears out quickly; pick up a fresh copy when you pass by. *Tokyo: A Bilingual Atlas*, available from English-language book shops, is full of clear maps of the whole metropolitan area on many different scales.

Numberless city **magazines** and tour companions, many of them little more than advertising supplements, are available. Only one is worth spending money on: *Tokyo Classified*, an excellent weekly magazine which combines comprehensive listings of art, theatre, music, film, restaurants, nightlife and festivals with witty features about Tokyo life.

Japan's **English-language newspapers** are all published in Tokyo, and the *International Herald Tribune, Asian Wall Street Journal* and *Financial Times* print Japan editions, available in book shops and news stands at large stations. Other foreign newspapers can be bought—at great expense—at big book shops like Maruzen and Kinokuniya. The English-language *Daily Yomiuri* carries a supplement from the British newspaper *The Independent* every Sunday.

The American Center, ✆ 03 3430 0901 (Exit A3 of Shiba Kōen subway station) and the British Council (Iidabashi subway or JR station) have **libraries** of English books relating to their respective countries. For books on Japan, try the Japan Foundation Library, ✆ 03 3562 3527, by Kojimachi subway station.

Tokyo Itineraries

Tokyo, like all capital cities, is an aberration. To come away with anything like a rounded picture of Japan, make sure that you spend at least half of your holiday outside it. What you see during your time here will naturally depend on personal interests. The following suggestions may help you establish priorities:

If you spend just 24 hours in Tokyo, go to Asakusa and (if you have time) Ueno in the day, and Shinjuku in the evening.

It makes a big difference to an experience of any city to know someone who lives there, and the people of Tokyo are kind and enthusiastic guides. As early as possible go to the tourist information centre to arrange a Home Visit (two days' notice is usually enough).

A very full but interesting day can be spent by visiting the Tsukiji Fish Market at 5am, having a *sushi* breakfast and then walking round Hama Rikyū garden. In the afternoon, you can either walk up to Ginza, or travel by boat from Hama Rikyū to Asakusa on the Sumida River.

Try to visit Yoyogi Park on a Sunday when the street performers are out.

Kitanomaru Park and Ueno Park each possess several museums, useful in bad weather. Remember that almost all museums close on Mondays, except when Monday is a national holiday, in which case they close the following day.

Festivals

The best Tokyo *matsuri* are living dramas of Edo history. *Tokyo Journal* has a festivals section, and the tourist information centre publishes a comprehensive pamphlet called *Calendar Events* which lists happenings big and small, inside and outside the city.

January

1–3	**New Year celebrations (*Hatsumōde*)** take place at shrines and temples all over town. The Meiji Shrine and Asakusa's Sensō-ji temple attract the biggest crowds.
2	The Palace grounds are open and the Imperial Family waves at the crowds from behind bullet-proof glass.
6	**Dezomeshiki.** This is a throwback to the Edo period when the guilds of firemen were the most heroic and dashing men in the city. Present-day firefighters in period dress perform cunning stunts on top of ladders in Harumi, a dock island on Tokyo Bay.
Early–mid-month	A fifteen-day **sumo tournament** (*sumō bashō*) takes place at the National Stadium in Ryōgoku.

February

3	**Setsubun.** Local worthies and members of the public mark the New Year (according to the old calendar) by throwing beans at temples and shrines like Asakusa's Sensō-ji.

March

18	**Asakusa Kannon Jigenhoyoe.** The Goddess of Mercy is honoured at Sensō-ji temple. There are parades, traditional dancing and huge crowds.

April

Early Performances of *gagaku* (ancient court music) take place in the Imperial Palace. Seats are available to the public; enquire at the tourist information centre well in advance.

Early–mid-month **Cherry Blossom Viewing** takes place all over Tokyo, but especially in Ueno Park, Shinjuku Gyōen garden, Yasukuni Shrine, Chidorigafuchi Park and Hama Rikyū garden.

21–23 Yasukuni Shrine has a **Spring Festival**.

May

Mid-month **Kanda Matsuri** is held at Kanda Myōjin Shrine. This is one of the great Edo townsmen's festivals held in full only on even-numbered years, in alternation with the Sannō Matsuri. Three *hōren* (palanquins) and 76 *mikoshi* (portable shrines) are paraded through the streets from dawn until late into the night by extremely drunk men in *happi* coats.

Mid-month Tokyo's biggest and most popular festival, the **Sanja Matsuri**, takes place at the Asakusa Shrine. A hundred portable shrines fill the streets; in the shrine itself, there are performances of weird and ancient music and dance.

Mid-month A fifteen-day **sumo tournament** is held at the Ryōgoku National Stadium.

June

Second Sunday **Torigoe Jinja Taisai**. The largest portable shrine in Tokyo, the *Sen-gan Mikoshi*, is paraded through the streets (Kuramae subway station).

10–16 The **Sannō Matsuri** alternates with the Kanda matsuri, being held in its full form only on odd-numbered years—an arrangement decreed after violent clashes between celebrants of the rival festivals. Held at the hilltop Hie Shrine. At its climax, mounted samurai accompany an ox-drawn carriage in a magnificent procession through the streets.

Late Displays of **irises** at the Meiji Shrine.

July

9–10 **Hozuki Ichi**. Wind chimes and plants are sold at the Asakusa Sensō-ji temple on a day when Kannon is believed to bring blessings of happiness.

13–16 **Mitama matsuri**. Music, dance and *nō* are performed at the Yasukuni Shrine.

Late	There are firework displays (*hanabi*) over the Sumida River near Ryōgoku. Both banks of the river become packed very early on; the alternative to the crowds is to purchase an expensive place on one of the sightseeing boats on the water (enquire at the tourist information centre).

August

Early	**Takigi Nō**. Torchlit *nō* performances take place at the Hie Shrine in Akasaka.
Late	**Asakusa Samba Carnival**. A bizarre modern innovation: Asakusa's inhabitants adopt the accoutrements of a Latin-American carnival (parades of ladies in sequinned bikinis, etc.).

September

Mid-month	A fifteen-day **sumo tournament** is held at the Ryōgoku National Stadium.

October

Early	Performances of ***gagaku*** in the Imperial Palace. Seats available to the public; enquire at the tourist information centre.
Mid-month –early Nov	**Chrysanthemum displays** can be seen at Asakusa Sensō-ji temple, Yasukuni Shrine, Hibiya Park and Shinjuku Gyōen garden.
17–19	Yasukuni Shrine has its **Autumn Festival**.
18	Offering of chrysanthemums and **dancing** at Asakusa Sensō-ji.

November

On the Zodiacal Days of the Cock	A traditional festival of courtesans and *geisha* of the Edo entertainment quarters, held at Otori Shrine near the old Yoshiwara district (check with the tourist information centre for dates and how to get there).

December

23	The Emperor waves at the crowds in the Imperial Palace on his birthday.

Central Tokyo

The Imperial Palace (Kōkyo)

The best place to view the Imperial Palace is from above, from the upper storeys of one of the many high-rise office buildings that line the avenues of the adjacent government and business districts. There, even more starkly than on a map, the strangeness of the city's structure becomes clear. Apart from the roofs of the Emperor's residence and the Imperial

Household Agency in its southeast corner, there is nothing palatial about the *Kōkyo* whatsoever, certainly not in the sense of Versailles or Buckingham Palace or even the palaces of Kyoto. It's a park, a shaggy forest of mixed trees with ponds and a few faint tracks visible in between. There used to be a nine-hole golf course there, built in the 1920s by the then Crown Prince Hirohito (he caught the bug on a visit to Britain). But years later—so the story goes—the biologist Emperor spotted a rare flower growing there, and decreed that the links should be allowed to return to their natural state. All around the palace grounds, pressing up against its moats like hungry predators, are the money palaces of Marunouchi and Kasumigaseki. Despite plummeting land values, this is among the most expensive real estate in the world and, at least according to the tour guides, the 130 acres are worth as much as the entire state of California.

The comparison is meaningless: this land, the green yolk at the centre of Tokyo's grey egg, can never be sold, developed or—by most people—even walked upon. It's tempting to see in this expensive nothingness an image of its inhabitant. Stripped of responsibility, divinity and power, the Japanese Emperor has survived, like the Imperial Palace, by doing precisely nothing. It is a space, not a place, just as he (to his subjects) is a symbol of state, not a human personality. But, like him, the palace grounds wield a symbolic influence far beyond their functional insignificance. Like a magnet, they transmit an invisible field that ripples through the city around them. From the imperial centre a whorl of moats and canals, partially filled in but still obvious on the map, spiral outwards to link up with the Sumida River. At a further remove is the circling Yamanote loop line. Aircraft flight paths, subway lines and expressways are all carefully routed to avoid encroaching above, below or upon the palace grounds. For years, building regulations forbade any structure which might be said to 'look down' upon the emperor.

Parts of the palace gardens are open to the public. In good weather the park is lovely; there are trees and plants to be enjoyed and history to be traced, and the whole thing can be adequately seen in a morning or an afternoon. But the Palace is interesting above all as a symbol, and one which provides clues to many aspects of Japanese culture and thought. 'One of the two most powerful cities of modernity,' wrote Roland Barthes in *Empire of Signs*, 'is built around an opaque ring of walls, streams, roofs and trees whose own centre is no more than an evaporated notion, subsisting here, not in order to irradiate power, but to give the entire urban movement the support of its central emptiness.'

History

All great capitals have their founding legends and Tokyo's is more bizarre than most. Ōta Dōkan, the 15th-century *daimyō* who unified the Kantō area, was sent here by Benten, the goddess who is worshipped on the island of Enoshima near Kamakura. As he was passing the mouth of present-day Tokyo Bay, a fish leaped from the waters and flopped onto the land at the foot of an adjacent hill. The fish was the kind called *konoshiro*; the words *kono shiro*, rendered in different Chinese characters, mean 'this castle'. Following the goddess's hint, Ōta constructed a fortification on the site in 1457, and it was passed down through the families who succeeded him. But it was as the seat of the shoguns and the capital of the Tokugawa state that Edo Castle achieved its greatest flowering.

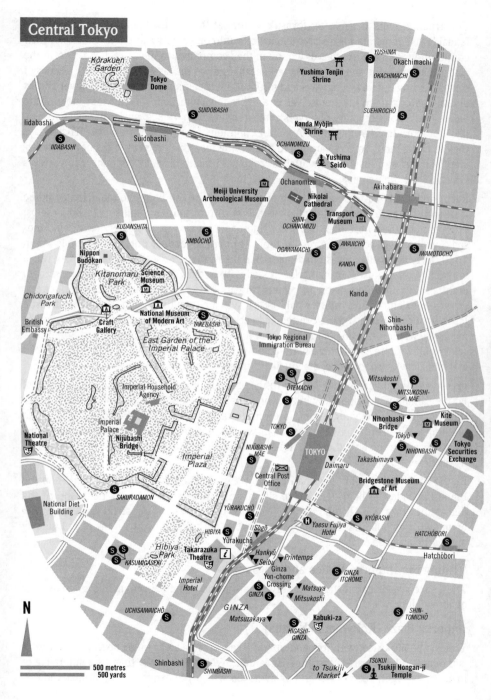

Central Tokyo

Kōrakuen Garden

Tokyo Dome

Yushima Tenjin Shrine

YUSHIMA

Okachimachi

OKACHIMACHI

Iidabashi

IIDABASHI

Suidobashi

SUIDOBASHI

Kanda Myōjin Shrine

SUEHIROCHŌ

OCHANOMIZU

Ochanomizu

Yushima Seidō

Akihabara

Meiji University Archeological Museum

Nikolai Cathedral

SHIN-OCHANOMIZU

Transport Museum

KUDANSHITA

JIMBŌCHŌ

OGAWAMACHI

AWAJICHŌ

KANDA

IWAMOTOCHŌ

Nippon Budōkan

Kitanomaru Park

Science Museum

Kanda

Chidorigafuchi Park

National Museum of Modern Art

TAKEBASHI

Shin-Nihonbashi

British Embassy

Craft Gallery

East Garden of the Imperial Palace

Tokyo Regional Immigration Bureau

Imperial Household Agency

ŌTEMACHI

Mitsukoshi

MITSUKOSHI-MAE

National Theatre

Imperial Palace

Nijūbashi Bridge

Imperial Plaza

TOKYO

Nihonbashi Bridge

Kite Museum

NIJŪBASHI-MAE

TOKYO

Tōkyū

NIHONBASHI

Tokyo Securities Exchange

Daimaru

Takashimaya

Central Post Office

Bridgestone Museum of Art

National Diet Building

SAKURADAMON

YŪRAKUCHŌ

KYŌBASHI

HATCHŌBORI

HIBIYA

Sōgō

Yūrakuchō

Yaesu Fujiya Hotel

Hatchōbori

Hibiya Park

Takarazuka Theatre

Hankyū

Seibu

Printemps

Ginza Yon-chome Crossing

Matsuya

Mitsukoshi

GINZA ITCHOME

KASUMIGASEKI

Imperial Hotel

UCHISAIWAICHŌ

GINZA

Matsuzakaya

GINZA

HIGASHI-GINZA

Kabuki-za

SHIN-TOMICHŌ

N

Shinbashi

SHIMBASHI

to Tsukiji Market

TSUKIJI

Tsukiji Hongan-ji Temple

500 metres
500 yards

Construction work began after Ieyasu's victory at the Battle of Sekigahara in 1600, as feudal lords, desperate for his favour, vied to outdo one another in the lavishness of their contributions and the number of workmen they committed to the project. Apart from the castle keep itself, the shogun's engineers set themselves the task of constructing a series of canals, serving both as waterways and fortifications, beginning at the Sumida River and its docks, and curling in on themselves in a tightening spiral to form the inner moat of the palace itself. Contemporary observers compared Edo with Venice, and many place names, like Sotobori-dōri (Outer Moat Avenue) commemorate these waterways. These days they're easier, and more rewarding, to find on the map than *in situ*—most have degenerated into malodorous drainage ditches, capped in many cases by concrete expressways which follow their course.

Reeds and sand had to be distributed over the swampy soil before foundations could be laid, and stones for the castle walls were ferried from the Izu Peninsula in 3000 ships. From the sea they were hauled by men and oxen, on carpets of slippery seaweed. Ships sank, walls collapsed and the retainers of rival *daimyō* feuded. But, by its completion in 1640, forty years after Ieyasu had made Edo his headquarters, the castle complex was a wonder. With boat-laden canals criss-crossed with bridges, waterside warehouses, smooth granite walls, fortified gates and guard towers, imperial and aristocratic residences, government offices and military barracks, it was a city within a city, the greatest castle Japan would ever see, and the centre of power and intrigue in the newly unified nation. At its heart was the keep, one of the biggest in the world: 40m above ground, and 84m above sea level, five storeys of sombre black tiles and plaster with a gleaming copper roof topped at its finials with *shachihoko*, dragon-like carp believed to ward off fire.

In fewer than 20 years it had burned to the ground. When the great blaze of 1657 swept Edo, a flaming whirlwind blew in the windows and quickly devoured the keep's wooden skeleton, igniting the gunpowder stores in the castle towers. Within two years the lesser buildings had been renewed, but Japan was by now at peace and, as a symbolic fist clenched above the city, the keep itself was unnecessary; apart from its stone foundation, it was never rebuilt.

By the Meiji Restoration, fires had done for most of the other buildings too. When the Emperor made the bold decision to site his palace here, in the very heartland of the defeated enemy, the Nishinomaru (Western Citadel) was chosen as the spot. The celebrated wooden buildings were praised by visitors, but they burned with the rest of the city during the air raids of 1945.

Visiting the Imperial Palace and Gardens

The palace grounds are divided into several areas with varying opening hours and degrees of accessibility.

Imperial Plaza (Kōkyo-mae Hiroba)

This is a public space, with free and unlimited access to all, except on special occasions. It is the most relaxed part of the imperial gardens, which isn't to say that it's comfortable or inviting: a roughly rectangular grid of lawns (on which you can at least sit, unlike those in the more popular Hibiya Park to the south) divided by broad gravel avenues and a busy road, **Uchibori-dōri**, which runs down the middle. In the winter, the unsheltered space is knifed by the wind; in summer, the gravel reflects the sun into a shimmering heat haze. It's a liminal place, a kind of annex to the palace, neither wholly imperial nor indisputably public. The Plaza serves as the official disaster evacuation zone for the Marunouchi business district. It's also the closest thing Tokyo has to a place of public assembly: demonstrations and open-air meetings are from time to time held here, and it's common to see the black vans of the *Uyoku*, the right-wing political groups, blaring their nationalist messages on the street in front of the moat. The most notorious incident occurred in 1952, just after the end of the American Occupation. A May Day assembly in Hibiya Park occupied the Plaza, and a frenzied battle broke out with police. Cars were overturned and burned, tear gas was fired, hundreds of police and civilians were injured, and two demonstrators were killed by police gunfire.

A turn around the Plaza is still something of a national institution for Japanese visitors. Whatever the weather, ant-like columns of uniformed schoolchildren troop backwards and forwards to have their photographs taken in front of **Nijū-bashi**, a double-arched iron bridge of 19th-century German design which, curiously, has become a sentimental symbol of the Japanese nation. Before 1945, young conscripts would come here to be photographed with their families before going off to war. Immediately after the surrender, ultra-nationalists chose the palace gates and bridges as the place to commit ritual suicide. The statue of the mounted warrior by the **rest house** in the southeast corner is **Kusunoki Masahige**, a 14th-century samurai, and a paragon of imperial loyalty.

Just beyond Nijū-bashi, and out of bounds, is the Fushimi turret, one of the few surviving Edo-period structures, apart from the walls. The **Sakashita-mon** gate, in the north part of the Plaza, is one of the main entrances into the palace. From the police box here, you can glimpse the roofs of the imperial residence and Household Agency.

Nishinomaru (Western Citadel)

The **Nishinomaru** is the private domain of the Imperial Family and Imperial Household Agency whose residences and offices it contains. Without an official invitation, it has always been difficult to enter this area: the cynical view has it that those commoners who have made it inside—the Empress Michiko and her daughter-in-law Princess Masako, for instance—are never seen again. However the Imperial Household Agency does run a little-known **group tour** of selected areas of the grounds and palace. Apart from the thrill of actually getting inside, there isn't much to get excited about. The original palace built for Emperor Meiji was burned by American bombers in 1945 and the oldest palace building dates from 1964. A new home for the Emperor and Empress was finished (for a controversial ¥5 billion) in 1993, and illustrated the problems of contemporary imperial taste: how to combine the simplicity and plainness of traditional Japanese structures with the opulence expected of international heads of state. The results—at least according to the official picture book released by the Agency—are bland in the extreme.

*For those set on going, the guided tour lasts about two hours and is in Japanese only; admission is likely to be granted only reluctantly to non-Japanese speakers unless accompanied by a Japanese friend. Securing a place requires a phone call to the Visitors' Office (Sankan-gakari) of the **Imperial Household Agency**, © 03 3213 1111 ext. 485, which will issue a permit to be picked up at least a day before the appointed time. Tours are conducted on weekdays and begin at either 10am or 1.30pm at the Kikyō-mon gate (one down from the Ōte-mon) on the east (Marunouchi) side of the moat. The tourist information centre has up-to-date information and may make appointments.*

The public are also allowed into the Inner Palace on 2 January and 23 December to pay their New Year and birthday respects to the Emperor. He can be seen with his family waving at the loyal crowd behind a sheet of bullet-proof glass, installed after an alarming incident when an over-excited subject hurled a steel *pachinko* ball at his sovereign.

Higashi Gyōen (East Garden)

The East Garden is the former site of Edo castle, the shogun's seat, and contains relics of the old keep, attractive gardens and good views of the city. You can enter or leave by three of the old palace gates: the **Ōte-mon** (the main entrance, near Ōtemachi subway station), the **Hirakawa-mon** (opposite the Mainichi newspaper building and near Takebashi subway station); and the **Kitahanebashi-mon** (which leads into Kitanomaru Park). (*Open 9–4 exc. Mon and Fri, but open when those days fall on a national holiday; closed 25 Dec–5 Jan; adm free—pick up a token at the admission booth which you surrender at the exit; last adm 3pm.*)

The most common entry to the East Garden is through the **Ōte-mon**, a 1967 reconstruction of the main gate of the shogun's castle, originally built over 420,000 man days by Date Masamune, the powerful *daimyō* of Sendai. Inside, you pass several buildings, modern and traditional: on the right, the new **Shōwa Memorial Hall**, currently under construction, and a couple of **rest houses**; on the left, the **Cabinet Library**, the headquarters of the imperial palace police division, and then a long, low wooden building in Edo style—the **Hyakunin-bansho** (Hundred-man Guardhouse).

The right-hand path just beyond here leads you to a stretch of the old **Hakuchō-bori** (Swan Moat), at the foot of an impressive section of walled rampart, constructed without mortar out of smoothly finished cyclopean blocks. The area in front of these is the old **Nino-maru** (Second Citadel), containing a stroll garden, with a pond and tea house, designed in the mid-17th century by the master landscaper Kobori Enshū. A steep path, just north of the Swan Moat, is called the **Shiomi-zaka** (Tide-Viewing Slope): from here you can see the buildings of Hibiya which was, in the early Edo period, a coastal inlet and port, before land reclamation drove back the waters of Tokyo Bay.

The slope leads up to the **Hon-maru** (Inner Citadel); you can also get there by returning to the Hundred-man Guardhouse and taking the left-hand turn. Following this route and keeping to the left you come, in the southernmost corner of the garden, to the **Fujimi Yagura** (Mt Fuji-Viewing Turret) which may once have lived up to its name, before the days of photo-chemical smog. When the decision was made after the great fire not to rebuild the main keep, this became the primary defensive point of the castle; finished in 1659, the three-storey building suggests in miniature something of the original architecture of the citadel.

At the north end of the Hon-maru, the huge stone pedestal is all that remains of the keep itself which, though splendid, was only intended for occupation as a last resort, and remained largely empty for its brief life. The residential and administrative base of the shogun and his court lay between here and the Fujimi Turret. At the south end were the halls used for state and ceremonial occasions including the **Ōhiroma** (Hall of a Thousand Mats), where distinguished petitioners, including the factor of the Dutch trading post in Nagasaki, were received in audience by the shogun. Twice a month all of the feudal lords serving their six-month stint in Edo also assembled in these chambers.

The second group of buildings contained the shogun's personal offices, and behind them were the inner chambers where no men, apart from doctors and a few guards, were allowed to trespass. This was the shogun's seraglio, a centre of profound intrigue, ruled over by his wife and the 500 to 1000 maidservants and concubines who served beneath her. In the 19th century, politicking in the inner chambers got particularly out of hand, despite the extraordinary precautions that were taken to avoid corruption—even at the most intimate moments between the shogun and his partners, at least two other ladies remained in discreet attendance to ensure that the concubine of the moment didn't abuse her power by asking for political favours.

The bizarre octagonal structure in the northeast corner, decorated with abstract mosaics, is the **Tōgaku-dō**, a private concert hall built in 1968 for the then Empress.

North of the Palace

Kitahane-bashi (the name means 'Northern Drawbridge', although the modern structure no longer lifts up and down) connects the East Gardens with **Kitanomaru Kōen** (North Citadel Park), a former territory of the Imperial Palace which was given to the nation on the Shōwa Emperor's 60th birthday in 1969.

In the south part of the park are four museums, although they don't measure up to those in Ueno Park to the northeast of the city. On the right, and before the Shutō expressway which makes a rare incursion into the Palace grounds, are the **National Archives** (Kokuritsu Kōbunsho-kan), of little use to anyone who can't read Japanese, and the **Tokyo National Museum of Modern Art** (Kokuritsu Kindai Bijutsukan, *open 10–5, 10–8 on Friday, closed Mon; adm ¥420 for permanent collection only*), which has a permanent display of paintings, prints and sculpture post-1868, and a space for visiting exhibitions. Of more interest is its satellite museum, the **Crafts Gallery** (Kōgei-kan), housed in a Meiji-period brick building, five minutes' walk west of the National Museum. The pottery, textiles, lacquerware and carvings on display here are a tribute to the subsidies and support which the Japanese government has given to its traditional industries. The select collection includes work by Living (and Deceased) National Treasures. Look out for Arakawa Toyozō's ceramics, and the beautiful raw silk kimono by Shimura Fukumi. The building, complete with chandeliers, used to be the headquarters of the Imperial Guard, who had the run of Kitanomaru Park after the Meiji Restoration. In 1878, in an event almost unprecedented in Japanese military history and symptomatic of the social turmoil caused by the Restoration, 200 privates mutinied against their officers, resentful at the division of rewards after the suppression of Saigō Takamori's Seinan rebellion. After attempting to petition the Emperor, they were defeated and 49 of them executed.

The **Science Museum** (Kagaku Gijutsu-kan, *adm ¥600*) is north of the others, and crowded with uniformed high school students at whom the beeping, button-pressing displays seem primarily to be aimed. At the north end of the park is a squat building with a gleaming octagonal roof topped with a gold mushroom: the 14,000-seat **Nippon Budō-kan** (Japan Martial Arts Hall), familiar to rock stars the world over as the venue for many of Tokyo's most lavish concerts. It was built for the 1964 Olympics, but achieved its greatest fame two years later when the Beatles sold out for five nights there. Profits were a hundred million yen; the 8,000 police deployed to protect the Fab Four from their fans cost another ninety million.

The **Tayasu-mon** (Tayasu Gate) at the northern end of the park is one of the oldest and most impressive portals in the castle grounds, built sometime in the 1620s, with two gates: a wide inner one to allow a mass of defenders to exit easily; and a narrow outer gate to impede the progress of attackers. The two stand at ninety degrees to one another, and between them is a square courtyard surrounded by turrets and high walls. Even if enemies did penetrate the first gate, they would be assailed by arrows and rocks as they wheeled round to face the second, sturdier portal. The inner courtyard is called the *masugata*, after the *masu*, a square wooden drinking cup whose shape it shares.

Yasukuni Jinja (Yasukuni Shrine)

Yasukuni Jinja (Shrine for the Repose of the Nation) is the area's controversial main attraction, entrance opposite the Tayasu-mon. This was founded in 1869 as the *shōkon-sha*, the 'shrine to which the spirits of the dead are invited'. Specifically, it enshrined the souls of those who had perished in the civil wars of the Meiji Restoration, and since then it has become a kind of Valhalla for all who have died in the service of the nation or—more controversially—the Emperor. Among the glorious dead honoured here are victims of the Boxer Rebellion, three Englishmen who died in the naval battle of Tsushima during the

Russo-Japanese War, and the fallen of the Pacific War, including the wartime Prime Minister Tōjō Hideki and eight others hanged by the military tribunals as Class A war criminals. It is the resort of right-wing extremists (the ultra nationalist assassins of at least one prime minister made solemn vows here before carrying out their crime); but it is also the closest thing in the popular imagination to a national Cenotaph or Tomb of the Unknown Soldier. Every year there is a tremendous fuss when members of the Cabinet are invited to pay their respects here. If they accept, they are accused by the left of violating the constitution which separates government and religion; if they decline they are noisily denounced by the right. Recently ministers have fudged the issue by attending the services but stating that they were doing so only as 'private individuals', not as members of the government.

For all this, the shrine is a pleasant place and a famous and beautiful cherry blossom-viewing spot with a number of different varieties primed to go off at various times over the April season. A 15m tall bronze **Ōtorii** (Great Gate) marks the entrance to a long, cherry-planted avenue, with the formidable shrine sanctuary (built in the Ise style, with jutting 'horns' at the finials) at the far end. There's a stage in front; at the **Mitama matsuri** (festival) from 13–16 July, traditional dances and candle-lit *nō* plays are performed on it.

East of the Palace

Hibiya, at the southeast corner of the palace, between Kasumigaseki and Ginza, was a tidal inlet in the early days of Edo—the name comes from a kind of oyster trap which was set on the mud flats by fishermen. After the land had been reclaimed, *daimyō* built their houses here. Today, it's a quarter of banks, theatres, concert halls and hotels, busy and purposeful during the day, rather still and empty in the evenings.

Hibiya Kōen (Hibiya Park) was laid out in 1903 on the site of a parade ground where the emperor used to review the troops. It was the city's first Western-style park. By day it is respectable, with a popular fountain plaza, a library and meeting hall. But quite early on it gained a night-time reputation, which it retains today, as a meeting place for couples who don't have the price of a love hotel, and the Peeping Toms who come in their wake.

On Hibiya-dōri, the avenue which runs along its east side, are the **Imperial Hotel** and the **Takarazuka Theatre** (under reconstruction until 2001), described later on. Just south of them, until its demolition in 1941, was the famous **Rokumei-kan** (Deer Cry Pavilion), which lends its name to that part of the Meiji period (the 1880s) when the craze for things Western was at its height. It was designed by Josiah Conder, the most famous of several British architects who more than compensated for their mediocre talents by simply being in the right country at the right time. Ochanomizu's Nikolai Cathedral and the Mitsui Club in Mita are the only designs of his to survive, but photographs and prints show the Rokumei-kan to have been more elaborate and pretentious than either.

It was built in brick on two storeys in an eclectic, vaguely Italian style with a high arcade of arched pillars along the front, and a Gallic tiled roof. Inside were 15,000 square feet of residential suites for visiting guests, a ballroom, and chambers for music, billiards, reading and cards. At the time of its completion in 1883, Japanese foreign relations laboured resentfully under humiliatingly unequal trade treaties. Shows of lavish modernity were part of the policy of convincing the West that Japan was just as civilized and enlightened as the next country; the Rokumei-kan, in other words, was a shameless act of international social climbing.

The Rokumei-kan era was intense but short-lived. For a while bustles, ballroom dancing lessons and charity bazaars were *de rigueur* among the wives of aristocrats, academics, politicians and diplomats. But the snobbery and naivety of Rokumei-kan diplomacy were transparent, and within a few years a reaction set in. The Prime Minister, Itō Hirobumi, was caught out in an affair with a married noblewoman; shortly before, he had been waltzing at a fancy dress ball attired as a Venetian prince. The two may not have been connected but, in the public mind at least, enough was enough. High jinks at the Rokumei-kan petered out of their own accord, and after an earthquake in 1893 the building remained in a state of semi-dilapidation until its demolition.

Yūrakuchō and Marunouchi

Ever since General MacArthur established his Occupation HQ in the present day Dai-Ichi Insurance building round the corner, **Yūrakuchō** has been at the heart of foreign life in Tokyo. Any exploration of the city should begin at the excellent **tourist information centre**, located in the new International Forum building a few metres from Yūrakuchō station. (The northernmost exit is called the International Forum exit; take this and you can't miss it.) Plenty of other international institutions are clustered in the blocks opposite, including the **American Pharmacy**, stocking foreign drugs, cosmetics and magazines, and the Foreign Correspondents' Club of Japan. Yūrakuchō means 'The Place Where Pleasure Can Be Had', and in the 1950s it was notorious for another kind of service available to visiting foreigners: the *pan-pan* girls, described by Fosco Maraini as 'painted harridans, with huge heels and misshapen legs, who shout, smoke, spit, chew gum, and call out "Hey, Johnnie!" at passers-by'. The *pan-pan* are less visible now, but parts of Yūrakuchō still have an agreeably raffish atmosphere, especially the underpasses beneath the railway tracks where tiny stalls serve cheap *yakitori* as the trains roll overhead.

Marunouchi means 'Within the Citadel', and *daimyō* built their houses here from the earliest years of the 17th century. By the late 19th century it had stagnated. 'Marunouchi was a place of darkness and silence, of loneliness and danger,' wrote the poet Takahama Kyoshi, 'the abode of foxes and badgers. Here and there were weed-grown hillocks from aristocratic gardens. The murder of Ōtsuya [a young local girl] was much talked about in those days.'

The area was called Mitsubishigahara, 'the Mitsubishi wasteland', after the family company which had bought the area for a knock-down price when no other buyer could be found. Mitsubishi commissioned Josiah Conder (he of the Rokumei-kan) to build their headquarters here, and slowly a crossroads of brick offices, 'Londontown' (Itchō Rondon), formed. In 1914 a student of Conder built Tokyo station which survives—minus its bombed domes and upper stories—to give some idea of **Itchō Rondon's** original appearance. At the time, everyone considered Mitsubishi to have made a stupid purchase; now, of course, Marunouchi is the corporate capital of Japan, and the most desirable business address in the country. Useful buildings in the heart of the district here include the credit card agent in the **Shin Marunouchi Biru** (New Marunouchi Building) on the west side of the station plaza, and the 24-hour, 365-days-a-year **Central Post Office** on its south side.

Ginza

Few urban districts in the world—Broadway, perhaps, or the Champs Elysées—have had such a hold on the national imagination as Ginza. Fifty-one popular songs, at the last count, contain the word *Ginza* in their titles. There are 500 regional Ginzas in towns throughout Japan, and countless Ginza Bars, Ginza Clubs and Ginza Shopping Centres. Ginza has become a brand name and an advertising slogan, a by-word for the most sophisticated shops, the most urbane cafés, and the most exorbitant property prices. Shifting exchange rates frequently prove such generalizations wrong, but it used to be said that if one took a ¥10,000 note, folded it as tightly as possible, and dropped it on the pavement at Ginza Crossing, it would not be enough to purchase the land it rested upon.

Ginza is also synonymous, of course, with Westernization and with the renewal and affluence that, until recently at least, were associated with the products of the West. It began to acquire this status in 1872 when the country's first railway line was opened between Yokohama and Shinbashi. Ginza, a few blocks to the north, found itself the natural disembarkation point for foreign goods, foreign ideas and foreign nationals as they arrived in Tokyo from the port. A few months earlier, a fire had destroyed the old wooden Ginza and the opportunity was taken to carry the new principle of Civilization and Enlightenment into bold practice. A British architect was hired and the quarter was rebuilt in expensive imitation of a Western city. Within a couple of years, two-storey brick houses with balconies flanked the main thoroughfares which were lined with trees, gas lamps and—another first—pavements. 'Bricktown', as it was called, drew crowds of sightseers, including woodblock artists whose prints show lively scenes of horse-drawn carriages and big-nosed foreigners strolling beneath the cherry trees and colonnades. But few Japanese, in the early days at least, were willing to live there. The houses harboured bugs and were damp and badly ventilated; rumours persisted that their inhabitants were prone to horrible diseases. Squatters and street entertainers with performing animals moved in, and the trees on the boulevards withered and died.

With generous subsidies the municipal authorities lured businesses back, and by the turn of the century Ginza was established as the place to buy Western-style suits, hats and other exotic goods like watches and spectacles. Newspaper offices, another foreign innovation, moved their offices here, and a *geisha* quarter was established by Shinbashi station.

Tram tracks (electrified in 1903) were laid down the main street, and horse-drawn omnibuses were seen earlier here than anywhere else in the city. Many of Japan's most famous department stores and venerable family businesses were established in Ginza at this time. The famous clock tower which still stands outside the Wakō store on Ginza Yonchōme appeared there in 1894.

It was also the place where the social fashions which spread through Japan in the early 20th century were most visible. Ginza was the habitat of the *moga* (modern girl or *gāru*) with her bobbed hair, gloves and earrings, and the *mobo* (modern boys) who hung out in cafés, milk bars, beer halls or ballrooms where, for one and a half yen, they could hire a 'taxi partner' to teach them the steps of the unaccustomed new dances. The street fashions were French in inspiration; the most famous cafés were the Plantain, the Lion, the Paulista, and the Colombin, with its 8m model of the Eiffel Tower. A new word was coined to describe the favoured activity of these spangled exotics: *Gimbura*, combining the first syllable of Ginza with the first syllable of *burabura*, meaning to loll or loiter or idle. While flappers were flapping in New York and London, their counterparts in Tokyo were loafing in Ginza.

The earthquake and fire of 1923 destroyed the crumbling remains of the old Bricktown, and between the world wars Ginza acquired a high-rise character, with the new multi-storey shops like Wakō, Mitsukoshi and Matsuya. The shortage of foreign goods during the war put a dampener on the district's traditional activities, but it suffered less from the bombing than many areas, and was reborn in the American Occupation, benefiting from the proximity of General MacArthur's HQ round the corner in Hibiya. Along with Akasaka, Ginza is one of the few places left in Tokyo where you just might see *geisha*, stepping in and out of taxis between the tea houses.

A Loaf through Ginza

The *burabura* approach is still the best one to take in Ginza. A stroll from the **tourist information centre** to the **Kabuki-za theatre** (try to time your walk to coincide with a performance there) can take anything from half an hour to a whole day, and even if the centres of youth fashion have shifted west to Shibuya and Shinjuku, Ginza still has a flourishing streetlife with Tokyo's most magisterial shops, some striking architectural oddities, and the smelliest drains in central Tokyo: despite their colossal expensiveness the streets have never been properly plumbed, and waste is still disposed of through open sewers.

Leaving the International Forum building (you will feel like Jonah emerging from the whale) and walking south along the railroad tracks, you will come to an underpass just on the other side of the station opposite the Yūrakuchō Denki Building. Take a left here and pass underneath the tracks (bullet trains pass overhead, as well as the more conventional JR trains). You remain technically in Yūrakuchō until the fly-over of the expressway, but the **Mullion Building**, between the railway and the road, is spiritually part of Ginza, with an exterior of vertical pieces of glass, and equally gleaming shops. Herein is a complex of banks, cinemas, subways, and a stunning, gravity-defying central atrium which ascends the full 12 storeys, dividing the **Hankyū** and **Seibu department stores**. At the front of the edifice, beneath the Japanized versions of American film posters, is a large innocuous-looking clock which every hour bursts into an animated display of electronic chiming. Ask for *Marion no tokei*, 'the Mullion clock'—it makes a useful Ginza rendezvous point.

Beyond the expressway, on the south side of the road, is the **Sony Building**, with its façade of 74 rectangular TV screens, a huge electronic canvas periodically reprogrammed with abstract designs by video artists. Inside are hands-on displays of the latest Sony gizmos like High-Definition TV and laser discs.

Ginza's most eminent institutions are concentrated around **Ginza Yon-chōme Crossing** where Harumi-dōri, the west–east street along which you have been walking, meets the north–south Chūō-dōri. On the southwest corner is the **San'ai Building**, a cylindrical sandwich of neon lights and glass-walled shops and cafés. Just behind here, on Chūō-dōri, is **Kyūkyodō**, a 300-year-old vendor of products made from *washi* Japanese paper. Upstairs are brushes and other paraphernalia associated with calligraphy.

Opposite the San'ai Building, on the northwest corner of the crossing is **Wakō**, a pricey department store which began life as a street stall, opened by an enterprising clockmaker's apprentice in the late 19th century, when gentlemen's watches were a badge of Civilization and Enlightenment. North of it, on Chūō-dōri, is the Tokyo branch of the **Mikimoto** pearl business whose patriarch invented the cultured pearl in 1893. On the east side of Chūō-dōri are three vast department stores: in ascending order of prestige, **Matsuya** (to the north), **Matsuzakaya** (to the south) and **Mitsukoshi** (on the corner).

The original **Kabuki-za** (Kabuki Theatre) couldn't have been more different from the present building (just beyond the next big intersection to the east). It was finished in 1889; surviving prints and photographs show what looks like an unusually attractive European-style structure, with columns, arches and large sculpted pediments. *Kabuki* had always been considered a rather vulgar, low city form, but in the posh new theatre *shitamachi* townspeople and high city toffs sat side by side. Then, in 1925, it was rebuilt in an ornate, bristling Momoyama style: the curved arches and heavy tile roofs were reproduced in modern materials which endow the building with a rather sinister, overbearing atmos-phere, unpleasantly appropriate to the authoritarian political regimes which grew to dominate Japan between the wars (*see* p.135 for details of tickets and times).

Nihonbashi

Before 1868, Nihonbashi was at the heart of *shitamachi*, the 'low city', where, in popular imagery, the salt-of-the-earth townspeople of Edo lived in rowdy contrast to the stuffy shogunal types over the moat. It was always the richest area of *shitamachi*, home—by virtue of the docks that once existed just to the south here—to the big shipping and retail businesses. Today, the area is indisputably high city, with flagship department stores and big financial institutions, but these days it has a rather dowdy, neglected atmosphere as if the rest of Tokyo has forgotten that it is there. Of the Edo period nothing remains, although there are a few Meiji buildings and some interesting, long-established shops.

Ginza becomes Nihonbashi just north of the expressway. Chūō-dōri, the main north–south street leading up from the Ginza crossing, is probably the closest Tokyo gets to the airy boulevards of European cities, and the further north you go, the more civic and respectable it becomes. There are occasional wacky touches: a giant paint pot with a brush sticking out on top of a building, and, a few blocks further north on the left-hand turning into Yaesu-dōri, a beautiful bronze giraffe, contoured in gold and wearing a gold crown; **Mon Coffee**, the café just above it, is a stylish place to watch the world going by. **Meidiya**, just north of the giant paint pot on the opposite side of the street, is the place to buy foreign groceries in Tokyo.

In the middle of Yaesu-dōri is a memorial, in Japanese and Dutch, to Jan Joosten, a ship-wrecked Dutch sailor of the early 17th century who settled in Edo, and lent his name—characteristically mangled first to Yayosu, then Yaesu—to the area on this side of Tokyo station, the east exit of which is the *Yaesu-guchi.*

On the other side of Chūō-dōri is the **Bridgestone Bijutsukan** (*open 10–6, closed Mon; adm ¥500*), an art museum which offers a superb short history of European painting and sculpture. The collection, owned by the tyre company, is small and select, with hardly a duff item and many masterpieces, beautifully presented. It begins with Greek and Roman statuary and a superb Egyptian corner, but the majority of the pieces are Impressionist or later: typically overripe Renoirs and Monets, a Cézanne of Mont St Victoire, an attractive faun by Rodin, paintings by Modigliani and Derain, some outstanding Picassos. Interesting too are the period works by Japanese artists, like Okada Saburosuke's 1907 *Portrait of a Lady*, a perfect example of the 'Japonesque' style that represented the only real attempt to meld foreign and native approaches to painting. The oriental elements—a *taiko* drum, a kimono, a gold screen—are clichés, mere decorative fancies. The other Japanese painters represented seldom ascend above pastiche: a Japanese Renoir, a Japanese Picasso, a Japanese Chagall.

Chūō-dōri continues, past **Maruzen** book shop, the **Takashimaya** and the old (now vacant) **Tōkyū** department stores (Takashimaya's lift attendants have the snappiest livery in Tokyo: mustard yellow suits and black straw hats), until it reaches the feature which gave Nihonbashi its name: 'The Bridge of Japan', which marked the meeting point of the five highways linking the capital and the provinces, including the great Tōkaidō between Edo and imperial Kyoto. All roads led to Nihonbashi, and all distances were measured from the marker in its middle. It burned and collapsed at regular intervals (on one occasion 1200 people who were escaping from a fire went down with it), and in 1911 was rebuilt in its present form: an elegant construction of low arches, paved in granite, guarded by four lions and four unicorns. The bridge should be a point of pride and a much-needed breathing space between buildings; instead it is dirty, seedy and in perpetual twilight. In 1962, in the rush for modernization before the Tokyo Olympics, an expressway was built right over the top of it, and the once lively Nihonbashi River was transformed into a subterranean canal.

Turning right on to a small street just after the defunct Tōkyū department store you will come, on your left, to the Taimeiken Building with a restaurant of the same name on the ground floor. On the fifth floor is the **Kite Museum** (Tako no Hakubutsukan, *adm ¥300*), an eccentric little place founded by the late Shingo Motegi, a kite enthusiast of international repute. The total collection numbers 3000; ten per cent are on display here, including kites in the form of birds, insects, warriors, demons and squid.

Mitsukoshi department store (closed on Mondays), on the north side of Nihonbashi bridge, went through numerous transformations from the Mitsui dry goods store founded in the 17th century. Mitsukoshi was the first of the merchant retailers to turn itself into a department store in the modern sense. From 1908 to 1914 it occupied a Western-style building inspired by London's Harrods. It was the first shop to display its goods in glass cases, rather than bringing them out of storage at the customer's request; it also installed Japan's first escalators in 1914. The present Mitsukoshi went up in 1935. The two great lions guarding the main entrance are imitations of those in Trafalgar Square, but the façade still has a decorative, distinctly oriental air about it.

You couldn't say the same for the building to the northwest, the old **Bank of Japan**, completed in 1896 on the site of the old gold mint, and next to **Tokiwa-bashi**, Tokyo's oldest stone bridge which is also still there. Its architect was Tatsuno Kingo who later designed Tokyo station, and its cobbled courtyard, solid columns and green bronze dome make it one of the most elegant and refreshing Meiji-era buildings in Tokyo.

North Tokyo

Between the Imperial Palace and Ueno Park is an interesting and subtle area, little frequented by tourists, with some of the most tranquil inner city escapes in the metropolis. This has long been a centre of scholarship in Tokyo: the Tokyo University (Tōdai) main campus is in Hongō just a few minutes' walk from the Yushima Tenjin, one of several important shrines and temples.

Akihabara

Akihabara (The Field of Autumn Leaves) is one of several places in Tokyo that are straight out of science fiction. It assumed importance in the Meiji period as a freight yard, and a market selling combs and accessories, and later bicycles, sprang up beneath the railway tracks. After 1945 it was the point at which army surplus goods entered Tokyo from the Chiba peninsula, and chief among these were radios, a prestige item in the post-war years. Technology students from the nearby universities set up their own stalls selling home-made gadgets, and Akihabara developed into the beeping, buzzing, whirring, electronic amusement arcade that exists today. In 1991, the turnover in these few blocks was ten trillion yen, fully 10 per cent of the national total in domestic electrical goods. Everything—from fridges and washing machines to pocket-sized computers and trans-lating machines—can be bought here, and bargained for. 'At Akihabara,' wrote Edward Seidensticker, 'and we who do not know must take the statement on faith, the electroni-cally sophisticated person can find anything that has been invented.'

For all its technological sophistication, the atmosphere of the black market still lingers around Akihabara: most of the traders are small and specialized, and you can tell at a glance what kind of goods they sell. Almost everything can be tried out in the shop. In recent years, Akihabara is said to have lost its competitive edge in goods like cameras to the discount chain stores in places like Shibuya and Shinjuku, and committed bargain hunters should shop around. Japanese goods may actually be cheaper back home, or in Hong Kong. Balance any savings against the inconvenience of adapter plugs and instruc-tions and warranties in Japanese (although international brands like Sony and Toshiba can be serviced and repaired anywhere). Above all, Akihabara is a fun place to shop, even if you don't buy: gizmos and innovations go on sale here before anywhere else in the world (*see* p.165).

Nikorai-dō (Nikolai Cathedral)

Open Tues–Sat, 1–4; donation expected.

This small cathedral, the headquarters of the Orthodox Church in Japan, is one of the most peaceful, calming and un-Japanese places in Tokyo. Officially called the Cathedral of the Holy Resurrection of Our Lord, it's popularly named after its founder, St Nikolai Kassatkin (1836–1912), who first travelled to Hakodate as chaplain to the Russian consulate in 1861. It was built between 1884 and 1891 from a design by the ubiquitous British architect Josiah Conder, and suffered badly during the Great Earthquake when the dome collapsed and the interiors were gutted by fire. The dome was lowered to avoid a repeat disaster; today, squatting beyond a high embankment wall, the building is certainly no beauty. But its Byzantine appearance and green copper roofs are unique in Tokyo and an Ochanomizu trademark; there's even a coffee shop by the station with its own version of the onion dome. The interior is surprisingly small, but the cool, echoic darkness is stunning after the noise and smog of Tokyo. Candles flicker on metal spikes before the languid icons—buy one in lieu of an entrance fee.

Yushima Seidō (Confucian Temple)

On the right, 100m north of Ochanomizu JR station east exit. Open 9.30–5; adm free.

Buddhism and Shinto (frequently the two were indistinguishable) remained the popular religions of Japan during the Edo period, but it was Confucianism—or rather a Japanese inflection of the teachings of the Chinese sages—which provided the ideological base for the Tokugawa state, and a code of ethics which is still discernible in Japanese society today. Just as Buddhism, with its concentric ranking of lesser *bosatsu* around a supreme deity, suited the centralizing policies of the early emperors, so the Confucian virtues of obedience, loyalty to elders and rulers, and sublimation of individual impulses in the interests of the group, were vigorously promoted and idealized by the shoguns. Scholarship, for a long time, meant only Confucian learning, and the centre of its practice and propagation was in present-day Ochanomizu.

One of Tokugawa Ieyasu's sons built a Confucian academy in Ueno in the 1630s, which was moved to this site in 1691 by the fervent Confucianist, Tsunayoshi, the fifth shogun. Promising sons of the samurai completed their military educations with study of the Chinese classics; the senior academicians were among the Tokugawas' closest and most esteemed advisers, and twice a year the shogun and his lords gathered here for lectures and ceremonies. What remained of the old complex burned utterly after the 1923 earthquake, and the present buildings, dating from 1935, include the **Nyūtoku-mon**, a black wooden gate with a green roof, and the concrete **Taisei-den** (Hall of Accomplishment) where Confucius and his followers are enshrined.

Kanda Myōjin Shrine

Ochanomizu contains institutions at the poles of Edo culture: on one block, the Confucianism of Yushima Seidō, the cold disciplinarian faith of the High City; over the road, the boisterous Shinto of the **Kanda Myōjin**, the Edo townsman's shrine whose biennial festival held on 9–15 May (odd-numbered years only) is one of the biggest and noisiest in the city.

The shrine was founded in 730 and was long associated with Taira no Masakado, a 10th-century lord who rebelled against the Kyoto court and declared himself Emperor. He was killed in battle, but his headless body was seen haunting Edo until he was enshrined, originally in Ōtemachi. In 1616 Tokugawa Ieyasu, no lover of emperors himself, moved him to Kanda and declared him guardian deity of the entire city. When the Emperor Meiji elected to worship there, however, the presence of this rebellious god was considered inappropriate. The shrine priests were prevailed upon to transfer his numen to a lesser shrine, and substitute that of an uncontroversial deity.

A copper *torii* gate behind the Seidō leads to the main shrine buildings, rebuilt attractively enough in concrete, with elegantly jutting tile roofs. Alongside them is the **Mikoshi-den**, the hall containing the ornate portable shrines paraded through the streets at festival time. The biggest is called **Sengan Mikoshi**, 'The Shrine Weighing 1000 *Kan*'—just under four tons. It's an exaggeration, but not by very much. During the festivities 400 porters in *happi* coats, often very drunk, are required to bear it through the neighbourhood.

Yushima Tenjin

Yushima subway station (Chiyoda Line); at the north end of Hongō-dōri, 800m from Kanda Myōjin.

Ten minutes' walk from the main campus of Tokyo University, this is Tokyo's principal shrine to Sugawara no Michizane, the 9th-century courtier deified as Tenjin, god of scholarship. These days he is worshipped principally as the god of passing exams (which isn't, of course, the same thing at all). During the entrance exam season, the precincts are crowded with candidates making supplications to the deity and buying the talismans (exam-passing amulets, even exam-passing pens and pencils) sold in the shrine shop. Wooden votive plaques festoon the grounds bearing detailed instructions to the deity on universities applied for and grades required. Late February and early March is also the season of the *ume* (plum) blossom, Tenjin's flower whose five-petalled crest adorns the 19th-century buildings.

Ueno

Compared to other districts of Tokyo, Ueno has a complicated and mixed atmosphere, and no one tribe holds sway. Ladies with Gucci handbags stroll beneath the trees at the northern end of the park, *en route* to piano recitals at the Festival Hall or exhibitions at the cluster of civic museums. At the southern entrance, the steps are crowded with homeless vagrants, pavement artists and Iranians dealing in various illegal goods. For a week or so in

April, the park becomes the most densely peopled spot in Japan, as tens of thousands gather for liquid picnics beneath the cherry blossoms. Ueno feels like a remnant of an earlier Tokyo, less self-conscious and squeakily affluent. The young are not so obviously dominant; older people feel comfortable here too.

History

Originally a headland jutting out into the sea, Ueno, by the time of the Tokugawa shoguns, was a feudal estate owned by Tōdō Takatora, the engineer of Edo castle. In 1624 the second shogun had a temple built on the hill and installed the monk Tenkai, a confidant of Tokugawa Ieyasu, who developed it into a huge complex of 36 sub-temples and 36 lesser halls. The temple's name was Tōeizan (Hiei-zan in the East) Kan'ei-ji, and its function was similar to that of the great Enryaku-ji on Kyoto's Mt Hiei: to protect the shogun and his city from the unlucky northeast direction, the source of plague, fire and evil spirits.

The temple flourished, despite being outside the city limits, and a thriving quarter of restaurants, workshops and brothels grew up around it. In 1868, however, Kan'ei-ji became one of the few significant casualties of the generally bloodless Meiji Restoration. As well as being commandingly situated on a hill, the temple grounds contained the tombs of six shoguns, and a band of about 2,000 Tokugawa loyalists, rejecting the surrender which had been agreed by their leaders, holed up here and dispatched patrols into the city. On 4 July the imperial forces on adjacent high land in Hongō mounted an artillery attack on the resisters. Many of the shells fell short, and fires were started. The remaining buildings were finished off in hand-to-hand fighting after the imperial troops breached the temple's main Black Gate. Three hundred men died and the ancient halls and temples were almost completely destroyed.

The land was due to be used for a medical school, but one Dr Bauduin, a Dutch adviser to the government, persuaded the authorities to create a park instead (a statue of the far-sighted doctor stands even today). For a while it became a popular spot for horse racing on a track which ran around the Shinobazu Pond. In 1882 the National Museum was opened, along with Tokyo Zoo, and a series of public-spirited concert halls, libraries and galleries. The pond was drained and, along with much of the park, given over to agriculture during the war, but it was restored during the Occupation. It was too late, though, for many of the zoo animals: as wartime food shortages became graver, they had to be put down. Those too big for bullets or poison, like the elephants, starved to death.

Ever since its station opened in 1883, Ueno has been the point of entry into the capital from the northern provinces. During the post-war period, poor farmers flocked to Tokyo in their thousands to start new lives in the city. Many of them never got further than Ueno which was for a couple of years a refugee camp for the homeless, a melancholy role which it hasn't entirely shaken off today.

Ameyoko (Candy or America Alley)

Hard left outside the Park Exit of Ueno station is the main relic of post-war hardship, a narrow alley of shops and stalls running beneath the tracks as far down as Okachimachi station, the next stop down on the Yamanote line. An apocryphal story tells of a Tokyo judge who, in the days of the tightest post-war rationing, refused to compromise himself by eating anything which had been obtained on the black market. He starved to death, along with dozens of others every day. Ameyoko, conveniently positioned on a busy corner out of sight of the local police boxes, was the solution to this dilemma. In the weeks after the war, farmers with sacks of contraband rice mingled with Tokyo people selling off the contents of their homes for cash or barter.

The second element of Ameyoko means 'alley' and the first is a pun. 'Ame' is Japanese for candy, and as life began to return to normal, it was this simple luxury that the market specialized in. Later, during the Korean war, GI surplus goods like jeans, watches, pens and belts appeared, and the name was painlessly adapted to reflect the change—from *ame* (sweets) to the first syllable of *Ame*rican.

After half a decade of turning a blind eye, the authorities legalized the market in 1950. It's still cheap, and shopping here is a salty contrast to the hushed atmosphere of Tokyo department stores. Stall keepers bellow their prices; shoppers bargain and jostle. Despite the superficial chaos of the tiny shops, it runs smoothly—lubricated, no doubt, by the discreet ministrations of the local *yakuza* gang syndicates.

Ueno Park

Shinobazu Pond, the wartime vegetable garden, is periodically threatened with plans to drain it and turn it into something else (a car park or a baseball stadium). You may utter a grateful prayer to Benten, the Shinto goddess enshrined on the **Benten-jima** island in the middle, that this has never been allowed to happen.

At the southeast corner is the **Shitamachi Museum**, Shitamachi Fūzoku Shiryokan (*open 9.30–4.40, closed Mon; adm ¥200*), with faithful reproductions of a range of typical low city houses (merchant's house, poor tenement, coppersmith's workshop, etc.) from the period before the Great Earthquake of 1923. English labelling is adequate, and you can enter the rooms and handle the everyday objects arranged inside. On the second floor is a children's area with Meiji- and Edo-era toys, plus rotating exhibitions of clothing, tools and festival objects.

Just above **Keisei-Ueno station** (shuttles depart from here for Narita Airport) is a set of broad steps leading into the heart of the park. As a foreigner, you might be accosted by young Iranians intent on selling you something illegal, but crackdowns have made this increasingly unlikely. A further set of steps on the right leads up to the park's most famous landmark and rendezvous point: a bronze statue of **Saigō Takamori**, the heroic Satsuma samurai who turned villain in 1877 by taking up arms against the Emperor whom he had fought so hard to restore eight years before. The shameful circumstances of Saigō's demise (he committed suicide in a cave, trapped there by attacking imperial troops) are reflected in the style of the charming statue, which was cast in 1893. Instead of a heroic martial pose, he is portrayed in clogs and informal kimono, casually walking his lap dog.

To the west of Saigō and his podium, a gravel avenue leads deeper into the park. On the east side is the **Kiyomizu Kannon-dō**, built in imitation of Kiyomizu temple in Kyoto and, a little further on, the original **Kuro-mon** (Black Gate) which once marked the entrance to the Kan'ei-ji complex, and still bears bullet holes from the siege of 1868.

Three shrines stand to the east, between the path and the Shinobazu Pond, from south to north: a shrine to the rice deity, Inari, reached, as usual, through a tunnel of orange *torii* gates and guarded by sleek fox statues; the **Gojōten**, dedicated to Tenjin, god of learning; and the Tōshō-gū which begins at the stone **Ōtorii** (Great Gate) and is reached by a long approach of stone and bronze lanterns.

The **Tōshō-gū** (*adm ¥200*), dedicated to the first Tokugawa shogun, Ieyasu, is one of the oldest in the park, founded in 1627 with a main hall dating from 1651. It was established by Kan'ei-ji's first abbot, Tenkai, who played an important role in Ieyasu's deification. The statues were donated by *daimyō* from all over Japan; the most ornate, closest to the shrine's outer wall, were the gift of junior branches of the Tokugawa family. These days, the delicate woodwork and opulently painted interiors are in a terrible state: the drapes are smoke-stained, the statues are mottled, and the shrine drum has a hole in its skin. Most shocking of all are the four famous lions by the master of Edo screen painting, Kanō Tanyū, worn to invisibility in places.

As you exit, notice the open-work depictions of the ascending and descending dragons on the **Kara-mon** (Chinese Gate), carved by the famous Hidari ('Lefty') Jingorō, who was also responsible for the famous 'sleeping cat' in Nikkō. The fabulous beasts are so realistically executed that in bygone days, of course, they used to slip off their gate at midnight and drink in the Shinobazu Pond; crowds of dragon-spotters used to gather from time to time to observe their movements.

The **Five-Storey Pagoda** (Gojū no tō) over the wall on the north side of the approach to Tōshō-gū is one of the few surviving relics of Kan'ei-ji, dating from 1647. To inspect it at close quarters you have to enter the **zoo** (famous for its pandas) whose entrance is a little further on to the north.

The northeast acres of the park are dominated by a number of public halls of culture, including the largest of Japan's national museums and the **Tokyo Metropolitan Festival Hall** (Tokyo Bunka Kaikan), opposite Ueno JR station, which hosts frequent musical events, including concerts by foreign artists. Next door, south of the **National Science Museum**, is the **National Museum of Western Art**, not as *bijou* as the Bridgestone in Nihonbashi, but with a big collection of Rodins and French Impressionist and Post-Impressionist paintings. The building is based on an old design by Le Corbusier.

Tokyo National Museum (Kokuritsu Hakubutsukan)

Open 9–5; adm ¥420 plus extra fee for special exhibitions.

In terms of the size of its collection (90,874) and its number of visitors (three quarters of a million annually) the **Tokyo National Museum** is the most important in Japan, although it's hardly the most beautiful or the best laid out. From the front, the three buildings compose a neat history of Japanese architectural tastes in the 20th century. On the left-hand side is the oldest wing, the **Hyōkeikan**, built in 1908, a languid European-style building with a green copper dome; in the middle is the **Honkan** (1937), the museum's main gallery, in a bristling neo-traditional style, half Greek and half Chinese temple; on the right is the **Tōyōkan** (1968), modelled after a temple hall, but constructed out of undisguised grey concrete.

Hyōkeikan

This houses vivid archaeological finds of the prehistoric periods (up to about AD 600), plus later excavations from cemeteries and cremation grounds. An unusually imaginative display on the ground floor demonstrates how the eponymous designs were applied to the pottery of the early Jōmon (Rope Pattern) period; there are perfect examples too of later Jōmon vessels, inlaid with ridges of clay which flow over their surfaces in irregular swirls and zig-zags, protruding above the lip to produce the famous 'flaming' pottery. The rear wing of the ground floor contains a small display of objects associated with the indigenous Ainu people of northern Japan, although anyone who has visited the Ainu museums of Hokkaidō will have seen far better examples of the wooden clubs, fur coats and geometric designs appliqued on to cotton.

The upstairs rooms contain finds from the *kofun* (tumuli) erected over the bodies of powerful chieftains in the 3rd to 6th centuries. The human and animal figures found there are among the most accessible objects of Japanese art, especially the *haniwa*, witty clay renderings of courtiers, warriors, houses and pets which took the place of human retainers who, at one time, were dispatched into the next world along with their master. Creepier and more stylized are the *dogū*, squat figures with elaborate head dresses and swollen limbs, identified by at least one writer as space-suit-wearing extraterrestrials.

Honkan

The **Honkan** contains the main body of the collection, two floors and 25 rooms of rotating exhibits, mapping a chronological course through all the main genres of Japanese art. Clear labelling and a good English map make it easy to find your way around here. Although there are many masterpieces, the vast size of the collection makes it difficult to say which will be on display at any one time.

The ground floor houses sculpture, metal work, arms and armour, textiles and ceramics. As well as many religious statues, there is a near-contemporary portrait of the 12th-century shogun, Minamoto no Yoritomo, in the striking style shared by paintings of the same period: an expressive, naturalistic face (in Yoritomo's case the look is one of wary cunning), combined with symmetrical and abstract treatment of his billowing formal robes. The next two rooms contain metal objects—Buddhist ritual bells and wands, and some cast metal kettles which display the painstaking attention to detail so prized in the tea cult. One, said to have been used by the 16th-century master, Furuta Oribe, was cast so as to boil with a melodious warble. Its decoration is subtle and stands out faintly on the purposely rough, rustic surface: horses gallop before the vague forms of hills; the lid handle is a dragon and rings on either side are in the form of fabulous beasts. Beyond the display of arms and armour is a long room devoted to textiles: *nō* and *kabuki* costumes, and scarcely less lavish examples of aristocratic dress and uniform. By the 17th century, Japan had its own silk industry and no longer needed to rely on imported textiles. A native idiom developed, drawing on the traditions of the past but adapting the conventions of painting and craft, and making use of what little imported material was available in Japan during the secluded Edo period. Outstanding among the exhibits is a *kosode* (short-sleeved robe) made for a courtesan during the early 19th century, with a striking design of a hawk and a dragon dramatically embroidered on black velvet (a very exotic fabric) and using gold foil.

Upstairs are paintings, prints, calligraphy and lacquerware and, again, the range defies brief summary. As well as the exquisite hand scrolls created by courtiers, there are admonitory depictions of the horrors of hell, like the famous *Hungry Ghosts Waiting to Feast on Faeces*, as graphic as its title. In the 15th century, monk artists painted ink landscapes to accompany poems, inspired by Chinese works of the Yuan and Ming dynasties: Shūbun's *Reading in the Bamboo Studio* shows a tiny figure, perched in a hut on a jutting crag, a kind of symbol of the monk philosopher, contemplating the void from his precarious earthly perch. Look out also for the penetrating, haggardly realistic portrait of the Zen master Ikkyū by Bokusai. (Be aware that the collection changes around, however, and don't search too hard.) The use of monochrome brush strokes to create elliptical, almost abstract landscapes gives many of the greatest Japanese paintings a very modern, or rather timeless, atmosphere. *Pine Forest* by Hasehawa Tōhaku, on two six-fold screens, is a superb example. Eighty-five per cent of their area is left blank, but the space between the smudged, erect pines breathes with the mistiness of dawn light.

Tōyōkan

The **Tōyōkan**, which houses art objects from other Asian countries, re-opened in July 1999 after a long period of refurbishment. The **Hōryū-ji Hōmotsuden** displays one of the greatest collections of ancient Japanese art: the treasures of Hōryū-ji temple, near Nara, founded by the 7th-century Prince Shotoku, father of Japanese Buddhism. The objects were displayed for only one day a week in the old building; because of their fragility, it was closed in case of rain or damp. A brand new building allows them to be displayed more freely.

West Tokyo

Shinjuku

Don't miss Shinjuku: if you spend only one night in Tokyo, try to spend it here. The other *sakariba* (roughly 'lively places')—Shibuya, Ginza, Roppongi, Ueno—are cities within a city. Shinjuku is better described as a metropolis within a megalopolis, a place of extremes, and the area which epitomizes the most dramatic features of modern Tokyo: teeming crowds (above and below ground), an epic railway station, visionary high-rise architecture, multiple department stores and a maze of neon-lit snuggeries devoted to *mizu shōbai*, the 'water trade' of drinking, entertainment and sex. On a Friday evening, Shinjuku station's east exit plaza, beneath the giant TV screen of Studio Alta, has to be one of the most exciting places in the world.

History

Shinjuku's associations with the pleasure industries go back a long way. It began life as an equestrian post station (the name means 'new lodging') founded in 1698 by five Asakusa brothel owners. Naturally, the refreshments on offer extended to more than just the horses, and in 1620 the stews were closed down for 50 years after a scandal involving a retainer of the shogun. For centuries after, Shinjuku was an insalubrious and unfashionable area, unfondly known as the anus of Tokyo on account of the queues of night-soil trucks which would form in the evenings, carting the city's waste out to the farms in the west. But it was spared the worst devastation of the 1923 earthquake, and slowly prospered on the backs of the refugees from the gutted districts of the Low City.

Like Shibuya and Ikebukuro, Shinjuku made its biggest fortune as the playground of commuters, who caroused and dallied in large numbers before returning to the western suburbs from Shinjuku station. The first national railway line was built here in 1885. Tram lines and private railways followed, and by 1928 it had become the busiest station in Japan; today, it is the biggest in the world. Twenty lines converge here, dispatching three million passengers every day. The metal clippers which the inspectors still use to punch tickets are said to wear out every three days.

Incineration in May 1945 proved little more than a minor inconvenience. The station was rebuilt and quickly established itself as the centre of Tokyo's black economy—the Ryūgū (Dragon Palace) Market was the biggest in the country. Japan's first strip show, The Birth of Venus, was held in the now defunct Teitoza theatre, and the banning of prostitution in 1958 caused barely a pause: the former *toruko* (Turkish baths) renamed themselves 'soaplands', and carried on as before. There was another clamp-down in 1985, but the *mizu shōbai*, controlled by the *yakuza* and tolerated by the police, remains cheerfully visible.

In the two decades after the war, Shinjuku became known as the hangout of students, journalists, writers and radical intellectuals, a reputation which still clings to parts of the area. In October 1968, student rioters, in emulation of their counterparts in Paris, began tearing up the paving stones and hurling them at policemen (the stones that remained were efficiently removed by the authorities and replaced by asphalt in the course of a single night).

Until the seventies, all the action had taken place on the innermost east side of the station. West of the tracks was a very different kind of water trade: a tract of grey reservoirs which were moved out west in 1965, suddenly releasing an expanse of untouched real estate. The first skyscraper, the then impressive Keiō Plaza Hotel, went up in 1971; since then it has been dwarfed by a battery of rivals, and several plots still remain vacant. In 1992 Shinjuku's transformation was completed by the opening of the new City Hall in a complex of extraordinary post-modern towers designed by Tange Kenzō. The remote suburban satellite is now the centre of Tokyo's government; Ginza/Marunouchi, the old centre, finds itself in the astonishing position of slipping to the margins. In little more than a hundred years, Tokyo's anus has become its heart.

Exploring Shinjuku

There are two mutually distinct areas. **West (Nishi) Shinjuku** is the skyscraper zone, a cool, impassive area of thrillingly tall hotels and office buildings which regularly disappear into the mist on cloudy days; the Odakyū and Keiō department stores are also on this side. Smaller shops, cinemas and street life are in **East (Higashi) Shinjuku**, as well as the pleasant **Shinjuku Gyōen** (Park), and **Kabukichō**, Japan's most famous red light district, which also contains numberless restaurants and bars offering innocent entertainment.

Shinjuku station is a unique cultural experience in itself, especially at rush hour and last thing at night. One writer suggested that 'you can find out more about the horrors and pleasures of modern Japanese life by spending ten gawping minutes in Shinjuku station than by reading a dozen industry textbooks.' Whether or not this is an exaggeration, for most people, ten minutes is quite enough. Long-term residents regularly get lost; if the constant buffeting crowds don't get you, then the profuse and mutually contradictory sign-posts will. The best advice is to get out, stay out and then take your bearings from the detailed enlargement of Shinjuku on the back of the tourist information centre's free Tokyo map. The west exit (*nishi guchi*) is closest to the skyscrapers, the east exit (*higashi guchi*) to Kabukichō, but even if you find yourself at the north or south exits, it's an easy matter to sidle round the station at street level. The second character in the Japanese word for exit, *guchi*, also means 'mouth': chewed up and spat out is how you will feel.

The smart way to avoid this bedlam is to take the Marunouchi or Shinjuku line to the subway station called **Shinjuku san-chōme**, 500m to the east of the main overland tracks. This is linked to an underground promenade (called 'Subnade' in Japanese English) which runs directly beneath the main street all the way to the station. Detailed maps, labelled in English, show exactly where you are in relation to the surface, and the stair exits for all the main landmarks are clearly indicated.

The most popular rendezvous points in Shinjuku are below the giant video screen of the **Studio Alta department store** (on the north side of the plaza by the east exit) and—less crowded, and with a bit more intellectual cachet—the **Kinokuniya** book shop, two blocks to the east.

West (Nishi) Shinjuku

The Escher-like convolutions of West Shinjuku continue even outside the station proper, with a subterranean walkway and multi-level roads making it difficult to know where exactly ground level is. **Chūō-dōri** (Central Avenue) is the road you want, a broad highway cutting through the centre of the skyscraper district.

The view from this approach will be familiar to aficionados (they do exist) of late-night Japanese monster films: the 'scrapers of Shinjuku are regularly trashed by Godzilla and his many adversaries. Individually, few of them are architectural works of art, and the combined effect is curiously unreal. Like many of the imported accoutrements of the West, there's something rather undigested about them, a self-consciousness that is difficult to put your finger on, as if one were viewing a display of skyscrapers, rather than the things themselves.

One at least—the newest, although not for long—is a wonder. The **Tokyo City Hall** by the grand-daddy of contemporary Japanese architects, Tange Kenzō, shows up most of its neighbours for the overgrown cigarette lighters they are. It is a fitting monument to the mighty but bizarre city over which it presides: dignified but never pompous, dynamic without being busy, witty but not corny. The wonderful check texture of the exterior—glass and contrasting shades of stone—is surprisingly warm, like an expensive tweed. Around 13,300 people, including the Governor of Tokyo, work in the linked complex of offices and (at the front) Metropolitan Assembly Hall. The tallest towers are both 243m high and contain 48 floors, and if they look familiar, they are: despite its relentlessly secular function, the hall is modelled on Notre Dame in Paris. The joke seems to have worked in a touching and unexpected way. Like the French capital, the City Hall has achieved a reputation among young Japanese as a place for romance. On clear evenings the twin **observation decks** on the 45th floor of each tower are busy with moony young couples enjoying one another's company, and the view.

Of course, the best view of the architecture is from outside the building itself, ideally in one of the flanking skyscrapers. The **Keiō Plaza Hotel** faces it (no one will mind you sneaking up if you do it discreetly); the handsome, triangular **Sumitomo Building**, to the northeast, has a free observation lobby and several cafe-type restaurants with excellent views on the 51st floor.

Nestling alongside all this magnificence, near the west exit of the station, is an alleyway of scruffy shopfronts and overhead wires possessing the rather sonorous Japanese name *Shomben Yokochō*: 'Piss Alley'. It may not have a fragrant aroma, but it's a lively place for tasty, and extremely cheap, *yakitori* and noodles, served in packed, noisy little restaurants.

East (Higashi) Shinjuku

Kabukichō

Kabukichō has countless bars, abundant cinemas, some great restaurants (especially Thai), but the commodity which animates it and gives it its character is unquestionably sex. Kabukichō is to sex what Tokyo's department stores are to shopping. It comes in all kinds of shapes and sizes, and most tastes and budgets are catered for. There are Kabukichōs in many Japanese cities, but Shinjuku's must be the most varied and densely-packed of them all. A survey revealed, in the southern quarter alone, 37 porn stores, 21 massage parlours, 21 nude shows, 17 'soaplands', 15 love hotels, 13 peep shows, 4 porn cinemas, 4 private video houses, a couple of strip theatres and two 'no-pants' coffee shops (the waitresses eschew underwear; the floors are mirrors)—all in the space of a few hundred metres.

By a crashing irony, Kabukichō (Kabuki Town) was christened and organized in its present form in an attempt to bring a touch of class and high culture to Shinjuku. Before the war it had been a characterless residential area. In its aftermath, a local notable named Suzuki pioneered a scheme to erect a *kabuki* theatre here, the centrepiece of an expensive project of reconstruction and gentrification. But the money ran out just as the water trade, which had always had a shadowy presence in the area, flowed in. By that time the name had stuck. Legal crackdowns—in 1958 and, most recently, in the so-called 'St Valentine's Day Massacre' of February 1985—have never put more than a temporary lid on its exuberant activities.

The best tactic, on a first visit anyway, is just to amble around and enjoy the unique, sinister-innocent atmosphere. Despite the superficial sleaze, Kabukichō is notoriously safe compared to equivalent quarters in other big cities—look at the crowds of high school age kids all around you. It would be hard to get into trouble, even if you did elect to sample some of the attractions on offer—the biggest risk would be running up a huge bill which you couldn't pay and couldn't argue with.

Kabukichō, in its broadest definition, consists of the blocks north of Yasukuni-dōri, between Seibu-Shinjuku station to the west and the small Hanazono Shrine to the east, which is especially pretty when lit up at night. To the northwest is **Shinjuku Plaza**, a scrappy square surrounded by multi-screen cinemas, some of them respectable.

Next to the shrine a honeycomb of tiny drinking and eating cells, known as the **Gōruden Gai** (Golden Block), has a particular reputation as the intellectuals' hangout. **Shinjuku ni-chōme** (in the blocks east of Shinjuku san-chōme subway station, a 10-minute walk from Kabukichō proper) is a lively area of gay bars and clubs, popular with customers of all orientations, and the abode of the famous *okama-san*, 'honourable transvestites'.

Shibuya and Harajuku

At first glance, **Shibuya**, western Tokyo's second great pleasure district, has little to distinguish it from its bigger brother Shinjuku, three stops up the Yamanote line: both were once outlying, semi-rural neighbourhoods; both contain baffling conglomerations of railway lines and department stores, and numberless hidey holes for drinking, eating and sex. But the ingredients combine in very different proportions, and the atmospheres of the two districts are distinct. Shibuya is teen city—trendy and 'cute'—where Shinjuku is raffish and seedy. In Shibuya, fashion replaces sex. The character swaggering down the sidewalks is less likely to be a *yakuza* touting for a peep show than a 15-year-old high school student in baseball cap and vintage $1000 Levi's. Young Japanese generally appear to foreigners to be younger than they are, but the immaculately dressed midnight crowds giggling, tottering and vomiting on the slopes of Shibuya look very young indeed.

Shibuya, and the areas immediately to the north and west of it, have more daytime attractions than Shinjuku: near **Harajuku station** is **Meiji Jingū**, Tokyo's biggest shrine, and the adjacent **Yoyogi Park**, which at weekends and national holidays becomes an open-air circus of musicians, teen fashion victims and street performers. Omotesandō-dōri, built as the shrine avenue, is more grown-up, an elegant boulevard of cafés and designer shops.

Shibuya

Shibuya station isn't as crowded as Shinjuku and for students of Tokyo streetlife there is only one important exit: **Hachikō Plaza**, on the west side of the station, near the JR tracks.

Hachikō

Hachikō (the name has been variously translated as 'Little Number Eight', 'Lord Eight' or, ingeniously, 'Octavius') was a very ordinary Akita dog whose sad little story has made him the most famous pet in Japan. He belonged to one Ueda Eisaburō, a professor at Tokyo University. Every day he would accompany his master to Shibuya station in the morning, and return to meet him off his regular train in the evening. One day in 1925 he found himself waiting for a very long time. Old Professor Ueda had died—but how could this be explained to little Hachikō? The family gave him away to friends in Asakusa, but every afternoon the faithful hound would cross Tokyo to wait in his accustomed spot for the master who never came home. Within a few years, Hachikō's dumb loyalty had made him a national institution. In 1934 he posed for a sculptor and a bronze statue was unveiled in front of the station. When he *was* reunited with his master a year later, his mortal remains were elaborately buried, minus his pelt which was stuffed and preserved in the National Science Museum. Hachikō's loyalty was tested to the limits during the war when he was melted down for gun metal, but the little chap has since been reinstated and remains Tokyo's most famous meeting spot.

Like many cult figures, however, Hachikō's reputation has been tarnished in recent years by revisionist historians. In his book, *Tokyo Rising*, Edward Seidensticker blasphemously suggests an alternative interpretation of the story. According to some eye witnesses, Hachikō didn't conduct his vigil in the evenings, but loitered around the station all day. His new owners, it seems, mistreated him, and once his reputation was established, there were rich pickings of food to be had from sentimental passers-by. The tale, Seidensticker suggests, is not one of trust and loyalty, but greed and cunning. Needless to say, this remains a deeply unpopular view. Japanese people of a certain age tend to adopt a very sad, wounded expression when they are told this version of the story.

The dog has now become such a popular rendezvous spot that it is often impossible to find the person you are supposed to be meeting there. Wait instead by the Hachikō *kōban* (police box) on the right-hand side as you exit the station; or by the Hachikō Wall, a ghastly relief of ceramic Hachikōs, which stands on the same side.

Exploring Shibuya

Five big roads, and several million people a day, converge on the crossing in front of Hachikō Plaza; when the lights change and the pedestrians stream across in a dozen

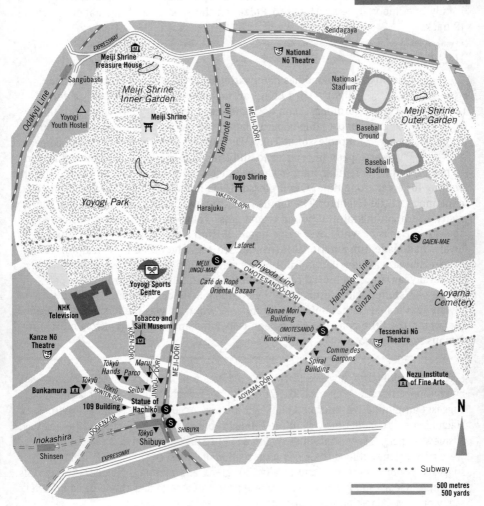

different directions, the scene is exhilarating. Standing on the edge of the road with Hachikō and the station behind you, a large department store called **109** is visible to your left. The road to the left of this is **Dōgen-zaka**, named after a famous 13th-century highwayman, Owada Dōgen, who preyed on travellers through what was then a dim and isolated valley.

At the top of the slope on the right is an extraordinary enclave: a village, clustered round several narrow alleys, of love hotels. Neon signs hum below mirrored, one-way windows; room charges—by the night or the hour—are discreetly displayed outside the covered entrances, and couples stroll around them in the evenings unselfconsciously looking for available rooms. At weekends, when the rates double, they are very often booked out. This air of lively innocence pervades the whole district. There are, no doubt, *yakuza* operating on the streets of Shibuya, but far more visible in their competition for the money and loyalties of its citizens are the huge department store and railway corporations which have effectively carved up the main highways between them. The road to the right of 109, **Tōkyū Honten-dōri**, leads up to the **Tōkyū department store**, the huge transport and retail conglomerate that first laid claim to the area. There aren't many activities in Shibuya that Tōkyū doesn't have a stake in. Attached to the store is the **Bunkamura** (Culture Village), a multi-level complex of cafés, restaurants, cinemas and a gallery which displays some of the best visiting exhibitions (largely of Western art) in the city, as well as the 2000-seat Orchard Hall, home of the Tokyo Philharmonic Orchestra, and the smaller Theatre Cocoon. The original Tōkyū store is in the station complex, above the terminus of one of the many Tōkyū commuter lines. To the east of the station (the other side from Hachikō) is another arts centre, the **Tōkyū Bunka Kaikan** (Culture Hall); the **Tōkyū Inn** hotel is a little to the north, beneath the railway tracks. Even 109 is another of Tōkyū's masks, the name a pun on the Japanese readings of the numbers 10 (*tō*) and 9 (*kyū*).

The competition begins on the avenue leading north, known commonly as **Jingū-dōri**, but officially as Fair Street. A few metres up on the left-hand side, joined across a side road by a bridge, are the trendy **Seibu** department store and its **Annex**, owned by the poet millionaire Tsutsumi Seiji. Opposite, and dowdy in comparison, are the **Marui** stores.

A left turn just after the Seibu B Building takes you to another big crossroads and—well, well, well—another department store, among the most exciting in Shibuya: **Parco**, a fantasy land of boutiques and designer concessions and an off-shoot of the Seibu corporation. Plainly, no self-respecting Shibuya *depāto* could make do with just one shop; Parco has three, all of them adjacent. It needs them, for lurking just up the road (turn left—i.e. west—at Parco) is an enemy stronghold: **Tōkyū Hands**, eight fascinating floors of household hardware, DIY materials and craft paraphernalia.

Continuing north over the crossroads in front of Parco, you enter **Kōen-dōri** which leads up to **Yoyogi Park**. On the second block on the right, opposite the Tōbu Hotel, is the **Tobacco and Salt Museum** (*open 10–6; adm ¥100*), a surprisingly interesting exhibition of artefacts relating to these former government monopolies. Apart from 2000 tobacco packets from around the world, there are biographies of famous smokers and displays relating the history of the weed, which was introduced into Japan at the turn of the 16th century. In the early days, pipes were smoked in much the same way as tea was drunk, with much solemnity and formal ritual. The floors devoted to salt are, as you might expect, less entertaining. No smoking, by the way, on the 2nd or 4th floors.

Harajuku

Harajuku station is one up from Shibuya and two down from Shinjuku on the Yamanote line. It has two exits; the Yoyogi Park one, at the south end, becomes impossibly congested at weekends.

Yoyogi Park

The scene in Yoyogi Park on a holiday or Sunday afternoon has almost become a Tokyo cliché. Spaced at intervals on the wide avenue are bands of Japanese youths dressing and behaving in a way that Western prejudice holds to be anathema to the polite Japanese. Spiky punks gob into their microphones, brilliantined Elvis impersonators croon, and the streets are filled with the sounds of over-amplified guitars and drum machines. Ever since the 1964 Olympic Village, which brought a flavour of hip cosmopolitanism to the area, was dismantled to create this park, it has been the assembly point of the Tokyo *zoku*.

The word means 'breed' or 'tribe', and *zoku*-spotting has been a popular activity for newspapers and magazines ever since the first 'modern girls' were identified 80 years ago on the streets of Ginza. There are the *takenoko zoku* (bamboo shoot tribe), named after the Harajuku shop which sells the tribe's uniform (baggy, androgynous trousers and smocks); and the more notorious *bōsōzoku* (speed tribe) who roar around in ferocious leathers on unthinkably expensive imported motorbikes, frightening old ladies. In the late 1980s many of the performances had real charm, with mime artists, *butō* dancers, folk and classical musicians—Japanese and foreign—sharing space with the inevitable rock'n'roll imitators and brutish thrash metal bands. On a recent visit, only the last were in evidence. But it may just have been an off day; change, after all, is in the nature of the place.

Yoyogi National Stadium

Two stadia, one large and one small, are mounted on a stone-flagged emplacement reached from Harajuku station by a network of spidery overpasses. Both were built for the 1964 Olympics, and both were designed by the Grand Old Man of Japanese architecture, Tange Kenzō. Great aluminium skins are swathed over a helix-shaped steel frame: the main stadium looks like the bit of a huge screw emerging from out of the earth. Look inside and up: the apex of the second, smaller gymnasium is a prodigy of swirling, geometric curves.

Meiji Jingū (Meiji Shrine)

For the two emperors who succeeded Emperor Meiji, no shrine has been dedicated. Taishō died mad in 1926, after only 14 years on the throne; Shōwa's long reign is too irrevocably associated with the Pacific War for any memorial to be other than controversial. But Meiji, or Mutsuhito as he was known during his 44-year reign, had presided over a revolution and, however much one might deplore aspects of it, no one could wish for, or even imagine, a return to the old days of the Tokugawa shoguns. Meiji died on 29 July 1912, an event as traumatic as the death of Queen Victoria a decade before. At his funeral, on the night of 13 September, the whole city fell silent as eight white oxen drew the Emperor's body to the station for transportation and burial in Kyoto. Within a matter of days, preparations had begun for his deification. **Meiji Jingū** was formally dedicated in November 1920. The entrance to the shrine grounds is just to the right of Yoyogi Park, down a long gravel avenue marked by two 12m high *torii* gates of unvarnished Taiwanese cypress, the biggest of their kind in Japan. The Emperor commandeered this land from the lords of Ii, and often spent time here. The June irises which bloom in the **Inner Garden** (*adm ¥300*) were the favourite flowers of his consort, Empress Shōken, and remain the shrine's most famous seasonal attraction. The shrine itself is a plain, rather blank set of buildings, impressive from the air but, from the ground, striking mainly for the green copper of the roofs, stained brown by fume-poisoned rain.

Behind the shrine buildings the grounds become overgrown and meadow-like; even at weekends they're rarely as crowded as Yoyogi Park. At the north end is the **Hōmotsu-den** (Treasure Museum, *open 9–4.30; adm ¥500*), built in 1921 in concrete emulation of the log cabin style of the Shōsō-in in Nara. As a man, Meiji is a distant and inscrutable figure; the personal objects on display here do not bring him any closer. A famous portrait by an Italian artist shows an intelligent-looking man with wispy hair and beard. Empress Shōken was a chinless lady who devoted herself to good causes like the Red Cross. Meiji reintroduced medieval formal court dress for ceremonial occasions, but is pictured with his wife in Western attire. Many of the exhibits here exemplify the schizophrenic tastes of the time—like the modern horse carriages topped with ornate traditional phoenixes, or the Emperor's dress uniform, a combination of Prussian twill and Japanese brocade.

East of Harajuku station, on the opposite side from the shrine and park, is **Takeshita-dōri** (Takeshita Avenue), shopping street of preference for the Harajuku *zoku*, and the closest thing Tokyo has to a Carnaby Street: a self-conscious higgledy-piggledy arrangement of cafés, record stores and boutiques, selling youthful fashions and trash accessories.

Omotesandō

This broad road (literally the 'avenue in front'—it was laid out as the formal approach to the Meiji Shrine) is one of the most elegant quarters of Tokyo, a place for café-hopping and boulevarding after a lazy afternoon spent in Yoyogi Park.

Three hundred metres down from Harajuku staion is the first big intersection. On the north side is the **Laforet department store** and, in a side street behind it, the **Ōta Memorial Museum of Art** (*open 10.30–5.30, closed Mon and from 26th to the end of each month; adm ¥900 for special exhibitions*), an attractive and intelligently curated museum displaying a small, scholarly selection of the 12,000 *ukiyo-e* (woodblock prints) collected by an insurance tycoon. Artists represented include Utamaro, Hokusai, Hiroshige and Kiyochika, as well as dozens of others less well known internationally.

Beyond the next main intersection on the south side of the avenue is **Café de Ropé**, a classic Omotesandō rendezvous. Just east of it is the souvenir shop **Oriental Bazaar**.

Omotesandō crossing is marked by two big stone lanterns. Southwest of here, down Aoyama-dōri, are **Anderson's Bakery** (opposite the prominent Fuji Bank), where Omotesandō ex-pats buy their bagels and patisseries, and further down (on the opposite side) the deluxe **Kinokuniya** supermarket. A quiet side road beyond here leads up to **Las Chicas**, with café, restaurant, bar, gallery and hair salon in a beautifully designed multi-purpose building. **Kottō-dōri** begins opposite Kinokuniya and leads down to Roppongi-dōri. Along it are more expensive shops, and the **Blue Note**, off-shoot of New York's famous jazz club. At the Roppongi-dōri end there are several excellent shops selling fine ceramics. Back at the crossing, Omotesandō continues southeast, past designer shops and cafés of chrome and frosted glass: impersonal, expensive and cool. Designers **Issey Miyake** and **Comme des Garçons** both have shops here. The glittering minimalist interiors of **Yokku Mokku** do for coffee and cakes what the designers do for clothes. Opposite is the trendy **Tessenkai Nō Institute** in a squat concrete building.

Keep going down and you come to another intersection. On the south corner, behind a wall, is the excellent **Nezu Institute of Fine Arts** (*open 9.30–4.30, closed Mon; adm ¥1,000*), an eclectic complex of galleries situated in a beautiful old garden. It was founded in 1940 and houses painting, calligraphy, sculpture, ceramics, textiles, lacquer and wood- and metal-work, including some of the most famous individual pieces of Japanese art, like the famous Shinto painting of the Nachi Waterfall. (The exhibits, however, are rotated so there is no guarantee of seeing the National Treasures on any one visit.) Some of the finest and most accessible objects are Chinese: stone Buddha heads with pigments still thick on their faces, and amazing bronzes from the Shang dynasty—furious-looking, 3000-year-old cauldrons studded with spikes, knobs and ridges, bristling with arrogant energy. Paths dip around a hilly garden filled with statues, stone pagodas and reproductions of famous art objects including, in the courtyard, the delicate 8th-century lantern from the front of Nara's Tōdai-ji temple.

South Tokyo

Tsukiji

A few minutes' walk from genteel Ginza, Tsukiji's main attraction—a huge, raucous, early-morning fish market—could hardly be more different in terms of atmosphere. The nearby Shiba and Hama Rikyū gardens are tranquil, inner city escapes: from the latter you can take a boat trip up the Sumida-gawa, Tokyo's historic, if grimy, main river.

History

Tsukiji means 'built land': like so much of Tokyo's coast it is polder, reclaimed in the 17th century using ashes from the great Long Sleeves Fire of 1657. Some interesting characters have lived here over the years, including Maeno Ryōtaku, an 18th-century physician who, despite the restrictions placed by the shogunate on foreign books, taught himself Dutch and translated into Japanese an influential book on anatomy. At his home in Tsukiji he assembled a clique of young specialists in what was then known as *rangaku*, 'Dutch studies' (the Dutch being the only nation allowed trading rights by the Tokugawa regime). An admirer of Maeno, Fukuzawa Yūkichi, set up his own school in the area in 1858; it grew into Keiō, one of Japan's most prestigious private universities. Fukuzawa, remembered as a pioneer of enlightened Westernization, is commemorated on the ¥10,000 note.

The foreign trade treaties of the same period brought numbers of foreigners to Tokyo, and in the earliest years of the Meiji period, a special walled settlement was built for them in Tsukiji. The American Legation moved here, but the experiment was not a success. Most foreigners chose to live in Yokohama and the hundred or so who remained in Tsukiji were mostly Chinese merchants and missionaries. The New Shimabara red-light district, thoughtfully established by the government for the convenience of the foreign gentlemen, closed within a few years. When the settlement was destroyed by the 1923 earthquake, no one felt the need to rebuild it.

Central Wholesale Market (Chūō Oroshiuri Ichiba)

The optimum time to arrive is about 5am, before the subway opens. Tell your taxi driver to go to **Tsukiji ichiba**. *On busy mornings the streets will be congested; get out and ask for the* **Sei-mon** *(Main Gate), opposite the offices of the* Asahi Shimbun *newspaper. Closed second and fourth Wed of every month and Sun.*

To someone who has never been to Tsukiji market, the idea of getting up at four in the morning to view buckets of dead fish may not be immediately appealing. It would be a pity to surrender to this disinclination. Tsukiji has as much in common with your local fishmonger as the Shinjuku terminus has with a country railway station. It's one of Tokyo's most unusual and exciting outings: vast, noisy and chaotic, and teeming with some of the strangest and most grotesque forms of life in Tokyo, human as well as icthyoid.

The market was moved here in 1935 from its centuries-old site in Nihonbashi. Fruit and vegetables are also sold here, but the principal attraction, to buyers and tourists alike, is marine produce, for which Tsukiji serves as supplier to the whole of eastern Japan. The statistics are staggering: 704,169 tons of fish were sold here in 1992, worth $5.9 billion (two and a half thousand tons—21 million dollars' worth—every working day), and fruit and veg add another billion dollars a year. Nine immense refrigerators have a combined capacity of 30,000 tons; there is parking space for 5000 vehicles, and the stalls get through 200 tons of ice daily.

The action starts early and continues through mid-morning, but the sooner you turn up the more there is to see. Walk straight through the main gate towards the large building directly in front of you. Inside are 1600 wholesalers' stalls arranged in avenues in a great quarter circle. For now, walk straight through to a set of concrete buildings on the far side. The fish have been arriving all night and from 5am they are auctioned in big rooms inside these annexes.

Freshwater fish go under the metaphorical hammer first, from about 5am, then live fish at 5.20, and crustaceans at 5.40. For three-quarters of an hour there's something interesting going on in almost every room, but the highlight is the tuna auction scheduled at 5.30am.

Deep-frozen, and with their tails chopped off, the tuna, each as big as a man, lie in steaming rows, like long aluminium bombs or pods from outer space. Yellow labels detail their weight and country of origin (as far away as Nigeria). The buyers prod and tap them (prime cuts, for the best sashimi, cost ¥25,000 a kilo), and a siren signals the beginning of the auction, a baffling drama of high-speed chanted prices and cryptic nods, hand-signals and gesticulations from the assembled

brokers. After the auctions, the fish are transported into the giant covered market building you passed through earlier. Watch your step in here: all the rules of Japanese courtesy and caution are discarded in this outer ring of Fish Hell. The two hazards of Tsukiji are the slippery floors (dress practically in trousers and flat, rubber-soled shoes) and the constant traffic of blaring, chugging, fuming vehicles: fork-lift trucks bearing pallets of twitching crustaceans; convoys of wagons distributing freshly-powdered ice; and bizarre, primitive scooters, like motorized planks. Even more varied is the produce: from familiar cod, mackerel and sardines, through squid and octopus wriggling vigorously in tanks and buckets, to sea slugs, giant clams and polychrome beauties from the China Sea. It's a tribute to the strict hygiene controls enforced here that, after 60 years filled with fish carcasses, the market buildings really don't smell that bad.

Breakfast in Tsukiji

For those who have an appetite this early in the morning, Tsukiji is the place to eat the freshest sushi in Japan. Between the market and Tsukiji Hongan-ji is the area called the **Jogai Ichiba** (Outer Market) with hundreds of little restaurants, shops and workshops supplying Tsukiji and its employees. Naturally, the fish sold is of the highest quality, although it's not always as cheap as you'd expect. The following open early:

Daiwa Zushi is a tiny shop in front of the big market area inside the market precincts, open from 5.30am; **Tatsuzushi** is just inside the northeast entrance of the market (not the main entrance), and opens at 7am. Both sell individual pieces of sushi for around ¥300–400, or courses from ¥2,000.

Just outside the northeast entrance, over the bridge and to the left, is **Tsukiji Sushisei**, an extremely popular bar founded in the Edo period which attracts long queues at lunchtime.

Individual pieces from just ¥150; it opens at 8am. Even cheaper is **Segawa Sushiten,** a stall situated just before Tsukiji Hongan-ji on the corner of Shin Ōhashi-dōri and Harumi-dōri, which sells only *maguro* (tuna) and also does take-aways, five pieces for ¥500.

If raw fish seems a bit ambitious at this time in the morning, try the 24-hour noodles at **Uogashi Ramen,** one block before Tsukiji Sushisei. The Outer Market has plenty of coffee shops doing breakfast sets of toast and coffee from around 7am.

Hama Rikyū (Beach Palace)

Between Tsukiji and Hamamatsuchō railway station to the south are two attractive water-front gardens, remnants of the private parks and hunting grounds of the shoguns and their lords. **Hama Rikyū** later became a palace for imperial receptions, and VIPs like the former US President General Ulysses Grant were put up here. It was filled with gun emplacements during the war and bombed to ruin, but today it's an attractive stroll garden based around a brine pond which swells with the tides of the Sumida River estuary, and has barnacle-encrusted rocks around its margins. The **Naka-jima (Central Island) teahouse,** reached by a zig-zagging wooden bridge, is a 1945 restoration of a surviving Edo-period building. The duck pond is still used by private shooting parties: turf-covered hides are dotted around the fenced-off perimeter.

Shiba Rikyū is smaller, less popular, and in some ways more striking, especially when viewed from the monorail linking Hamamatsuchō station with Haneda Airport to the south. The *shinkansen* tracks have encroached upon it, but the contrast between the still, green garden and the shimmering steel multi-storeys around it is dramatic.

Shiba Park Area

North of Hamamatsuchō station, a road leads west to **Daimon,** the gate of the once great Zōjō-ji. Down a side street to the south of here is the private **Tolman Collection** (*open daily except Tues 11–7*) of contemporary Japanese prints, run for the last 20 years by a talkative American couple. Thirty artists sell their work here, among them the American Clifton Karhu, famous for his boldly coloured scenes of Kyoto, and the octogenarian Shinoda Toko. Prices go up to ¥10 million, but you can pick up a print for ¥5,000 or a book of Karhu postcards for ¥1,480. Anyone with an intelligent interest is welcomed; call ✆ 03 3434 1300 for precise directions.

Shiba Kōen, beyond the Daimon, is the site of one of the most overused photographs of Japan: the stately eaves of **Zōjō-ji** and, behind, looming above it like a headless Godzilla, the vermilion girders of Tokyo Tower. The caption for this picture is usually something like 'Tokyo: city of contrasts', but in fact the contrast is not what you'd expect. The tower opened in 1958; the hall went up 16 years later, replacing the temporary structure erected on the fire-bombed ashes of the old Zōjō-ji.

The park, now little more than a collection of golf greens and hotels, with a few Buddha halls in between, was once the greatest temple complex in Tokyo, covering 660,000 square metres, with 48 sub-temples and 150 schools, housing 3,000 priests and novices, plus their servants and the pilgrims who made their way here along the Tōkaidō highway from Kyoto. **Zōjō-ji** was founded in 1393 by the Jōdō sect and became the chief burial place for the Tokugawa family. Today, what remains is rather a jumble and only the 21m high **San-mon** gate (1612) is of any antiquity.

Tokyo Tower

Kamiyachō, Daimon or Shiba Koen subway stations. Open 9am–7 or 9pm depending on season; adm ¥800 main observatory; ¥1,400 includes upper observatory. Other attractions have a separate admission fee.

According to its pamphlet, this is 'the world's tallest self-supporting iron tower'—333m high, although the highest that tourists can go is the upper observation deck at 250m. Eight TV and four radio stations broadcast their signals from Tokyo Tower, although its primary purpose may simply have been, as Edward Seidensticker suggests, to be higher than the Eiffel Tower, which it mimics slavishly. Tokyoites certainly seem to love it dearly and almost any organized tour of the city will end up here. Crammed into the lift with a horde of over-excited schoolchildren, ¥1,400 lighter in pocket, the tower is best appreciated for what it is: a Japanese folly, and a monument to urban kitsch. Solicitous stewards and stewardesses, wearing the Tokyo Tower livery (dark green suits with cream lapels), give the impression of being in a holiday camp, a vertical Butlins. At the low levels are the Tokyo Tower Aquarium, the Tokyo Tower Wax Museum, and the Tokyo Tower Holographic Mystery Zone. At 150m the lower of the two observatories is a bazaar of overpriced snacks, offensive souvenirs and Tokyo Tower tat (kitsch-lovers on a budget should look out for the set of five Tokyo Tower fridge magnets). The only half-decent reason for wasting your time and money here is the view. Visibility is rarely good enough to see more than a few kilometres, but there is always something horribly compelling about the sprawl of Tokyo seen from the air.

Shitamachi (The Low City)

For years the decline of *shitamachi* (pronounced 'sh'tamachi') has been the great theme of writers on Tokyo, and no history of the city is complete without a nostalgic lament for the 'Low City', a lost paradise of folk culture, obliterated by earthquakes and bombs, and by the relentless march of Japan's modernization. *Shitamachi* was the home of the *Edokko* (Children of Edo): the merchants, traders, artisans, fishermen, cooks, entertainers, prostitutes, apprentices and housewives who formed the mass of the Edo population at a time when it was the biggest city in the world. The *Edokko* were Tokyo's Cockneys: raucous, fun-loving rascals with an eye for the main chance, and a tearful fondness for sentimental love stories and old tales; chirpy under-dogs, contemptuous of their pompous masters in the ruling military class, but fiercely proud and insular, with a conservative suspicion of novelty and change. *Kabuki* was their drama, in the days before it became respectable and artistically regarded. Woodblock prints and scandal sheets, produced in bulk out of tiny workshops, were their reading. Yoshiwara, the licensed brothel quarter which so many print artists commemorated, was their recreation. Edo culture, the popular entertainment of the *shitamachi* townsman, is one of the great artistic achievements of the feudal period. 'Asakusa people are old-fashioned', wrote the novelist Kawabata Yasunari in the early part of our own century. 'They look after others and others look after them, they care for people and have a sense of duty, all of them, the dealers and hawkers at the top to the tramps and beggars at the bottom...the toughs in Shibuya and Shinjuku are a newer sort than the ones we have here. They don't have a tradition, but Asakusa does.'

Asakusa

> Asakusa of the myriads flings everything forth in the raw. All manner of desire dances there naked. All classes and all races mix into one great flow, limitless, bottomless, not distinguishing day from night. Asakusa is alive. The masses edge forward. Asakusa of the masses, melting down old forms to be cast into new ones.

> Soeta Azembō, quoted in Edward Seidensticker's *Tokyo Rising*

From the mid-19th century until the Pacific War, Asakusa was the capital of *shitamachi*, and the liveliest of Tokyo's *sakariba*, 'lively places'. Contemporary chroniclers, like the one quoted above, describe it in almost mystical terms, but its attractions were simple and earthy: large crowds, a big temple in a park, and entertainments spanning every degree of respectability and taste. In 1920 the novelist Tanizaki Jun'ichirō, later to win the Nobel Prize for Literature, enumerated the attractions of Asakusa: 'old theatre, new theatre, moving pictures, things Western, things Japanese, Douglas Fairbanks, Onoe Matsunosuke [the Japanese Fairbanks of the day], ball riding, equestrian acrobatics, *Naniwa* ballads, girlie theatre music, merry-go-rounds, Hana Yashiki funfair; the Twelve Storeys Tower; air-gun shooting, prostitution, Japanese food, Chinese food, Western food, *Rairaiken* restaurant, wonton, noodles, oysters, rice, horse meat, snapping turtles and eels.' These days Asakusa's temple and old shops make it an essential day out on any holiday in Tokyo, but the fun does tend to peter out after sunset. When the temple grounds empty and the shopping alley is boarded up, the streets become empty and echoic. The films in the cinemas are second-run; the old-style monologists attract small audiences. You can still get eels and snapping turtles at interesting old restaurants, but seldom after 8pm. All the other twenty-four-hour attractions of Tanizaki's list have moved west, and Asakusa has entered its old age.

History

Asakusa's existence is a paradox: it became the heart of Edo by virtue of its isolation, beyond the pale of the old city walls. The Sensō-ji temple, with its ancient statue of Kannon, has been a centre of pilgrimage since the 7th century, positioned on the main road to the north by an important crossing point on the Sumida River. In 1657, the shogunate took advantage of a disastrous fire to expel from the city the prostitutes of the Yoshiwara pleasure quarter who were held to be injurious to public morals. The site chosen for their new home was well out of harm's way, among deserted paddy fields to the north of the old temple. Asakusa soon became a handy refuelling stop for thirsty townsmen on their way to, or from, the delights of Yoshiwara. In 1841, a similar decree forced the *kabuki* theatres, also held to be hot beds of licentiousness, to up sticks and move to Asakusa. The district now had the most popular temple in the city, as well as a virtual monopoly on the two great traditional recreations of the Edo townsman: plays and tarts. There was no looking back.

Tanizaki's list gives some idea of Asakusa's variety, but it represents only a fraction of the circus acts, story tellers and freak shows which encamped there in the temple grounds in a permanent, informal funfair. There were tea shops, stalls selling cosmetics and combs, quack doctors, wild animals and performing monkeys, magicians and fortune tellers, acrobats and jesters, and oddities like a spider man, a woman who smoked a pipe through her navel, and a man who ate and drank through a hole in his stomach. Notorious were the proprietresses of the 'archery stands' which provided flimsy cover for much simpler sport in the tents at the back, and provoked the anger of the licensed ladies of Yoshiwara. Westerners who witnessed the fun in the early Meiji period noticed a new attraction: life-size papier-mâché puppets of foreigners, with livid red hair and staring blue eyes.

Asakusa reached its peak of excitement in 1890 with the opening of a 60m tower, the highest in all Japan, containing art galleries, exotic shops filled with international goods, and an observatory reached via the country's first lift (perhaps rightly, this was considered dangerous and closed after two months). The edifice, octagonal in shape and built of red brick, was called the Ryōunkaku (Cloud-Surpassing Pavilion), but everyone knew it as the Jūnikai (The Twelve Storeys). Nearby was the Panorama-kan, which contained life-size models of soldiers against panoramic backgrounds of painted battle scenes. In 1903 the first cinema, the Denki-kan (Electric Hall), opened amid great scandal. Asakusa youths, it seems, were taking advantage of the darkness to do what couples have traditionally done in the back rows of cinemas all over the world. Strict rules were introduced, segregating the sexes and insisting that the usherettes should, at all times, wear underwear. In the days of silent cinema, the picture houses employed flamboyant performers known as *benshi* who, like the narrators in the *bunraku* puppet theatre, declaimed all the parts as well as narrating the story in alternating couplets of five and seven syllables. Realistic touches were added, like the burning of incense during funeral scenes. When the talkies arrived, the *benshi* went on strike in a vain attempt to save their unique profession.

In 1917 Asakusa theatres began to put on 'opera', although the word encompassed a wide range of forms from *The Magic Flute* to musical frivolities like *The Women's Army Is Off For The Front*, a kind of Carry-On-Up-The-Trenches set in Europe during the First World War. Performers attracted claques of fierce partisans called *peragoro*, 'opera ruffians', who would cheer and applaud passionately for their favourite singer, then beat up the fans of her rivals after the show. After the earthquake (which toppled the top two floors of the Twelve Storeys cloud-scraper, but left the temple unharmed), opera yielded in popularity to live cabaret in the style of the Parisian Folies-Bergère. This, like the movies, attracted fierce moral scrutiny. The dancing soubrettes were not allowed to kick in the direction of the audience or wriggle their hips (only *swaying* was allowed); their costumes had to cover their breasts and upper bodies, and below the waist the top 10cm of thigh must be concealed by fabric which could not be flesh-coloured. Troupes were regularly summoned to the police station to have the length of their drawers measured by frowning officers.

In 1927 the first subway line ran between Asakusa and Ueno (today's Ginza line), but the district lacked an overland railway station and this contributed to its decline in favour of Ginza, Shibuya and Shinjuku. The war put on hold the pleasures which Asakusa specialized in, and in 1945 the great temple was finally razed by American bombs. Afterwards, the ponds of the park were filled in. Having slipped from opera to cabaret, the new staple of the Asakusa theatres was strip shows. These days even those are dwindling, and no new popular entertainment is there to take their place.

Tourist Information

Asakusa has its own **tourist information centre** (opposite the famous Kaminari-mon gate, a few minutes from the subway stations) with English-speaking helpers, pamphlets on the *shitamachi* area, and a touch-screen video guide which will print out information sheets on individual places and events.

Senso-ji (Asakusa Kannon)

As with all of modern-day *shitamachi*, the pleasures of Senso-ji are in its atmosphere. Most of the buildings are concrete; few are more than 40 years old. But this is a living temple: the human circus of shoppers, worshippers and fun-seekers is as vigorous as any in the country.

Archaeological remains on the site of Senso-ji—better known as Asakusa Kannon—go back to the Nara period, but traditional history is much more precise. On the morning of 18 March AD 628, two fishermen, Hinokuma Takenari and his brother Hamanari, found a tiny gold statue in their net which was enshrined by their lord in a temporary sanctuary. Twenty years later, the 5cm image was sealed inside an altar where it is said still to remain, a survivor of the temple's destruction by fire bombs in 1945. No human has laid eyes on it since that time, although a copy was created for public display.

Begin at the famous **Kaminari-mon** (Thunder Gate), site of a million tourist photos, a huge red portal crowded with people, flanked on either side by two snarling deities. On the right is Fūjin, God of Wind, his

garments flapping about his body. On the left is Raijin, God of Thunder: in his hands he clutches gold dumb-bells with which he beats a halo of *taiko* drums. The huge red lantern beneath the gate bears the characters for 'Thunder Gate'; a dragon is carved in wood on its base.

The street beyond here is called **Nakamise** (Inner Shops). There are no freak shows anymore, but by day, and especially during festivals, the human traffic jam that develops here still suggests the atmosphere of Asakusa during its glory days. This is one of the best places in Tokyo for buying souvenirs. In the tiny, crammed shops which line the pedestrian arcade there is plenty of tat, but also old establishments producing hand-made goods by traditional techniques—swords, seaweed crackers, lucky cats, paper balloons (*see* pp.166–7 for shopping guide).

The Main Compound

At the end of Nakamise is the two-storey **Hōzō-mon** (Treasure Storing Gate) containing the temple's sutra library, 5428 volumes of it. Beyond lies the courtyard, with the **Hondō** (Main Hall) ahead.

Savour the scene from this end. The Hondō, rebuilt in 1958, is nothing special close-up, but from a distance, with its steeply raked roof and milling crowds of worshippers, visible through a haze of incense smoke, it's a stirring sight. Visitors waft the smoke over their heads and hands as a rite of purification; the temple stalls sell talismans, postcards and fortunes. Inside the Hall is the Gokūden, a gold plated inner shrine which contains (we must take it on trust) the original Kannon statue of 628. Aizen Myō-ō and Fudō Myō-ō, two of the Fierce Kings, are enshrined to the left and right. On the ceiling are modern paintings of soppy, lily-toting angels and a dragon; the walls bear impressive Edo-period votive paintings of bloodthirsty scenes from Japanese literature.

The shrine to the right and rear is **Asakusa Jinja**, a good illustration of the symbiotic relationship between Shinto and Buddhism. While the temple contains the Buddhist Kannon, the shrine deifies the two fishermen who hauled her out of the waters of the river, along with their lord who installed her in the first temple building. The pleasingly weathered building survived the bombs and dates back to 1649. The famous Sanja Matsuri festival in May centres on this shrine. Behind it, there is the smaller **Hikan Inari** shrine to the rice deity. It was established in 1854 by a local fireman as a thanksgiving for his wife's recovery from illness. At the back, a little house on stilts contains hundreds of clay figurines of foxes, messengers of Inari.

West of the main Kannon Hall, a five-storey pagoda is visible over an enclosed wall. These are the precincts of the **Denbō-in**, the abbot's residence, but gaining admittance is not straightforward. Ask at the Temple Office on the west side. You may be lucky and get in that day, but the chances are you'll have to return for a later appointment. Inside is the **pagoda**, rebuilt in 1973 (it looks it), and a fine 17th-century garden by the landscape artist Kobori Enshū.

South of the Denbō-in compound a road runs west, and a gate leads into the small **Chingō-dō temple**, dedicated to the *tanuki* (racoons) who once inhabited the grounds of

Sensō-ji. The grounds contain numerous statues of these comical, plaintive-looking creatures, famed for their round bellies and their unfeasibly large testicles—apart from this indelicate feature they could have been designed by an oriental Beatrix Potter. On the other side is a black statue of Jizō *bosatsu* (*see* p.95) being supplicated by tiny children in red bonnets, and surrounded by offerings of milk, pop and sweets.

Kappabashi

Seven hundred metres west of the temple, a road called Kappabashi-dōri runs north to south, lined with shops devoted to kitchen and restaurant supplies. For tourists, this is the place to buy a unique Japanese souvenir: the glistening plastic food models displayed in restaurant windows. Surreal favourites are the forks levitating above a bowl, suspended only by a thin strand of noodles or spaghetti. The Asakusa tourist information centre has a useful map of the street detailing the products sold in each shop.

A Note about Directions

In the listings which follow, every effort has been made to provide clear, accurate directions which the reader can follow on the ground. This an almost impossible task: the streets have no names; the building numbers are not consecutive; the signs are in Japanese; landmarks (noodle shops, car parks, petrol stations, etc.) are regularly torn down and converted into something completely different.

If the directions to some of these establishments appear infuriatingly vague, it's not for want of trying. Even if they appear precise, don't take them for granted. The best one can ever do in Tokyo is to aim the reader at roughly the right area. After that, a few simple urban survival skills are required (*see* p.14).

(✆ *03–*) *Shopping*

art

Haguro-dō, ✆ 3815 0431, opposite Yushima Tenjin shrine, displays and sells *nikuhitsu*, paintings of the Edo period.

Ōya Shobō, ✆ 3291 0062, is near the junction of Yasukuni-dōri and Ochanomizu-dōri. It sells woodblock prints and illustrated books, old and new.

Tokyo Ochanomizu Kottōkan, ✆ 3295 7110, is an antique hall containing a dozen different dealers.

Tolman Collection, ✆ 3434 1300, by Daimon subway station, is a private gallery of contemporary Japanese prints run by a larger than life American couple.

books

Maruzen, ✆ 3272 7211, in Nihonbashi (just a few minutes from exit B3 of the subway station or the Yaesu exit of Tokyo station) is biggest and best of the Tokyo bookstores. It has a good crafts floor for gift-buying as well as foreign books on the 2nd and 4th floors.

The **Yaesu Book Centre**, ✆ 3281 1811, is a few minutes south of Tokyo station. It often has sales of cheap and attractive reproduction antique maps.

South of here, in Ginza (within walking distance of the tourist information centre) is **Jena** which stocks a lot of glossy foreign magazines and art books.

Kinokuniya (5 minutes from Shinjuku station east exit), a useful meeting place, has foreign books on the 6th floor. A larger flagship store, also in Shinjuku, has recently opened next to Takashimaya Times Square on the vast elevated boardwalk that parallels the train tracks south of Shinjuku station. There's another branch in Shibuya in the Tōkyū Plaza, beyond the bus terminal at the west exit of the station.

Kanda-Jinbōchō is the traditional bookselling quarter of Tokyo. In the old days there were tales of foreigners picking up uncut first editions of *Ulysses* for a few yen: the shop keepers couldn't read the titles. These days they know exactly what they're doing; prices aren't cheap, but it's still a fascinating place to browse.

Kitazawa, by the A1 exit of Jinbōchō subway station, would be a fine English-language bookshop in any city, selling antiquarian works of literature and travel, and modern editions of literature, the humanities and social sciences. A 10–15 minute walk east down Yasukuni-dōri and on the same side of the road (the south) is **Charles E. Tuttle** with a large stock of paperbacks on Japan. Just beyond here is **Sanseidō** with a large general selection.

clothes, jewellery and accessories

The department stores are the best places for scouting out traditional Japanese dress, like kimono. Even if you eventually buy elsewhere, it's worth visiting one of them to get an idea of the available fabrics and prices.

Hayashi Kimono, ✆ 3591 9826, in the International Arcade, near Yūrakuchō station, has a range of second-hand kimono, and long experience of dealing with foreign customers.

Grand Back, ✆ 3478 6942, is Japan's equivalent of 'High and Mighty', a chain, with branches in several Japanese cities, specializing in large sizes. A life-saver for the businessman whose shoe bag has been mislaid by the airline. It is on Aoyama-dōri, east of Gaien-mae subway station.

Mikimoto, ✆ 3535 4611, is the Tokyo saleroom for the exquisite cultured pearls, invented and cultivated in Toba, near Nagoya.

crafts and ceramics

Again, the department stores are the best place to get your bearings. **Maruzen**, in Nihonbashi (*see* 'books'), has a good crafts floor.

On the north side of Roppongi-dōri, towards Roppongi, are a few shops selling excellent souvenirs, such as **Washikobo**, ✆ 3405 1841, which sells dolls, wallets and books made from traditional paper, as well as plain sheets in various colours. There are several excellent, if pricey, ceramic shops on Onotesandō, a little north of the intersection with Roppongi-dōri.

Taketori Monogatari, ✆ 3954 3395, facing the Yamanote line tracks north of Mejiro station, specializes in Japanese dolls for festivals like Girls' Day on 3 March, and also sells Western-style dolls. It is expensive.

department stores

Most of the items you may want to take home from Japan can be bought in department stores, plus a good many that you never dreamed of. They're not always the cheapest places to shop (look out for the sales in June–July and Jan–Feb), but for choice, convenience and service, they're unrivalled. Ask about tax free discounts for tourists. Every sizeable station in Tokyo has at least one *depāto*; the following are the most famous:

Ginza, the birthplace and spiritual home of the Japanese department store (*see* pp.133–35), boasts **Wako**, ✆ 3562 2111; **Mitsukoshi**, ✆ 3562 1111; **Hankyū**, ✆ 3575 2231; and **Matsuya**, ✆ 3567 1211.

Shibuya is the *depāto* battleground, with the Seibu and Tōkyū chains competing for customers on adjacent blocks (*see* pp.148–51): **Seibu**, ✆ 3462 0111; **Tōkyū**, ✆ 3477 3111; **Tōkyū Hands**, ✆ 5489 5111; **Parco**, ✆ 3464 5111.

Harajuku and **Omotesandō** have **Laforet**, ✆ 3475 0411, with boutiques and accessory stores in the heart of Harajuku, next to Meiji-jingū-mae subway station; the **Hanae Mori Building**, designed by Tange Kenzō, isn't technically a department store but contains a number of classy, independent designer fashion shops.

Go to **Shinjuku** (*see* pp.144–8) for **Isetan**, ✆ 3352 1111.

Ikebukuro offers **Seibu** and **Parco**, ✆ 3981 0111.

electronics and music

Akihabara is still the most spectacular and varied place to buy electronics in Japan. The main stores are west of the station. Biggest and most convenient for foreigners is the **Laox** (Japanese pronounce it *Raokkusu*) chain with eight stores (*open seven days a week, 10–7*): there's a main store, two **conpyūtā-kan** (computer buildings; number 2 sells second-hand machines) and satellite shops specializing in audio, musical instruments, and computer games. Just northwest of the station, on the station side of Chūō-dōri, is the **Duty Free-kan**, which specializes in goods adapted for export to the overseas market. Staff here speak English, but are sometimes surprisingly ignorant about their stock. If you have a particular item in mind, shop around and don't take no for an answer: the gizmo of your desire almost certainly *is* here, if you have the energy to track it down.

Recently a number of discount chains have sprung up, claiming to rival Akihabara in price, if not in choice:

Dynamic Audio, ✆ 3478 5881, is an alternative to the Akihabara stores, with bargains in used stereo equipment. The nearest subway is Meiji-jingū-mae.

Wave (*Ueibu*), ✆ 3408 0111, west of Almond, on the south side of Roppongi-dōri, is the shopping equivalent of a Roppongi nightclub (*see* p.180): every kind of pop music available on tape, CD, video, laser disc, DVD and DAT. On the 4th floor is classical music, plus expensive interior design novelties.

food

For an overview of Japanese comestibles, the department store food halls (always in the basement), once again, are the most accessible. Matsuya in Ginza has a particularly graphic fish section.

Musashiya, ✆ 3821 1687, specializes in that quintessential, but acquired, Japanese taste, *tōfu*—red pepper *tōfu*, ginger *tōfu*, *tōfu* croquette, to name but a few. In an old *shitamachi* area between Nippori (Yamanote line) and Sendagi (Chiyoda subway line) stations.

markets

Tsukiji's Central Wholesale Market (for fish) and Ueno's **Ameyoko** (an old black market site) are attractions in themselves (*see* pp.154–7 and pp. 140–1). *Tokyo Journal* lists irregular and one-off flea markets and sales.

souvenirs and miscellaneous

The **Nakamise**, the long avenue leading up to Asakusa's Sensō-ji temple, is lined with shops selling dolls, swords, fans, kimono, Japanese snacks and other useful souvenirs. **Bairindō**, on the left-hand side of the first block, sells nuts and crackers with various flavourings—sesame seeds, seaweed, beans and pistachios. A little further on is **Kazusaya**: kimonos and accessories, *yukata* (cotton kimonos) from about ¥3,000, and *noren*, the short cotton curtains, blazoned with calligraphy or designs, which hang down from the doors of traditional shops and restaurants. The third shop on the left of the second block sells eels and prawns, pickled. On the left-hand side of the third block is **Bunsendō**, selling decorative fans and paper products. Just after the third block down on the left-hand side are two ivory-carver's shop—predictably expensive given the worldwide hunting ban. Hyodanya, the one nearest the shrine, offers decidedly better quality goods. From old ivory are carved shoe horns, cigarette holders, tiny figures of priests, pilgrims, gods and skeletons. A pair of chopsticks costs between ¥15,000–¥42,000, a chopstick rest only a little less. The second to last shop on the right is **Sukeroku**, a tiny room filled with miniature dolls of Edo types, expensive and cutesy. On the far side of the same block is an appealing shop called **Fujiya** which specializes in *tenugui*, cotton hand towels with designs from traditional sources like *kabuki* and *ukiyo-e*.

Oriental Bazaar, ✆ 03 3400 3933, is an unashamedly touristy shop with a conveniently wide selection of souvenirs for those in a hurry. It is fine for small items, but if you're investing in anything expensive, then shop around. It's on the south side of Omotesandō-dōri slightly nearer Meiji-jingū-mae than Omotesandō subway station.

International Arcade, beneath the railway tracks behind the Imperial Hotel, contains stalls selling clothes, craft souvenirs and electronic novelties like computer dictionaries and translating machines. Fun and touristy.

American Pharmacy, ✆ 03 3271 4034, sells US brand-name drugs, cosmetics and magazines. Behind the Yūrakuchō Denki Building, near the American Express offices in Yūrakuchō.

Kiddyland, ✆ 03 3409 3431, on the south side of Omotesandō-dōri, east of Meiji-jingū-mae subway station, is a mind-boggling seven storeys of toys with samples for test-play.

(✆ 03–)   *Where to Stay*

Having spent 13 or more hours in a plane and schlepped your way into town from Narita Airport, the last thing you'll want to worry about is finding somewhere to stay for the night: Tokyo is one place where you'd be well advised to make a booking before you arrive, at least for the first night or two. Reserve especially early for late spring and late autumn. In February thousands of students converge on Tokyo to take university entrance exams, and cheaper accommodation gets booked up. Hotels in Tokyo are expensive: you get less for your money, and in a less convenient position, than anywhere else in the country. Having said that, Tokyo's deluxe hotels are no more expensive than their counterparts all over the world. Standards of service, if a little impersonal, are uniformly high.

Those with business to do and tourists on generous budgets will want to stay in one of the central areas: Ginza, the Tokyo station area, Akasaka or the districts around the palace moat. Shinjuku has fine hotels and is well connected with the rest of the city, but its station is a horror: unless you can afford to take taxis, this will add to your journey times. Shinagawa, on the southern reaches of the Yamanote line, is also a bit out of the way. Visitors on a tighter budget and those whose main interest is sightseeing should consider one of the quieter, older, more outlying areas like Ueno or Asakusa.

Almost every kind of accommodation in Tokyo, even down to the lowliest hostel, will have someone who speaks English.

Numbers refer to map, pp.168–169, which shows hotel locations.

Key for Tokyo Hotels
(*See* listings pp.170–4)

1. Ryokan Asakusa Shigetsu Bekkan
2. Kikuya Ryokan
3. Ryokan Sansuisō
4. Ryokan Sawanoya
5. Imperial Hotel
6. Hotel Ōkura
7. Tokyo Hilton
8. Century Hyatt
9. New Ōtani Hotel
10. Capital Tōkyū
11. Akasaka Tōkyū
12. Ginza Tōkyū Hotel
13. ANA Hotel Tokyo
14. Roppongi Prince
15. Keiō Plaza Intercontinental Hotel
16. Tokyo Station Hotel
17. Yaesu Fujiya Hotel
18. Hotel Kokusai Kankō
19. Ginza Capital Hotel
20. Shinjuku Washington Hotel
21. Fairmont Hotel
22. Shinjuku Park Hotel
23. Asia Centre of Japan
24. YMCA Asia Youth Centre
25. Suigetsu Hotel
26. Kimi Ryokan
27. Tokyo International Youth Hostel
28. Yoyogi Youth Hostel

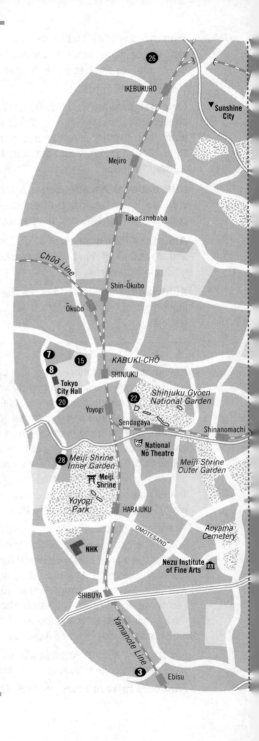

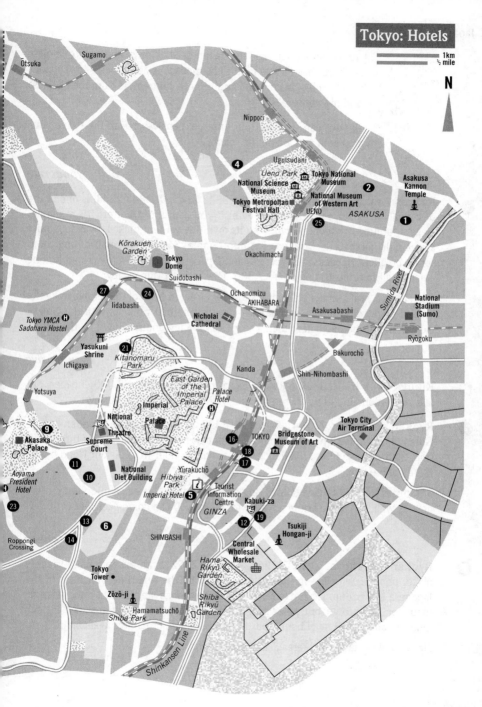

Tokyo: Hotels

1km
½ mile

N

Ōtsuka

Sugamo

Nippori

Uguisudani

④ Ueno Park

National Science Museum

Tokyo National Museum ②

National Museum of Western Art

Tokyo Metropolitan Festival Hall

UENO

Asakusa Kannon Temple ①

ASAKUSA

㉕

Sumida River

Okachimachi

Kōrakuen Garden

Tokyo Dome

Suidobashi

National Stadium (Sumo)

㉗ ㉔ Iidabashi

Ochanomizu

AKIHABARA

Asakusabashi

Ryōgoku

Tokyo YMCA Sadohara Hostel ⑪

Nicholai Cathedral

Yasukuni Shrine

Ichigaya

㉑ Kitanomaru Park

Kanda

Bakurochō

Shin-Nihombashi

Yotsuya

East Garden of the Imperial Palace

Palace Hotel

Imperial Palace

National Theatre

Supreme Court

Tokyo City Air Terminal

⑨ Akasaka Palace

⑪ ⑩ National Diet Building

⑯ TOKYO

⑱

⑰

Bridgestone Museum of Art

Aoyama President Hotel

㉓

Yūrakuchō

Hibiya Park

Imperial Hotel ⑤

Tourist Information Centre

GINZA

Kabuki-za

⑫ ⑲

Tsukiji Hongan-ji

⑬ ⑥

⑭

SHIMBASHI

Central Wholesale Market

Roppongi Crossing

Tokyo Tower ●

Zōzō-ji

Hamamatsuchō

Shiba Park

Hama Rikyū Garden

Shiba Rikyū Garden

Shinkansen Line

169

Japanese-style

Tokyo has disappointingly few Japanese-style inns, and no world-class ones; those that survive tend to be modest establishments in the older districts, full of history and atmosphere, but remote from the business and nightlife areas.

If you plan to splash out on an expensive *ryokan* then save your money until you are out of Tokyo.

moderate

① **Ryokan Asakusa Shigetsu Bekkan,** ✆ 3843 2345, 🖷 3843 2348, is one of the best deals in town, recommended even if you can afford better. It's a simple, elegant, unfussy wooden *ryokan*, with its own tiny garden, tucked away in a quiet street right next to the Asakusa Kannon temple, Sensō-ji. A small dining room serves breakfast (Japanese or Western) and Japanese dinner. A *tatami* room for one person (without meals) begins at ¥7,300. There is an 11pm curfew.

To get there, walk up the Nakamise shopping street in front of the temple; take the second road from the end on the left—not the one that runs beneath the wall of Denbō-in, but the one before that. The *ryokan* is a few metres down on the left.

inexpensive

② **Kikuya Ryokan,** ✆ 3841 6404/4051, also in Asakusa, is ¥2,000 cheaper, but less convenient and in a concrete building. There is a midnight curfew.

③ **Ryokan Sansuisō,** ✆ 3441 7475, 🖷 3499 1944, is a plain wooden inn in Gotanda, an unusual place for tourists, although not inconvenient: it's three stops from Shibuya, five from Shinjuku, and only half an hour from distant Ueno by the JR Yamanote line.

5 minutes from Gotanda station; ring for directions. There is a midnight curfew here as well, but if you ask in advance for a key, you can come back later.

cheap

④ **Ryokan Sawanoya,** ✆ 3822 2251, 🖷 3822 2252, is an exceptionally friendly place, popular with foreign tourists, and run by the one-time president of the Japanese Inn Group. It's in Nezu, an old *shitamachi* district near Ueno, inconvenient for downtown but possessing its own eccentric attractions like a clock museum and an old neighbourhood shrine (free guide brochures available).

Nezu subway station is nearest; ring for directions.

Western

luxury

5 The **Imperial**, ✆ 3504 1111, opposite Hibiya Park, is the city's most famous and historic hotel, although it's lost a lot of its atmosphere since the old Frank Lloyd Wright building (which survived the Great Earthquake) was replaced by a predictable shiny edifice in 1968. The Imperial Suite must be the single most expensive room in Japan: ¥800,000.

6 **Hotel Ōkura**, ✆ 3582 0111, 🖷 3582 3707, south of the Imperial Palace, is the most prestigious Tokyo hotel, the address to impress, the place for top-level business, receptions and the swankiest weddings.
The nearest subway station is Toranomon, but if you can afford to stay here then you can afford to take a taxi.

expensive

7 8 The **Tokyo Hilton**, ✆ 3344 5111, 🖷 3342 6094, and the **Century Hyatt**, ✆ 3349 0111, 🖷 3344 5575, are both grand, meticulous, and slightly cheaper than the above, but lose out in terms of convenience by their position in Shinjuku (unless that is where you want to be).

9 The **New Ōtani Hotel**, ✆ 3265 1111, 🖷 3221 2619, near the Akasaka Palace (Nagatachō subway station), is one of Tokyo's biggest, the venue for top level international conferences. It has beautiful gardens.

The Tōkyū chain has three fine hotels in central Tokyo. In descending order of expense:

10 The flagship **Capitol Tōkyū Hotel**, ✆ 3581 4511, 🖷 3581 5822, is close by Kokkai-gijidō-mae subway station, between the Hie Shrine and the Diet Building. It has a plush atmosphere, very comfortable rooms and excellent secretarial and translation facilities.

11 A few hundred metres away is its little brother, the **Akasaka Tōkyū**, ✆ 3580 2311, 🖷 3580 6066, on top of Akasaka Mitsuke subway station, another glamorous city hotel with its own arcade of élite shops.

12 On the other side of town, just round the corner from the Kabuki-za theatre and Higashi Ginza subway station, is the refurbished **Ginza Tōkyū Hotel**, ✆ 3541 2411, 🖷 3541 6622, an elegantly glitzy hotel in a useful position.

13 **ANA Hotel Tokyo**, ✆ 3505 1111, 🖷 3505 1155, is in Ark Hills, a huge gleaming agglomeration of apartments, offices and a concert hall, just east of Roppongi.

(14) More convenient for the dedicated nightlife animal is the **Roppongi Prince**, ✆ 3587 1111, a bizarre creation built by the architect Kurokawa Kishō around a central swimming pool with transparent sides like a goldfish bowl. From the poolside area you can see the door of everyone's room; even the lifts are glass. A voyeur's dream, low on privacy, but high on humour, favoured by visiting rock bands who appreciate its proximity to the bright lights, and its stern ways with trespassing groupies and autograph hunters.

(15) **Keiō Plaza Intercontinental Hotel**, ✆ 3344 0111, ⌨ 3343 8269, was Shinjuku's first skyscraper, and purveys all the usual comforts, with fine views of Tange Kenzō's splendid City Hall opposite.

moderate

(16) The **Tokyo Station Hotel**, ✆ 3231 2511, ⌨ 3231 3513, is as convenient as its name suggests and, if the rooms are nothing special, it does have atmospheric bars overlooking Marunouchi, and is housed inside the old Meiji-period station building.

(17) The **Yaesu Fujiya Hotel**, ✆ 3273 2111, ⌨ 3723 2180, is at the other (east) side of Tokyo station, past the Yaesu Book Centre: an efficient, modern business hotel.

(18) The **Hotel Kokusai Kankō**, ✆ 3215 3281, ⌨ 3215 1140, is a similarly workman-like place, on the same side, nearer the station.

(19) **Ginza Capital Hotel**, ✆ 3543 8211, ⌨ 3543 8211, is a business hotel with a nearby annex, and small cheap rooms, near Tsukiji or Shintōmichō subway stations.

(20) **Shinjuku Washington Hotel**, ✆ 3343 3111, ⌨ 3340 1804, 8 minutes' walk from Shinjuku station, has a dehumanizing façade—hundreds of equally-spaced, identical portholes—but the rates are good, the restaurants numerous and the service warm.

(21) The **Fairmont Hotel**, ✆ 3262 1151, ⌨3264 2476, near Chidorigafuchi Park on the northwest bank of the Imperial Palace moat, has one of the loveliest settings in Tokyo, especially during the cherry blossom season.

inexpensive

(22) **Shinjuku Park Hotel**, ✆ 3356 0241, ⌨ 3352 2733, is a very good deal at the top end of *inexpensive* (verging on *moderate*). It is a cosy city hotel, south of Shinjuku station, overlooking Shinjuku Gyōen park.

(23) **Asia Centre of Japan**, ✆ 3402 6111, ⌨ 3402 0738, is a plain, clean business hotel near Nogizaka and Aoyama Itchōme subway stations.

(24) **YMCA Asia Youth Centre**, ✆ 3233 0631, ⌨ 3233 0633, near Jinbōchō and Suidōbashi subway stations, takes both sexes and has a 1am curfew.

(25) **Suigetsu Hotel,** ✆ 3822 4611, 📧 3823 4340, close to Nezu subway station or 15 minutes from Ueno JR station on the west side of the park (near Ueno Zoo) is a foreigner-friendly hotel, with attached *ryokan*, near old Ueno.

cheap

(26) **Kimi Ryokan,** ✆ 3971 3766, is Tokyo's best backpackers' hang out, with a famous notice board of news about jobs and travel; it's well worth consulting even if you don't actually stay here.

Tokyo has two principal youth hostels, both of which get booked up and have a (loosely enforced) three night maximum per guest:

(27) **Tokyo International Youth Hostel,** ✆ 3235 1107, is near Iidabashi station.

(28) **Yoyogi Youth Hostel,** ✆ 3467 9163, is the part of the old Olympic Village near Sangūbashi station. Guests e are expected to be International YHA members.

Gaijin Houses

Occupying the lowest step of the accommodation ladder is the Tokyo *gaijin* house, so called because no Japanese would be so unhygienic as to live there. The best of them offer extremely cheap accommodation (usually by the week or month, rather than the day) and a friendly, communal life with self-catering kitchen facilities. The worst are prodigies of squalor and inconvenience (some of the horror stories you hear—dishes unwashed for a year, dead monkeys in the bathroom—are exaggerations, but *some* are true). Most are just cheap and messy. While many people are grateful for them for a short while, no one is ever sorry to leave.

The following looked all right at the time, but no promises. A fuller list can be had from the tourist information centre. Remember that *gaijin* houses generally cater for long-term visitors to Tokyo, renting by the week or month. Daily terms may not be available at all and the best (i.e. least vile) often have waiting lists.

Marui House, ✆ 5952 1090, is at least close to a major Yamanote line station (Ikebukuro).

Tokyo House, ✆ 3391 8808, is also in Ikeburo, but further from the station.

Taihei House, ✆ 3940 4705, is 5 minutes from Komasoma station on the Yamanote Line.

Love Hotels

Friday and Saturday nights are the busiest for love hotels when rates double and rooms book out. At other times, they are a rather economical—if bizarre—form of one-off accommodation, as long as you don't mind a late check-in and early check-out. Rooms are rented by the hour during the day and evening, but from about 10pm nightly rates apply. These are generally no more than the cost of a single room in a business hotel, with the advantage that you pay by the room, not per person. In theory, the whole family could bed down in a room costing ¥10,000.

Love hotels are identifiable by their gaudy neon signs, opaque windows and discreet entrances screened from full view of the street. Once you can recognize them, you'll start spotting them everywhere, especially in quiet back streets near major stations and nightlife areas. Shinjuku's Kabukichō has a large number, as you'd expect; Dōgenzaka, near Shibuya, has an extraordinary love hotel village set back from the road. For straightforward budget accommodation, you'll want the plainest and cheapest possible. Couples with something more adventurous in mind might want to visit one of the many 'themed' love hotels, including the following:

Rosa Rossa, in Dōgenzaka, features boudoirs in the style of a 19th-century French brothel.

In **P&A Plaza**, ℂ 3780 5211, also in Dōgenzaka, the top rooms contain miniature swimming pools with transparent walls.

Hotel Alpha Inn, ℂ 3583 3655, in Higashi Azabu, caters for athletes of a different inclination: 26 S&M zones fully equipped with riding horses, uniforms and a fearsome collection of whips and leather goods.

Hotel Japan, ℂ 3461 1303, in the Maruyamachō district of Shibuya, has rooms with tanning beds, karaoke machines, and built-in ceiling planetariums.

(ℂ 03–) **Eating Out**

Tokyo is rich in good restaurants and dining out is one of the city's great pleasures, for the huge number of foreign and ethnic restaurants, as well as native dishes. The key word in contemporary Japanese cooking is *mukokuseki* (meaning 'no nationality' or 'eclectic') and refers to the interesting twists which Japanese-born, foreign-trained chefs give to imported recipes. Like cars, buildings and fashion, European and Asian-style food in Tokyo rarely turns out to be quite the same as the model which inspired it.

Most of the establishments classed here as *expensive* and *moderate* are one-offs for holiday treats and special occasions; excluded are the numberless chain restaurants and anonymous local noodle bars and *yakitori* shops which provide thoroughly decent, modest nourishment at much cheaper prices. Remember that even the flashiest restaurants usually do inexpensive lunchtime sets for a fraction of their evening tariffs (on which the following listings are based). To save money, treat lunch as the main meal of the day, and fill up on something cheaper and simpler in the evening.

Tokyo Classified has good restaurant reviews. Rick Kennedy's book, *Good Tokyo Restaurants* (Kodansha International), lives up to its title.

Japanese

 Botan, ✆ 3251 0577, in Kanda, between the Transport Museum and Awajichō or Ogawamachi subway stations, was founded a century ago by a man who once worked in a button factory, hence its name. It's a simple, comfortably old-fashioned place specializing in chicken *nabe* (stew) cooked at the table on a charcoal brazier.

Fukuzushi, ✆ 3402 4116, is behind the Roppongi Roi Building: from Roppongi subway station, take the main road to the left of Almond, it's a few minutes' walk on the right. This is a flamboyant and trendy *sushi* restaurant in a tiny bamboo garden which stays open until 11pm.

Jiro, ✆ 3535 3600, in the basement of the office opposite the Sony Building in Ginza, has the most expensive, meticulously prepared and highly praised *sushi* in Tokyo.

Kakiden, ✆ 3352 5121, is just south of My City, the department store on top of Shinjuku station. It is an elegant, innovative restaurant serving *kaiseki*, the delicate, bitty *haute cuisine* of Kyoto. Moderately priced menus are also available.

Yama no Chaya, ✆ 3581 0656, by the Hie Shrine, Akasaka-Mitsuke subway station, is a simple, exquisite and extremely pricey (well over £100 a head) teahouse restaurant serving a delicate sea food course based around *unagi* (eel).

Yūsan, ✆ 3237 8363, is north of Yama no Chaya, a relaxed and unstuffy *kaiseki* restaurant, near the Akasaka Prince Hotel.

Soul, ✆ 5466 1877, in Aoyama, is a *mukokuseki* ('no nationality') restaurant in which the Japanese influence still remains strong: Chinese, Cambodian and Korean dishes, light but fiery, plus native dishes like fried noodles.

Robata, ✆ 3591 1905, below the railway tracks, just south of the tourist information centre in Yūrakuchō, serves superb farmhouse cooking in an atmospherically dingy wooden building, frequented by poets and other bohemians.

Tomoegata, ✆ 3631 6729, specializes in *chanko nabe*, the high-protein wonder food which makes sumo wrestlers look the way they do. It's two blocks south of Ryōgoku in the heart of *shitamachi*, not far from the National Sumo Stadium.

Kaotan Ramen, ✆ 3475 6337, on the right, coming down the Aoyama Cemetery hill from Nogizaka subway station, is a deliriously popular *ramen* shack which is open until 5am.

Komagata Dojō, ✆ 3842 4001, is on the west side of Edo-dōri avenue, three blocks south of Asakusa station on the Asakusa line. It is an old Edo-style restaurant specializing in *dojō* (loach), stewed (*dojō nabe*) or in an omelette (*yanagawa*).

Kujiraya, ✆ 3461 9145, on Shibuya's Tōkyū Honten-dōri, just past the 109 Building, is the more famous, more conveniently positioned, but less interesting of Tokyo's two whale restaurants. Dishes like *kujira sukiyaki* are in the *moderate* price category, but there are cheaper sets, especially at lunchtime.

Maisen, ✆ 3470 0071, near Omotesandō subway station (ring for precise directions), is a big, bustling restaurant devoted to *tonkatsu*, crispy battered pork cutlets, with a variety of accompaniments.

Nanaki, ✆ 3496 2878, third on the right from the overhead tracks as you walk west from Ebisu JR station, is an esteemed, but very affordable, shack serving *soba* (buckwheat) noodles.

Negishi, ✆ 3232 8020, northwest of the cinema-filled square in Shinjuku's Kabukichō, near the tracks of the Seibu Shinjuku line, is a cheap and cheerful diner serving beef and vegetable stew.

Sweet Paozu, ✆ 3295 4084, on Suzuran-dōri, parallel and to the south of Yasukuni-dōri, in the heart of the Jinbōchō book selling district, is an authentic Chinese *gyōza* (dumpling) shop, more than 60 years old and utterly without frills. It closes at 8pm.

Taruichi, ✆ 3208 9772/3, is one of Tokyo's two *kujira* (whale) restaurants, and the more lively by far. The menu consists of a cross-sectional diagram of a whale with arrows pointing to the various different cuts which range from whale steak (the most expensive, almost like rich beef) to whale penis (the cheapest, served in thin slices, very chewy). The cheerful proprietor, Mr Sato Takashi, is a whale-meat evangelist, and a passionate believer in the humanitarian benefits of killing and eating as many whales as possible. The minke whales swim around in a tank at the front of the restaurant—you decide which one you want, and harpoon your own (only joking). Taruichi is near Shinjuku station, but takes a little finding. From the central east exit, walk out into the plaza so you are facing the giant video screen of Studio Alta. Take the road just to the left of here, and continue down it across the next main road, Yasukuni-dōri, between a games arcade on the left and the Daiwa bank on the right. The restaurant is on the 5th floor of a rather dingy building a few metres down on the left.

Yabu Soba, ✆ 3251 0287, is in Kanda between the Transportation Museum and the Tokyo Green Hotel Awajichō (Awajichō or Ogawamachi subway stations). It is the mother restaurant of another famous Tokyo chain, this time specializing in *soba* noodles served in a traditional atmosphere.

Sushi Tochigi-ya, ✆ 3291 9426, a minute from Ochanomizu station, serves dirt cheap *sushi* until 1am.

expensive

Nobu, ✆ 5467 0022, is located on Roppongi-dōri about halfway between the JR Shibuya station and Roppongi subway station. Internationally acclaimed chief Nobu Matsuhisa has opened up a Tokyo branch of his successful partnership with Robert De Niro. The cuisine is decidedly Japanese, but spiced up with eclectic influences from France to Peru. Highly recommended is the *omakase*, or chef's selection (dinner from *¥10,000*; lunch from *¥6,000*), which changes every day depending on the chef's mood and ingredients.

1066, ✆ 3719 9059, is tucked away near Meguro station on the Yamanote Line (ring for precise directions). It is a British restaurant with roasts, puddings, dozens of British ales, and live folk music on the first and third Wednesday of each month.

L'Orangerie de Paris, ✆ 3407 7461, in the striking Hanae Mori building near Omotesandō station, is one of Tokyo's best French restaurants—and in a great position on Omotesandō-dōri, the closest Tokyo has to a continental boulevard.

moderate

Aux Bacchanales, ✆ 5474 0076, located just down the crowded Takeshita-dōri from Harajuku station, is an excellent place to cap off a day of traipsing about the area. There are two sections; the larger is a sidewalk café serving light brasserie-type food, while the other more discrete section is a French restaurant serving good traditional French food (*expensive–moderate*). For enthusiasts, there is also '*baby-foot*' (table football) inside.

El Castellano, ✆ 3407 7197, on Aoyama-dori towards Shibuya station, serves superb Spanish food in a congenial atmosphere, presided over by the witty and urbane Mr. Vicente Garcia.

Granata, ✆ 3582 3241, next to TBS TV, north of Akasaka subway station, is a popular, informal Italian restaurant with its own built-in pavement café.

Angkor Wat, ✆ 3370 3019, is a bit off the beaten track (between Yoyogi and Minami-Shinjuku stations), but serves sweet, spicy Cambodian dishes in a noisy, fast-moving atmosphere.

Ban-Thai, ✆ 3207 0068, in the Dai-ichi Metro Building, next to the Shinjuku Prince Hotel, in the southwest corner of Kabukichō, is one of Tokyo's oldest and most popular Thai restaurants; reservations are recommended.

Brasserie Bernard, ✆ 3405 7877, is next to the Ibis Hotel on Gaien-Higashi-dōri, the road that leads north opposite Almond coffee shop near Roppongi subway station: an unpretentious French restaurant serving beefy stews, black puddings etc. in a hearty provincial style.

Las Chicas, ✆ 3407 6865, at the end of a sidestreet west of the Kinokuniya supermarket (Omotesandō subway station), is the best outdoor café in Tokyo, with an eclectic European menu, and good *café au lait* in French-style bowls. There is more formal, expensive food inside, as well as a bar, art gallery and hair salon.

Mugyodon, ✆ 3586 6478, is a few minutes south of Akasaka subway station. It serves unglamorous but wholesome Korean food (hotter and more garlicky than Japanese) in an otherwise forbiddingly expensive part of town.

inexpensive

The most atmospheric cheap food in Tokyo is to be had in the nameless, phone-less, unreservable *yakitori* stands under the railway tracks just south of the tourist information centre in Yūrakuchō. Service is fast and noisy, tables and chairs are tin and wobbly, and if they ask you to shove up and make room for another party, there's no arguing. Still, as the smoke wafts off the grills, and the trains rattle over-head, it's irresistible: a flavour of Tokyo during the 1950s.

Le Mange-Tout, ✆ 3268 5911, nearest stations Kagurazaka or Ichigaya, though neither are particularly near (ring for directions), is a Tokyo secret that's becoming increasingly well known: a studenty and very *inexpensive* French restaurant serving good portions.

Johnnie Rockets, ✆ 3423 1955, is generally regarded as the best burger in town. Two pieces of advice, however: 1) don't expect too much from Japan's best burger; 2)don't bother working out how much Japan's best burger is costing you. Located on the southeast corner of Roppongi crossing opposite the Almond Café.

Bindi, ✆ 3409 7114, in Nishi Azabu, on an alley off Roppongi-dōri, opposite the Fuji Film building, is a trendy but informal Indian.

Chao! Bamboo, ✆ 5466 4787, is on the alley behind Café de Ropé on the west side of Omotesandō-dōri, near Harajuku, and serves cheap, eclectic southeast Asian dishes at open-air tables.

Ganga Palace, ✆ 3796 4477, off Gaien-Higashi-dōri, between Nogizaka and Roppongi subway stations, is dramatically decorated (fountains, columns) and moderately expensive if you pile on the dishes, but substantial Indian curries can be had for under ¥2,000. When the food stops at 11pm, the place turns into a trendy bar, open until 5am.

Ichioku, ✆ 3405 9891, near the Defence Agency (Bōeichō), Roppongi subway station, is a classic *mukokuseki* ('no nationality') restaurant, although the attributed influence is Balinese. The *gyōza* (traditional Chinese and Japanese meat dumplings) filled with mozzarella are celebrated.

Ninnikuya, ✆ 3446 5887 (call for directions from Ebisu station on the JR Yamanote and Hibiya subway lines), is another original, a restaurant whose menu is based entirely around garlic (the name means 'Garlic Shop'); it gets very busy and bookings are recommended.

Pas à Pas, ✆ 3357 7888, is on a sidestreet to the east of the main road between Yotsuya san-chōme and Akebonobashi subway stations. It is a simple, cosy, tiny French restaurant, the best value of its kind in town.

Tompo, ✆ 3405 9944, just off Meiji-dōri, east of Harajuku station, specializes in cheap Chinese stir-fry.

Zuien Bekkan, ✆ 3351 3511, on Shinjuku-dōri, a couple of blocks east of Shinjuku-gyōenmae subway station, is another cheap, rowdy Chinese place: snapping turtle soup, sea slug in soy sauce, and the usual staples.

cheap

When maximum bulk at minimum cost is your priority, try the following:

Shakey's Pizza has branches in Harajuku, Shibuya, Ikebukuro, Shinjuku, Ginza and various lesser places where, between 11am and 2pm (except Sun), you can eat as much pizza, potatoes and spaghetti as you like for next to nothing.

Takeya, ✆ 3836 3679, on the 6th floor of the Beklitas Building, a minute from the Shinobazu exit of Ueno station, has a similar deal for *shabu-shabu* and *sukiyaki* (plus extras). Men ¥2,200, women ¥1,980.

Tokaien, ✆ 3200 2924, is 3 minutes from Shinjuku station east exit. It is a Korean barbecue restaurant with an all-you-can-eat-type menu: for ¥950, you can have 15 dishes; for ¥2,250 you can have 40 dishes.

Branches of **MacDonalds**, **Kentucky Fried Chicken** and **Subway Sandwich** can be found all over Tokyo.

Nightlife

After-dark fashions in Tokyo change by the week, so the publishers take no responsibility for social embarrassment suffered by anyone using the following guide—for up-to-date fashion victimology, consult *Tokyo Classified* or ask on the street. To dispense with confusing directions, phone numbers only are given for the more obscurely located places—most of them should have someone who speaks English.

Roppongi

During office hours, Roppongi crossing is an untidy crevasse of record shops, cheap cafés and fast food joints, pervaded by the migraine hum of the overhead expressway. But when the lights come on, above all at weekends, it's transformed into a neon carnival, the traditional party place of Tokyo's expatriate tribes. Icy European models, bullet-headed marines, Brazilian cocktail waiters, beer-chugging city bankers, Israeli street traders and Iranian bricklayers swarm the all-night bars, restaurants and clubs, along with the ubiquitous blue-suited 'salarymen' and armies of Japanese girls in ferociously slinky, 'body-conscious' dresses. The diversity of the mix means that, however hard it tries, Roppongi is still nothing like Paris or L.A. But foreign influence definitely shows in the design of its bars and restaurants: compared to the more traditional entertainment districts, there are plenty of places on ground level with big windows that allow you to form some idea of what's inside before blundering in. Roppongi is open, tolerant and accessible and, wherever you end up, you will never be far from an English menu.

Almond, a nasty pink coffee shop on the southwest corner of Roppongi crossing, is Tokyo's second most famous meeting place, after Shibuya's Hachikō. Nightlife is mostly concentrated in the streets behind it, to the south.

Gas Panic, ✆ 3405 0633, and **Gas Panic Club**, ✆ 3402 7054, are the archetypal hang-outs of young *gaijin*, with a grungy and unpredictable adolescent atmosphere. For a more mature (some would say staid) atmosphere, try the **Lexington Queen**, ✆ 3401 1661, a Tokyo institution, the first stop for visiting showbiz royalty (preferential treatment given to models).

Immediately to the left of Almond as you face it, a busy road leads towards Tokyo Tower. Two hundred metres down it, on the right, is the **Roi Building** (pronounced 'Roa'), another useful rendezvous point. Just before it, a road leads right to a cluster of American restaurants: **Spago's**, **Tony Roma's** and the ubiquitous **Hard Rock Café**.

The nearby **Charleston** is an inexpensive bar restaurant serving pizza and snacks at open air tables. Next door is **Salsa Cariba**, an unpretentious Latin American bar, full of real Latin Americans. Signs forbid dancing; everyone ignores them.

Café Mogambo, ✆ 3403 4833, is a friendly African bar.

Salsa Sudada, ✆ 3405 1967, has Latin music.

Nishi-Azabu

A 15-minute walk from the nearest subway station, Nishi-Azabu is isolated enough to avoid the worst of the Roppongi crowds.

Hobson's, a blue and yellow ice cream parlour on the southwest corner of Nishi-Azabu crossing is the rendezvous.

Acaraje, ✆ 3401 0973, is a Brazilian bar serving powerful cocktails.

Club Jamaica, ✆ 3407 8844, is a self-consciously cool reggae bar.

Shibuya and Omotesandō

The multi-storey buildings around Shibuya station are a honeycomb of restaurants, bars and clubs catering for Japanese students. Omotesandō has more sophisticated, cosmopolitan clubs.

Bar Dark Side, ✆ 3476 2193, is a sleek, matt black cocktail bar on the 5th floor of the Brither Building, a few minutes' walk from Shibuya station.

DJ Bar Inkstick, ✆ 3496 0782, is an elegant, well-established music venue formerly in Roppongi.

Blue Note Tokyo, ✆ 5485 0088, *www.bluenote.co.jp*, is an offshoot of the famous New York jazz club with world class visiting acts. Consult *Tokyo Journal* for the current programme.

Maniac Love, ✆ 3406 1166, is located on a side street off Aoyama-dori, and has a terrific sound system, and the best DJ's.

Club Quattro, ✆ 3477 8750, in Shibuya, is the place to catch more cutting edge rock acts, and indie pop.

Shinjuku

Kabukichō is the sex capital of Tokyo with some of the most eye-popping shows, bars and theatres in Asia, but there is plenty of good entertainment of a conventional nature. Shinjuku ni-chōme is famous as the stomping ground of the *okama-san*—Tokyo's transsexuals and transvestites.

DX Kabukichō, ✆ 3232 9946 (only Japanese spoken), has a commercialized live sex show well used to gawping foreigners. Look out for the discount coupons in free English language papers like the *Tour Companion*.

Performance

Tokyo is a popular and lucrative stop for theatre companies from all over the world—avant-garde experimentalists, as well as Andrew Lloyd Webber—but the following list focuses on uniquely Japanese forms. *Tokyo Journal* and English-language papers like *The Japan Times* contain comprehensive monthly listings of drama (Western and Japanese), dance, ballet, opera and musicals.

The Ticket Pia booking agency has an English-language line, ✆ 5237 9999.

National Theatre (Kokuritsu Gekijō), ✆ 3265 7411, features alternating programmes of *bunraku* and *kabuki*, with English programmes and earphone commentaries. Nagatachō and Kojimachi subway stations.

Takarazuka Theatre, ✆ 5251 2001, near the Imperial Hotel and Hibiya subway station, is usually the home of the Takarazuka girls, a unique and extraordinary Japanese phenomenon. Young women, intensively trained for years at a special school, play male and female roles in achingly sentimental pastiches of Hollywood musicals. The building, however, is being renovated and the troupe are based (until January 2001) in the 1000 Days Theatre, just on the other side of the railway tracks from the Tourist Information Centre.

Kabuki-za, ✆ 3541 3131, the bristling 'Japanese Gothic' palace on the edge of Ginza, is the best place to sample traditional Japanese theatre. The programmes have English plot summaries, and earphone receivers with a simultaneous English commentary can be hired. A full *kabuki* programme lasts most of the day, but at Kabuki-za, you can pay to see just one act, from ¥2,500. The nearest subway station is Higashi Ginza.

National Nō Theatre (Kokuritsu Nōgakudō), ✆ 3423 1331, is a beautiful theatre near Sendagaya station. Check the press for performance times.

Kanze Nō Theatre (Kanze Nōgakudō), ✆ 3469 5241, is near Shibuya JR station.

Tessenkai Nō Institute, ✆ 3401 2285, is a fashionable theatre in a modern concrete building, popular with a young audience. It is near Omotesandō station.

Kyoto

Kyoto is one of the most beguiling ancient capitals in the world, but it is a beautiful city rather than a splendid one, and its charm takes some adjusting to. Here are no etched skylines, broad boulevards or monumental architecture. Kyoto's marvels are quiet and interior. The important things, like much else in Japan, are on the inside, hidden from public view: temples, shrines, palaces, villas, treasure houses, gardens. They are the finest of their kind anywhere. For anyone remotely interested in Japan's visual art and architecture, this is the place to start. The complaint that 'temples all look the same' doesn't stand up; the lesson of a few well-spent days in Kyoto is what contrasts of mood, style and setting Japanese art affords.

In 1994 Kyoto celebrated its 1200th birthday. For a good ten of those centuries visitors have been shaking their heads and promising one another that it wouldn't be there for much longer. The Japanese idea of *mono no aware*, nostalgia for the transience of things, was born in Kyoto and has flourished here ever since. It was invented by the courtiers of Heian-kyō (Capital of Peace and Tranquillity), as the city was originally called, and finds its fullest expression in *The Tale of Genji*, but the sentiment lives on in every contemporary discussion of the city, especially among foreigners. You should have seen it before the economic boom! You should have been there in the Occupation! You would have loved it before the War! In Kyoto it is axiomatic that Things Aren't What They Used To Be.

Don't be fooled. Things never have been what they used to be. They never will be. The image of a once perfect, now sullied Kyoto is a myth. Compared to the violence and unpredictability of earlier eras, the 20th century has been good to the city; there are better reasons than usual for believing in its survival for another 1200 years.

In the 10th century, priests and aristocrats got into quite a lather about the supposed imminence of *Mappō*, the End of the Law, a long period of decline and decadence which would culminate in the Buddhist Apocalypse. For decades it seemed as if they might be right, especially in the 15th century when feuding nobles torched the city during the Ōnin Wars. But Kyoto rebuilt itself, and came relatively unscathed through political reorganization under the Tokugawa shoguns and the transfer of *de facto* government to Edo (Tokyo). The next crisis was in the late 19th century when the Emperor moved out too, and when industry and Westernization were drastically altering the look of urban Japan. But the changes were absorbed and quickly became inseparable from the city's charm: when the streetcar system was torn up in the 1970s it was mourned by the same people whose grandparents fought so bitterly against its introduction 80 years before. It's a city that inspires deep love and loyalty: Kyoto's most recent brush with destiny came during the Pacific War when, against all logic, it was spared the incendiary bombs which devastated every other large Japanese city. The story goes that a Japan-educated art historian, Langdon Warner, talked the US War Secretary out of including it on the shortlist of targets for the atom bomb.

The newest threat is not war or apocalypse but development. In 1894 Kyoto celebrated its 1100th anniversary with the unveiling of the bold Heian Shrine. The 1200th birthday was marked in very different style: with the construction of the colossal new Kyoto Hotel and a thunderous new station development, both far exceeding previous height restrictions of 30m. Protesters foresee a nightmare escalation of skyrise construction which will overshadow the temples and block out forever Kyoto's mountain panorama. The city, they fear, will never be the same again.

History

From its foundation until the early 17th century, when **Shogun Tokugawa Ieyasu** moved the seat of administrative power to Edo, the history of Kyoto was the history of Japan (*see* pp.59–60). Political power might be bandied between emperors, courtiers and regents, wars and natural disasters might drive them from the city from time to time, but it was always Kyoto to which they returned. The Minamoto family tried to escape in 1185 by establishing their military headquarters (the *bakufu*, 'camp office') in the coastal town of Kamakura and appointing governors to keep a beady eye on Kyoto and its imperial occupants. It didn't work and, in the 1330s, the Kamakura rulers were toppled by a clever emperor whose schemes had been allowed to develop unchecked. Their successors, the Ashikaga shoguns, adored Kyoto and maintained its position as capital when it was burning about their ears. Always, power hovered over the Emperor's city, even if it rarely rested in one place for very long.

Kyoto's dominance of Japanese history is all the more remarkable when one remembers that, until 794, no capital had lasted for more than 75 years. In 784 Nara was abandoned by **Emperor Kammu** in an effort to escape the big Buddhist monasteries which had become greedy for a slice of power. A new palace was established at Nagaoka-kyō, a few miles southwest of present-day Kyoto, but the place gave everyone the creeps. There were murders and portents and court intrigues, and within a few years Kammu was scouting around for somewhere else to pitch his palace.

The choice of an auspicious site was a complicated business, made according to the strict rules of Sino-Japanese geomancy. *Feng shui*, as it's called in Chinese, conceives of the world as a system of energy flows uniting humans and nature, the animate and the inanimate. Any potential interruption of these 'dragon lines'—from a city, to an individual house or even a marriage bed—has to conform to their flow or risk misfortune to the place and its occupants. Kyoto's splendid position, like Nara before it (and like their common ancestor, the mighty capital of Tang China, Chang-an), is no accident.

The principles behind the city's location are best appreciated from perches like **Mt Hiei** or the platform of **Kiyomizu Temple**. It sits on a plain, sloping south towards Ōsaka and the sea, and bordered to the north, east and west by mountains—the back and arm-rests of a great geographical armchair supporting and protecting the emperor and his people. A river, the **Kamogawa**, flows south and west, and a mountain, Mt Hiei, deflects the evil forces which were believed to emanate from the northeast.

Internally, too, the new city followed Chinese models. Like Buddhist temples, it was constructed on a north–south axis. Just as the stars in the night sky revolve around Polaris, the great north star, so life in Heian-kyō (as Kyoto was then known) revolved around the Emperor's palace compound (*daidairi*) in the centre of the northern city. The streets were arranged in a five-by-four kilometre grid of intersecting avenues; one of these (on the site of the present day Senbon-dōri) was 85m wide and ran from the main gate in the south to the palace, dividing the city into an east and west district. Placed symmetrically on either side of this street were an east and a west market, east and west reception halls for visiting dignitaries and two temples which flanked the main southern gate.

The city has sprawled far beyond these limits, and the size and position of many of Heian-kyō's avenues and institutions have changed. But one of the attractions of Kyoto is how precisely the ancient avenues still frame the most modern developments. **Tō-ji**, the temple of the eastern district, survives on its original site today, and its reconstructed halls house statues carved during the lifetime of Emperor Kammu's son. The **Imperial Palace** has moved its position, but traces still remain of the great Heian pond garden which filled its southern stretches. Even when changes have been forced on Kyoto they have been made with the symbolism of its history firmly in mind. When the Tokugawas built **Nijō Castle** as a symbol of their power in Kyoto, they relished the fact that it had once been the site of a Fujiwara lord's villa, and before that the palace of Kammu himself.

Like Nara before it, Kyoto broke out of its neat frame and began to crawl east over the Kamo River. Communities naturally developed around temples, and these tended to cluster in the foothills at the edge of the city, especially **Higashiyama**, the Eastern Mountain. The western part of the city, prone in any case to flooding and poor drainage, atrophied and died. These days, the area west of Senbon-dōri is a dreary industrial zone with virtually no sites of cultural interest; before the Pacific War large parts of it were uninhabited marshland.

The grid pattern, though it survived, quickly became blurred about the edges. **Fires** made this inevitable: Kyoto was rebuilt virtually from scratch after huge conflagrations in 960 and 1180, and almost no original structures pre-date them. The greatest surviving Heian temple, **Byōdō-in**, is south of the city in Uji. **Kōryū-ji's Kōdō** is probably Kyoto's oldest hall, dating from 1165—**Sanjūsangen-dō** temple was originally constructed the year before but burned and was rebuilt a hundred years later.

Large-scale construction in Kyoto has come in phases, as successive rulers sought to establish their legitimacy. In the 13th century the ruling military class adopted the new Buddhist sect, **Zen**, and temple complexes like Tōfuku-ji and Nanzen-ji were founded, although much wealth and power was concentrated in the camp HQ, Kamakura. The

Ashikaga shoguns brought power back to Kyoto in the 14th century, although the many beautiful temples and gardens created at this time—including Saihō-ji and the Gold and Silver Pavilions—were overshadowed by the civil wars which convulsed Japan during the Muromachi period. The ten years between 1467 and 1477 were the most wretched of Kyoto's history. By the time the Ōnin Wars (*see* **History**, p.58) petered out—due more to sheer exhaustion than outright victory and defeat—200,000 buildings had been destroyed, Kyoto's population had dwindled from half a million to 40,000 and its *raison d'être*, the Emperor, was literally homeless, subsisting on noodle soup and flogging off furniture and even samples of the imperial handwriting. 'Today much of Kyoto lies in ruins', reported Francis Xavier in 1551. 'Many people have told us that it once had 18,000 houses, and it seems to me that this must have been true, to judge from the very large size of the city.'

Around this time, Japan's fortunes began to rise again under the great warlord **Oda Nobunaga** who began the slow job of uniting Japan. Nobunaga's talent, however, was war; the benefits he brought to the country as a whole were often at the expense of its capital. He razed the troublesome monasteries on Mt Hiei, burned the northern part of the city when it withheld its taxes, and only managed to build a Kyoto castle by stealing the heads of carved Buddhas to use as building stones. It was his low-born successor, **Toyotomi Hideyoshi**, who gave Kyoto the attention it deserved and lavished money on the biggest and most concerted restoration of the city in its history.

Hideyoshi's ambition and ebullience gleam through the magnificent structures which rose in the city during the Momoyama ('Peach Mountain') period, named after the hill in southern Kyoto where he built the second of his extravagant palace-castles. Both these structures were dismantled shortly after his death and their gates and halls distributed, piecemeal, to the temples of Kyoto, where they remain today as the most dramatically opulent buildings in the city. Momoyama architecture is recognizably 'Chinese' in appearance, with curved gable roofs and deep eaves sheltering elaborate carved and painted woodwork. Interiors are dimly lit and decorated with gorgeously colourful screen paintings applied to canvases of gold leaf. Later on, the ostentation of Momoyama art was taken to excess in the bristling vulgarity of buildings like the Tokugawa shogun's mausoleum at Nikkō. Under Hideyoshi, in buildings like the audience chambers of **Nishi Hongan-ji** or **Daigo-ji** temples, it struck its perfect note: assertive and confident, bold but never shrill.

Hideyoshi's lively extravagance found expression in other ways. He overturned the exclusive conventions of the tea ceremony by holding a giant tea party lasting ten days, to which all the tea lovers in Japan—*daimyō* (feudal lords) and peasants alike—were invited. Often these artistic diversions served a practical end, like the 52m Buddha (destroyed in an earthquake long ago) which he built in Higashiyama. Like Nobunaga he commandeered the materials of its construction; unlike his predecessor, they were not religious icons, but swords which were confiscated from the peasants and melted down. In 1591 Hideyoshi accomplished what Emperor Kammu had planned but never completed: 23km of city wall, a military necessity since the introduction of firearms by Portuguese sailors. Hideyoshi didn't follow the old plan in every respect though. The new fortification was not rectangular but irregular, reflecting the evolved shape of the contemporary city.

Kyoto didn't die under the Edo-based **Tokugawa shoguns,** but its character changed. The buildings wrought by Hideyoshi were demolished or dispersed by the new dynasty and the walls were left to crumble so that no sign remains of them today. Nijō Castle was the Tokugawas' main contribution to Kyoto's architecture, a lavish but little-used symbol of authority, a snub and veiled threat to the imperial house. Instead of being the centre of the empire, Kyoto became one terminal of the Tōkai-dō, the great arterial highway linking the emperor's capital with the shogun's power base in Edo. Kyoto was under the cultural influence, if not the authority, of the old court aristocracy, who built great melancholy stroll gardens for themselves at Katsura and Shūgaku-in, and dreamed of the halcyon Heian period. Edo, on the other hand, was the home of the warrior, as well as the ascendant merchant class who grew in importance as the population swelled and communications improved. This perceived distinction between the two cities survives today and the contrast—between the fey aristocrats and bonzes of Kyoto and the brusque warriors and rascally merchants of Edo—inspired much of the period's literature and drama.

Merchants thrived in Kyoto too; the richest endowed temples of their own, and financed civil engineering projects to alleviate the flooding of the Kamo River and link Kyoto and Ōsaka by canal. The leisure needs of this newly-moneyed class were provided for by pleasure quarters like the one at **Shimabara,** west of Nishi Hongan-ji temple, which was surrounded by its own wall, a city within a city. Crafts like weaving and ceramics became established too, and are still practised in the Nishijin and Kiyomizu areas respectively.

Commodore Perry always gets the credit for 'opening' up Japan and forcing the Meiji Restoration but, in fact, anti-shogunal feeling had been growing in Kyoto for decades. In the 1780s a samurai called Takayama Hikokuro had symbolically decapitated the statues of three Ashikaga shoguns and dumped them on the bed of the Kamo river. Ashikaga-bashing became a popular way of expressing indirect discontent with the ruling shogunal dynasty, and the plotters of the Restoration gathered their forces around the emboldened emperor. When the shogun was humiliatingly ordered to Kyoto to explain his dithering over Perry to Emperor Kōmei, it was the beginning of the end for the Tokugawas. In 1867 Kōmei's son, Meiji, received the shogun's resignation in the Great Audience Chamber of Nijō Castle. The following year, 1074 years after the city's birth, the Emperor left Kyoto for Edo (now renamed Tokyo) taking with him the status of capital city. Ironically, the triumph of Kyoto's Restoration forces spelt the end of the city's historic role.

Getting There
getting to Kyoto from the airports:

Kyoto is served by Kansai International Airport and Ōsaka Itami Airport. The latter mainly handles domestic flights. An airport limousine bus from Itami will deposit you at Kyoto station in about an hour and costs ¥1,260.

From Kansai International Airport, there are a number of options. The quickest and most comfortable route is the JR Haruka limited express (*tokkyū*) train which takes only 75 minutes from the airport to Kyoto station and costs ¥3,490, but is free if you exchange your Japan Rail Pass voucher before leaving the airport (see p.9).

An ordinary JR train departing from the airport takes about an hour and 40 minutes to reach Kyoto station. There is also an airport bus which takes over two hours and costs ¥2,200.

If you are flying back home from Kansai Airport, it is very important to remember that you must have ¥2,600 for the departure tax, which can only be paid in yen.

arriving by train

Almost everyone coming from Tokyo will arrive by train. The shinkansen takes about 2 hours and 40 minutes, and is free with a JR Rail Pass (¥13,220 otherwise). Unless you are willing to spend some serious time in trains (and some serious time working out connections etc.), the shinkansen is your only rail option. From Ōsaka, the trip by shinkansen takes a mere 16 minutes (and costs ¥1,350 without the rail pass). However, there are cheaper ways to make the trip. The regular JR Tokaido (Sanyo) Line runs from Ōsaka to Kyoto in about 30 minutes if you catch an express train (¥540). If you take the JR train, do not get a train that stops at every station (*kakuekiteisha* or *futsū*) which will significantly increase your travelling time. You can also take one of two cheaper, but slightly more time-consuming, private lines. The Hankyū-Kyoto Line from Umeda station to Kyoto costs ¥390. The Hankyū train does not actually stop at Kyoto station but comes north via Katsura and then traverses Shijō-dōri, stopping at Ōmiya, Karasuma and Kawaramachi. You can also take the Keihan Line from Yodoyabashi station in Ōsaka to one of several stops in Kyoto, including Sanjō (where it connects with the subway), Shijō, Gojō and Shichijō for ¥400. Both the Keihan and the Hankyū Line trains take about 45 minutes if you get express trains.

arriving by bus

There is an overnight bus from Tokyo to Kyoto which costs ¥8,180 and takes eight hours. It is not a comfortable option; do it only if money is a real issue. Not only do you save marginally on the price of your ticket (¥5,000 cheaper then the shinkansen), you save substantially on a night's accommodation.

Orientation

Arriving in Kyoto by train is a shock from which many visitors never recover. This, they have been led to believe, is one of the most elegant cities in the world. When they finally fight their way out of the station they are confronted, not with cherry blossoms and pagodas, but with a concrete plaza of jammed buses surmounted by the wretched Kyoto Tower, the stupidest civic monument in Japan. It doesn't even have the teeming ant-like quality of Tokyo's sub-cities. It looks like what it is—an abject failure of city planning, a monument to petty cost-cutting and short-termism. At least nothing of particular value has been sacrificed to produce this mess—the southern quarter of the old capital was always one of its least savoury. But it does make one thing essential: get away from the station as soon as possible. Check into your *ryokan* or hotel, then escape quickly to a big temple or garden (**Kiyomizu** is ideal—*see* p.219).

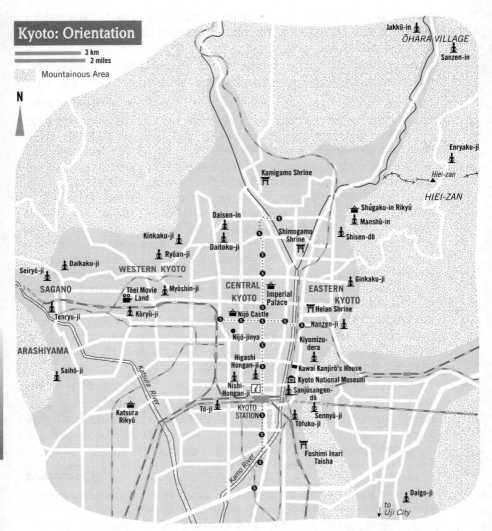

Kyoto: Orientation

3 km
2 miles

Mountainous Area

N

JakkŌ-in
ŌHARA VILLAGE
Sanzen-in

Enryaku-ji

Kamigamo Shrine

Hiei-zan

HIEI-ZAN

Daisen-in

Shūgaku-in Rikyū

Manshū-in

Kinkaku-ji

Shimogamo
Shrine

Shisen-dō

Daitoku-ji

Ryōan-ji

Daikaku-ji

WESTERN KYOTO

Seiryō-ji

SAGANO

Tōei Movie
Land

Myōshin-ji

CENTRAL
KYOTO

Imperial
Palace

EASTERN
KYOTO

Ginkaku-ji

Heian Shrine

Tenryu-ji

Kōryū-ji

Nijō Castle

Nanzen-ji

ARASHIYAMA

Nijō-jinya

Kiyomizu-
dera

Saihō-ji

Higashi
Hongan-ji

Kawai Kanjirō's House

Kyoto National Museum

Nishi-
Hongan-ji

Sanjūsangen-
dō

Katsura
Rikyū

Tō-ji

KYOTO
STATION

Sennyū-ji

Tōfuku-ji

Fushimi Inari
Taisha

Daigo-ji

to
Uji City

Ancient Heian-kyō's grid layout makes navigation simpler than in any other Japanese city—which isn't to say it's easy.

Nine numbered avenues, running east–west, formed the old city's lines of latitude. The northern boundary, **Ichijō-dōri** (First Avenue), is on the approximate level of today's Imperial Household Agency. The southern limit, **Kujō-dōri** (Ninth Avenue), runs just south of Tō-ji temple. All nine of these avenues exist today and, if you know your numbers, they are a useful indication of relative north–south position: thus **Shijō** (Fourth Avenue) station is north of **Gojō** (Fifth Avenue) and **Shichijō** (Seventh Avenue) stations, but south of **Sanjō** (Third Avenue) and **Nijō** (Second Avenue) Castle.

Unnumbered avenues form the north to south longitudes. The most important of these are **Karasuma-dōri** (directly north of the station and above Kyoto's subway line) and **Kawaramachi-dōri** (parallel with the Kamo River). Major junctions are named after the avenues whose intersection they mark, and these compounds are often used for bus stops. So, for the teeming crossroads in front of Hankyū and Takashimaya department stores, you should get off at **Shijō-Kawaramachi**.

The bad news is that most of the places you want to visit were built outside this helpful grid. Big tourist attractions are well known and well sign-posted. For private addresses and smaller establishments the usual rules apply: ask for precise directions or a hand-drawn map with directions in Japanese which you can show to passers-by; collect business cards, match books and anything with a Japanese address on; allow plenty of time for getting lost and seeking directions; and carry a phone number in case you have to call and ask to be met.

This chapter is divided up as follows: **Central Kyoto**, with entertainment, conveniences and a few good temples and palaces; the few attractions of **Southeastern Kyoto**; **Eastern Kyoto**, the rich historical area on the far side of the Kamo River, enough for a holiday in itself; **Northeast Kyoto**, with a couple of rustic temples and an isolated imperial villa; **Western Kyoto** and **Arashiyama and Sagano**, really a series of separate, scattered attractions; and **Outer Kyoto**, describing the best of many day (or even half-day) trips possible from the city.

Getting Around
by bus

Since the demise of Kyoto's trams, buses have become the main form of transportation within the city. As the bedlam in front of the station demonstrates, they are numerous, and you can take them almost anywhere if you have time and don't mind the crowds and slowness. As well as **Kyoto Eki-mae** (in front of Kyoto Station), there's a big bus station called **Kitaōji Bus Terminal**, on Kitaōji-dōri in the north central part of the city.

The standard fare is ¥220 and you feed your money into the driver's box as you get on. At bus and subway stations you can buy a **one- or two- day unlimited pass** (*ichinichi jōshaken* means 1-day pass, *ninichi jōshaken* means 2-day pass) for the price of five or so journeys. You can also purchase the pass at some hotels.

A pass for buses alone costs ¥700 for one day; a joint bus and subway pass is ¥1,200. However, you should look into the two-day bus and subway pass for ¥2,000, as with the one-day pass you are constricted to the Kyoto city limits. Sights like Saihō-ji, Arashiyama and Ōhara actually fall outside this limit. With the two-day pass you can go anywhere you like. Ask at the TIC for details, as the rules are liable to change now and again. Both the International Community House and the tourist information centre maps carry colour-coded plans of all major bus routes. A more comprehensive map is available, but only the major stops are transliterated into Roman characters.

by subway

Kyoto has just two subway lines. The most useful one runs north to south, through Kyoto Station, beneath Karsuma-dōri, and cuts through the centre of the city up to Kitayama station. The newer Tōzai Line runs east to west from Nijō station to Daigo-ji in the eastern suburbs of Kyoto. This is primarily a commuter rail, but will connect you to the sights of Eastern Kyoto and to Nijō Castle. The east-west line intersects with the north-south line at Karasuma-Oike station. Fares begin at ¥200; and the one- or two-day bus and subway pass can be used.

by train

As well as the inter-city JR lines and private services linking Kyoto with the rest of Kansai, there are useful commuter trains connecting points within the city (main stops only listed):

JR Sagano Line	Kyoto–Nijō Castle–Uzumasa–Saga
Keifuku Arashiyama Line	Shijō–Ōmiya–Uzumasa–Saga
JR Nara Line	Inari–Uji–Nara
Keihan Main Line	Demachiyanagi–Marutamachi–Sanjō–Shijō–Gojō–Shichijō–Tōfuku-ji–Fushimi Inari–Ōsaka
Eizan Line	Demachiyanagi–Shūgaku-in–Yaseyuen
JR Biwako Line	Kyoto–Ōtsu (Lake Biwa)
Hankyū Kyoto Line	Kawaramachi–Karasuma–Uniya–Katsura

by taxi

Taxi drivers charge a bit less than their Tokyo counterparts, but are no more likely to speak English. **MK Taxis**, ✆ 075 721 2237/4141, has English-speaking drivers who, for ¥ 2,000 an hour plus the meter rate, will act as guides to the city.

car hire

Mazda Rent-A-Car, ✆ 075 681 7779.
Nippon Rent-A-Car, ✆ 075 681 0311.

Both are near the south exit of Kyoto Station. Before hiring a car, enquire at the tourist information centre. They sometimes have English-language leaflets which entitle the bearer to big reductions (up to 20%). Even without the reduction, prices are fairly cheap with economy class cars going for about ¥6,000 a day.

Note: driving in Kyoto is no fun.

bicycle hire

Both of the hire firms listed below are aimed at tourists and charge around ¥1,000 a day. A daily rate means 9–5 at Yasumoto and 9–7 at Heian. Hourly rates are also available, starting at ¥200, at both places. At Heian you can get yourself a slick mountain bike for double the regular rate.

Rent-A-Cycle Yasumoto, ✆ 075 751 0595, is just behind the noticeable Sanjō Keihan Kita building, which stands on the northeast corner of the big intersection at Sanjō Keihan station.

Rent-A-Cycle Heian, ✆ 075 431 4522, is on the corner of Shimocho-jamachi and Muromachi streets just to the west of the Imperial Palace grounds.

tours

Coach tours with English-speaking guides run daily except for New Year, and can include a trip to Nara as well as the big Kyoto sights. They're an expensive way of fitting a lot of superficial sightseeing into a short time: expect to pay ¥5,000 plus for half a day and at least ¥10,000 for a full day. The biggest company is JTB's **Sunrise Tours**, ✆ 075 341 1413. Many hotels and inns act as agents for JTB and will make reservations for you.

Cheaper but, if anything, more irritating, are **Japanese-language tours** leaving from Kyoto Station. Enquire at the tourist information centre.

Even if you do not think you are really interested in a tour, it is worth checking out the charismatic **Johnnie Hillwalker (a.k.a. Hajime Hiroka)**. Mr. Hillwalker's unusual four-hour tour covers about 3km on foot, with one short bus ride. You will see an intriguing array of backstreets and local craft shops, cemeteries and obscure shrines. It is highly recommended and very reasonably priced (*¥2,000 for one person, ¥3,000 for two, children free*).

Tourist Information

The excellent **tourist information centre** (*open Mon–Fri 9–5, Sat 9–12 noon*; ✆ 075 371 5649) is underneath Kyoto Tower, on the west side of Karasuma-dōri, the main avenue stretching north directly in front of the station. The multilingual staff provide up-to-date maps, timetables, price lists, magazines, pamphlets and advice. They keep information on the rest of the country too. From outside Kyoto you can ring them free on the **Japan Travel Phone** Line, ✆ 0120 444800, or ✆ 0088 22 4800.

Student **Goodwill Guides** can also be arranged from this office, an excellent free service which you should take advantage of, especially for sites like the Palaces and Nijō Jinya which can only be visited on a Japanese-language guided tour.

If you'll be in Kyoto for more than a week, pay a visit to **Kyoto International Community House** (*open 9–9; adm free*; ✆ 075 752 3010), near the approach road to Nanzen-ji, a few minutes southeast of Okazaki Park and the museums (Tōzai subway line to Keage station). The material here is really aimed at longer-term residents, but the bulletin board advertises events open to all. There's a CNN TV link, an inexpensive French restaurant, and a library of foreign newspapers, travel guides and books on Japan.

The ICH also runs Japan's biggest **Home Visit** system, with 100 families who between them speak English, French, German, Chinese, Italian and Spanish. Make your application a couple of days in advance.

English-language bookshops sell maps, but a perfectly adequate one of Kyoto and Nara is available free from the tourist information centre. Bigger and more comprehensive is the handsome map given away by the International Community House. They're not supposed to give these to casual tourists, so you may have to exaggerate the time you're planning to stay.

The long-established monthly **Kansai Time Out** has features aimed at tourists and residents as well as comprehensive listings for theatre, cinema, music, TV, festivals, sport, meetings and exhibitions and hundreds of classified ads.

There are countless English free sheets and events guides; best is the tourist information centre's **Monthly Information**, a newsletter listing festivals, markets, exhibitions, performances and special openings.

Kyoto Itineraries

If your stay here is limited (likely if you have a rail pass from which to extract value), the following suggestions may help you divide up your time:

Day One—**Eastern Kyoto**

AM: Kiyomizu-dera and/or Sanjūsangen-dō (temples)
PM: Philosopher's Walk to Ginkaku-ji (canal and temples)

Bad weather alternative: Kyoto National Museum, Kawai Kanjirō's House (potter's traditional house), Museum of Traditional Industry (crafts).

Visit the tourist information centre and Imperial Household Agency to make reservations for special temples, palaces and Nijō Jinya.

Day Two—**Northwest Kyoto**

AM: Daitoku-ji (Zen temple compound)
PM: Ryōan-ji (Zen garden) or Kinkaku-ji (gold temple)

Bad weather: Kōryū-ji Treasure House (sculpture), Tōei Movie Land (theme park), Nishijin Textile Centre.

Day Three—**South Kyoto and Uji**

AM: Uji's Byōdō-in (temple)
PM: Fushimi Inari Taisha (hillside shrine)

Bad weather: Kyoto National Museum, Kawai Kanjirō's House.

Day Four—**Central Kyoto**

AM: Nijō-jō (castle)
PM: Nijō Jinya (*ninja* house)/ Sentō Gosho (Retired Emperor's Palace).

For the Jinya and Sentō Gosho you must make a reservation. Both of these and Nijō Castle are good in wet weather.

Day Five—**Western Kyoto**

AM: Katsura Rikyū (Imperial Villa) and/or Saihō-ji (temple moss garden)
PM: Arashiyama and Sagano (pretty local neighbourhood)

Katsura and Saihō-ji require reservations; the latter is very expensive. You could spend a whole day in Arashiyama and Sagano.

Day Six—**Northeast Kyoto**

Early: Shūgaku-in Rikyū (Imperial Villa)
Rest of Day: Mt Hiei (scattered mountain temples)

Uncomfortable in bad weather. Shūgaku-in requires a reservation. Exploring Mt Hiei could fill a whole day.

Day Seven—**Day trip to Ōhara village**

Festivals

Every week there are several festivals going on somewhere in Kyoto (see the tourist information centre's *Monthly Information Newsletter* for a comprehensive list). Those given here are just the most famous *matsuri* which you might want to time your visit to coincide with. Bear in mind that big festivals always mean big crowds, and that accommodation, tours and everything else get booked up early at such times. Restricted temples and treasure houses are most likely to be open in the autumn, and most likely to be closed in the winter months.

January

1–3   Millions congregate at Fushimi Inari Shrine for **New Year** celebrations. Everything else is closed.

15   Edo period **archery** marathon at Sanjūsangen-dō temple.

21   **Hatsu Kōbō.** Lively festival, the first of the year, at Tō-ji temple, held in memory of the Buddhist saint Kūkai, posthumously known as Kōbō Daishi.

February

2–3   New Year according to the old calendar. Capers involving dancers in demon costumes, beans and fire (both to drive out the demons) go on at several shrines and temples. Check at the tourist information centre for times and places.

March

15   The anniversary of the **death of Shaka**, the historical Buddha. Numerous commemorative services and performances of religious drama. Giant torches are lit at Seiryō-ji in Sagano.

April

All month   Geisha and their **maiko** apprentices perform **traditional Kyoto dance** at the Gion Kaikan theatre.

Mid-month   Kyoto goes on a week-long drinking binge beneath the **cherry blossoms** which come out all over the city. Famous spots are the Heian Shrine, Imperial Park, Arashiyama, Maruyama Park and Philosopher's Walk.

May

15   **Aoi Matsuri** (Hollyhock Festival). Riders in Heian court costume process from the Imperial Palace to Shimogamo Jinja and Kamigamo Jinja, two ancient shrines in the north of the city, re-enacting a 6th century rite of thanks to the deities who saved Kyoto from a plague.

Third Sun   **Mifune Matsuri**. Musicians and actors perform on river boats at Arashiyama.

June

1–2   *Nō* plays performed by torchlight in the Heian Shrine.

July

All month   **Cormorant fishing** (Ukai) at Arashiyama and Uji. Trained cormorants dive for river fish from torch-lit boats.

14–17   **Gion Matsuri**. Kyoto's most important festival attracting millions of visitors, and featuring famous floats offered by the old merchant quarters. Music, lively costumes and carnival atmosphere.

August

All month   **Cormorant fishing** continues at Arashiyama and Uji.

Various days **Rokusai Nembutsu Odori**. Dances, noise and acrobatics to drive away demons throughout the month.

7–10   **Rokudō Pilgrimage**. Families welcome the spirits of the dead with lanterns and gongs in various temples near Kiyomizu-dera, an area where corpses used to be buried.

16   **Daimonji**. At the end of **Ō-bon**, the festival of the dead when families honour the visiting spirits of their ancestors, five huge bonfires are lit on the mountains surrounding the city. The most famous two form the character for great, *dai*. They can be seen simultaneously from tall buildings and hillsides in the north of the city.

September

Full moon   Moon-viewing ceremonies at Daikaku-ji and Uji.

October

22   **Jidai Matsuri** (Festival of the Ages). Thousands of people in historical costume parade from the Imperial Palace.
Hi-matsuri (Fire Festival). Fiery torches are carried through the village of Kurama, to the north of Kyoto.

November

All month   Maple and ginkgo trees blaze into spectacular autumn colours all over the city, especially beautiful in Hōnen-in, Tōfuku-ji, Shūgaku-in Imperial Villa, Ōhara and Saihō-ji. Chrysanthemums in Nijō Castle.

First week   Several temples and halls which are usually closed admit members of the public. Check at the Tourist Information Centre

December

1–26   **Kaomise *Kabuki*.** Annual *kabuki*-fest at the Minami-za theatre.

21   **Shimai Kōbō.** Last market of the year at Tō-ji temple, in honour of Kōbō Daishi.

31   **New Year's Eve** celebrations, including a fire ritual at Yasaka Shrine.

Visiting Temples and Villas

Admission fees and opening hours for Kyoto temples are fairly standard; only the exceptions to the general rules will be noted.

Try to start early. After 11am the famous temples become choked with crowds even off season. Buddhist monks rise at dawn and no one will mind a few discreet early visitors wandering around the grounds. However, halls and treasure houses, and anything involving admission fees and tickets, generally open between 8am and 9am and close between 4pm and 5pm. Many shut at 4pm during the winter months. Expect to be refused admission if you arrive less than half an hour before closing time. Kiyomizu-dera opens at 6am and closes at 6pm (occasionally even later), so it can be usefully fitted in at the beginning or end of a day's sightseeing. Dawn and dusk are in any case the best times to view this great temple.

Shinto shrines like Fushimi Inari Taisha and Heian Jingū never really close, although the Heian Jingū's garden does.

Certain smaller temples and sub-temples receive visitors for only a few days a year, usually in the autumn colours season at the beginning of November (the best time to visit Kyoto, if you can stand the crowds). In the pages that follow, **Anraku-ji** and **Reikan-ji** on the Philosopher's Walk, and **Daitoku-ji** fall into this category. Several of the Daitoku-ji sub-temples not described in detail here also open only for that week, and if you're in Kyoto in November you should certainly pay them a visit. Full details are always available from the Kyoto tourist information centre.

Temple **entry fees** are between ¥300 and ¥500 unless otherwise stated; the November special openings generally cost ¥600. Only **Saihō-ji**, the Moss Temple, charges exorbitantly: ¥3,000 per person (*see* pp.234–5).

Special Arrangements

Most of the places listed in this chapter can be freely visited without appointment but a few, among them some of the most worthwhile places in Japan, limit visitor numbers and require you to make a booking on a guided tour.

The procedures are quick and straightforward and no one should be discouraged by them: the limitations on numbers actually make these places a more pleasant experience by eliminating the human traffic jams which clog many temples. At busy times of year such as public holidays, August weekends and the cherry blossom and maple leaf viewing seasons, tours may become full in advance. Make your enquiries as early as possible and be prepared to offer alternative times and dates. Tokyo and Kyoto tourist information centres can help out with arrangements; so will the JNTO office in your home country (*see* p.45), or a good agent like Nippon Travel Agency or JTB (*see* pp.6–7).

The Imperial Household Agency (Kunai Chō)

Subway to Imadegawa station. Inside Kyoto Imperial Park, just to the southeast; open Mon–Fri, 8.45–4, closed 12–1; © 075 211 1215.

This should be one of your first stops on arrival in Kyoto. The Agency issues permits for the **Kyoto Imperial Palace**, **Retired Emperor's Palace** (both in Kyoto Imperial Park in the centre), the **Katsura Imperial Villa** (southwest) and the **Shūgaku-in Imperial Villa** (northeast). Bookings for the Imperial Palace can be made up to 20 minutes before the tour leaves. A tour of the Retired Emperor's Palace can usually be arranged on the morning of your proposed visit, and tours of the villas within a couple of days, but the Agency does not guarantee this and to be absolutely sure, you should make arrangements in advance. Outrageously, it is much easier for foreigners to see the palaces and villas than for Japanese, who often have to wait weeks for their applications to be processed.

One member of your party must put in a brief personal appearance at the office in Kyoto Imperial Park, and be prepared to list the full name, passport details and ages of everyone who wishes to be included—extras who turn up on spec at the last minute will not be admitted. For the Imperial Palace, children must be accompanied by an adult, which in Japan means over 20. In the other three, no one under 20 is allowed—though tall Westerners in their late teens probably won't be challenged. There is no admission fee to any of these places.

Your permit will usually be issued on the spot. Arrive promptly bringing it and your passports, which may be checked.

Tours are available at the following times:

Kyoto Imperial Palace (Gosho)—50min tour. Mon–Fri, and every Sat in May, Oct and Nov only: 10am and 2pm. During other months, every third Sat only: 10am. This is the only one of the imperial properties which sometimes offers tours in English. Ask when you make your application.

Retired Emperor's Palace (Sentō Gosho)—50min tour. Mon–Fri, and Sat only in May, Oct and Nov: 11am and 1.30pm.

Katsura Imperial Villa (Katsura Rikyū)—60min tour. Mon–Fri, and Sat only in May, Oct and Nov: 10am, 11am, 2pm and 3pm.

Shūgaku-in Imperial Villa (Shūgaku-in Rikyū)—60min tour. Mon–Fri, and Sat only in May, Oct and Nov: 9am, 10am, 11am, 1.30pm and 3pm.

Nishi Hongan-ji—tours of the *treasures* depart at various times between Mon and Sat. Reserve in English at the **Reception Office** (*Sanpaibu*), ✆ 075 371 5180, the modern block at the far left as you enter the Horikawa Avenue gate.

Nijō Jinya—45min tours at 10am, 11am, 2pm and 3pm every day. ✆ 075 841 0972. Phone in Japanese to make a reservation. The tourist information centre, a travel agent or your hotel can do this for you.

Saihō-ji—the tourist information centre issues a sheet showing exactly how to apply for this temple. From a post office purchase a return postcard (*ōfuku hagaki*) which is two-sided. On the 'send' side write the temple's address in the space below the blue stamp: Saihō-ji Temple, 56 Jingutani-chō, Matsuo, Nishikyō-ku, Kyoto 615–8286. On the 'return' side (bearing a green stamp) write on the left-hand side the address in Japan where you wish to receive your appointment card. On the right-hand side list the names of your party, their occupations and ages, and a choice of two or three possible dates. The 'return' postcard will be sent back to you with an explanation in Japanese and English. Turn up promptly on the specified date with this card and ¥3,000 per person in cash.

Central Kyoto

Today's downtown Kyoto occupies the eastern half of Emperor Kammu's old capital, Heian-kyō. Not much of the imperial peace and tranquillity remains today, but the gridiron layout is obvious, and this area is still Kyoto's centre of power and leisure. The main rail and bus terminals, the subway line, and the mass of its cinemas, hotels and department stores are located in a two and a half kilometre square north of the station and west of the Kamo River. Banks, department stores, travel agencies and airlines are all concentrated in the station area, and around the intersection of Shijō-dōri and Kawaramachi-dōri.

Equally abundant are heavy traffic, dense pollution and chaotic city planning. Few historical sites have survived the city's frequent levellings and the pressure to exploit this expensive land. With the exception of a few of the old wooden quarters, mostly around the canals near the Kamo River, this is the part of Kyoto most like every other Japanese city. Change your money here, stop by the Tourist Information Centre, and visit a few of the places listed below. After that, get out of the city centre to the east and west margins, where Kyoto is at its most distinctive and elegant.

Central Kyoto

500 metres
500 yards

•••••••• Subway

N

IMADEGAWA-DŌRI

Nishijin Textile Museum

S IMADEGAWA

13

Imperial Household Agency

Imperial Palace

Kyoto Gyōen

Ōmiya Palace

Sentō Gosho

SENBON-DŌRI

HORIKAWA-DŌRI

14 Prefectural Government

KARASUMA-DŌRI

MARUTAMACHI-DŌRI

S MARUTAMACHI

KAWARAMACHI-DŌRI

HIGASHIŌJI-DŌRI

Nijō Castle

NIJŌ S

NIJŌ-MAE S

OIKE S

City Hall

16

OIKE-DŌRI S

2 1

KYOTO SHIYAKUSHO-MAE S

Sanjō Keihan Bus Terminal

SANJŌ-DŌRI 5

Keihan line

Nijō Jinya

PONTOCHO

Sanjō Keihan

4 GION

15

Maruyama kōen (Maruyama Park)

Chion-in

Ōmiya

Haňkyu line

Karasuma

6 Kawaramachi

Shijō

Yasuku Jinja (Gion Shrine)

SHIJŌ- DŌRI

S SHIJŌ

Takashimaya Dept. Store

Hankyū Dept. Store

Minami-za Theatre

Gion Corner

to Arashiyama

Shijō Ōmiya

Keifuku Arashiyama line

HORIKAWA-DŌRI

KARASUMA-DŌRI

Kano River

Kennin-ji

Yūzen Textile and Dye Museum

GOJŌ- DŌRI

S GOJŌ

Gojō

ŌMIYA-DŌRI

SHIMABARA

Costume Museum

7

9 10

3

Shichijō

Kawai Kanijirō's House

Kiyomizu-dera

Nishi Hongan-ji

12

8

Higashi-Hongan-ji

Kyoto National Museum

SHICHIJŌ- DŌRI

Tourist Information Centre i

Keihan line

Sanjūsangen-dō

Locomotive Museum

Kyoto Tower 19

SHIOKŌJI-DŌRI

Post Office

Kyoto Eki-mae Bus Terminal

S KYOTO

17

to Hakata

KYOTO STATION

18

HACHIJŌ-DŌRI

Tōfuku-ji

Tō-ji

KUJŌ-DŌRI

S KUJŌ

Sennyū-ji

Tōfuku-ji

200   Kyoto

Key for Kyoto Hotels

(For listings *see* pp.256–260)

1	Tawaraya	**11**	Kiyomizu Sansō
2	Hiiragaya	**12**	Matsubaya
3	Seikoro	**13**	Takaraga-ike Prince
4	Shiraume	**14**	Brighton Hotel
5	Yachiyo	**15**	Miyako
6	Kinmata	**16**	Kyoto Hotel
7	Riverside Takase	**17**	Hotel Granvia
8	Ryokan Kyōka	**18**	New Miyako
9	Ryokan Yuhara	**19**	Kyoto Tower Hotel
10	Ryokan Hiraiwa		

Tō-ji (East Temple)

> *Bus 17 to Tō-ji Nishi-mon-mae, or 18 or 207 to Tō-ji Higashi-mon-mae, or Tō-ji station on the Kintetsu-Nara Line.*

Tō-ji's mighty five-storey pagoda used to be the first landmark glimpsed by travellers from the nearby port of Sakai, the symbol of arrival in Kyoto; nowadays it is overshadowed by the grotesque Kyoto Tower. The exhaust-singed quarter immediately southwest of the station is one of the least appealing in the city, but at the time of its founding it was key, marking the capital's southernmost boundary.

Emperor Kammu decreed that there would be no temples within Heian-kyō itself (turbulent priests, after all, had been the main reason for quitting Nara), except for one on either side of the great southern gate, **Rashō-mon** (later the title of a novel by Akutagawa Ryūnosuke, filmed by Kurosawa). **Sai-ji** (West Temple) had burned down by 1233 and nothing of it survives. **Tō-ji**, its eastern twin, was luckier: in 823 it was entrusted to the care of Kūkai, the great founder of Shingon Buddhism (posthumously canonized as Kōbō Daishi).

Shingon, with its colourful pantheon of deities arrayed hierarchically around a divine central essence, was a useful doctrine for a ruler trying to establish his authority in a new, permanent capital. Tō-ji was awarded the title **Kyōō Gokoku-ji**, Temple-for-the-Transmission-of-the-Teachings-to-the-King-and-for-the-Protection-of-the-Nation. This special status, and the undying popularity of Kōbō Daishi, ensured rich patronage and survival as one of the finest repositories of Heian art.

The temple buildings are classically arranged on a north–south axis, although the most interesting are fenced off and entered via a ticket booth. (The rest of the wide grounds are open to all, and there is a big market here on the 21st of each month, the Daishi's traditional birthday.) The **Kon-dō** (Main Hall) is the biggest building in the temple. It was rebuilt around 1600 in stern majestic style, and has an interesting middle roof between the upper and lower eaves at the front. Within, a gold-covered statue of Yakushi Nyōrai, Buddha of Healing, sits between Nikkō and Gakkō, *bosatsu* (see p.95) of the sun and moon. The statue is 3m tall but the great hall, flagged in diagonal stones, gives an impression of space and tranquil emptiness.

The single-roofed **Kōdō** (Lecture Hall) north of it is similar: from the outside, grand and rather haughty; inside, dim, voluminous and often very cold. The Lecture Hall, however, is transfigured and overwhelmed by its contents: an awe-inspiring, three-dimensional mandala, created through the arrangement of the temple's finest statues, many of them carved in the 9th century by Kōbō Daishi himself. Even without a precise knowledge of the identity and iconography of the 21 figures, the effect is profound and suggestive of the theological complexities of Esoteric Buddhism.The statues form three distinct groups of five deities, with three guardians at both the east and west (right and left as the viewer faces them). In the middle of the central group, Dainichi Nyōrai, source and essence of all things, sits in his royal crown, right hand clasping his left index finger in the sexual, 'All-Is-One' *mudra* (sacred hand gesture). Around him are four *nyōrai* (Buddhas), including Amida at front left—all date from the Momoyama period.

The flanking groups follow the same pattern but these are original Heian period National Treasures. To your right are five *bosatsu*, earthly manifestations of the *nyōrai*, their worldly status indicated by their crowns and jewellery. To the left, the show is stolen by a superb phalanx of the **Go Myō-ō** (Five Fearful Kings), many-armed, multi-headed bruisers, mounted on bulls or stomping wrong-doers beneath their feet, whose role is to intimidate evil and deliver the short, sharp shocks all mortals occasionally require. The mandala is protected at its corners by the Four Directional Guardians, the most handsome and familiar of which is **Bishamonten**, at back right, his miniature pagoda held high. Two of the finest statues are interpretations of Indian deities, standing between the pairs of Guardians, one at either side: on the right **Bonten** (Brahma), four heads and four arms supported on a lotus borne by four geese; and **Taishakuten** (Indra) elegantly astride a Shetland-pony-sized elephant. The **Treasure Hall** opens in the autumn for a special exhibition of its Tibetan art, as well as distressing examples of statues charred and mutilated in a recent fire. You may well see the restorers at work on them around the temple.

Nishi Hongan-ji (West Temple of the Primal Vow)

Buses 9 or 75 to Nishi Honganji-mae, or a short walk from Kyoto station.

Northwest of the station, off Horikawa-dōri, is another big temple, although stylistically and doctrinally it could hardly be more different from Tō-ji. **Nishi Hongan-ji** is a centre of Shin, one of the most popular Buddhist sects in Japan, a simple and accessible creed and the antithesis of Esoteric Shingon. Hongan-ji was founded in the late 13th century at the mausoleum of the sect's founder, Shinran Shōnin. For centuries, it was dogged by misfortune and persecutions, repeatedly burning to the ground to be rebuilt on half a dozen different sites. In 1591 it finally found a patron in the 16th-century warlord Toyotomi Hideyoshi, who donated the plot of land on which it now stands; the most notable of the present buildings were built over the next few years or moved here after his death from Hideyoshi's palaces. Hongan-ji's abbots buckled down and did as they were told during the Edo period; consequently, it has survived virtually undisturbed as a matchless example of Momoyama architecture and decoration.

Note

Make sure you get the correct Hongan-ji. There's a **Higashi (East) Hongan-ji** too, offshoot of a 17th-century rift, and unmissably positioned on the main road in front of the station, two blocks up from the tourist information centre. The layout of the halls is virtually identical to the West temple, but the buildings here date from only 1895 when they were rebuilt after a fire. Such was the popular devotion inspired by the sect that female followers offered their hair to be plaited into great ropes used to haul building materials. One of these can still be seen, coiled in a glass case by the eastern temple's Amida-dō (Hall).

Touring Nishi Hongan-ji

At Nishi Hongan-ji, the Amida Hall, Founder's Hall and courtyard are open to all from dawn until dusk, but the treasures can only be seen on a special tour. This is straightforward to arrange (*see* pp.200–1). No photography is allowed in the interiors. The temple **book shop**, left of the main gate, sells an excellent brochure with information about Hongan-ji and the Shin sect.

The Shoin

The chambers and *shoin* (studies) of Nishi Hongan-ji contain all the traditional elements of Momoyama architecture, but compared to later examples of the style they are relaxed—pure heady opulence, unmotivated by the paranoia and obsession with hierarchy which pervades Nijō Castle. The temple's policy of limiting access has paid off: the condition of the wooden structures and, particularly, the colours of the paintings are outstanding. Look out also for the carved openwork transoms above the partitions; the panels of the coffered ceilings, each one hand-painted with an individual design, often humorous; and the ornate nail covers and sliding door handles. The tour guide passes a gravel courtyard with a 17th-century *nō* stage to begin in the **Great Audience Hall**, a 203-mat room with the classic *shoin* arrangement of raised floor, staggered writing-shelf and *tokonoma* alcove, viewed from the main part of the room through a fan-shaped window. The paintings on the doors are by the great Kanō school, and illustrate the acts of good and evil Chinese emperors.

Next to it are small waiting rooms, each with a decorative motif. The **Chamber of Geese** follows the progress of these birds from the morning (right-hand side) to the evening (left); if you stand at the right-hand corner of the room and look up at the top left transom, the geese carved into it appear to be flying against a rising moon. The **Shiro Shoin** (White Study) is a jewel, with peacocks on fields of gold and unfathomably complicated carvings of birds and peonies. Opposite this room is the **Northern Nō Stage**, the oldest in the world, built in 1581 and set in black pebbles for enhanced acoustics.

The **Kokei Garden** is a curiosity: a dry gravel 'lake' with bridges and boulders but, remarkably, no pine trees. Instead, cycad palms lend the scene a spiky, un-Japanese air. Look at the ceiling panels in the corridor running alongside here: among the books, scrolls and scholarly appurtenances is a single cat, painted, your guide will explain, to protect the paper from mice. The **Hiunkaku** (Pavilion of Floating Clouds), in the southwest corner of the temple grounds, came from Hideyoshi's Juraku-dai Castle and is ranked for its perfection alongside the Golden and Silver Pavilions; unfortunately it's closed to casual visitors. The **Kara-mon** (Chinese Gate), north of the main entrance in the temple's east side, is a typical Momoyama structure of curving roofs and rich woodwork.

Nijō-jō (Nijō Castle)

Buses 9, 12, 50, or 101; or subway to Nijō-jō-mae subway station.

The buildings of **Nijō-jō** ('the most ornate, materialistic structures that a Japanese man ever raised for himself', as Gouverneur Mosher called them) form one of the least typical and most fascinating castles in all Japan, more of a palace than a military installation, the ultimate expression of the aspirations and paranoias of the Tokugawa family. It was begun in 1602 by the first shogun, Ieyasu, soon after his victory at the battle of Sekigahara, and extended under his two successors until 1625.

Even its construction was laden with historical symbolism. Parts of Nijō-jō were recycled out of Fushimi Castle, the seat of Toyotomi Hideyoshi from whose son Ieyasu had recently seized power. He positioned them on the site of an old Ashikaga palace, hoping, justifiably as it turned out, that some of that dynasty's longevity would rub off on his own. The turrets looked insolently down on the Imperial Palace, just blocks away. In 1626 Emperor Go-Mizuno'o actually paid a visit there, an unprecedented act of submission. 'The castle is a symbol of...occupation by a group of outsiders,' wrote Mosher. 'Nothing could have less to do with Kyoto.' Having made their point in stone and wood, the shoguns lost interest in Kyoto. Tokugawa Iemitsu, shogun number three, marched 300,000 men into the city in 1634 but, as the Edo police state established itself, blatant muscle-flexing became unnecessary, and Nijō-jō spent the next two centuries in political mothballs.

Then, in the crisis years of the late Edo period, a curious reversal took place. In 1863, with the foreign powers clamouring to be allowed in, the penultimate shogun, Iemochi, was summoned to Kyoto and instructed by the Emperor to resist all barbarian demands. His successor, Keiki, spent most of his beleaguered two-year rule in Nijō-jō, and the edict abolishing his office was promulgated from the Ōhiroma reception room. The very symbol of shogunal power was hijacked by the emperor; with satisfying irony, the Tokugawa dynasty came to a humiliating end in the very building designed to glorify it.

The Grounds

The main **East Gate** (Higashi Ōte-mon) is on Horikawa-dōri. Once inside, turn left then right to approach the **Chinese Gate** (Kara-mon), a preview of the decorative pageant within. The beautifully painted carvings (look especially for the tiger among the bamboo on the inside beam) will remind anyone who has been there of the Tokugawa mausoleum at Nikkō (north of Tokyo)—both were crafted by the left-handed artist Jingoro, nicknamed *Hidari* ('Lefty'). But to appreciate fully the hyperbole of Nijō-jō, take a look at the baroque metal ovals set into the wood at regular intervals on this gate and throughout the palace. Eagles and chrysanthemums soar and bloom on them in copper and gold; they look like the shields of midget warriors. In fact, inasmuch as they have a practical function, they are nail covers, exaggerated beyond recognition.

In most Japanese castles it is the central defensive keep, the *Hon-maru*, which provides the focus of interest, and the outer buildings—the residences and administrative rooms occupied during peace time—which fall victim to fire and dismantling. Here the reverse happened. Nijō-jō's *Hon-maru* burned in 1750 and the site is occupied by a 19th-century replacement, brought from the Imperial Palace in 1893. It opens occasionally to the public, but the real attraction here is the **Ni-no-maru Palace** opposite the Chinese Gate.

Externally, the structure is unusual: five separate Momoyama-style buildings, joined by corridors at their corners, and staggered diagonally from southeast to northwest. Inside, the 33 *tatami* rooms compose a unique architectural map of the rigid social structure which the shogunate imposed upon the whole country. Everything was built on a grand scale, but the grandeur was carefully calibrated according to the rank of those for whom the room was intended, the outer block being for humble messengers, the fifth and inner room for the shogun alone.

The screen paintings, for example, were all done by members of the Kanō school, but different artists were assigned different chambers depending on the richness of their style. The carved transoms above the partitions sometimes depict different scenes on their twin sides: the more gorgeous one, with peacocks and thick gold leaf, faced into the room of higher rank. Above all, the buildings resonate (literally) with the Tokugawas' obsessive fear of assassination. Doors between the buildings can be unlocked only from the higher-ranking side; the 'nightingale floors' of the corridors sing squeakily when the slightest pressure is applied to them; and each of the five buildings has at its centre a concealed, windowless room where bodyguards lurked.

The first block, the **Tozamurai-no-ma** (Retainers' Room), was an administrative and reception area where low-ranking visitors were frisked and made to wait. The paintings are big, bold and symbolic: lions and leopards representing courage romp among the bamboos of moral rectitude. Here and elsewhere, many of the ceiling panels are damaged and crudely repainted: the vandalism occurred during the Meiji period when shoguns and their works were fair game.

Much the same style is seen in the adjacent **Shikidai-no-ma** (Reception Room) block where shogunal ministers carried out their business. The climax of opulence is in the central **Ōhiroma** (Grand Chamber), though this was not designed for the most honoured guests. Here the shogun received the outer circle of his *daimyō*, the feudal lords who had failed to back Ieyasu at the Battle of Sekigahara and whose loyalty might be in doubt: the intention was to awe and intimidate as much as to delight.

A tableau of mannequins dramatizes the magnificent scene. In the lower part of the room the shogunal ministers and visiting *daimyō* kneel opposite one another. Above, on the raised *tatami* mats, the shogun and a single page sit in front of a glorious *tokonoma* alcove, its shelf made from a single 5m plank of zelkova. To his left, a pair of bright red tassels advertise the presence, in the lightless room behind, of the shogun's bodyguards—tactfully kept out of the way, but no secret. The big chamber painted with pines and a hawk, on the other side of the Ōhiroma (viewed from the other side, on your return journey from the inner sanctum), was where these men armed themselves.

The **Kuro Shoin** (Black Study), where the *Fudai-daimyō* (inner lords) were received, is friendlier, quieter, more delicate in style; its painting of pines and herons on a golden beach by Kanō Naonobu is beautifully preserved, one of the finest in the palace. Sparest of all is the shogun's private apartment, the **Shiro Shoin** (White Study), accessible only to him and his female attendants. The partitions bear delicate ink paintings of misty Chinese scenes, and the hand-painted ceiling panels are of flowers, supplied as tribute by different *daimyō*. Even in use, the rooms would have been devoid of furniture, with tables supplied from the kitchen, and bedding carefully stowed.

Before leaving, glance at the **garden**, as sumptuous and expensive in its way as the palace. Its appearance has changed over the years and one theory holds that it was originally a huge dry garden, without water or even trees. The reason for this says a lot about the vulnerability of the Tokugawas even at the height of their splendour—the shogun, it seemed, didn't want to be reminded of the passing of the seasons.

Nijō Jinya

One and a half blocks south of Nijō-jō.

It's hard to translate the word *jinya*—'encampment house' is something like it, although really they were unique institutions, products of the state apparatus during the Edo period. The Tokugawas' hegemony stood or fell by their handling of the *daimyō*, the feudal barons who governed the regions by proxy, and who were perpetually scrutinized for signs of over-ambition and revolt. Certain barons were permitted to build castles; the rest made do with smaller headquarters which developed in time into the fortified house known as the *jinya*. Another shogunal management technique was to keep the barons busy (and broke) with twice-yearly journeys between Edo and their regional seats. So commercial *jinya*, hired by the night, sprang up along the principle routes, where *daimyō* and their samurai could put up in the comfort—and security—to which they were accustomed. It's in this last category that **Nijō Jinya**, one of the most dastardly buildings in Japan, falls.

Touring Nijō Jinya

The house is privately owned and visitors must join the 40-minute tours which depart regularly (*see* p.201). The tourist information centre can also arrange student **Goodwill Guides**, and the *jinya* is a worthwhile place to take advantage of this free service—the tour commentary is extremely detailed and in Japanese only.

History

The *jinya's* first master, an intriguing character called Ogawa Hiraemon, had been a *daimyō* himself with a castle in Shikoku, but blew it all by backing the wrong side at the battle of Sekigahara in 1600. In Kyoto he re-established himself as a rice merchant and apothecary, and his aristocratic connections won him powerful customers who developed the habit of staying at his house—ideally positioned for both Nijō Castle and the Imperial Palace. Over the course of 30 years, Ogawa remodelled the place as a purpose-built *jinya*, cramming the tiny area with anti-espionage devices, unique decoration and brilliant defences against fire. It's tempting to see it as an early example of the Japanese genius for miniaturization—a capsule castle. At any rate, it survived incineration on numerous occasions, including the Great Fire of Temmei in 1788, and is still owned today by the 13th generation of Ogawas.

Inside the Jinya

Positioned in the heart of the capital city, Nijō Jinya was never designed to withstand full-frontal military assault. What Ogawa and his expensive clients feared most of all was stealth: the eavesdropping of spies, and the surprise attacks of *ninja* or disguised assassins. How real these threats were, and whether or not the ingenious snares were ever put to the test, we don't know: one of the interesting things about the *jinya* is that it probably says more about the atmosphere of paranoia fostered by the shogun, than about the actual dangers which *daimyō* faced. The *jinya's* first line of defence is its unobtrusiveness. Even today, with a sign mounted outside for the tourists, it's easy to miss: a modest old merchant's house with sections of its walls constructed out of fireproof clay in the style of a *kura* (store room). It's also misleadingly compact: there are actually three separate levels within, although the roofs suggest only one.

The tour proper begins in the **Ōzashiki** (Main Parlour), a 15-mat room (*see* '*tatami*', p.304) where visiting *daimyō* could receive visitors, and the most lavish in the house. The floor of the shelf alcove here is a single 2m plank of maple, said to cost as much as the rest of the house put together; the screens are painted with a panorama of eastern Kyoto. The incense alcove to the left is inlaid with mother-of-pearl and also glass, an exotic commodity at the time; the porcelain nail covers would have struck Edo-period visitors as equally bold. But the room's most exciting feature is above your head: an opening in the ceiling, apparently just a skylight, which gives on to a sound-proofed hidden room where four bodyguards could lurk, listening in to their master's audiences below, ready to leap down on any aggressor.

By the garden south of this room, and at points throughout the house, hooks project beneath the eaves of the roof where wet mats were hung to repel the heat of neighbourhood fires. East of the **Ōzashiki** you will be shown a smaller room whose *tatami* could be lifted to uncover a miniature *nō* **stage**, complete with jars beneath the floorboards to absorb sound. Secret conferences may also have been held here: the screens contain an elaborate, sound-proofing combination of paper and wood, designed so that the shadow of any eavesdropper would be cast on to the partition.

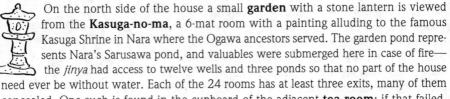 On the north side of the house a small **garden** with a stone lantern is viewed from the **Kasuga-no-ma**, a 6-mat room with a painting alluding to the famous Kasuga Shrine in Nara where the Ogawa ancestors served. The garden pond represents Nara's Sarusawa pond, and valuables were submerged here in case of fire— the *jinya* had access to twelve wells and three ponds so that no part of the house need ever be without water. Each of the 24 rooms has at least three exits, many of them concealed. One such is found in the cupboard of the adjacent **tea room**; if that failed, defenders could hop through to the corridor outside, where the ceiling flips down to reveal a staircase to the second storey.

The upper floors of the *jinya* are even more cramped and shin-barking than the ground floor. The most interesting room is the novelty **Tomabune-no-ma** (Boat Room) which juts out over the former site of a large pond; its floor, now too weak to support visitors, is said to make a 'rowing sound' when stepped upon. There's another **tea room** with a raised floor, beneath which is a concealed hidey-hole. Various other chambers are reached via a narrow corridor made deliberately low and dingy to hamper swordsmen. At the eastern end, for attackers who made it that far, is an especially painful sequence of dirty tricks: two unguarded staircases, one of them leading only to a dead end, down which unwary pursuers would topple; and a series of removable floor-boards designed to trip enemies up before pitching them into the open pit below.

Kyoto Imperial Park (Kyoto Gyōen)

A few minutes' walk south of the east exit of Imadegawa subway station. Buses 59, 201 and 203 to the Karasuma-Imadegawa intersection.

This large public park contains the **Kyoto Gosho** (Imperial Palace) and the **Sentō Gosho** (Retired Emperor's Palace). All the coach tours come here, but visitors who are short of time can confidently skip them in favour of the outlying Katsura and Shūgaku-in Imperial Villas. You will have to come to the park in any case, though: permits for all four places are dispensed by the **Imperial Household Agency** whose office is here. *See* 'Special Arrangements' (pp.200–1) for details of the tours and how to apply for them.

Imperial Palace (Gosho)

Visitors who come to the Imperial Palace expecting the Japanese equivalent of Versailles or the Forbidden City will be disappointed. Of all Kyoto's major attractions, this is the least vital: a series of impressively large, but listless, beige 19th-century buildings, set amid oceans of raked gravel. Since 1990 when Emperor Heisei discarded tradition to be enthroned not in Kyoto but in the Tokyo Imperial Palace, it's become little more than a museum. But even in its heyday, it was a self-contained private area closed to all but a few, and never intended to inspire public awe. The resemblances between these buildings and Shinto architecture, notably the Ise Shrine in Aichi Prefecture, are no coincidence. The buildings here embody not worldly power, but ceremonial authority, and above all the importance of ritual purity, expressed in the unvarnished natural materials and the empty courtyards of severe white stones. In the old days all forms of perceived uncleanliness—death or menstruation, for instance—were rigorously excluded from the palace grounds. No one bothers with such minutiae today, although you might detect a faint echo in the solemn entrance procedures and the exclusion of visitors from various areas of the palace.

History

The original Imperial Palace was west of the present site, part of a huge compound of ministries and pavilions accounting for one-fifth of the entire area of Heian-kyō. A permanent imperial home, to be used continually by successive emperors, was one of the cornerstones of Emperor Kammu's new city. But the place seemed ill-starred and fires and earthquakes eventually drove the emperors out altogether, back to the 'village palaces', temporary dwellings between which the itinerant court could move at its convenience.

In 1331 one such village palace became the new permanent *gosho*, narrowly avoiding destruction in the civil wars of the 15th century. The present buildings are based on original designs, but the oldest of them were rebuilt in 1855.

Touring the Imperial Palace

The main gate of the palace, the **Kenrei-mon**, is in the south wall. Until quite recently only the Emperor could enter here; now the gate is open to state guests. George Bush was the first to receive this honour on his famous visit to Japan when he beame ill at a state dinner. Prince Charles and Princess Diana were not so lucky when they visited the palace; they humbly ambled in through the **Kenshun-mon**, a gate formerly used by imperial messengers, but now reserved for run-of-the-mill nobles and foreign premiers. Several other gates round out the stratified entrance system. The **Seisho-gomon**, where tourists are allowed to enter, was formerly reserved for children of the royal family.

The tour passes by a number of tall porches where carriages and palanquins deposited their distinguished burdens, before wheeling to the left to pause between the thatched **Kenrei-mon** and a lower gate with tiled roof and vermilion columns, the **Jōmei-mon**. Rarely are tours allowed to pass through here, but take a look: this is the most important part of the palace. The enclosure, filled with raked gravel, was the venue for state ceremonies like the New Year Audience and religious services involving the emperor; architecturally, it echoes the pristine courtyards of the Ise Shrine. At the far side, built into the roofed corridor which surrounds the yard, is the **Shishin-den** (Pure Dragon Hall) where the thrones of the Emperor and Empress still stand, great inlaid platforms, with curtains and a canopy topped by phoenixes. The hall is 30m wide and 21m deep; its rippling roof is thatched with 40 layers of cypress bark, half a metre thick. In front is a broad staircase where nobles would stand, one step for each of the 18 ranks. To the east a cherry blossom, and to the west a mandarin tree, represent the Ministries of the Left and the Right.

The **Seiryō-den** (Pure Cool Hall) was the emperor's daily home in the Heian period and still contains chambers for the Empress and her maids, and a bedroom for the Emperor with a 20cm thick mattress of *tatami*. Later it became a ceremonial space: the rectangle of white marble in the corridor at the front was where prayers were offered to the imperial forebears at Ise. The **Kogosho** (Lesser Palace) belonged to the Crown Prince. The court-yard and garden in front of it were the venue for courtly entertainments like poetry-writing parties and *kemari* or 'kick ball', a Pythonesque game played by men in court costume with a sphere of deer- and horse-hide.

Retired Emperor's Palace (Sentō Gosho)

The **Sentō Gosho** was a product of the Japanese abdication system whereby emperors, while still young, could pass on the ceremonial responsibilities of state to their infant heirs. Early retired emperors sometimes wielded considerable influence as back-stage power brokers, a state of affairs which the newly-empowered Tokugawas were determined to avoid. They set about putting the imperial family in its place, first by marrying off one of their daughters to Emperor Go-Mizuno'o, and then by having him visit them in the ludicrously opulent Nijō Castle. A series of squabbles led to Go-Mizuno'o abdicating in favour of his half-Tokugawa daughter in 1629. For the shoguns it became essential to keep him busily occupied and out of harm's way.

The third shogun, Iemitsu, gave the plot known as the *Sentō Gosho* as a permanent home for the Retired Emperor and his consort. Originally it was divided into two by a wall running from east to west, the Emperor and his entourage living in the south, the Empress and her ladies in the north. But the palaces burned repeatedly and after the last blaze in 1854 the southern palace was not rebuilt. So the Sentō Gosho does not actually exist—the buildings that stand today in the northwest corner are the Empress's **Ōmiya Palace**, where an old Dowager lived until 1872. With the abolition of the abdication system in 1909, the supply of retired emperors dried up forever, and the buildings were remodelled and used to accommodate visiting dignitaries, including the Prince of Wales in 1922.

But it is the **garden** that visitors come here to see. Go-Mizuno'o was a cultured man and with his fat allowance from the shogun he was able to indulge his artistic interests to the full. He hired as his chief adviser Kobori Enshū, the outstanding landscape architect of his age. The garden has been changed and augmented by successive occupants, but the basic 17th-century plan remains the same. Two lakes, joined by a narrow channel, are circled and bridged by a network of carefully laid out paths in the manner of the classic stroll garden. This style, not so ladenly symbolic as the Zen dry garden, is artful nonetheless. The paths lead the walker through a series of carefully plotted viewing positions: vistas open up dramatically, framed by trees or the banks of artificial valleys, to direct attention to the terrain ahead or to give a new perspective on what has just been passed. The garden begins simply with the plain tree-fringed **North Pond** and gathers detail and artifice as one moves south. The two lakes are divided by a bridge between two lovely banks of maples; another, more ostentatious stone bridge reaches an island in the south lake. It zig-zags beneath a sheltering wisteria trellis, turning the stroller's gaze one way and then another. The most stylized and interesting area is around the southern lake which has a striking 'shore' of mango-sized pebbles, gifts from a *daimyō*, said to have been delivered individually wrapped in squares of silk.

Southeast Kyoto

Fushimi Inari Shrine

Train to Inari station (JR Nara Line) or Fushimi-Inari station (Keihan Oto Line); bus no.5 to Inari Taisha-mae. There is north no.5 bus and a south no.5 bus: make sure you take the south bus.

The flat, smoky sprawl south of Kyoto Station is grim, but on its eastern side is Mt Inari, home of the photogenic **Fushimi Inari Taisha** and Kyoto's best urban escape. It's the chief shrine of what has become one of the most ubiquitous and popular of the Shinto cults—partly through the importance of its deity (Inari, God of Rice, and hence money and commercial prosperity), and also because of the inherent fascination of its symbols; the cute-sinister foxes, servants of Inari, which cluster the thousands of lesser shrines dotted over the mountainside.

The rice god has been worshipped here since the 8th century when the Hata, the local clan who donated the land for Heian-kyō, founded a shrine on the peak of Mt Inari. It was moved down to the present site in 816; the present **Sha-den** (Main Sanctuary) dates from a post-Ōnin War rebuilding as long ago as 1499, although it hardly looks it beneath its rich vermilion paint. The other structures in the precincts are a bit of a jumble: a big two-storey **gate**, a **stage** for shrine dancers, a **tea house** donated from his palace by Retired Emperor Go-Mizuno'o. The **Main Sanctuary** and **Worship Hall** are in the **nagare style** (*see* p.77), with broad eaves sweeping out horizontally to shelter the worshipper. Elsewhere, and all over the mountain, you will encounter sub-shrines in every idiom imaginable: roofs curved and straight, in tile, copper and shingles, with and without *chigi*, those projecting 'horns' characteristic of early Shinto architecture.

But the shrine's most famous feature is to be found above these, on the paths leading up the slopes of the mountain. Clustered together, as close as they will stand, are thousands of red **torii** gates forming a series of low tunnels beneath which all climbers must pass. The *torii* are tax-deductible: those characters painted on them in black are not prayers or sacred texts, but the names of the companies which erected them (a supermarket, a swimming school), all hoping to win recession-proof divine favour.

Inari-san, the mountain behind the shrine, is one of the stillest places in Kyoto, especially lovely in the early morning. Tracks criss-cross the woods and bamboo thickets and you can amble for hours without taking the same path twice. Among the numberless miniature shrines stacked on top of one another you will find various deities represented, jumbled randomly among thickets of statuary—Kannon, for instance, and the fierce Buddhist king Fudō Myō-ō. But the mountain belongs to the foxes which, even within their basic pointy-eared, sharp-nosed design, take on an amazing variety of forms. Many of them are canine, but some are more like snakes, or even dragons. They can be seen grimacing, jumping, galloping or just sitting alertly to attention, like demonic greyhounds, 'snickering weirdly at mankind' (Lafcadio Hearn).

The lanes leading up to the front gate of the shrine are notable for their pilgrim shops selling miniature *torii*, ceramic fox statuettes, and Fushimi *ningyō*—painted clay dolls sold as symbols of good luck. The pathetic-looking corpses on wooden skewers are another local speciality: broiled quails and sparrows.

A note for the adventurous: the shrine never closes, nor do the mountain paths to the top of Inari-san. In fact, the trails are always lit, though not too brightly. An after-dark—even a midnight—stroll here can be an exciting way to experience some of the Shinto mystery and you are almost guaranteed not to run into another tourist. You may, however, encounter members of the nationalist right wing, so watch your step.

Tōfuku-ji (Eastern Good Luck Temple)

Buses 202, 207 or 208 to Tōfukuji.

This big Zen compound was founded in 1236 by an ambitious nobleman in emulation of the great Nara temples, **Tōdai-ji** and **Kōfuku-ji**, and christened by combining a character from each of their names. By the 14th century it rated alongside Daitoku-ji as one of the five great Zen temples of Kyoto, although the two can hardly compete today. **Tōfuku-ji** is justly famous for its matchless autumn colours which flare beautifully in November in a gorge of maples crossed by a wooden bridge. Otherwise the compound is sprawling and unkempt, with only one or two interesting buildings among the parked cars and empty paths.

The finest of these is the Kamakura-period **San-mon** gate, a National Treasure, although more immediate amusement is to be had from nosing round the long building to the west (i.e. left) of this as you walk in. This is the magnificent 14th-century **Tosu**, or lavatory block. You can still peer through the wooden slats and make out the rows of latrines which would originally have been partitioned into individual cubicles. Sadly, they appear to be unused these days—more than one has well-fertilized foliage protruding from within.

The **Hōjō** (Abbot's Quarters) dates only from the Meiji period, with unusual geometric gardens laid out in 1939. Cross the maple gorge by the **Tsūten-kyō** (Bridge to Heaven) to the **Kaisan-dō** (Founder's Hall) which has its own 17th-century garden: on one side mossy mounds, planted with shrubs and rocks; on the other, a chess board of squares raked into the gravel.

Sennyū-ji (Temple of the Bubbling Spring)

Buses 202, 207 or 208 to Sennyū-ji-michi.

This little-visited temple was founded as a hermitage by the Buddhist saint Kōbō Daishi and rebuilt in 1218 on a spot where a miraculous spring appeared. Sixteen emperors are buried here, and the grounds have a regal air with broad quiet avenues and tall trees. The **Goza-sho** contains imperial apartments furnished in quasi-Western style with carpets, tables and chairs; beyond an expanse of gravel is the enclosed mausoleum containing the remains of the emperors, from the 13th-century Shijō to Kōmei, father of Emperor Meiji and the last of his line to live in Kyoto. Just inside the main gate, on the left, is a small hall devoted to the **Yōkihi Kannon**, a Chinese image of a famous beauty and imperial consort of the Tang dynasty. This placid, rather cow-like sculpture receives the kind of attention commonly devoted to European images of the Virgin, with half a dozen different postcards and even Yōkihi paperweights on sale.

Eastern Kyoto

Sanjūsangen-dō (Hall of the Thirty-Three Bays)

Buses 206 and 208 to Hakubutsukan-Sanjūsangendō mae.

This extraordinary temple presents one of the most awe-inspiring sights in Kyoto. Ranged ten deep, in 100 diagonal rows, are 1000 gilt statues of the Buddhist deity of mercy **Kannon bosatsu**, all of them subtly different in the carving of their draped garments, in the arrangement of the ritual objects in their many hands, and in the texture of their ageing over 800 years.

Sanjūsangen-dō was founded in the 12th century by Go-Shirakawa, a brilliant and manipulative emperor who acceded at the age of 29, abdicated at 31 to take the tonsure, and died in his sixties after three decades of *de facto* rule as *Ho-o* or retired emperor-priest. Go-Shirakawa was born into the vacuum left by the decline of the Fujiwara, when the Taira and Minamoto clans played out the epic struggle that was to mark the end of the Heian Period. By keeping his allegiances cunningly flexible, he held on to power through a series of bloody wars and succeeded in wresting back some of the authority that had slipped away from the throne. Sanjūsangen-dō was the fruit of his friendship with the doomed Taira chief, Kiyomori. In 1164 it burned down, eighty-five years after its foundation; the present building, and all but 156 of the statues, were replaced in 1266.

Its official name is Rengeō-in, Temple of the Lotus King, but everyone knows it as Sanjūsangen-dō, Hall of the Thirty Three *Ken*—the bays between the pillars in which the statues are arrayed. Their vast number, all of them facing in the same direction, gives the building unusual dimensions, only 16m deep, but 119m wide. Originally the outer woodwork would have been brightly painted; the dignified exterior gives little hint of the complex opulence within.

Sanjūsangen-dō was a response to the widespread belief in the coming of *Mappō*, the period of earthly decay which would herald the end of the world. To counteract its effects, seen in the civil wars of the late 12th century, priests and rulers placed their faith in sheer weight of numbers. Many new temples were built, monks spent lifetimes chanting the name of Amida Buddha, scribes repeatedly copied out sutras to be buried in special mounds. And in Sanjūsangen-dō the 1001 statues of Kannon were individually assembled out of wood, lacquer and gold leaf.

The arrangement and design of the statues are riddled with numerological conceits, best observed in the large seated central image. Like its companions, it represents **Jūichimen Senjū Kannon**, eleven-headed thousand-armed Kannon, a common manifestation of the deity who is also well known as a graceful feminine figure, the popular goddess of mercy. The eleven smaller faces are arranged around the crown of the head. Count the arms and you will find only 21 pairs: but these represent 1000, because every hand has the power to save 25 worlds (Buddhist arithmetic, it is true, leaves something to be desired). Each Kannon, what's more, can metamorphose into 33 different forms, depending on the needs of the supplicant. So the hall effectively contains 33,033 deities each capable of saving 1000 worlds—powerful allies, even in the age of *Mappō*.

There they wait like a Buddhist version of the US Cavalry, ready to sweep into action to save the world from the circling forces of darkness. The 42 visible hands pray or grip symbolic objects—a trident, a staff, statues of Amida, an axe, a wheel, a skull, a bell, a mirror, a lotus, a sword, a bow and arrow, a rosary, a flaming jewel. The sculptors, both at the original founding and the reconstruction, were all members of the family workshop which included Kōkei, Unkei and Tankei. Many of their works are signed, all are slightly different, and the game played by Japanese visitors is to search out a face resembling that of a loved one, often the recently deceased. More individually fascinating, however, are the **Nijūhachi bushū**, the 28 attendant deities, flanked by the gods of wind and thunder, which stand in front of the Kannons. These masterpieces of Kamakura vigour derive from Hindu deities. They include the winged, beaked birdman **Karuraō (Garuda)**; **Magoraō**, the five-eyed lute player; and **Basūnennin**, a deathly, emaciated old sage.

Since 1606 an annual archery contest has been held at Sanjūsangen-dō, with contestants firing the 390ft width of the hall at a target for 24 hours non-stop. The record was set in 1686 when a 22 year old shot 13,053 arrows (544 an hour) and hit the target with 8,133 of them. These days a shorter exhibition match takes place on 15 January every year.

Kyoto National Museum (Kyoto Kokuritsu Hakubutsukan)

Opposite Sanjūsangen-dō. Open 9–4.30; closed Mon; adm ¥420.

Across the road from Sanjūsangen-dō, to the west of the junction of Shichijō-dōri and Higashiyama-dōri, this fine, compact museum provides a historical overview of Japanese art in all media, from the Jōmon to late Edo periods. It was established as the Imperial Museum in 1889 'for the purpose of collecting and protecting the cultural properties which had been kept in the old temples and shrines'. This, remember, was the mid-Meiji period when state-sponsored persecution of Buddhism was in full swing. It is true that many temples were selling off their works to foreign collections (mainly to compensate for the financial restrictions which were suddenly imposed on them), and the sturdy museum was much less vulnerable to the fires which every year carried off a few more masterpieces.

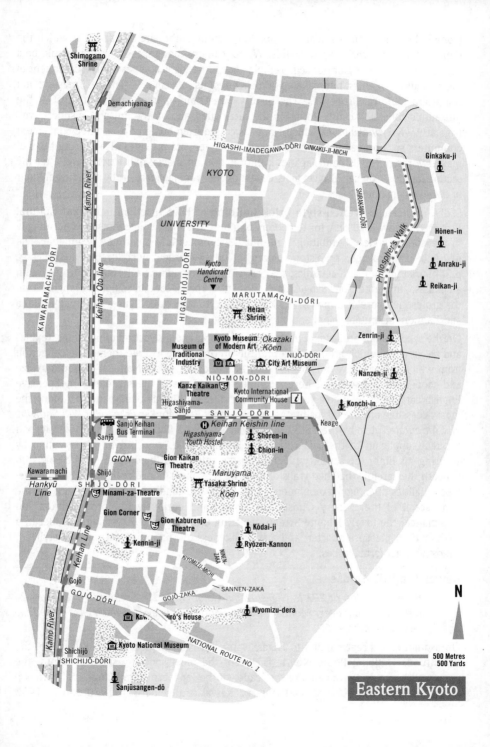

Eastern Kyoto

Nonetheless, more than a whiff of coercion surrounds the circumstances in which the temples 'handed over' their treasures. Without them, though, the museum would be a shadow of its present glorious self. Temple and shrine loans compose only 16 per cent of the museum's holdings, but make up 80 per cent of its collection of National Treasures and Important Cultural Properties. The displays are changed frequently, but most of the museum's collection can be found in the catalogues, and on the museum's superb web page at *www.kyohaku.go.jp*, which can be accessed from home or from three convenient computers set up near the front entrance. This web site provides clear descriptions of masterworks in English and Japanese, information on special exhibitions, and a terrific section for kids. You can also get an excellent overview of Japanese art by spending an hour or two with this site.

Sadly, the famous **French-style brick building** of 1895, itself an Important Cultural Property, is now used only for temporary exhibits. The main collection sits rather dingily in the concrete New Exhibition Hall, but it's compact and pleasingly negotiable. The first floor contains good prehistoric pieces, including a large clay coffin from a *kofun* (*see* p.54) burial mound, and ceramics, the best of them, including a winsome court lady with a Pekinese, imported from Tang China. The central rooms contain sculpture, ranging from the grotesque figure of Emma-ō, the king of Hell, to large-scale figures of Amida Buddha and Kannon, inscrutably aloof and inward-looking.

On the second floor are lacquerware and metalwork, and a selection of paintings, textiles and calligraphy which are replaced monthly in order to conserve them. The collection from which they are drawn is second only to that of the Tokyo National Museum in size and scope, and a few hours here, accompanied by one of the museum's inexpensive English catalogues, will give you a good grounding in painting of all periods. Among the most accessible are the ink paintings, many of them by monks. *Priest Hui Kuo Showing His Amputated Arm* by the 15th-century master Sesshū illustrates a famous Zen legend about a supplicant of the sect's founder, Bodhidharma, who proved his devotion by severing his limb; the scroll, with the ghostly, thickly outlined figure of the patriarch beneath the carefully hatched walls of the cave, combines horrid realism with the archetypal qualities of an icon. Anonymous, but equally outstanding in their medium, are the hand scroll of the Hungry Ghosts, a poignant and curiously humorous admonition to penance; the lovely Hikone Screen depicting musicians, gō-players and stroller in a 17th-century pleasure quarter; and a stern likeness of Minamoto Yoritomo in stylized, almost abstract formal robes.

Kawai Kanjirō's House

Buses 202, 206 or 207 to Higashiyama Gojō. Open 10–5; closed 10–20 Aug, 24 Dec–7 Jan, and every Monday (except national holidays in which case closed the next day); adm ¥700.

On a quiet side street parallel to Higashiyama-dōri, on the second block south of the tumultuous National Route No. 1, is one of the most soothing spots in Kyoto, the preserved home and workshop of the leader of the Japanese *mingei* (folk crafts) movement, and one of his finest works of art. Kawai settled here in 1920 and in 1937 redesigned the house in a beautifully relaxed, hybrid style. The basic model is the traditional wooden rural cottage with floors of both wood and *tatami*. The furniture has the lovely rough elegance of *mingei*, but much of it is upright in the Western style—a fine line to be treading in the 1930s when foreign influences were vigorously discouraged. It's a relaxed, tactile place: you can browse through books and magazines on well-worn wooden chairs. At the back is Kawai's great multi-chambered 'climbing' kiln, deified as a Shinto god with a straw apron and paper zig-zags, but rendered unusable by anti-pollution laws. Arranged about the house are original pieces in bronze, wood and ceramics, many of them featuring a recurring motif: the mystical clenched hand with pointing index finger which obsessed Kawai in his later years.

Kiyomizu-dera (Pure Water Temple)

The traditional pilgrim's approach to Kiyomizu begins via Kiyomizu-michi or Gojō-zaka, two bustling alleys lined with souvenir, craft and ceramic shops. Ask a taxi driver for either of these by name or take buses 202, 206 or 207 to Kiyomizu-michi. Open 6–6.

A more dramatic approach to **Kiyomizu-dera** is by the little path which climbs the hill from the south side and suddenly reveals the temple buildings and the famous precipitous gallery across the gaping ravine, 'like being in a small boat on a calm sea and suddenly encountering a battleship under full steam' as Gouverneur Mosher wrote in the 1960s. In those days the path led 'through a small village, a quiet wood, a peaceful isolated graveyard'. The peace and isolation is today compromised by National Route No.1, but if you can put up with the fumes for a few minutes the detour is worthwhile. Starting at the Higashiyama-Gojō intersection, walk along the left-hand pavement of the National Route for 600 unpleasant metres. A lesser road leads up from here to the path for Kiyomizu. You know you are nearly there when you reach a small but elegant three-storey pagoda. The best view of Kiyomizu is from just in front of here, and a path leads down into the gorge, past restaurants and noodle shops, and up to the temple via the main stone stairs. The description of the precincts below follows the crowds from the main gate. Those coming from the back should simply read it in reverse order.

Kiyomizu-dera is to Kyoto what St Paul's is to London or Notre Dame to Paris: a religious institution that is also a national icon, a place famous for being famous, and known to people who have never been near it. Japanese visitors to Kyoto come here before anywhere else, and you too should make it a high priority. You could spend most of the day here, but the temple is close enough to the station for a taxi excursion between trains.

Many Kyoto temples are famous for just one hall or treasure: Kinkaku-ji's Gold Pavilion or Byōdō-in's Phoenix Hall. Kiyomizu has its postcard image too—the gravity-defying flying platform—but the temple's charm is pervasive, and there are no dull or disappointing parts. At first glance the precincts are a jumble, though a fascinating one. Steep, narrow streets crammed with noisy craft shops suddenly open out before a great red gate. Climbing through it, you encounter a three-storey pagoda, and an asymmetrical line of gates and halls overshadowed at the far end by the great roof of the main hall. From inside the latter, the reasons for the temple's informal arrangement become clear: the buildings occupy the ridge of a hill and below the main hall is a precipice over which it projects on wooden stilts. From this platform a huge tract of Kyoto can be seen, lapping at the feet of the surrounding mountains to west and east. Pilgrims have been climbing the hill to take in this scene since before Kyoto was founded. It is this spectacle, and the relationship it has fostered with the city below, that makes Kiyomizu such a special place.

History

The origins of Kiyomizu lie in the 8th century and a legendary meeting between two men: Enchin, a Nara priest, and the warrior Sakanoue Tamuramaro, the first man to receive the title of *sei-i-tai-shōgūn*, 'great barbarian subduing generalissimo', for his victories over the Ainu aboriginals of the north. Enchin came to the remote mountain as a novice after dreaming of a golden stream—the 'pure water' of the temple's name, beneath which worshippers practise austerities to this day. There he encountered a mysterious old man meditating beneath a tree. The hermit persuaded Enchin to take his place for a while, and entrusted him with a log, telling him that he should carve it into a statue of Kannon. The man, inevitably, was not what he seemed. He disappeared, heavenwards, leaving only his shoes at the top of the mountain. Plainly young Enchin was going to be waiting for a very long time. Twenty years later he was still keeping his promise to the mountain deity, and wondering what to do with the log, when General Tamuramaro entered the picture. His wife was pregnant, and Enchin caught him in the act of killing a deer, the skin of which was thought to ensure safe delivery (Kiyomizu still has a nationwide reputation as an efficacious spot for the prayers of expectant mothers). The monk was horrified, and delivered an electrifying sermon on the evils of killing animals. The effect on Tamuramaro was remarkable. He became Enchin's patron and gave over his own house to be reconstructed on the mountainside as the first Kiyomizu Temple. The troublesome log was duly carved and installed as its principal image.

Enchin was a priest of the Hossō sect which, being based in Nara, was exempt from the destructive internal feuding of the later Kyoto temples. There were fires of course, but perched on its magic mountain the temple quickly became popular with the inhabitants of the new capital, and there were always eager benefactors willing to donate new halls and raise them from the ashes. In 1629 all but four burned down; the present buildings date largely from the second Tokugawa shogun's rebuilding of 1633, but they're believed to follow the old designs closely. By Kyoto standards, Kiyomizu's buildings, though distinguished, are young. They are only a part of its complex charm which, like a Shinto shrine, depends as much on nature as on architecture, and on the numinous beauty of the place itself.

The Precincts

The 1629 fire did its greatest damage in the east, and several of the buildings at the west end predate it. The red **Niō-mon** (Gate of the Two Kings) and its guardian deities are 15th century, and the bell in the facing **bell tower** was cast in 1478, making these the oldest features of the temple. The bell tower itself and the **Sai-mon** (West Gate) are about a hundred years younger: the carved animal heads and deeply curved Chinese gables are typical features of Momoyama architecture. Beyond the West Gate is the three-storey pagoda followed, in an irregular line, by the **Sutra Hall** and **Tamura-dō**, honouring the temple's heroic founder. The latter building was originally Kiyomizu's main hall, and it still contains statues of the *dramatis personae* of the founding myth: Enchin, the hermit-deity, Tamuramaro and Takako, the pregnant wife.

Just before the Main Hall, and swarming with schoolchildren on most days, are the curious *geta* **(clogs) and staff of Benkei**, the sidekick of the 12th-century warrior Minamoto Yoshitsune.

Benkei and Minamoto Yoshitsune

Countless legendary accounts of heroism and strength feature the heroic pair, who were finally hounded to their deaths by Minamoto Yoritomo, Yoshitsune's jealous older brother. In several ways they resemble Robin Hood and Friar Tuck. Just as in the English legend, the young warrior won the holy man's respect by defeating him in a staff fight on a bridge—the Gojō-bashi in Kyoto. In one version of the legend, Benkei was so confident of beating the young Yoshitsune that he braggingly swapped his wooden staff and clogs for ones made of iron, thus ensuring his own humiliation. The giant set displayed here, actually 19th-century reproductions donated by a grateful blacksmith who was cured of his blindness, commemorate the famous incident.

Kiyomizu's present **Hon-dō** (Main Hall) dates from 1633, but its unique structure bears the traces of centuries of growth and adaptation. The famous jutting platform, suspended above the ravine by five layers of interlocking wooden scaffolding, was not, of course, designed as an observation platform. It is actually a stage for shrine dancers—its wings can accommodate an orchestra—and the feat of engineering which enables it to hang suspended in mid-air was actually a brilliant piece of improvisation. When this became the site of the first worship hall, Kiyomizu was a remote and little-visited temple. Buddhism, too, was then a much more self-contained and inward-looking religion, centred upon the rites of a few priests and not requiring space for lay worshippers. When these started to arrive in large numbers there was only one direction in which to build from the crowded hillside—out, into space. Tales are told of worshippers who jumped off the edge to survive or break their necks, according to their faith or sinfulness.

Kiyomizu's eccentric development also shows in what many consider to be its finest feature—its immense shingle roof, best appreciated from the slope leading to the small shrine behind. The original roof structure—with its thick ridge and hipped ends—is still apparent, but has been augmented by the hip-and-gable projections which cover the orchestra wings. It's the interplay of these two elements—the great, massy, convex roof and the lighter, perpendicular, concave extensions—which gives the hall its restless energy.

Inside, the principal image of eleven-headed, thousand-armed Kannon is said to be the one carved by Enchin from Gyōei's log, and is so sacred that it is displayed only once every 33 years, even to the temple's priests. The visible statues include Jizō and Bishamonten, and the 28 disciples of Kannon, but more appealing are the big weather-beaten **ema** (votive plaques) which hang beneath the wide eaves. Several depict horses, three show early Edo period ships and are famous for the supposedly occidental faces among the sailors on deck. *In situ* they are hard to make out; reproductions can be seen in the nearby **pilgrims' shop**.

Other Buildings

The priests' lodgings and administrative headquarters of Kiyomizu are in a sub-temple called **Jōju-in** (Achievement Temple), closed to tourists for most of the year but worth seeking out during its brief open season in early November. Tucked away in the north part of the compound is a famous **pond garden**, unreliably attributed to the 17th-century master Kobori Enshū, which makes famous use of the 'borrowed scenery' of the Yuya Valley at its rear. There are more fine views from the **Jishū-gongen**, an independent Shinto shrine within the Kiyomizu precincts, said to have been founded at the same time in 798. The buildings, with curved Momoyama-style gables, are pleasant enough, but the shrine's greatest pull is its self-proclaimed status as a 'Love Shrine'. Charms and amulets promise amorous success, and the yard in front contains two stones which are said to bring fortune in love to anyone who can walk between them with eyes closed.

The Eastern Halls

To the east of the main hall a set of wide stairs descends into the ravine, and a row of smaller halls stands above it, their backs against the hillside. The northernmost of these, and the smallest, is dedicated to Jizō, the *bosatsu* (*see* p.95) who protects travellers and children. Next to it the **Shaka-dō** honours the historical Buddha, and next to that is the hall of Amida Buddha (**Amida-dō**), an unusual example of a Jōdo sect hall in a Hossō sect temple. The hall next to it, **Oku-no-in** (Inner Temple), also raised up on piles and housing a statue of Kannon, is one of the most important in Kiyomizu, and the focus of much of its symbolism. This was the spot where Enchin first met the supernatural hermit. The golden spring of his dream, **Otowa-no-taki** (Sound of Feathers Waterfall), flows out of the mountain just below it, and behind the hall is another emblem of water and purity: an image of Kannon standing in a flowing basin which worshippers anoint as an act of devotion.

Gion

Centred upon Shijō-dōri, between the Kamo River to the west and Maruyama Park to the east, **Gion** is celebrated as the home of Kyoto's most famous **geisha**—or *geiko*, to use the local word. Kyoto *geiko* become older and fewer every year and, unless you have expensive connections, the innocent pleasures they provide (singing, dancing, joke-telling; *geisha* are not prostitutes, although they may become mistresses of their well-established clients) are beyond the reach of tourists. The few still left are most likely to be seen in the early evening when they walk or are driven to the tea houses where they perform their entertainments; or at the annual Miyako Odori dance season in April (it's said that these days non-*geiko* are recruited for these displays to swell numbers)—*see* p.198.

Other peak times for visiting Gion are the **cherry blossom season** in April, when Maruyama Park becomes a human carpet of drunken picnickers; **New Year's Eve**, when the entire city seems to converge on the Yasaka Shrine to light tapers of rope from a sacred fire; and 17 July when the city stops for the **Gion Matsuri** parade of ancient shrine floats. Gion also has Kyoto's greatest concentration of traditional shops; the best of these are listed in the 'Shopping' section (pp.256–8).

Exploring Gion

Walking east from **Shijō station**, the first notable building is the **Minami-za** theatre on the right, a bristling tiled structure where the country's top *kabuki* actors perform their December *Kaomise* (Face-showing) season. Three hundred metres down, the road is crossed by Hanami-kōji, an attractive street of old **tea houses**, many of them fronted with the angled bamboo slats called 'dog-repellers'. To the south is **Gion Corner**, which presents a nightly show of traditional arts for tourists, and **Gion Kaburenjō** where the *geiko* perform their spring dance season. On the southeast corner of the Hanami-kōji crossing is **Ichiriki-tei**, an old and exclusive tea house and a prime *geiko*-spotting point.

Shijō-dōri ends at a T-junction opposite the heart of the district, the **Yasaka Jinja** (Yasaka Shrine, also known as **Gion Shrine**), and one of the liveliest spots in the city, especially on summer evenings when food and souvenir vendors erect stalls under the trees. The shrine is said to have been founded in the 7th century by Korean immigrants, and the surviving buildings show a strong Buddhist influence, diluted somewhat after the 19th-century Meiji Restoration when Shinto-Buddhist syncretism was discouraged. **Maruyama Kōen** (Maruyama Park) is just behind here, and northeast of it **Chion-in**, temple head-quarters of the Jōdo sect, a huge and rather overbearing place, with the biggest temple gate in Japan (the **San-mon**, dating from 1619), and a famous bell rung 108 times at midnight on New Year's Eve.

Walk north of Shijō-dōri where the streets parallel to it take on a sleazier and altogether more contemporary tone. **Shinbashi-dōri**, east of Hanami-kōji, is slick with hostess bars and love hotels; to the west, along the **Shirakawa canal**, are old houses and *ryokan*. **Shinmonzen-dōri**, the next east–west street up, is a good place to look for antiques and unusual souvenirs.

Heian Jingū (Heian Shrine)

Bus no.5 to Kyoto-kaikan Bijutsukan-mae.

Due north of Maruyama Park is **Okazaki Kōen** (Okazaki Park), a worthy civic affair containing several museums of limited interest to first-time visitors. The **City Museum of Traditional Industry** (Dentō Sangyō Kaikan), in the southwest corner, is the most accessible, with displays and practical demonstrations of regional crafts. The **City Art Museum** (Shiritsu Bijutsukan) and the **Kyoto National Museum of Modern Art** (Kokuritsu Kindai Bijutsukan) both feature modern and contemporary Japanese work, but most visitors will pass by beneath the vast vermilion *torii* gate which straddles the road between them. This marks the approach to the **Heian Shrine**, raised in 1894 to mark Kyoto's 1100th birthday and boost civic morale in the decades after the departure of the Emperor. The imperial connection is obvious in the profusion of chrysanthemum crests on walls, pillars and regalia. Two descendants of the sun goddess are worshipped here. As late as 1937, the last of the Kyoto-based sovereigns, Emperor Kōmei (1831–66), was enshrined here by the proponents of state Shinto. The principal deity, though, is Emperor Kammu, 50th ruler, who presided over the founding of Heian-kyō, as Kyoto was then called. The shrine was designed, after much consultation with archaeologists and ancient plans, in imitation of the Daigoku-den (Hall of State) of Heian-kyō's first Imperial Palace. The mimicry is imperfect, but this is still the best place to get an idea of what an early Heian building would have looked like in mint condition.

Once inside the **Oten-mon** gate, the structure will be familiar to anyone who has seen the present Imperial Palace or the Phoenix Hall at Byōdō-in temple in Uji. On the far side of a vast gravel courtyard is the Outer Sanctuary, 15m high and 30m wide. Two covered corridors sweep to either side, enclosing the rear half of the courtyard like arms, topped at their ends by bristling turrets. The initial shock, especially after the aged silvery wood of authentic Heian buildings, is one of colour: the pillars and outer woodwork are vermilion-orange, the walls brilliant white, and the roofs greeny-blue. They are roofed in tile which contributes to the Chinese look of the place, in contrast with the softer smooth textures of Japanese cypress shingles. The scale of the buildings is all the more impressive when you realize that they are actually only two-thirds the size of the originals. This shows rather absurdly in the small terminal turrets, which would have been cramped anyway but which become, in this diminished replica, Munchkin-sized.

At the back of the Shrine is a five-acre garden, laid out in the Meiji period in a nostalgic style. The East Garden strives hardest after an antique effect: a roofed bridge with a central moon-viewing pavilion alludes to the Gold and Silver Pavilions of the 14th and 15th centuries; the famous stepping stones were taken from the piers of the old bridges built across the Kamo River in the 16th century. Still, the imprint of Westernization is unmistakable: this is more of a park than a garden, whose outstanding features are not rocks, bridges or gravel beds, but trees and plants—although it is no less attractive for that, and in the spring the blooming parasols of pink cherry blossom are idyllic.

Nanzen-ji

Bus no.5 to Nanzen-ji Eikan-dō michi.

Politically, Nanzen-ji was one of the most powerful and important of the Kyoto Zen temples and still serves as headquarters of the Rinzai branch sect. But fires and war have jumbled the compound's layout; today it lacks the cloistered, microcosmic appeal of Daitoku-ji, although for its great gate, screen paintings and an intriguing sub-temple, it's still a worthwhile stop for those in the area.

The pine forest in which Nanzen-ji was raised was originally claimed by the Retired Emperor Kameyama as the site for a detached palace, after he fell out with the Kamakura shoguns. The place acquired a reputation for being jinxed, and when a priest of Tōfuku-ji successfully exorcized it in 1291, the Emperor was impressed enough to reward him with one of the imperial halls. Later Kameyama converted the entire palace into a temple, in emulation of Tōdai-ji in Nara, and personally carried earth used in its construction.

The monks of Mt Hiei set fire to the temple in 1393, and it was Hideyoshi Toyotomi who rebuilt it in the late 1500s after another bonfire during the Ōnin Wars. Nanzen-ji's greatest century was the 17th, when it gained its present **Hōjō** (Priests' Quarters), several sub-temples, a number of fine paintings, and its garden, attributed to Kobori Enshū.

The **San-mon**, rebuilt in 1626, is famous as the gate which, in the manner of a Zen paradox, leads from nowhere to nowhere. The paths pass around rather than through it; its presence is largely symbolic, but it is one of few such gates which visitors can pay to ascend. The view from the top is excellent, and the paintings of phoenixes, angels and tentacular waves on the ceilings and pillars of the worship hall are remarkably colourful and well-preserved, although irritatingly obscured by chicken wire. This was the legendary hiding place of Ishikawa Goemon, a popular outlaw who holed up here before being captured and boiled alive in a cooking pot.

The **Hōjō** (Priests' Quarters) is a chimera of two halls, both reconstructed here in 1611: the Seiryō-den from the old Imperial Palace and a smaller hall from Hideyoshi's Fushimi Castle. Their sliding doors contain fine paintings by the Kanō family, including a beautiful sequence of surly tigers and leopards prowling and sleeping in a bamboo forest.

There's a dry Zen garden by the Hōjō, although it's not as interesting as the one in **Konchi-in** (entrance to the right, just before the entrance to the Nanzen-ji compound), the most accessible of Nanzen-ji's sub-temples. It came to prominence under a powerful priest called Sūden, a henchman of Tokugawa Ieyasu and one of those who kept an eye on affairs in the emperor's city after the shogun moved the seat of government to Edo (Tokyo). After the ticket booth, signs lead you past tall hedges to the **Tōshō-gū** which Sūden built in his boss's honour. The *gongen*-style shrine is schizophrenically decorated— to its rear are the gaudy colours and carvings suggestive of the head Tōshō-gū shrine at Nikkō; at the front, the worship area is a forbidding matt black. The shrine is thought to have been deliberately placed near the entry point into Kyoto of the Tōkai-dō, the great road from Edo—an effective warning to travellers that, however distant they felt themselves to be from the power of the shoguns, Big Brother was always watching them.

To the right-hand side of the shrine, a gate leads on to narrow stone steps and past a small chapel dedicated to Sūden. Opposite here is Konchi-in's own Priests' Quarters, and the **temple garden**, a subtle and cunning work of abstract art. A sea of raked gravel stretches in front of the temple veranda to a pair of rock islands, and beyond them to a thickly planted embankment. The right hand 'crane' island consists of solid upright stones and a tall upright regular pine; the left one is a 'turtle' shape with low, round stones, stumpy shrubs and a gnarled tree. The two are linked across the gravel by a long, flat rock in a pool of dark pebbles. The crane and tortoise have long been symbols of longevity, but in this arrangement they seem suggestive also of one of those oppositions of two archetypal principles—male and female, mind and spirit, yang and yin.

Philosopher's Walk (Tetsugaku no Michi)

Start from Nanzen-ji in the south or Ginkaku-ji to the north.

North of Nanzen-ji, the small **Shishigatani canal** curves between a pair of tree-lined paths, right up against the foothills of Higashiyama. In the early years of the century, Nishida Kitarō, a professor at Kyoto University, used to take his morning constitutional here. Fifty years after the philosopher's death, his modest walk has become the most famous in the city, and a definite tweeness surrounds the perfumed tea rooms and craft shops which have sprung up here. Just above the canal, though, on the slopes of the mountain are three of the most secluded temples in Kyoto, and the walk ends just outside **Ginkaku-ji**, the eccentric and fascinating Temple of the Silver Pavilion.

The walk can be made in either direction, and takes a leisurely hour excluding breaks. Proceeding from south to north, the first of the temples, seldom open to the public, is **Reikan-ji** (Sacred Mirror Temple), a small imperial convent whose abbess is always a member of the old aristocracy (before 1868 she would have been a princess). The two simple buildings, one of them housing the eponymous mirror, are rarely open even when the grounds are, but the sloping garden is exquisite: raked gravel blends into sand and moss which merges in turn into a grove of flowering trees on the upper level.

A few yards up the same road, and smaller still, is **Anraku-ji**, a neat, secluded temple with something of the atmosphere of an English country churchyard. It belongs to the Jōdo sect, an off-shoot of Tendai Buddhism which gained a vast and rather unruly popularity during the time of the ex-emperor Go-Toba at the end of the 12th century.

Concubines and Converts

In 1206 two priests of the sect, Anraku and Juren, were preaching in this area where they won two distinguished converts—the Emperor's favourite concubines, Pine Beetle and Bell Cricket, who were so impressed by the charismatic monks that they took the tonsure and never returned to the palace. Whether it was conversion, or something more like seduction, is a matter of legendary conjecture. Either way, the news that his mistresses had deserted him for a pair of upstart bonzes drove Go-Toba into a frenzy. He had both the monks arrested and, when they refused to recant, executed. Anraku was beheaded on the shore of the Kamo River. Miraculous purple clouds gathered over the spot and the monk's fearless tranquillity won many more converts to Jōdo—although the unhappy nun-concubines committed suicide.

By 1212, the Jōdo sect became acceptable once more, and the temple was founded in memory of the tragic events. A pile of boulders at a crossroads of paths just inside the temple points to the graves: to the right are formal stones marking the resting place of the priests; ahead, at the end of the path, the smaller memorials of Pine Beetle and Bell Cricket. The small **Main Hall** contains images of Amida Buddha, the Jōdo founder Hōnen and, to the right, statues of the monks and their ladies. Anraku-ji is open during the cherry blossom season, the beginning of November, and at odd times during the year.

Hōnen has his own temple, the **Hōnen-in**, beyond a dense bamboo wood a few strides north of here. The buildings can't generally be entered, but the grounds are open daily and in the maple-viewing season you will have to run the gauntlet of kimono-clad ladies and their tripod-laden husbands obsessively photographing one another beneath the beautiful trees. Despite a return to imperial favour at the end of his life, Hōnen's Jōdo sect was persecuted in Kyoto after his death. For years the image of Amida worshipped here sat naked on the hillside after zealots destroyed its chapel; the present arrangement is 17th century. Peer into the back of the **Main Hall** and notice the 25 *bosatsu* (*see* p.95), represented not by statues but by 25 fresh flowers strewn on the polished floor in front of the weather-beaten Amida Buddha. By the main gate is another lovely curiosity: two raised rectangular beds of sand raked into the shapes of leaves, petals and patterns of water, depending on the season.

Ginkaku-ji (The Temple of the Silver Pavilion)

Bus 32 to Ginkaku-ji-mae or buses 5 or 204 to Ginkakuji-michi.

Ginkaku-ji, with a little exaggeration, might be called the Nero's palace of Imperial Kyoto. Nero was Yoshimasa, not an emperor himself but a shogun, eighth of the Ashikaga dynasty which seized power in the 14th century. Japan during this period was remarkable in two respects: under the shoguns' patronage, the gentle arts—painting, gardening, drama, the tea ceremony and flower arrangement—achieved standards of sophistication unmatched since Heian times. Politically, anarchy—bordering on outright civil war—prevailed under a government which had shed all pretence of authority. Fires and floods, earthquakes, plagues and famines fanned persistent riots and petty rebellions, and for ten years between 1467 and 1477 the wretched Ōnin Wars razed large sections of the capital.

It was in this atmosphere, with bodies unburied in the charred streets, that Yoshimasa made his plans for the Temple of the Silver Pavilion. He built it as a retirement villa, in emulation of the Golden Pavilion erected on the other side of the city by his grandfather Yoshimitsu, the third shogun. The landscape artist Sōami designed the grounds; the finest craftsmen and materials were requisitioned—although the silver leaf covering for the principal hall, which gives the temple its popular name, was never actually applied. When Yoshimasa died in 1490, the complex became a Zen monastery known as Jishō-ji and was used, at various times, as an army camp and battle ground; intermittent restorations, notably in the 17th century, prevented the gardens melting completely into the hillside.

The Grounds

The hedonistic origins of Ginkaku-ji—pleasure villa turned Zen monastery—are obvious even before you are inside the grounds. Instead of the monumental portal and north–south avenue of approach common in purpose-built temples, a modest tiled gate opens onto a sandy lane bound with hedges and a bamboo fence. Round a corner and past a miniature grove of trees and sand, the garden is glimpsed, just, through the arched window of a **Chinese gate**. The intention is to tease visitors: by depriving them of a panoramic view until the very last moment, Yoshimasa played with his guests and whetted their sophisticated appetites.

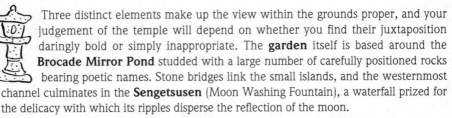

Three distinct elements make up the view within the grounds proper, and your judgement of the temple will depend on whether you find their juxtaposition daringly bold or simply inappropriate. The **garden** itself is based around the **Brocade Mirror Pond** studded with a large number of carefully positioned rocks bearing poetic names. Stone bridges link the small islands, and the westernmost channel culminates in the **Sengetsusen** (Moon Washing Fountain), a waterfall prized for the delicacy with which its ripples disperse the reflection of the moon.

The main body of buildings is to the left of the visitors' entrance. The only original one here is the **Tōgū-dō** (special permission required to enter), beyond the Main Hall and joined to it by a roofed corridor. Here Yoshimasa lived, and here he installed the simple **Dōjin-sai**, a prototypical tea ceremony room, the first one ever built to the now standard size of four and a half *tatami* mats. The shogun's play-house, the **Silver Pavilion** (Ginkaku) itself, stands next to the pond, a dreamy, fine-boned, unobtrusive building that makes even Kinkaku-ji (the Golden Pavilion) look coarse by comparison. Architecturally it's a hybrid, with a villa-style ground floor of screens and moveable walls, and an upper storey with swing doors and bell-shaped Chinese windows. The notched corners of the lower roof and the surmounting phoenix add a touch of tasteful flamboyance. Significantly, Yoshimasa had it facing to the east, away from the charred city of which he had washed his hands.

But the temple's dominant and most controversial feature is not its buildings or greenery. Beyond a bamboo barricade, between the Ginkaku and the Tōgū-dō, are two weird **sand mounds**, one a decapitated cone, Mt Fuji-style, the second a flat irregular blob said to imitate the shape of a famous Chinese lake. The material used to fashion them is much finer than the gravel found in classic Zen gardens: the edges and curves of each mound are as sharp as if they had been planed out of wood, or freshly tipped from the jelly mould. They appeared at some point during the Edo period: nobody knows who put them there, or why, although there's no shortage of theories. The 'lake' is said to have been created to enhance moon-viewing parties—the light sand would naturally reflect the moonlight thus illuminating the rest of the garden. The Fuji mound might have originated in the piles of sand which the temple gardeners kept in reserve to replenish the paths. Whatever the original intention, the sandcastles have become their own justification—bizarre, almost grotesque, but essential. You would never add features like this to an existing garden. But this one would be completely different—and not half so intriguing—without them.

Northeast Kyoto

Bus no.5, 北 8 (north 8) or the private Eizan Line to Ichijōji station will drop you in the general vicinity of Shisen-dō and Manshū-in. From there a short journey in a taxi would save time.

The stretch of foothills between Ginkaku-ji and the Shūgaku-in Imperial Villa has a sleepy small town atmosphere. It doesn't have the calculated picturesqueness of Arashiyama or the Philosopher's Walk, but it's not on the tour bus trail either, and there will always be fewer crowds here than in the more famous temples of the city. Public transport in this area isn't especially good and it's easy to lose your way among the ambling lanes.

Shisen-dō (Hall of the Poets)

Buses 5 or north 8 to Ichijō-ji Sagarimatsu-cho.

The palpable melancholy that surrounds Kyoto's hillside retreats must have something to do with the fact that so many of the men who built them were failures—forgotten princes, unpopular shoguns, retired emperors gelded of all real power. The founder of **Shisen-dō** was no exception. Nominally a temple, Shisen-dō was actually an exquisite private hermitage created by Ishikawa Jōzan, an ally of Tokugawa Ieyasu, who fell out with his boss over the siege of Ōsaka in 1615. He was exiled to Kyoto where he devoted many years to the care of his ailing mother. He built Shisen-dō in 1636 and lived there, as a poet and full-time dilettante, until his death in 1672 at the age of 89.

The villa shares the exquisite idleness of Katsura and Shūgaku-in, but on a much smaller and more intimate scale. The deliberately modest 'rustic' entrance opens on to a little stone path which minces through a bamboo grove to a second small gate. The twists and turns in the path create an impression of exaggerated distance from the everyday world outside. The villa itself is small, and painted beneath its ceiling are images of the **Shisen**, 36 famous poets of China and Japan. The **garden** is the villa's main attraction and falls into two parts. The lower section, a stroll garden with paths of fine white sand, is pretty enough. But the best view is from the veranda. Beyond a conventional gravel 'sea', are 'mountains', not of stone, but azalea bushes, clipped into smooth orbs, and blending skilfully into the forested mountains behind. The effect is very different from a Zen-style stone and gravel garden—cosier, more emotional, in keeping with the secular, dandified atmosphere of the whole villa.

Manshū-in

Buses 5 or north 8 to Ichijō-ji Shimizu-cho.

This is a mercifully isolated temple, well off the tourist beat, but all of its features are better exemplified elsewhere, especially in the Katsura Imperial Villa with which it is contemporaneous. It was originally founded in the 8th century on the top of Mt Hiei, and after several changes of scene, the monks constructed the present buildings here at the beginning of the Edo period (early 17th century). Prince Yoshihisa, for a while the adopted son of Tokugawa Ieyasu, was dispatched here when the shogun no longer needed him; the temple has ever since enjoyed *monzeki* (imperial temple) status. The **Daishoin** (Large Study) shares the ornate decoration and foppish detailing (sliding door grips in the shapes of gourds, fans, etc.) of Katsura. The more interesting **Koshoin** (Small Study) is unfortunately closed to visitors.

Shūgaku-in Rikyū (Shūgaku-in Imperial Villa)

Bus no. 5 to Shūgaku-in Rikyū-michi or the Eizan Line to Shugakuin station

The biggest of the imperial villa complexes, **Shūgaku-in**, outshines even Kiyomizu in the splendour of its setting: built around an artificial lake, with sweeping views of the city below and the foothills of Mt Hiei above. A big proportion of the 70-acre site consists of **paddy fields** which are leased out and farmed privately even today. Compared to the refined literariness of Katsura Rikyū, Shūgaku-in has a gentler, more authentic air which you may prefer. The two palaces were built by men in the same predicament—imperial figureheads robbed of power by the ruthless Tokugawa shoguns. But where Katsura's designers turned inwards (self-consciously filtering and reshaping nature according to a fixed set of aesthetic principles), in Shūgaku-in the viewer is thrust outwards into a natural world which is allowed to speak for itself. Frail, uncomplicated buildings, open to the breezes and to boundless views, gave an illusion of space and dominion to an emperor whose authority was a charade, and whose movements and freedom were sharply controlled by the very men who posed as his servants.

History

The genius behind Shūgaku-in was Retired Emperor Go-Mizuno'o, a thorn in the side of shogun Tokugawa Hidetada whose daughter, nonetheless, he was pressured into marrying. When this reluctant union produced a son, Go-Mizuno'o's Tokugawa brother-in-law tried to force him to resign in the child's favour. But the boy died, and the Emperor held out until 1629 when he abdicated in favour of his daughter. Relations with the shoguns thawed and Go-Mizuno'o was allowed to begin two big building projects. Sentō Gosho (Retired Emperor's Palace) was his city address; Shūgaku-in was his country cottage. He visited it more than 70 times between its completion in the 1650s and his death in 1680.

For 200 years thereafter its customary state was tangled neglect. From time to time emperors took a passing interest, and there was a big spring clean in 1824 when many of the present buildings were erected. The Emperor Meiji took over in 1883, and the grounds have been immaculately tended ever since.

Touring Shūgaku-in Imperial Villa

Reservations for the regular tours (conducted in Japanese only) should be made in advance at the Kunai Chō *(Imperial Household Agency), see pp.200–1.*

Shūgaku-in was built as a pleasure park, and was never intended to house the Retired Emperor for more than a short visit. Its buildings are frail and less playful and innovative than those at Katsura, but look out all the same for the storm shutters which fold away into a discreet case, and the paper screens which, instead of sliding horizontally, hinge upwards to create an awning. Notice, too, a small but important distinction as you are admitted to the villa grounds: you enter by a door in a gate, not by the gate itself, which is opened only for emperors and distinguished guests.

The Lower Villa

This sheltered grove served as a reception area, and is built around the **Jugetsu-kan**, an 1824 reconstruction of Go-Mizuno'o's original. Three of the *tatami* in the biggest room are raised, and beside them is a *tokonoma* (alcove) and shelves, and another smaller narrow alcove. This was where the Emperor sat; the extra space was designed to hold his beloved *biwa* (lute). On the little island in the pond is a famous **lantern** called, for its shape, 'kimono sleeve' or, more puzzlingly, 'alligator mouth'.

The Middle Villa

At the back gate, the comforting enclosure of the Lower Villa gives way to a sudden expanse of mountains, paddy fields and stern gravel paths—these used to be simple tracks through the rice, later primped up by the Meiji emperor. The path forks and your party is led to the right into the **Middle Villa** through a series of gates. The last of these has the thick tiles and gables of a temple gate, which it is. This villa was built later than the other two for Princess Ake, Go-Mizuno'o's eighth daughter; the **Rakushi-ken**, with its tile and shingle roof, was her residence and survives from 1668. In 1680 she became a nun and the small temple next door, **Rinkyu-ji**, was built for her. The most interesting structure is the **Kyaku-den**, once the dressing room of Go-Mizuno'o's empress, rebuilt in Shūgaku-in after her death. The doors bear beautiful paintings of floats from the Gion Festival and a famous family of crafty-looking carp. The fish, it is said, were so lifelike that they used to escape from the wall during the night and play in the pond. A later artist solved the problem by painting a net over them, but the carp have already chewed holes in it.

The Upper Villa

 Returning to the junction of paths, the alternative fork leads through the paddy fields past a huge **hedge** which crowds thickly around the track. This huge buttress of vegetation is one of the garden's glories. It contains 40 different kinds of shrub which flower in season; enormous razor-sharp scythes are specially forged to keep them trimmed.

The hedge was planted to cover the stone dam beneath, but it also serves to conceal the view of the lake until the visitor has reached the highest point. It's a breathtaking view and the symbolism, given Go-Mizuno'o's historical circumstances, is poignant. Since the earliest rulers, the ceremony of climbing a mountain and viewing the land from on high had been an important expression of kingly authority. This garden creates an illusion of the same power. On the horizon, seamlessly incorporated into the composition as 'borrowed scenery', are the mountains, the abodes of the gods. Below is the pond with its islands, landing stages and pleasure pavilions—the domain of the emperor and his courtiers. On the lower slopes come the farmers in their rice fields, and in the plain is the city of Kyoto lapping, these days, at the very gates of this one-time retreat.

The pavilion at this high point is called **Rin'un-tei** (Pavilion in the Clouds). At the front is a porch called the **Senshi-dai** (Poem-Washing Platform) where the Emperor sat painting and writing. Around the pond are waterfalls and lanterns, and **tea huts** designed by Go-Mizuno'o, some of them decorated with name plaques in his own hand. The pond's islets are linked by bridges, the most striking of which is the **Chitose-bashi** (Bridge of Eternity), a splendid Chinese-style structure with two roofed platforms and a gilt phoenix on the top. The story behind it says a lot about the surveillance under which the emperors lived. It was donated during the renovations of 1824 by a regional governor, much to the annoyance of the shogun who reacted paranoiacally to any perceived liaison between his nobles and the imperial house. The bridge was allowed to remain; its donor was ordered to disembowel himself.

Katsura Rikyū (Katsura Imperial Villa)

A permit must be obtained from the Imperial Household Agency (see p.200–1). Travel by train to Katsura station (Hankyū Line), or by bus 33 to Katsura Rikyū (a 30-minute journey; be warned that the buses are infrequent).

Three miles west of Kyoto Station, on the far bank of the Katsura River, lies an outstanding product of Kyoto imperial taste and Edo military money. Its creator was Prince Toshihito, another of those potentially troublesome aristocrat-aesthetes who were richly pensioned off in the early decades of the Tokugawa regime. He was an emperor's younger brother and had been adopted by Toyotomi Hideyoshi, only to be discarded a few years later when one of the general's concubines bore him a son. The consolation prize, awarded by the Tokugawa shogun, was the Katsura plot and permission to build a villa here. Work on the park began in 1615 and was continued by Toshihito's son, Toshitada—also a cultivated man, and also in the pocket of the shoguns (his wife was a daughter of the Maedas, one of the richest and most favoured of the *daimyō* families).

The earliest villa buildings were raised in the 1620s, at the same time as Nijō Castle; the contrast between the two expresses the aesthetic paradox of the age. While *arriviste* generals were raising sumptuous palaces, the true aristocrats—with no power to flaunt and nobody to cow or impress—took for their inspiration the humblest of models: the simplicity and poverty of the rural farmer.

Katsura is an oriental Arcadia, an aristocrat's idealization of the Chinese and Japanese countryside, replete with learned allusions to myth, famous places, classical poetry, and the vernacular literature of the Heian court such as *The Tale of Genji*. Architecturally, the villas here fostered a new type of building: the *sukiya* style (*see* p.81), combining the lightness and fresh simplicity of the tea house with the traditional elements (desk, alcove, staggered shelves) of the *shoin* (*see* p.81) study. The buildings, unfortunately, are undergoing renovations until the end of the year 2000. The tour route is still the same and you will be able to appreciate the garden and some aspects of the architecture, although there is no entrance into the buildings until the renovations are completed.

The Katsura buildings depart in almost every respect from the orthodoxies enshrined so portentously in Nijō Castle. Instead of coloured tigers on gold leaf, the alcoves and partitions bear graceful ink sketches, or crisp and unusual wallpaper designs; in contrast with the baroque metalwork of Nijō Castle, the door pulls and nail covers are slim and unobtrusive, fashioned in the shape of hats, pine needles, etc. The sliding doors in many of the rooms can be removed altogether, opening the traditionally enclosed tea room completely to the garden. The pillars are frequently no more than rough, unplaned logs, further blurring the distinction between inside and outside, building and garden. The *sukiya* style is plain where the old *shoin* were gorgeous; light and witty where they were dense and oppressive. It was the classic response of aristocracy to the usurpation of its mannerisms by the *nouveaux riches*. As soon as the soldier shoguns could afford to build and live like emperors, the rules of imperial taste were changed again. The Tokugawas built their gaudy castle only to discover that it had just stopped being fashionable.

 The grounds themselves were also innovative, combining the glittering other-worldliness of the Heian Paradise style with the sophisticated rusticity and minute detailing of the tea garden. This is one of the very earliest stroll gardens, and the path which visitors follow around the pond is famous for embodying the principle of *shin-gyō-so* (formal–semi-formal–informal). At different points the path is composed in three different combinations: smooth, geometrically cut slabs (formal); coarse, randomly-spaced stepping stones (informal); or a crazy paving of cut and natural rocks (semi-formal). The lumpy informal arrangement is often employed very deliberately: for visitors in kimono and wooden clogs, these stretches would be tricky to negotiate. Forced to keep their eyes on the ground, they would look up a few moments later to find a new vista had assembled itself before their eyes.

Other features of the garden embody similar exquisite refinements and hint at the idleness of the idle rich who devised them. Early on in your tour you pass a thatch-covered bench where participants in the tea ceremony waited while the master made his preparations. Facing it is a low hillock planted with cycads, specially raised in order to block the view of the garden and prevent the surprise from being spoiled. A little further on is one of the garden's most famous allusions: a stone bridge and miniature spit of gravel intended to represent the coastline at Amanohashidate, a famous beauty spot on the Japan Sea coast. This is best viewed from the **Shokin-tei** (Pine Lute Pavilion), the most interesting of Katsura's tea houses. It faces water on three sides, and each of its four faces looks quite different so that each view of it seems to reveal a different building. Thus the garden designers expanded space and made four imaginary places out of just one. Within, the tea room arrangement of hearth and alcove is enlivened by the bold blue check *tokonoma* alcove. The entrance into the room is an unusually low narrow opening called a *nijiriguchi* (literally 'wriggle door'), which forced participants to prostrate themselves and enter the small room in an appropriately humble state of mind.

Large, shapely and well-cut pieces of stone were objects of great prestige and value; among the tributes given by *daimyō* to successive proprietors of the villa are many of the stone bridges and lanterns seen around the garden. The latter are especially interesting. A couple of them, which your guide may or may not point out, were given by the Christian garden artist Furuta Oribe, and bear an image of Mary and the Latin fragment 'Fili' on their bases.

The destination and focus of the path you follow is the *shoin* villa complex which, sadly, is rarely opened to tourists. The experience of sitting inside has been described as 'like looking at the world from inside cubist sculpture'. Even from the outside it's easy to see what has excited 20th-century architects about the place. The three distinct sections, which link corners in a diagonal zig-zag pattern said to imitate the flight of wild geese, were built separately over nearly 40 years, but they ripple gracefully into one another and, if steel and concrete replaced wood and bark, they would have a very modern air.

Saihō-ji (Temple of Western Fragrances)

Bus 29 to Kokaderu-michi (buses are very infrequent); buses 63 and 73 also go near, but a taxi from Katsura station is easiest. Permission to view the garden must be obtained in advance by post (see p.201).

The garden of **Saihō-ji**, also known as **Koke-dera** (Moss Temple), is one of the most extraordinary in Japan. Even if the eerie moss forest doesn't stun you, the admission fee will: ¥3000, as much as a night's accommodation in a modest *ryokan*. Is it worth it? If Japan is bleeding you dry, then forget it: Kyoto offers ten other unique temples for the price of this one. But if you've already seen the inner ring of famous sights, or just crave some megaphone-free peace and seclusion, then Saihō-ji is worth saving up for, especially during the June rains which are said to bring out its colours at their most beautiful. In fact, the high price is what preserves the special atmosphere of the place: there are no crowds, no school parties, no cheeping tour guides. Even if you have no interest in gardens, the spectacle is astonishing. Think of it as the horticultural equivalent of a night at the opera, priced accordingly. Perhaps in order to reinforce the point that the ¥3000 fee is a 'donation', not an entrance charge, the temple also requires visitors to participate in a short religious service before being shown the garden. No one need feel intimidated by this, and plenty of your Japanese fellow worshippers will be just as baffled by the experience as you.

History

The original Saihō-ji was celebrated as much for its architecture as its garden. The famous Rurikaku, which stood on the very edge of the lake, provided the inspiration for both the great Ashikaga pavilions at Kinkaku-ji and Ginkaku-ji, but it was burned, along with countless others, during the 15th-century Ōnin Wars; today a simple tea house is the only architectural antiquity. A temple originally founded here in the Nara period was rebuilt and landscaped in 1339 by Musō Kokushi, a famous Zen master and one of the earliest garden designers to be known by name. The story is told of a simple priest who would come to the temple every day to help with the back-breaking work of remodelling the hillside. No one, it seemed, knew who he was, and when Musō followed him one evening he disappeared into a roadside chapel to metamorphose back into a stone statue of Jizō, the ubiquitous *bosatsu* (p.95) who guards roadways and travellers in the form of a tonsured monk.

Touring Saihō-ji

After presenting your appointment card and parting with your money, you will be ushered into a hall where you sit cross-legged before a low writing desk. Sutras will be chanted for twenty minutes 'for happiness and ancestors', and you'll be asked to write a short prayer on a wooden tablet with a calligraphy ink brush (a vague, non-denominational piety in English is fine). After that the congregation is led into the garden and for an hour or so you are left to your own devices.

Even without tales of stone Jizōs that walk, the moss garden would be an enchanting spot with all the qualities of a secret garden: a place to meet fairies or— as was intended—Enlightenment. The layout is simple: a series of linked pools, said to model the strokes of the character *kokoro* (heart), and surrounded by hills on three sides. Above, the light is filtered and dappled by a thick forest canopy; below, every surface—earth, rock, the banks of the lake, the root boles of the trees—is coated with moss, a luminous green fleece of 120 different varieties. Between the leaf ceiling and the moss carpet it's almost like being indoors. You feel you should take off your shoes—indeed stepping off the paths onto the delicate moss is strictly forbidden.

Theologically, Saihō-ji is a bit of a mixture. The garden around the pond suggests an earthly realization of Amida's Western Paradise, the Pure Land of Jōdo Buddhism. But Musō was a Zen priest, and it was also intended as an aid to *zazen* meditation. The upper part of the garden in particular, northwest of the lake, is very Zen in spirit. Beyond a small thatched gate and up stone stairs the moss is left behind and the garden becomes rocky and austere. Behind the **Shito-an**, a small chapel enshrining a statue of Musō, is a dramatic cascade of boulders, one of the earliest examples of the so-called 'dry waterfall', and a precursor of the famous Zen gravel gardens.

Arashiyama and Sagano

The area is well served by public transport. Take the JR San-in Main Line to Saga station from Kyoto Station, or Keifuku Electric Railway's Arashiyama Line to Keifuku Arashiyama station. Buses 11, 28, 73 and 93 all stop at Arashiyama.

The flat land to the northwest of Kyoto narrows towards a ravine, and sandwiched between the Ōi River and the hills is an ambling, autumnal neighbourhood of expensive tea shops, little country temples and beautiful, timeless bamboo groves. Once this was a secluded village, the retreat of writers, abandoned court ladies and artistically-inclined emperors. Today it's still one of Kyoto's most pleasant suburbs, although the lazy, Sunday-afternoon atmosphere is hardest to enjoy at weekends when the restaurants and streets clog with yelling toddlers and wobbly 'office ladies' on rental bikes. The heart of Arashiyama is the **Togetsu-kyō**, an attractive concrete incarnation of an old arched bridge. On clear days, eagles wheel above the wide river; below is **Nakanoshima**, 'Middle Island', once just a spit of river sand, but now home to some fine and expensive *kaiseki* restaurants.

Tenryū-ji

There's nothing special about the Meiji-period buildings at **Tenryū-ji** (Temple of the Heavenly Dragon) just to the northwest of the bridge, but it has an old garden and a history as interesting as its name. It was built in superstitious response to the death of Go-Daigo, the 14th-century emperor who famously attempted to restore direct imperial rule, and who was revered during the Meiji period as a revolutionary hero. Go-Daigo was aided and finally betrayed by Takauji, first of the Ashikaga shoguns, and the news of the Emperor's death in exile—clutching the Lotus Sutra and the imperial sword of office—caused great anxiety to the new regime. The Zen priest Musō Kokushi dreamed that the Emperor's spirit sprang from the Ōi River in the form of a golden dragon. In order to placate it, Heavenly Dragon Temple was built here in 1340 on one of the dead Go-Daigo's favourite spots; Takauji himself carried stones and timber to the site in a display of obeisance to the shade of his old enemy.

The **garden** doesn't compare with Kinkaku-ji or the Imperial Villas, but it's historically important in providing a link between the courtly Heian pond and the Zen contemplative garden. From the veranda of the **Hōjō** (Abbot's Quarters) one faces a cluster of tall, upright rocks representing the mythical Chinese Isles of the Blest and suggesting the influence of Sung Dynasty ink paintings which were admired in Japan at this time. It is also thought to be the earliest surviving garden to incorporate 'borrowed scenery'—the Arashiyama mountain behind. The temple kitchens serve Buddhist vegetarian lunches between 11 and 2.

Several lesser sights lie at the base of the hill east of Tenryū-ji. **Ōkōchi Sansō** is a 20th-century garden built for a celebrated actor of black-and-white samurai flicks. In **Rakushisha** (The Hut of the Fallen Persimmons), a straw raincoat and traveller's umbrella hat commemorate the *haiku* poet Bashō who holed up in this hermitage in the 1690s and composed his *Saga Diary*. Ten minutes' walk away is **Giō-ji**, named after a concubine of Taira no Kiyomori, the famously ruthless Heike leader. When Kiyomori tired of Giō, she retreated to this hermitage, leaving behind a sad little poem about the transience of love and beauty. It was discovered and read by the general's new girlfriend, who was so struck by it that she dumped him on the spot and joined her predecessor in the temple.

Seiryō-ji, a kilometre to the east, is worth visiting only on the 8th and 19th of the month when a secret image of Gautama Buddha (*Shaka* in Japanese), which gives the temple its popular name, **Shaka-dō**, is displayed to the public. The 1.5m sandalwood image, with its stylized drapery chiselled into thick grooves, is cruder than anything which exists in mainstream Japanese art but is considered profoundly holy. It was carved by a Sung Chinese sculptor as a copy of an Indian original said to have been modelled from the Buddha's own features. In the black days of the 12th century, the rumour spread that the statue, disgusted by the perpetual civil wars, was planning to do a runner back to China. Hordes of the panicking faithful turned up at the temple to beg for its continued protection; dozens of copies were carved just in case, and survive today all over Japan.

One kilometre northeast of Seiryō-ji, the five white bands on its outer walls and abundant chrysanthemum crests give **Daikaku-ji** away as an imperial temple. It used to be Emperor Saga's country villa and was converted into a Shingon temple in 876. Architecturally it's still closer to a palace, with a wide gravel forecourt before a **shinden** (p.81) hall that was moved here by Emperor Go-Mizuno'o from the Imperial Palace. The style is identical to that of the Kyoto Imperial Palace—cypress shingle roof with a protruding central lip, and two trees (an orange and a plum) flanking the stairs. The interior has Momoyama period screens of hawks and peonies by Kanō Sanraku; behind it, a network of covered corridors (another feature of palace architecture) leads through the grounds to the **Worship Hall**. The **Godai-dō** enshrines the Five **Myō-ō**, the Fierce Kings of the Shingon sect, and its veranda faces the **Ōsawa Pond** where moon-viewing parties are still held in the autumn. The concrete octagon to the rear is a repository containing sutras inscribed by Emperor Saga in a successful attempt to avert plague. You'll see pilgrims following his example in the temple's halls today.

Kōryū-ji

By train to Uzumasa station, either by Keifuku Arashiyama Line or JR Sagano Line. The Keifuku Arashiyama station is nearer to the temple.

This lovely temple set in lush, informal gardens predates the founding of Heian-kyō, and has the oldest **Lecture Hall** (1165) in the city, as well as a 13th-century chapel to Prince Shōtoku. All these, however, are eclipsed in popularity by the modern concrete **Reihōkan** (Treasure House) and its statue of **Miroku Bosatsu**, the Mona Lisa of Japanese art, and one of the most celebrated oriental sculptures in the world.

History

The statue (the first object to be officially designated a National Treasure, in 1953) has always been considered remarkable, and the temple was purpose-built to shelter and enshrine it. It was almost certainly carved by a Korean (there are nearly identical pieces in bronze in the Seoul National Museum), but no one seems to know whether he lived in his own country or was one of the many immigrant settlers who thrived as weavers and craftsmen in central Japan. In 603, at any rate, the statue was given by the great Buddhist reformer Prince Shōtoku to the chief of the Sino-Korean Hata clan which occupied the Kamo River area. The temple was built around the time of Shōtoku's death in 623, and survived the next millennium relatively unscorched; its treasure house was constructed as a 1300th birthday offering in 1923. The statues and their admirers are constantly scrutinized by security men but even so—like the Temple of the Golden Pavilion and Michelangelo's David—the Miroku Bosatsu has suffered from the depredations of the mentally unbalanced. In 1961 an enraptured student reached out to touch it, and snapped a finger off its left hand.

Reihōkan (Treasure House)

Miroku is the Japanese version of Maitreya, a lesser *bosatsu* (Sanskrit: *bodhisattva*) who will one day be reborn as the *nyōrai* (Buddha) of the future, the saviour of all beings. The statue here represents the deity's most familiar form: like the one in Nara's Hōryū-ji, it shows a slim, graceful boy (considered to be a likeness of the young historical Buddha) meditating on the nature of things, exuding an air of profound gentleness.

He is a Christ-like deity, suggesting compassion, meekness and the absence of desire. Originally, the surface of the statue was covered in gold leaf. Thirteen and a half centuries later only the simple crested crown indicates the Buddha's royal origins. The red pine has been burnished to a deep irregular lustre. The 'half-lotus' pose—right leg folded across the left thigh, left foot on the floor—suggests the Miroku's dual nature: both in the world and outside it, human saviour and divine principle. The carving becomes simpler and purer as the eye moves up the statue: from the stylized but involved drapes of the skirt, to the smooth arms and impossibly slender torso, to the plain crown and beatific face. The upper body is sometimes compared to that other emblematic sculpture, *The Thinker*, although Rodin's modelling is crude and melodramatic next to this. The face inclines towards the fingers of the right hand but isn't quite supported by them, so that there is an unresolved quality to the pose: the tranquillity of enlightenment is set against the tension of deep concentration; the smooth plumpness of the shoulders and face is balanced by the sharp nose and pointed fingers. The statue is curiously lit, perhaps for conservation reasons: half of its face and body are in darkness so it is difficult to make out the warm archaic smile which the postcards reveal.

There are more than 50 other statues in the hall, many of them National Treasures. To the right as you face Miroku is an image of **Hata-no-Kawakatsu**, who received the statue from Prince Shōtoku and built the temple. He and his wife are carved in the simple, rather heavy style used for aristocrats and Shinto deities in the Heian period. To your left, seated on a large carved throne, is a posthumous rendering of the 16-year-old **Shōtoku**. Opposite are several huge and dramatic statues of multi-armed Kannons. The seated **Senju Kannon** in the middle, although in bad condition, is compelling. A crack visibly divides the middle of its face and body emphasizing the figure's powerful symmetry, despite the raddled and crumbling limbs flailing on either side.

Tōei Movieland (Tōei Eigamura) also called Kyoto Studio Park

Behind Kōryū-ji. Open 9–5; 9.30–4.30 in winter; adm adults ¥2,200, children ¥1,300/1,000.

Japanese theme parks can, as a general rule, be avoided like the plague, unless you take pleasure in long queues and egregious cuteness. **Tōei Movieland** is different, though: tatty enough to be charming, and with an amusing (and possibly unintentional) sense of irony, a refreshing oasis of tackiness in Japan's most elegant city.

The site still serves as a working studio for the Tōei Film Company. When the park is closed (and when they have the financial backing, an increasingly rare state of affairs) the recreated historical streets and façades are used for filming the samurai movies which are a staple of Japanese TV schedules. Something of the production values of these endeavours is conveyed by the sign which stands in front of a reconstructed Edo period bridge. 'Simply by changing the name on its signpost,' it explains, 'this bridge is magically transformed for the camera into any famous bridge in Japan.' As in movie museums all over the world, the sets are brought to life by energetic bands of out-of-work actors who mount bloodthirsty battles and displays of *ninja* stunts.

Attractions include a street of Edo period merchants' houses, a reconstruction of the famous Yoshiwara pleasure quarter of old Tokyo, and a room full of small screens showing excerpts from classic films and the careers of famous actors. Sadly, these are not subtitled, but press the bottom left-hand button in the central panel of the black and white section for a scene famous even in the west—the showdown in the rain from Kurosawa's superb *Seven Samurai* (*Shichinin Samurai*). Outside again there are several cinemas (one showing non-stop cartoons), a *kabuki* theatre, and a hilariously feeble special effects corner where fibre-glass monsters judder hydraulically out of murky paddling pools. All of these are included in the admission price, but there are plenty of ways of spending more money: shops selling photographs of old Japanese idols, remote-controlled boats, and a costume studio where you can pay large sums to be made up and photographed as a variety of historical characters. It's no Disneyland, but it's fun if this kind of thing is your cup of tea.

Ryōan-ji (Dragon Peace Temple)

Bus no.59 to Ryōanji-mae or the Keifuku Kitano Line to Ryōanji-michi.

Ryōan-ji is another temple eclipsed by its greatest treasure: its garden, the purest and most famous example of the *karesansui* rock and gravel style, as satisfying and suggestive a piece of abstract art as any in the world. Unfortunately it's one of the least well-kept secrets in Kyoto, and the covered veranda from which the garden is viewed frequently resembles a football terrace with standing room only. Arrive as close to the 8am opening time as you can, or choose a rainy day when it will be less crowded and just as enjoyable.

History

The old aristocratic estate which preceded Ryōan-ji passed in the 15th century to Hosokawa Katsumoto, a leading general in the Ōnin Wars which devastated Kyoto in the 1470s. On Hosokawa's instructions, the ravaged site was converted into a Zen temple after his death. The garden seems to have been constructed around 1500; of its origins, that is as much as we know.

Tradition attributes it to Sōami, but for no better reason than that he is conventionally considered the finest gardener of his age. Unusually, the long low rock by the back wall has two names—Kotarō and Jirō—carved on it, and it's conjectured that these might belong to *kawaramono*, the low-caste 'river bank workers' who became the first professional gardeners. Whoever put them in their place, the stones of Ryōan-ji have spent most of their existence in obscurity. For 400 years they quietly gathered moss, attracting almost no attention from outside. Then, in the 1930s, the garden was suddenly discovered. It became a popular subject for black-and-white photography, and the Western architectural theorists who were writing with such excitement about Katsura Imperial Villa found in it another example of brilliant spatial manipulation using the simplest of elements; it's as a precocious example of modern art that the garden has become famous. These days the temple is one of the most visited spots in Kyoto.

Despite its meteoric rise to fame, the site can hardly have changed at all in its 500 years. Zen gardens must be the most robust works of art in the world. In 1797, fire swept through the Ryōan-ji compound destroying screens, paintings, musical instruments, sculptures, scrolls and buildings. The rock garden survived unaltered.

Viewing the Garden

Because the garden is wide and can only be viewed from close up, it is impossible to photograph properly. Lenses inevitably chop the corners off or distort its flatness with neck-cricking camera angles. It has to be visited in person, and it is always a surprise.

The first surprise is its small size; the second its extreme plainness. The garden consists of a rectangular bed of raked gravel 31m by 15m, surrounded on three sides by a low wall. Set into the gravel are boulders, none of them particularly massive, none taller than a couple of feet. There are 15 of them altogether, arranged in five groups of (from east to west) five, two, three, two and three. They can only be viewed from the broad veranda of the **Hōjō** (Abbot's Quarters) on the garden's north side; no more than 14 of the stones can ever be seen from any one position.

The gravel is framed by a stone rim, a pebble-filled drainage channel, then the small flagstones from which the temple buildings rise. The walls to the south and west are made of clay baked in oil which over the years has oozed to the surface to form intriguing irregular patterns. At least three different kinds of tree overhang the shingle roof of the wall, and shed their leaves onto the gravel. Within, there are no plants at all, apart from tiny lichens on the surface of the rocks, and the haloes of moss into which they are set.

The garden is compelling, but its austerity and barrenness defy conventional notions of horticultural prettiness. Its appeal is intellectual, not sensual. Few people who take the time to contemplate it deny its unique power and fascination. But no one seems able to agree what its effects are or how they are achieved.

There's no shortage of interpretations. The more literal-minded see the rocks as mountain tops above clouds, curves of a dragon protruding from the water, a stylized Chinese character, or even a tigress leading cubs across a river. In truth, of course, you see what you want to: staring at the garden is as hypnotic as staring into the flickering flames of a fire.

The garden's shape and form suggest other archetypes. It shares, for instance, the 2:1 proportions of the standard *tatami* mat—the symbol of sleep, repose and the home. The long raked grooves might suggest the weave of the matting, or even the pattern of planted rice in the paddy—or the waves of the sea, or currents of a river, even the swirling patterns of iron filings around a magnet. Certainly, the rock groupings appear in some mysterious way to be locked into one another: to move even one would destroy the coherence of the whole. Countless other gardens have been constructed using the same materials. None has matched the tension of Ryōan-ji.

Like the Zen meditation which it was designed to aid, all this is very difficult to convey in words. The garden can be thought of as a Zen *koan*, a riddle or paradox designed to provoke and jolt the rational mind but without a straightforward answer. 'In Ryōan-ji, objects (the rocks) are so perfectly arranged in space (the sand) that the viewer eventually ceases to experience them as separate,' wrote the garden scholar Günter Nitschke. 'It symbolizes nothing, in the sense that it symbolizes *not*... It belongs to the art of the void.'

Kinkaku-ji (Temple of the Golden Pavilion)

Buses 12 or 59 to Kinkajuji-mae.

> *The Golden Temple, about which I had dreamed so much, displayed its entire form to me most disappointingly.*
>
> Mishima Yukio, *The Temple of the Golden Pavilion*

Every coach party in Kyoto passes through the Temple of the Golden Pavilion, and anyone visiting as the guest of Japanese hosts will almost certainly be taken here. Kyotoites are very proud of **Kinkaku-ji**, perhaps because its central attraction (a building coated in gold leaf) seems to correspond to Western ideas of grandeur and opulence. In fact, after a bizarre arson attack in 1950, the pavilion was completely rebuilt. It may have cost $7 million, but it's new, and it looks it—many visitors will experience the same first reaction as Mishima's narrator, Mizoguchi. Blasphemous though it is to say so, the Golden Pavilion can be skipped by anyone spending fewer than four days in Kyoto.

History

The 14th-century general Yoshimitsu led the life of an archetypal Ashikaga shogun: he succeeded to the title when barely an adult, held power for a few violent, famine-racked years, then retired gratefully in 1394 to rule from behind the scenes as a priest. Yoshimitsu was then 36; the son who succeeded him was ten. His last 14 years were largely devoted to the artistic activities which are his great legacy. He studied Zen and the tea ceremony, hosted boating parties and *nō* plays, collected

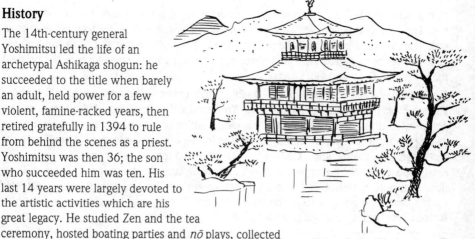

the newly fashionable art of Sung China, and built a marvellous palace retreat for himself on the northwest outskirts of the city which was converted into a Zen temple on his death.

It was christened, and is still officially called, Rokuon-ji (Temple of the Deer Park). The Golden Pavilion (finished around 1398) was only one building among many, but it was the most splendid and, thanks largely to its position on top of a large pond, it was the only one to survive subsequent fires and dismantlings. Contemporaries compared its beauty to that of Amida's Western Paradise. Even the Emperor condescended to pay a visit there, just before Yoshimitsu's death in 1408. His grandson, Yoshimasa, sought to emulate it with his Temple of the Silver Pavilion (Ginkaku-ji) in the east.

The English pamphlet handed to foreign visitors explains that 'during recent years...the structure has become damaged, and has required extensive repairs.' Even by Japanese standards this is some understatement. In 1950 Kinkaku-ji was deliberately burned to its foundations. The arsonist gave himself up immediately, and was imprisoned after a sensational trial. He was a temple novice, a loner and a stutterer, who had become psycho-pathically envious of the beautiful pavilion. His intention had been to die with the building; at the last minute he lost his nerve and attempted suicide on a nearby hill. Mishima Yukio's claustrophobic novel was based closely on the case, and also provided material for Paul Schrader's 1985 film, *Mishima*. Fundraising for the new Golden Pavilion began immediately, and the building was opened in 1964. Even today, it's the most conspicuously guarded and security conscious temple in Kyoto.

Touring Kinkaku-ji

Viewed from a distance, in photographs or across the reflecting pond, the Golden Pavilion is a splendid sight: two broad sweeping roofs crowned with a copper-gold phoenix, the upper two storeys—pillars, hand rails and eaves—glimmering even in the thinnest light, perched on the brink of the water 'like some beautiful ship crossing the sea of time'. Closer up, you begin to have doubts. The woodwork is smooth and unweathered, the shingles are regular and free of moss. Even when new, it would never have looked like this. The gold (20kg in all) is, as the guides proudly boast, five times as thick as the original leaf, which would in any case have worn to transparency centuries before the fire. No expense has been spared and, undoubtedly, no replica could come closer to the original than this one. But it still looks ersatz.

For its time it was a bold and unusual building, an architectural hybrid which reflected the various roles of the retired shogun-priest Yoshimitsu. The first floor, **Hōsui-in**, is in the *shinden* (*see* p.81) style of an imperial residence with a broad veranda facing the pond and *tatami* rooms divided up by sliding screens; to its right is a covered pier for mooring pleasure boats. The middle floor, **Chōon-dō**, is more like a temple hall or samurai house. The small top storey has bell-shaped windows and swing doors in the style of a Zen cell. Each floor thus reflects one of Yoshimitsu's duties: on the first he was a courtier and aesthete; on the second, a politician; on the third, a priest. The bird on the roof is the phoenix, entirely appropriate for a building risen, literally, from the ashes.

Daitoku-ji (Temple of Great Virtue)

> Buses nos.1, 12, 92, 204, 205 or 206 to Daitoku-ji-mae, or bus no.59 to Senbon Kitaōji then a short walk east, or subway to Kitaōji then a 10–15 min walk west.

A mile west of Kinkaku-ji, on busy **Kitaōji-dōri**, is the greatest of Kyoto's big Zen temples, a monastic city within a city and an essential stop for anyone seeking to understand the social and political character of Zen. **Daitoku-ji** is popular with tourists, but its quiet avenues and twenty-odd sub-temples are broad and numerous enough for it never to feel crowded, and there isn't a vending machine in sight.

Zen was introduced into Japan from China in the 12th century and, like all successful foreign imports before and since, it was quickly modified to suit Japanese habits and traditions. The head temple of the typical Zen *garan* (monastic compound) was constructed on Chinese lines, with a Messenger's Gate, Main Gate, Buddha Hall and Lecture Hall formally aligned on a south–north axis, and a Bathhouse, Sutra Repository and Bell Tower to their west. At Daitoku-ji, these prominent public buildings still echo the Chinese Zen style, with diagonally laid flagstones and benches instead of the native *tatami* mats. The main doors swing on wooden blocks rather than slide, and the windows are curved arches, almost Islamic in shape, a style possibly imported into China from the Middle East.

The abbot's and priests' private living quarters, on the other hand, are Japanese in their *tatami* floors, sliding screens and irregular arrangement, and the same goes for the numerous sub-temples which form the true heart of Daitoku-ji and comprise most of its area. These lesser institutions were founded by priests of the sect after they had graduated from the main temple, usually at the behest of a rich patron. Where the head temple was formal, geometric and Chinese, they were personal, higgledy-piggledy and traditional. Like miniature Oxford colleges, they developed their own traditions, laid their own gardens, commissioned and collected their own works of art, and prospered or declined according to the wealth and taste of their individual patrons. Daitoku-ji should be thought of not as a single sight, but as a collection of fine temples behind one wall. You can easily pass the entire day here; a long morning is the minimum.

History

The great Zen master Daitō Kokushi founded Daitoku-ji in 1319, after 20 years living as a beggar under Gojō Bridge. Among his early converts were the Emperors Hanazono and Go-Daigo, and Daitoku-ji's prosperity was guaranteed in 1333 when it became an officially designated imperial temple. It was razed in the Ōnin Wars, but rebuilt from scratch in the 1470s by the colourful priest Ikkyū. The popularity of Zen among the samurai class brought bountiful patronage during the Momoyama and Edo periods when many of Daitoku-ji's sub-temples were endowed. At one time there were as many as 80 of them; they dwindled to the current level during the anti-Buddhist persecutions of the Meiji period.

Visiting Daitoku-ji and its Sub-temples

Unfortunately, Daitoku-ji itself and a number of the most interesting sub-temples, as well as the Abbot's Quarters of the main temple, are closed to the public for most of the year, apart from a ten-day opening for the autumn colour viewing season at the beginning of November. Serious aficionados can apply in advance for special permission at other times. Start with your nearest JNTO office and ask their advice.

Main Temple

Although you cannot actually go inside any of the buildings of the main temple, you can see the order and arrangement of the seven buildings as described above. You can also go up and peer inside the Buddha hall, and get a good view of the second and larger of the two gates, the orange-red **San-mon**, was rebuilt in 1526; the upper storey was added in 1589 by Sen-no-Rikyū, Hideyoshi's artistic mentor and (tea) drinking buddy. He made the mistake of placing inside it a statue of himself, an act of hubris which so angered the general that he forced Sen to commit suicide and nearly destroyed the entire temple.

To the north of the **Lecture Hall** (presently under reconstruction) is the **Hōjō** (Abbot's Quarters; *occasionally open to the public, ask at the tourist information centre for more information*) which dates from 1636 when ceremonies were held to commemorate the 300th anniversary of Daitō Kokushi's death. The rooms are decorated with ink screen paintings by the great Kanō Tanyu. To the south and east are two Zen gardens. The smaller east one was designed to incorporate the 'borrowed scenery' of the mountains beyond, but smog and telephone wires have done for that idea. The larger garden contains two mysterious cones of sand. Opposite them is a lovely Momoyama period gate, intricately carved. It was brought here from one of Hideyoshi's Kyoto castles and is nicknamed **Higurashi-mon** (All Day Gate) because of its carvings—considered so flawless that one could spend all day admiring them.

Daisen-in (Temple of the Great Hermit)

The monks here are showmen and you may find the chirpy, Big Top atmosphere irritating, although at times it borders on the hilarious. Framed examples of the chief priest's aphorisms, some of them translated, decorate the walls alongside stills of his TV appearances. 'Do not take the monastic for granted,' advises one proverb. 'For underneath that robe may be a badger in sheepskin.' The one benefit of this self-consciousness is the detailed, if wordy, English pamphlet which is sold here.

Large crowds gather on the viewing platform for the austere rock garden in the front of the temple, noisily hooping it up to the priest's witty speech. Notice how much money changes hands at the end these performances. Aside from its charismatic chief priest, the temple has become famous on the strength of its **garden**, an extraordinary literal rendering of a Chinese Sung landscape, a collaboration between founding priest Kogaku and the artist Sōami, who painted some of the sliding screens in the **Abbot's Quarters**.

 Gardens surround the **Hon-dō** (Main Hall) on three sides; their heart is the small and crowded section in the northeast corner. After more conventionally austere rock gardens, the number and variety of elements here appear chaotic. Hundreds of rocks bristle against a background of shrubs and white wall, overwhelming the white gravel between them. Many have individual titles and the best of these are brilliant; once you've heard the name it's impossible to see the stone in any other way. The **Darumaishi** looks just like the hunched figure of the Zen founder Daruma as he is always depicted in folk art; the **Tiger's Head Stone** is like the smooth head of a cat surfacing above the water. The most dramatic rock, and the one around which the garden was designed, is the **Treasure Boat Stone**, once the proud possession of the shogun Ashikaga Yoshimasa. It's a dense, noisy scene with none of the pregnant emptiness of Ryōan-ji, and none of its inscrutability either. The garden, it's generally agreed, is to be read as an allegory for the course of human life. It begins at **Mt Hōrai**, the Chinese mountain of the immortals, represented here by the big camellia bush in the corner. In front of this are several upright and very obvious **foothills**, and to the right a **spring** (sand) plunges over a **waterfall** to fan out into the **island**-studded (rock-filled) **river** (gravel), suggesting the obstacles and difficulties which the soul encounters on its journey. The river flows to the west and south and in both cases empties into a broad empty **sea** of gravel, suggesting the void which comes with the end of life.

Kōtō-in (Temple of the Tall Paulownia)

Kōtō-in is a classic sub-temple, more like a private house than a place of worship, with a lovely moss lawn and spectacular autumn maple leaves. The **altar room** contains an image of Shaka, the historical Buddha, as well as members of the Hosokawa family, founders of the sub-temple and forebears of Hosokawa Morihiro, the Prime Minister who ended 38 years of rule by the Liberal Democratic Party in 1993. Kōtō-in's chief benefactor was Hosokawa Tadaoki, a gifted samurai who served all three of the great 16th-century warlords before ending up with Tokugawa Ieyasu in 1600. His wife, a famous beauty, took the name Gracia after becoming a Catholic in 1587. In 1600, in obedience to her husband, if not her priest, she killed herself to escape capture during a siege. The character of Mariko in the James Clavell novel *Shogun* was based on her.

Ryōgen-in

This is a compact and interesting sub-temple with good English captions and a pamphlet. It was built in 1502 and has five gardens. The **Totekiko**, jammed between a rectangle of verandas, is the smallest in Japan. The **Kodatei** was built out of rocks plundered from Hideyoshi's Jūrukutei villa, and has two stones representing the sounds 'a' and 'un', the alpha and omega, the passive and active principles of oriental religion.

Outer Kyoto

Kyoto's public transport network puts once out of the way places within easy reach of the centre. None of the following is more than an hour and a quarter from central Kyoto. **Uji's** Byōdō-in is an outstanding and ancient temple; **Ōhara** is an evocative old village, rich in history and anecdote; **Hiei-zan** should be visited as much for the pleasure of its forested slopes as for the historic monastic complex, Enryaku-ji, which it houses.

Uji

From Sanjō station take the Keihan Line to Keihan Uji, with a change at Chūshojima. From Kyoto Station take the JR Nara Line to Uji.

Uji was a Heian holiday camp, where rich courtiers built their villas and decamped in the summer to escape the heat of the capital. It was on the main road to Nara and became famous for two things: its green tea, still the best in Japan, and the strategically important Uji Bridge, the site of many bloody showdowns and last stands, several of them recorded in the 12th-century warrior epic, *Tales of the Heike*. In 1180, during the stewardship of the great general, Taira no Kiyomori, troops of the rebellious Minamoto family were pursued here as they fled towards Nara. The rebel leader, the 74-year-old Minamoto no Yorimasa, tore down the bridge and held off the army of 20,000 with a band of 200 loyal samurai. As his sons and comrades dropped around him, Yorimasa was finally persuaded to retreat to **Byōdō-in** where he laid down his fan, and composed his farewell poem:

> *How sad that the old*
> *Buried tree should die without*
> *A single blooming.*

There he committed *seppuku* on a spot still known as the Fan-Shaped Lawn.

Byōdō-in (Temple of Equality and Impartiality)

Byōdō-in is about 10 minutes' walk from the JR station in Uji, over a reconstruction of the famous Uji Bridge, widely signposted in English and Japanese.

Since the 1950s Byōdō-in's **Hōō-dō** (Phoenix Hall) has become one of the most famous buildings in Japan, but when Yorimasa spilt his guts here it was a lonely and neglected place. Its survival is almost inexplicable—few comparably important Heian structures made it much beyond the 1400s. For centuries at a time, and even until the war, the Hōō-dō was derelict; squatters sheltered here and lit fires beneath its wooden beams. Today, its fluttering roofs and fragile timbers are a nationally familiar archetype of Heian beauty. If you notice a lot of visitors reaching into their pockets and scrutinizing their small change, then this is the reason: the Hōō-dō adorns the flip side of the ¥10 coin.

History

The site of Byōdō-in was originally a pleasure villa owned by Minamoto no Tōru, a Heian courtier who probably inspired Lady Murasaki's hero, the shining Genji. (The final sequence of *The Tale of Genji*—the so-called Uji Chapters—is set around here.)

It came into the possession of Michinaga, the greatest of the Fujiwara regents whose policy of marrying off their daughters to successive emperors had made them the most powerful family in the land. In 1052 his son, Fujiwara no Yorimichi, converted the place into a huge private temple complex dedicated to the Fujiwara clan, with seven pagodas and 26 halls. The Emperor himself paid a visit here in 1067.

A century later the Fujiwara were history, their power broken by the contending Taira and Minamoto clans. With no one to tend it, the temple fell into disuse. Those melodramatic battles over the neighbouring Uji Bridge took their toll on the temple complex. Only the Phoenix Hall, surrounded and protected by its symbolic pond, survives to the present day.

The Hōō-dō (Phoenix Hall)

The hall has weathered over 940 years, the waters and garden around it have been altered beyond all recognition, but their combined effect is still uniquely majestic and delicate. It takes its name from a supposed resemblance to the great mythical bird, hovering above the pond with wings outstretched, in the act of taking off or landing, but never quite touching down.

In the time of the Fujiwaras, worshippers prayed from a floating platform on the water; musicians would perform from decorated barges. The far shore of the pond is still the best place to appreciate the **Hōō-dō**'s extraordinary construction, although these days you can also enter the Buddha hall. It's been described as sculpture, rather than architecture, because so many of its spaces are wholly unsuited for any human use. The famous wings, for instance, which unfurl from the central hall on raised stilts surmounted at their corners by roofed turrets, are purely ornamental. They lead nowhere, contain nothing, there is no access to them, and their ceilings are too low for a man to stand up, let alone worship. The 'tail'-corridor at the back (whose Zen-style bell windows give it away as a later addition) serves no purpose, and even the stone lantern in front of the hall is useless—its openings are too wide to shelter a candle. In the best traditions of the Heian court, where an inappropriately coloured kimono sash meant social death to its wearer, appearances are all. The Hōō-dō may be as practical as a chocolate fireguard, but it looks out of this world. Symbolically, that's just what it was intended to be. The temple's dedication ceremonies coincided exactly with the imagined onset of *Mappō*, the End of the Law, when worldly decadence outstrips all human bids for salvation, and the best that men can do is to put their trust in the mercy of Amida, Buddha of the Western Paradise. It's this heavenly realm which Byōdō-in represents and which forms the main theme of its famous paintings: the pond is the sea across which souls must journey to the Pure Land; on its far shore, Amida sits in his hall, facing east.

You can just make out his dully glinting face through the open doors of the central hall. The roof above it is raised, accentuating the opening and drawing the eye towards it. Inside, the 3m statue dominates the surprisingly small area. Amida looks down through drooping lids; the statue was designed so that only one man kneeling at the very base of his pedestal (i.e. Fujiwara no Yorimichi) can meet his gaze. The statue, together with the exquisite figures of the 52 heavenly musicians arrayed on the upper walls, is the only authenticated work of the priest-sculptor Jōchō who pioneered a new technique: instead of carving out of a single block, the figure was assembled from several smaller pieces of cypress glued together, allowing for much greater detail (see for example the delicate instruments and finely nuanced poses of the musicians).

Even if big, impassive Buddhas don't do much for you, the room itself is a pageant of decorative art. The arrangement of lotus leaves in the dais is unusual: instead of being staggered and interleaved, they are stacked in sets of four, reinforcing the impression of weightlessness. Amida's intricately carved halo dates from the Kamakura period; its flame-like peak laps at a flower-shaped medallion of great intricacy suspended from the square canopy above. The poles which hang from the latter would once have supported curtains.

The chamber still glints with the remnants of gold leaf replenished during various restorations. Once it would have shone: as well as the gold, the beams and pillars were studded with bronze mirrors which survive on a few of the roof beams. The base of the pedestal used to be inlaid with pearls and gold, which were picked off during the hall's period of service as a doss house; the coffered ceiling was gilt; and the panels, walls and pillars were painted with scenes of *raigō*—the moment of reunion between the dying man's soul and Amida in the Pure Land. There were nine of these, corresponding to the Western Paradise's nine levels (even Heaven has class distinctions). Some of these paintings have been skilfully reproduced, others can be made out amid the worn wood and centuries of graffiti, particularly to the immediate left and right of the statue.

Treasure Hall (Hōmotsu-kan)

The best of the surviving paintings have been moved here, along with the temple's famous bell, allegedly the most beautiful in Japan, and the original bronze phoenixes from the roof of the Phoenix Hall. The paintings are important to art historians as early examples of *yamato-e*—intimate, literary depictions inspired by the gentle, rolling landscapes of Yamato, the Japanese heartland, rather than by the craggy Chinese scenes which had influenced earlier artists. All of them show Amida and attendant *bosatsu* in action, sweeping down from the heavens to beam their celestial light at dying mortals of the nine classes. The heavenly host is conventional, but the earthly landscapes are warm and recognizable—horses gambol in the corner of one picture, and the buildings vary from an opulent winged villa (not unlike the Phoenix Hall itself) to humble thatched cottages still seen in mountain areas today.

Mt Hiei (Hiei-zan)

*Unnumbered **express buses** reach Hiei-zan in 1hr 10mins from stop no. 1A in front of the post office by Kyoto Station. They are infrequent in winter. This is the most convenient option but check for departure times.*

*__Trains__ on the Eiden Eizan Main Line (from Demachiyanagi station) terminate at Yaseyuen station; from here a **cable railway and ropeway** transfer visitors to the top, some distance from the temple precincts.*

*A more convenient, centrally-placed **cable car** links the east slopes of the mountain with Sakamoto on the shores of Lake Biwa, a couple of miles north of Ōtsu. This cable car is a 10–15min walk from the Keihan Sakamoto station on the Ishiyama-Sakamoto Line. From Kyoto take a train bound for Hama-Ōtsu that shares the same track as the Tōzai subway line. (Do not get on a subway train bound for Daigo.) At Hama-Otsu change trains—across the platform—for the Keihan Ishiyama-Sakamoto Line.*

Note: at 2800ft, Hiei-zan is at least one layer of clothes cooler than the city below it.

Among the superstitious considerations which made Kyoto an ideal site for Japan's capital was Hiei-zan, the great mountain which dominates the northeast skyline. The northeast has always been an ill-omened direction in Japan, the *Kimon* or Devil's Gate, through which the forces of bad luck, fire and pestilence enter a house or city. This may be a folk memory of the early struggle between the Japanese settlers and the aboriginals who occupied large areas of northeast Japan before they were driven into Hokkaidō. Even the walls of the Imperial Palace have a notch in their top-right hand corner to confuse the evil spirits, and a guardian monkey just in case they break through anyway.

Emperor Kammu's solution for Kyoto was on a grander scale altogether. A temple on Hiei-zan, established by the priest Saichō, posthumously canonized as Dengyō Daishi, was formally appointed to protect and watch over the city. It was a fateful decision. The mountain temple, **Enryaku-ji**, soon became one of the most powerful and troublesome institutions in the country. The mountain location, far from isolating the bonzes, effectively fortified them against external control. Until the 16th century, violence and death often did visit Kyoto from the northeast—in the shape of the very monks who were supposed to guard it.

Enryaku-ji's long period of power ended, as you might expect, in devastating retribution. Today, most of the temple buildings are 17th-century and none has the individual charisma of the great city temples. Collectively though, they form one of the biggest temple complexes in Japan, scattered across a forested mountain with popular walks and fine views of Kyoto and of Lake Biwa to the east.

Enryaku-ji

Adm ¥550; another ¥450 is necessary to enter the Kokuhō-den (Hall of Secret Treasures), but you can buy a combined ticket for ¥850.

History

Enryaku-ji, named after the historical period (782–806) of its founding, quickly became more powerful than any temple before it. Cunningly, the monks incorporated Shinto gods into their worship, claiming them as primitive avatars of existing Buddhist deities and thus establishing an authority over the 'descendants' of the gods, the imperial family. As the principal centre of learning, Mt Hiei became Japan's greatest university, having educated many of the great priests and thinkers of Japanese history and given birth to all the subsequent major Buddhist sects (apart from Zen which was imported directly from China).

Enryaku-ji was the founding temple of the Tendai sect, established by Saichō as an attempt to improve on the schools of Nara Buddhism which had become worldly and doctrinally slack. But by the 10th century, the same judgement was being made of Tendai. Successive splinter groups broke away, to the violent fury of the parent monastery. The first of these made its headquarters, unwisely, in Mii-dera on the shores of Lake Biwa, directly below the glowering peaks of Mt Hiei. For 600 years these two temples were the Tweedledum and Tweedledee of Japanese Buddhism, invariably taking opposing sides on any issue of contention. But Enryaku-ji had the strategic advantage of height and regularly stomped on its rival, razing Mii-dera to the ground 9 times in 250 years.

At the height of its power, Enryaku-ji comprised 3000 temples—a state-within-a-state, immune to external authority, with its own army and the power to tip the balance in secular as well as spiritual matters. Of the alternative sects which emerged in Kyoto during the Heian period—the Jōdo of Priest Hōnen, Shinran's Shin sect, Nichiren's Hokke—all endured persecution and suppression masterminded on Mt Hiei. Imperial authority was also flouted. When disagreements with the emperor arose, Enryaku-ji's private army would march on the palace—because they carried the portable shrine of the Shinto deity Sanno, no one dared to challenge them physically. 'There are three things which I cannot bring under obedience' lamented Emperor Shirakawa (1056–1129) famously: 'the waters of the Kamo River, the dice of the *sugoroku* game, and the bonzes on the mountain.'

If anyone was going to put an end to this it was Oda Nobunaga, the notoriously brutal unifier of late 16th-century Japan. In 1571 he assembled an army at the foot of the mountain. Here, patently, was a man with no qualms about upsetting the odd portable shrine. 'Surround their dens and burn them,' he commanded, 'and suffer none within them to live.' The soldiers stormed the temples, torched their buildings and massacred their inhabitants, including a good many women and children besides the recalcitrant priests.

Nobunaga's successor, Toyotomi Hideyoshi, rebuilt Enryaku-ji, limiting the number of temples to 125, its approximate strength even today. But the stuffing had been knocked out of it and Kyoto's northeast front has been quiet for the last 400 years.

Visiting Enryaku-ji

Enryaku-ji's mountain-top position hasn't saved it from crowds or commercialization, which are excessive. Grit your teeth through the recorded commentaries, bus fumes and souvenir emporia in the Eastern Compound, and escape at some point to the Western Compound and Yokawa down the road, which still maintain a measure of their ancient tranquillity. Mudō-ji Dani (Valley of the Still Temple), just below the eastern (i.e. Sakamoto) cable car station, lives up to its name; the half dozen modest temples have good views over Lake Biwa.

Eastern Compound (Tō-tō)

Passengers from the express bus disembark in a horrible car park by the eastern compound entrance. The modern building on the left just after the ticket booth is the **Kokuhō-den** (Hall of Secret Treasures) where an early Heian statue of thousand-armed Kannon is housed. Further on, on the same side, is the **Daikō-dō** (Great Lecture Hall, originally built in 1634) which burned in 1956 and was replaced by the present building, carried up from the bottom of the mountain beside Lake Biwa. Just to the west of here (i.e. to the right as you walk south from the car park) is the **Kaidan-in** (Ordination Hall, 1604), with attractive curving gables and bell-shaped Zen windows. Saichō fought throughout his career for his own *Kaidan-in*. After his death permission was finally granted, and Enryaku-ji gained an important degree of autonomy from the Nara temples who had until then enjoyed exclusive rights of ordination.

The most important building is on a lower level, and the best overall view of it can be had from the back of the Great Lecture Hall where you can look down on the gable end with its intricately carved medallions and gold-fanged demons. This is the **Konponchū-dō** (Fundamental Central Hall), the first hall ever built by Saichō, and the cell from which the whole great monastery city grew. The statue of Yakushi Nyōrai enshrined here (hidden— only a copy is displayed) was dedicated in 794 in a much simpler building.

The present hall dates from 1642 and is surrounded by an outer cloister with carvings of animals and birds beneath the eaves. Time, and centuries of candle and incense smoke, have done a good job in elegantly muting the once bold colours inside; the whole structure has an air of symmetry and purpose despite the intricate carvings on the transoms and the faded flower paintings in each panel of the coffered ceiling. The inner sanctuary is eerily beautiful. Its floor is much lower than that in the front worship area, so that the altar beyond seems to rise floating out of nowhere. The priests sat down there to conduct services, symbolically linking the void between man and god who, though on the same level, are unbridgeably separated.

The central image is Yakushi, Buddha of healing, a copy of Saichō's original which is hidden in the closed altar behind (complete with its own miniature roof and gables). He is flanked by Nikkō and Gakkō, deities of the sun and moon. Three gold lanterns in front of them contain flames said to have been kindled by Saichō and to have remained unquenched ever since—though they have certainly been swamped by greater fires in the intervening 1200 years.

West of the main buildings, paths and a fast road cut through the forest towards the Western Compound. The bright vermilion **Amida Hall** and two-storey **pagoda** are both 20th-century reconstructions. Past a small chapel to Kannon called **Sanno-in** (after the Shinto deity which the monks used to carry down the mountain on their punitive raids), steps lead down to **Jōdo-in**, a small sub-temple with a main hall, a phoenix-topped Amida hall, and the grave of Saichō. This beautiful and other-worldly place owes its unbelievable neatness to the curious austerities practised by the monks here. Nicknamed 'sweeping hell', they involve intensive brushing of the temple and its ground for up to six hours a day. Some monks spend 12 years on the mountain, never leaving and doing little else.

Western Compound (Sai-tō)

Beyond Jōdo-in, the Western Compound begins at **Benkei no Ninai-dō** (The Halls Benkei Lifted), two identical temples joined by a covered corridor which bridges the path. Benkei was the sidekick of the 12th-century hero Yoshitsune no Taira, renowned for his Herculean feats of strength: the story goes that he hoisted the halls by shouldering the bridge between them like a yoke. Both buildings are designed for religious walking ceremonies which play an important part in Tendai worship: monks pace around the outer corridors, chanting or reading from the sutras.

The next building, the **Shaka-dō**, is not so grand as the Konponchū-dō, but is much older. It was originally built in the Kamakura period as part of Mii-dera, the breakaway monastery at the foot of the mountain which naturally supported Oda Nobunaga against Enryaku-ji. Nobunaga's successor, Hideyoshi, had it rebuilt here—the interior layout is very similar to Konponchū-dō, but it enshrines instead a Saichō-carved statue of Shaka, the historical Buddha, flanked by the Four Directional Guardians. On an isolated mound north of the Shaka-dō is a weird object, something like a pagoda that has sunk into the earth under its own weight leaving only the golden spire on the top. This is the **Sōrin-tō**, a rare example of a zero-storey pagoda, mounted on a stone vault containing sutras.

The road continues to **Yokawa**, the third and northernmost compound which has no buildings of particular interest. The two and a half mile walk is pleasant enough; intermittent buses link it with the main car park.

Ōhara

Kyoto buses 17 or 18 from Kyoto station; 16 or 17 from Sanjō station. Be sure that you get a Kyoto bus and not a city bus.

Like many naturally beautiful villages in this crowded country, Ōhara has become a little self-conscious over the years. Once it was famous for the 'Ōhara wenches', simple rustic maids with the endearing habit of walking round with bundles of sticks on their heads—

these they would carry into Kyoto to sell in the markets. Nowadays, the *Ōhara-me* have neat little uniforms and jobs in the tasteful craft and souvenir shops which line the winding lanes.

Apart from its lazy, rural atmosphere, the village is visited for the two lovely temples on either side of the Ōhara River: **Jakkō-in** to the west, and **Sanzen-in** to the west on the slopes of Gyō-zan—Fish Mountain.

Sanzen-in (Three Thousand Temple)

History

These days Sanzen-in is a *monzeki*, an imperial temple traditionally administered by an imperial prince; at its foundation, a thousand years ago, it was an altogether humbler place. A hall was built on the side of Fish Mountain by Eshin, a famous son of Enryaku-ji temple on Mt Hiei, in 985. This was a period of crucial intellectual change for Japanese Buddhism when the complex theology and rituals of the Tendai sect, accessible only to an educated few, were actively simplified and demystified for the benefit of the illiterate masses. Eshin was one of those who developed the doctrine of the **Nembutsu**, a chanted formula (*Namu Amida Butsu*, simply, 'Save me, Amida Buddha'), the mere utterance of which was said to guarantee the sincere worshipper's entry into Paradise. Amida, the merciful Lord of the Western Paradise, was depicted more and more in religious art, and the comfort which he offered after death to long-suffering souls became the great theme of late-Heian Buddhism. Simple rural temples, with only a few buildings and a single priest, were the places where this grass roots evangelism took place; because of the eminence of its founder Eshin, Sanzen-in—in spite of its remote location—became one of the most important and well-known.

Touring the Temple

Thirty years ago, Sanzen-in could only be approached on foot, but today a metalled road leads up Fish Mountain, to the right-hand side as you approach from Kyoto. The immediate approach to the temple runs beneath a fine wall like those built around 16th-century castles. In May, this approach becomes a tunnel of pink and white cherry blossom. Inside the **Goten-mon** gate is an extensive garden of cryptomeria trees rising like pillars out of a carpet of moss.

The three main temple buildings are linked by covered walkways which lead you first into the **Kyaku-den** (Guest Palace), a 16th-century structure built as a residence for the temple's Imperial abbots. Display cases contain treasures brought to Ōhara by these men (notice the ubiquitous imperial chrysanthemum embossed on swords and lacquerware). The interiors were comprehensively restored in the early years of the century, and the door paintings date from the same time, including an intriguing image of white-bearded Shaka Buddha, praying fiercely on a mountain-top accompanied by a kneeling follower. A crazily distorted pine tree writhes beside them. Its branches form the shape of a dragon—look for the beady eyes in the top left corner.

The second building, the **Shinden**, burned, and was built anew in 1926, but the objects it contains are ancient. The west room enshrines the temple's abbots. On the left is a millennium-old statue of the 'Fierce King' Fudō Myō-ō, with much of the original colour of his cloak of flames preserved. In the centre is Amida, and to the right a lovely Guze Kannon with a metal crown, found to contain a letter inside its hollow body, dated 1246.

But it's the **Hon-dō** (Main Hall), also known as the **Ōjō Gokuraku-in** (Temple of Rebirth in Paradise), which you've really come to see. The plain, shingle-roofed building dates from the 12th century, but the main image of Amida Buddha was carved by Eshin at the time of the hall's original construction in 985. In themselves, the three sculptures are stiff, rather cool figures, but their state of preservation is remarkable, and they're beautifully set off by the snug, smoke-blackened interior. The ceiling is on two levels: the upper, accommodating Amida's head and halo, is shaped like an upturned boat and was originally painted with images of his 25 *bosatsu* (*see* p.95)—these can just be made out using the electric torch which is usually at the front of the altar. The lower beams are on a level well below Amida's head so that the statue, although far from huge, appears to loom impressively in the limited space. A few surviving fragments of mural survive behind protective frames, but at one time the walls teemed with the images of 3000 Buddhas, *bosatsu* (*see* p.95) and heavenly beings, plus countless flowers and geometric designs, all evocative of the Pure Western Land where Amida welcomes the souls of the dead. Seishi *bosatsu* (*see* p.95), to the viewer's left, prays for the dying mortal; Kannon, on the right, proffers a lotus flower to scoop it up into paradise. The two flanking statues, possibly later than the main image, both kneel and lean forward slightly, adding to the dynamic, swooping quality of the whole composition.

The gardens extend above and behind the Hon-dō where a **tea arbour** stands, selling the ultimate beverage for the man who has everything: salty tea laced with flakes of gold dust.

Jakkō-in (Solitary Light Temple)

This secluded little convent, reached by winding lanes on the west side of the Ōhara River, is a simple, unspectacular place, the scene of one of the most famous and pathetic scenes of Japanese literature. It is described in the *Tales of the Heike* (translation below by A. L. Sadler), a chronicle of the struggle at the end of the 12th century between the Minamoto (or Genji) clan and the Taira (Heike) who, under the powerful stewardship of their leader, Kiyomori, had in the space of a few decades become the rulers of Japan. Then, in 1181, Kiyomori died and the Taira's supremacy was challenged by the descendants of his old enemies, the Minamoto. The two sides played a cat-and-mouse game with one another on land and sea, until 1185 when the Taira fleet was destroyed in the straits of Dan no Ura at the westernmost tip of Honshū. At the climax of the battle, with the enemy closing in, Kiyomori's widow, Lady Nii, seized hold of her grandson, the infant Emperor Antoku, and jumped with him into the sea followed by her ladies-in-waiting.

All but a handful drowned. Among those dragged from the waves against their will was Kenreimon-in, daughter of Kiyomori and widow of the previous puppet emperor, Takakura.

She had watched her mother, Nii, and child, Antoku, drown before her eyes. After the battle, the sole surviving member of her immediate family, she was taken to Kyoto, 'bereft of all her old companions like a fish on the dry land or a bird torn from its nest'.

She was twenty-eight this year, and the beauty of her face was not yet dimmed; neither was the elegance of her slender form impaired; but what now availed the loveliness of her hair?

Kenreimon-in took the tonsure and offered the tiny robe of Antoku, still scented with his perfume, at Chōraku-ji temple. But the cell where she was living was destroyed in an earthquake, and the nun-empress resolved to escape from the capital and the gaze of curious passers-by. In the autumn of 1185 she was conveyed out of Kyoto to an obscure convent in the northern mountains.

The place she had chosen to dwell in was ancient and surrounded by mossy rocks. The reeds in the garden were now covered with hoar-frost instead of dew, and when she gazed on the faded hue of the withered chrysanthemums by the wall, she could hardly fail to be reminded of her own condition...still the image of the late Emperor was impressed on her mind, and wherever she might be, and in what world soever, she thought she could never forget it. They built for her a small cell ten feet square beside the Jakkō-in, and in it were two rooms; in one she put her shrine of Buddha and in the other she slept.

In the summer of 1186, more than a year after the catastrophe that changed the whole course of Kenreimon-in's life, she received a visitor, the last old friend she would ever see. It was the retired emperor Go-Shirakawa, at various times the ally of both Taira and Minamoto, whose shifty power-broking had added much to the confusion of the civil war. Now, though, he came to Ōhara out of compassion. When Kenreimon-in first appeared, he didn't recognize her, such was her poverty and gauntness. All afternoon they talked about the unfathomable changes that had come to pass.

Formerly she had lived delicately in the Jewel Halls, and couches of brocade had been spread for her in the Golden Palace, but now she dwelt in a hut of brushwood and thatch, and the sleeves of her robe were dishevelled and tear-stained.

When the Retired Emperor left with his retinue,

the former Empress, her mind occupied in spite of herself with thoughts of bygone days and shedding tears she could not restrain, stood watching the Imperial procession until she could see it no more.

She lived for another 27 years. On her death bed she followed the convention of grasping a cord of five colours, attached at its other end to a painting of Amida in his Pure Land.

As the sound of her prayer grew weaker and weaker, a purple cloud of splendour unknown grew visible in the west, and an unknown perfume of wondrous incense filled the cell, while celestial strains of music were heard from above. Thus, in the middle of the second month of 1213, the former Empress Kenreimon-in breathed her last.

The Temple

It was the plainness and simplicity of Jakkō-in that made it such a poignant place for an empress to end her life; in 800 years, not a great deal has changed and the atmosphere of melancholy is still palpable. There isn't much to describe: a wooded garden with a waterfall cascading into a pond planted with azaleas, camellias, pines, cherries and maples; and a handful of worn old buildings, some open only intermittently to public view. The **Hon-dō** (Main Hall) was reconstructed in the early 17th century, but the rear part of the building contains timbers dating from the time of the Minamoto and Taira. Inside are statues of Kenreimon-in and her faithful lady-in-waiting, Awa no Naiji, a former concubine of Go-Shirakawa—who hurtfully failed to recognize her when he visited the convent that summer afternoon. The **Shoin** (Study), said to occupy the site of the empress's hut, is a 19th-century restoration; some of the interior screens are illustrated with scenes from the *Tales of the Heike*.

Traditional Arts and Crafts

For a lively survey of Kyoto regional crafts, visit the **Museum of Traditional Industry** (Dentō Sangyō Kaikan) in the southeast corner of Okazaki Park.

textiles

The Chinese immigrant family, the Hata, wove silk on the Kyoto plain even before the foundation of Heian-kyō in 794, but the Ōnin Wars drove the weaving guilds out of the city in the 15th century. After the wars petered out, the old military camps were colonized by the returning merchants. **Nishijin** (West Camp), north-west of the Imperial Palace, is the area with the greatest concentration of looms and textile shops and, although techniques have developed, it still produces some of the finest brocades in the world.

The **Nishijin-ori Kaikan** (Nishijin Textile Centre, *bus 9, 12, 59, 101, 201 and 203 to Horikawa-Imadegawa junction; open 9–5; adm free, exc. certain exhibits*) has a museum of textile history, a shop, weaving demonstrations and displays of treasured fabrics.

The **Orinasu-kan** (Weaving Centre, *bus 201 to Imadegawa-Jōfuku-ji*) has a smaller display, unstifled by coach parties, in a traditional Japanese house.

Kodai Yūzen-en (*Takatsu-ji-dōri, south of Ōmiya station*) demonstrates the techniques of **Yūzen dyeing**. Devised in the 17th century, this involves painstakingly painting silken garments by hand (or today by variously coloured stencils) and then washing out the excess dye in exceptionally pure water. The banks of the Kamo River used to be the place for this; it was said you could judge the prosperity of the city from the colour of the stained water as it passed out of Kyoto.

tea ceremony

If you are interested in learning about the tea ceremony Ura Senke holds classes at the Kyoto International Community House (*see* p.195). Arrangements to simply observe a tea ceremony can also be made through the International House.

(*✆075–*) **Shopping**

Like any other big Japanese city, Kyoto has its covered arcades, sunless underground malls and immaculate department stores, but it is also a major centre for the manufacture and sale of traditional Japanese goods. Small craft items are not expensive, but in the older shops you get what you pay for, and for the best you will pay a lot. Generally, the more venerable-looking the shop, the higher its prices. (Venerable in Japan doesn't necessarily mean opulent, just old and traditional-looking.)

For bargains the best places are Kyoto's **markets**. A full list of these can be found in the tourist information centre's monthly bulletin. Of the big ones, the most famous are on the 25th of the month at the **Kitano Tenman-gū shrine** (at the west end of Imadegawa-dōri, southeast of Kinkaku-ji); and on the 21st of the month at **Tō-ji temple**. The latter, held in commemoration of the Buddhist saint Kōbō Daishi, is particularly lively in December and January.

art and antiques

Shinmonzen-dōri, a small street north off of Higashiōji-dōri just north of Gion, is the place to browse for art and antiques even if you have no intention of buying. Of particular note is **Kawasaki Bijutsu**, run by friendly Shinji Kawasaki, who speaks impeccable English.

Nishiharu, ✆ 211 2849, on the corner of Teramachi-dōri and Sanjō-dōri, two blocks west of Sanjō-Kawaramachi junction, is the oldest and most respected of Kyoto's **ukiyo-e** (woodblock print) sellers, with prices to match (there is very little priced under ¥10,000).

Yamazoe Tenkō-dō, ✆ 561 3064, on Nawate-dōri, just south of Sanjō station, sells scroll paintings and calligraphy. There are reasonably priced pieces in boxes in front of the shop; more expensive scrolls are inside.

books

Maruzen (east side of Kawaramachi-dōri, 5 minutes north of Hankyū department store) devotes its entire sixth floor to foreign books; magazines are on the first floor. The **Izumiya Book Centre** has a smaller selection; it's a bit nearer the station, in Avanti department store, on the south side of the tracks.

ceramics

Asahi-dō, ℂ 531 2181, on the right-hand side of Kiyomizu-zaka (the slope leading up to Kiyomizu temple) towards the top, is the biggest dealer in Kyoto's local pottery, **Kiyomizu-yaki**.

Tachikichi, ℂ 211 3141, on Shijō-dōri, 7 minutes' walk on the right-hand side going west from Kawaramachi station, is a 250-year-old, large-scale vendor of Kyoto ceramics. The shop accepts many credit cards and will ship all over the world.

clothes and accessories

Kikuya, ℂ 351 0033, stocks kimono and accessories, new and second-hand, in a wide range of prices and conditions. From Karasuma-Gojō intersection, walk a block north and then six blocks east. The shop is on the right.

Aizen Kobo, ℂ 441 0355, a block south of Imadegawa and two blocks east of the Nishijin-ori Kaikan, sells beautiful, if pricey, clothing dyed with indigo using semi-traditional methods. The shop also affords you the opportunity to peer inside a traditional Japanese home long inhabited by the Utsuki family of weavers and dyers (although not by the current generation, a husband and wife team). The wife speaks English well and is very proud that the Victoria & Albert Museum in London has purchased some of her designs.

Kasagen, ℂ 561 2832, on the north side of Shijō-dōri at the Yasaka shrine end, sells hand-made oil-paper umbrellas in myriad designs.

crafts and toys

Yamato Mingei-ten, ℂ 221 2641, is next to Maruzen bookshop, on Kawaramachi-dōri, north of the Sanjō-dōri junction. This *mingei* (folk crafts) shop was opened shortly after the war by a member of the influential Folk Crafts Movement. It sells hand-made ceramics, glassware, lacquerware, basketry and textiles.

Maruzen bookshop (east side of Kawaramachi-dōri, 5 minutes north of Hankyū department store) has a floor devoted to traditional crafts.

Hirata, ℂ 681 5896, just north of Tō-ji temple, is a small, fascinating shop crammed with folk toys from all over Japan and owned by one of the leading authorities on the subject.

department stores

Hankyū and **Takashimaya**, on the southeast and southwest corners of Shijō-Kawaramachi respectively, are the most convenient of Kyoto's *depato*.

food

Murakami-jū, ℂ 351 1737, is on the block just to the southeast of Hankyū department store. For an edible souvenir that will keep in your suitcase, and *isn't* made of seaweed, try the delicious *tsukemono* (pickles) from this graceful old shop.

Hōrai-dō, ✆ 221 1215, on Teramachi, the fourth turning on the right as you walk west from Shijō-Kawaramachi junction, sells caddies, ladles, whisks, bowls and other tea ceremony utensils, as well as green teas in powder or leaf form.

Tsukimochi-ya Naomasa, ✆ 231 0175, is on Kiyamachi-dōri, the street running east of the Takasekawa canal, just north of Sanjō-dōri. If you really want **manjū**, those dreary sponge cakes stuffed with bean jam, this is *the* place to buy them. They make a good present for Japanese friends.

household and miscellaneous items

Aritsugu, ✆ 221 1091, in Nishiki Food Market, near the junction with Gokomachi-dōri, has traditional hand-made kitchen hardware—buckets, tureens, graters, strainers, steamers, and *sushi* knives as sharp as samurai swords.

Hirata, ✆ 561 1776, on Yamato-ōji-dōri, north of Shijō-dōri, and east of the bridge, is the place to buy beautiful bamboo and reed blinds, made to order.

Miura Shōmei, ✆ 561 2816, on the north corner of Shijō-dōri and Higashi-ōji-dōri, opposite Yasaka Shrine, sells hand-made lanterns, including some in bold modern designs.

Naitō, ✆ 221 3018, on the north side of Sanjō-dōri, between the Kamo river and the Takasekawa canal, sells brushes and brooms for every conceivable cleaning job—ashtrays, kettles, nostrils, shirts and desk-corners.

Kungyoku-dō, ✆ 371 0162, is on Horikawa-dōri, opposite Nishi-Hongan-ji temple. Here you will find countless flavours of incense, in sticks and chips, plus incense-burners and traditional *rōsoku* vegetarian candles.

Where to Stay

Compared to Tokyo, accommodation in Kyoto is varied, interesting and (relatively) inexpensive. If you haven't tried it already, this is one of the best places to stay in a Japanese-style *ryokan*. The cheapest of these are clean, friendly and elegantly simple. The most expensive are an extraordinary experience: like owning your own antique samurai house for the night, complete with world-class Japanese restaurant and full domestic staff. Old inn buildings were not designed for privacy: for sound-proofed rooms, as well as English-speaking staff and post-feudal gimmicks like faxes and international telephones, you'll be better off in a Western-style city or business hotel. Remember to book in advance for Fridays and Saturdays, the autumn maple leaf season, and the evenings of big festivals (*see* pp.197–9). Kyoto, as you'll see for yourself, is used to foreigners and you shouldn't have too much problem making yourself understood. The tourist information centre can make reservations only for the (generally good) establishments listed in the Welcome Inn brochure. The most convenient locations for transport and amenities are, in general, the most urbanized and noisy. If big cities oppress you, then consider seriously the possibility of staying in Nara, just 35 minutes away by train.

Numbers refer to map, p. 200, which show hotel locations.

Japanese-style

Ryokans (see pp.47–8) in Kyoto generally fall into two categories: luxury and basic. Some of the luxury *ryokans* may be more spartan than others and correspondingly less expensive, but do not expect the *ryokans* in the inexpensive category to even come close to the elegance of a Tawaraya or a Hiiragiya. What you can and should expect from even the inexpensive *ryokans* is a clean communal bath, *tatami*-mat rooms (some of which may look out onto a garden), and friendly, respectful service. Even the inexpensive *ryokans* will give you far more insight into the Japanese way of life than a normal hotel.

luxury

1 Tawaraya, ✆ 211 5566, @ 211 2204 (English spoken), is centrally situated on Fuyachō-dōri, two blocks west of Kyoto City Hall, on the south side of Ōike-dōri. This is probably the best *ryokan* in the world, patronized for over 300 years by international celebrities from the Rothschilds and the King of Sweden to Saul Bellow and Marlon Brando. No glitz here, though, just 19 rooms furnished with the finest antiques, private cedar baths and lovely gardens (*from around ¥40,000–¥90,000*). You will need to reserve weeks in advance.

2 Hiiragiya, ✆ 221 1136, @ 221 1139, is just about as famous as Tawaraya and just about as expensive. If Tawaraya can boast Marlon Brando and the King of Sweden, then Hiiragaya can boast Charlie Chaplin and the Japanese royal family. A room without a bath here is a relative bargain at *¥28,000*. Rooms with a bath are in the Tawaraya range.

expensive–moderate

The following four *ryokans* are all top-notch and priced accordingly. Each will have a range of rooms available at a range of prices, generally about *¥20,000– ¥65,000*, though you may find bargains in the off season. Variables affecting the price of a room include view (of a garden or river), private bath, size, and whether you take your meals in or eat out.

Though each of these places will have somebody on hand who speaks at least some English, it is usually better to ask someone who speaks Japanese to make the initial call on your behalf.

Although the price may seem steep, *ryokans* can offer better value than hotels when you consider that meals and service are included. Of the four, Yachiyo and Shiraume seem to have more moderate availables.

3 Seikoro, ✆ 561 0771, @ 541 5481, is conveniently located close to the Keihan Gojō station and within walking distance of many of the Eastern Kyoto sights. (The Kawai Kanjirō house, in particular, is only a few minutes' walk). The owner is congenial, and the décor, like the clientele, is a mix of Western and Japanese.

④ Shiraume, ✆ 561 1459, 🖂 531 5290, in the east of the city on the south side of Shirakawa canal, is a former *geisha* house in the heart of Gion with rooms overlooking the gurgling waterway. Of all the *ryokans,* this is perhaps the most beautifully situated. A private bridge leads you across the canal. It is hard to believe that the nightlife district of Gion bustles outside the walls.

⑤ Yachiyo, 🖂 771 4140, is located across from the Kyoto International Community House on the road leading to Nanzen-ji. This may be the best value amongst the more luxurious *ryokans* at ¥20,000 per person per night with two meals. A newer annex detracts only slightly from its charm.

⑥ Kinmata, ✆ 221 1039, 🖂 231 7632 (English spoken), is centrally situated on Gokomachi-dōri, three blocks west of Kawaramachi station. Kinmata opened in 1801 as an inn for travelling quack doctors whose advertising boards still stand in the entrance. It has superb food and exquisite décor, although the nine rooms don't afford much privacy and only one has a private bath. Reservations required. The price here drops significantly if you take your meals elsewhere.

inexpensive

The best bargains in Kyoto are a string of simple *ryokan* on the banks of the Takasegawa stream, a picturesque trickle to the west of the Kamo River which used to carry trading barges to Fushimi and Ōsaka to the south. Ten minutes' walk from Kawaramachi-Shijō crossing, five minutes by bus from Kyoto Station, this is the quietest and most convenient neighbourhood in central Kyoto, with an authentic local atmosphere and a colourful local populace of *mama-sans*, sweet-potato vendors, curious children and squalling cats. A couple of doors south of Riverside Takase is a wonderful *sentō* (public baths of three different temperatures, plus sauna) where gentlemen with punch perms and dragons tattooed on their backs cackle villainously and soak away the strains of a hard day's...business.

Except for **Yuhara**, the following are members of the Japanese Inn Group. Rooms are plain *tatami* with communal bath or showers and meals are not generally served.

⑦⑧ Riverside Takase, ✆ 351 7920 (English spoken), is three minutes' walk from Kawaramachi-shōmen bus stop, the third one after Kyoto Station on bus 205. It is the annexe of the slightly more expensive **Ryokan Kyōka**, nearer Kyoto station, ✆ 371 2709.

⑨ Ryokan Yuhara, ✆ 371 9583, is a few yards south of Riverside Takase.

⑩ Ryokan Hiraiwa, ✆ 351 6748 (English spoken), is between the last two, one block to the east.

⑪ Kiyomizu Sansō, ✆ 561 6109, 🖂 561 6109, is a tiny inn on the east of the city, on Sannen-zaka, the street of craft and souvenir shops which is the traditional pilgrims' route to Kiyomizu Temple. Reservations required. Reserve meals in advance at the front desk.

12 **Matsubaya**, ☎ 351 3727, 🖷 351 3505, set in the shadow of Higashi Hongan-ji, just east of Kawaramachi-dōri, is run by a very kind-hearted old lady, assisted by her daughter and a troop of students who are quite proficient at English. The inn used to be a favorite with Sumo referees, and above the doorway to the reception desk you will see a framed piece of yellow paper with the imprints of five Sumo wrestlers. Now the clientele is almost entirely made up of foreigners, especially visiting academics.

Western

luxury

13 **Takaraga-ike Prince**, ☎ 712 1111, 🖷 712 7677, *www.princehotels. co.jp.* If you are attending a conference at the Kyoto International Conference Hall and money is no object, this is the place for you. Next to the Ritz in Ōsaka, the rooms here have to be the largest in Japan. Located on the northern fringe of the city, most rooms have good views of the beautiful mountain scenery. The service is excellent, the restaurants are fine, and there is a nearby park for jogging and pleasant evening walks. Although comparitively remote, a 25-minute subway ride will take you to the heart of the city.

expensive

14 **Brighton Hotel**, ☎ 441-441, 🖷 431 2360, is two blocks east of the Imperial Palace on Nakadachiuri-dōri. Many consider the Brighton to be Kyoto's finest western-style hotel; with a huge six-storey atrium, fountains, miniature trees and glass elevators, it is certainly the airiest. It is also the most expensive in this category with doubles starting at ¥26,000. The best rooms have a view of the Imperial Palace and its grounds.

15 **Miyako**, ☎ 771 7111, 🖷 751 7111, *www.miyakohotel.co.jp*, is in the east, by the International Community House and very close to the Keage stop on the Tōzai subway line. The Miyako has been in business for over a hundred years and has served Queen Elizabeth II, Ronald Reagan, and Al Gore. The atmosphere here is restrained and the décor comfortably out of date (*from ¥19,000*). Behind the hotel is a pleasant walking path with good views of northeastern Kyoto.

There is also a *ryokan* attached to the main hotel that is every bit as good as the other fine *ryokans* listed above. If you are a little apprehensive about your first *ryokan* experience this might be a good place to start, as the familiar comforts of a hotel are only 100 metres away. Rooms in the *ryokan* start at ¥30,000.

16 **Kyoto Hotel**, ☎ 211 5111, 🖷 254 2529, *www.kyotohotel.co.jp*, is located right at the Kyoto Shiyakusho stop of the new Tōzai subway line. Although the rooms do not match the luxury of either the Brighton or the Miyako, it is cheaper and more centrally located. It is also the tallest building in Kyoto (17 stories), and many rooms, particularly those facing east, have terrific views. Even if your room does not have a great view, take solace in the Sky View restaurant that looks out on the Kamo river and the Higashiyama mountains.

moderate

⑰   **Hotel Granvia**, ✆ 344 8888, @ 344 4400, *www.hotels.westjr.co.jp/kyoto/*, forms part of the gargantuan and recently completed station complex. This may or may not appeal to you, but the Granvia certainly has luxury. The rooms are well designed in a contemporary style with tasteful lighting and good views of the city *(from ¥14,000)*.

⑱   **New Miyako**, ✆ 661 7111, is the Miyako's poor relation across town, located just southwest of Kyoto station. It boasts a good selection of restaurants, and excellent service. Rooms are a bit cheaper than the Miyako, and a bit less luxurious. There is a convenient Miyako courtesy shuttle which will deliver you to Sanjō Keihan, and the Miyako proper, which is walking distance from the main sights in eastern Kyoto.

⑲   **Kyoto Tower Hotel**, ✆ 361 3211, @ 343 5645, *www.keihan.co.jp/kyotower/ index.html,* is located beneath the hideous Kyoto Tower near the station. It describes itself as 'practical for all tourists, businessmen and other transients' (*singles from ¥8,500*).

(*✆ 075–*)   *Eating Out*

Noodle shops and other places to grab a quick bite offer consistently good food. The places listed here all have something special to recommend them.

Japanese-style

expensive

Kyoto is the birthplace of **kaiseki ryōri** (*see* p.30), the haughtiest of Japanese *haute cuisine,* but like every Japanese city it teems with cheaper establishments, serving food and drink in every style. The area around the station is poorly served; for a better choice start at **Shijō-Kawaramachi junction**, near Takashimaya and Hankyū department stores. Along the stretch of Kawaramachi-dōri north of here are numerous chain restaurants, pizza parlours and fast food joints, their plastic models displayed in the windows. The streets just south of Hankyū are calmer, and there are a handful of **nomi-ya** drinking places around there. A few yards east, towards the river, you cross the Takasegawa canal; bars, restaurants, noodle shops and clubs cluster on both of its banks. Many of the latter, especially in the area south of Shijō-dōri, employ 'hostesses' offering a variety of different services to their customers. They're harmless enough, except to your finances. If you choose to enter one of these places, make sure you know what you are spending.

Nakamura-rō, ✆ 561 0016, is by the stone gate south of the Yasaka Shrine. The oldest buildings of this classic Kyoto *ryōtei* (first class *kaiseki* restaurant) are 400 years old, making it the oldest in Japan. Princes have eaten here, the architects of the Meiji Restoration plotted here, and there are screen paintings by the 17th-century painter Ogata Kōrin.

Minokō, ✆ 561 0328, is one block south of the stone gate of Yasaka Shrine. Minokō serves both regular and *cha* (tea) *kaiseki*, a highly formal accompaniment to the tea ceremony. Lunchtime *bentō* are served overlooking a beautiful garden.

Minokichi, ✆ 771 4185, in eastern Kyoto, just off Sanjō-dōri on Dōbutsuen-mae-dōri, the road that leads north to the zoo, is a big, popular restaurant with a relaxed and unintimidating atmosphere. It is popular with foreigners; English is spoken.

Kyoto's other cuisine, distinct from *kaiseki*, is **shōjin ryōri**, the delicate and surprisingly varied vegetarian food prepared by Zen monks out of *tōfu*, herbs and vegetables. The commercial restaurants specializing in this style are generally found in the vicinity of Zen temples, a number of which serve *shōjin ryōri* to their visitors at lunchtime.

The most famous restaurant, and one of the most expensive, is **Ikkyū** (by the east gate of Daitoku-ji temple), where reservations are essential. Better value is **Izusen** (in Daitoku-ji's Daiji-in sub-temple). Both are closed by the early evening. Izusen is, in fact, a chain, but a very high quality one. Only the Izusen located inside the Daitoku-ji grounds serves *shōjin ryōri*; the others serve various types of Kyoto cuisine, with a vegetarian slant. Lunches are *moderate–inexpensive.*

moderate

Nishiki, ✆ 871 8888, lies at the southeastern end of Nakanoshima, the river island at Arashiyama. It serves good value **kaiseki** meals in a very attractive area. The **oshukuzen** meal, a cross between a *bentō* lunch box and a formal meal, is especially reasonable.

Sagano, ✆ 861 0277, just to the south of Tenryu-ji temple, is a great choice for lunch or dinner if you are in the Arashiyama area. Dishes focus on *tōfu* made by Morika, Kyoto's most renowned *tōfu*-maker.

There is a delightful bamboo grove and a garden outside the wall on the north side. If you have seen enough austere rock gardens and precious stroll gardens, seek out this parody of *karesansui* (*see* p. 303). The ocean is mimicked with the usual white stones, islands with the usual larger stones, but in the centre looms a large, blue aluminum submarine. A joke? It is hard to say: the man who designed the garden claims that the submarine is atomic and is aimed at America. A set course is ¥3,800.

Yoshikawa, ✆ 221 5544, directly west of the Hiiragiya ryokan, just south of Oike-dōri, offers both Kyoto-style **kaiseki** and simpler *tempura* dishes in a slightly stiff ambience. The food is always delicious, but lunch here is more highly recom-mended, as it is more moderately priced.

Okina-tei, ✆ 221 0250, opposite Vivre Hall (pronounced *Bibore Hōru*), one block north, then one and a half blocks west of Shijō-Kawaramachi junction, has *sukiyaki* beef dishes in a 120-year-old restaurant.

Okutan, ✆ 771 8709, in the Chōshō-in sub-temple of Nanzen-ji, is one of several restaurants around Nanzen-ji which serve *yudōfu*: *tōfu* (bean curd) stewed in a pot and dipped piping hot into flavoured sauces, with side dishes.

Hirano-ya, ✆ 561 1603, at the north gate of Maruyama Park, specializes in *imobō*, the dried and salted fish which were a staple of local cuisine until fast roads and refrigeration put the city within reach of the sea. It is authentic, but not to everyone's taste.

Izujū, ✆ 561 0019, on the corner of Shijō-dōri and Higashiōji-dōri, opposite Yasaka Shrine, is a century-old *sushi* shop decorated with Imari ceramics.

Kappa Nawate, ✆ 531 4048, is on the right-hand (east) side of Gion's Yamato-ōji-dōri, as you walk north from Shijō-dōri. It is a *robatayaki* grill: choose small dishes of fish and vegetables (from the English menu or by pointing at the counter) and watch them being cooked before your eyes. A snack here can be very inex-pensive; it depends how many dishes you order.

These two restaurants, one in central, one in eastern, Kyoto, serve *bentō* box meals in the Kyoto style:

Tagoto, ✆ 221 1811, has a tiny entrance in an alleyway on the north side of Shijō-dōri, opposite Takashimaya department store.

Rokusei Nishimise, ✆ 751 6171 (English spoken), overlooks the canal on the west side of the Heian Shrine.

Agatha is a modern Japanese restaurant that serves anything—from meatballs to fruit—grilled on a skewer. There are two branches, separated by only a few yards, on the east bank of the Takasegawa canal south of Ōike-dōri. Main branch: ✆ 223 2379; northern branch: ✆ 255 2279.

inexpensive

Omen, ✆ 771 8994, located just south of Ginkaku-ji, is a perfect way to end or begin a stroll down the Philosopher's Walk. The house speciality is thick white noodles served with several different kinds of vegetables. The place has become so successful that they have opened a branch in New York (in SoHo on Thompson Street).

Matsuno, ✆ 561 2786, on Shijō-dōri, a few metres east of the Minami-za theatre, serves delicious broiled eels, painted with sweet sauce and served over a bowl of rice (*donburi*) or in a set (*teishoku*).

Kawamichi-ya, ✆ 231 8507 (English spoken), is a lovely garden-fringed **soba** shop, started 300 years ago to sell noodles to pilgrims climbing Mt Hiei. Walking east from Kawaramachi-Ōike junction, Fuyachō-dōri is the third street on the left. Turn down here; the restaurant is in the middle of the second block on the right.

Takasebune, ✆ 351 4032, is in an alleyway, just east of Hankyū department store. Look out for the large oar at the front of the building. This renowned **tempura** restaurant is run by an old Takasegawa canal boatman.

Tsukimura, ✆ 351 5306, situated south of Hankyū department store, is a small, friendly drinking spot which serves rice dishes cooked in the pot (*kamameshi*).

Foreign

expensive

Dio Diva, ✆ 256 1326. You will find little Italian restaurants all over Japan with the plastic food outside, and the red, green and white of the Italian flag. This place is absolutely different; the chef is a true artist, the food world-class Italian food. The occasional Japanese flourish, like shiitake mushrooms, is smoothly integrated into delicately prepared appetizers, pastas and main courses. Try the house special for dessert—a fig cake without sugar, baked in a traditional Tuscan fashion. Located behind Daimaru department store off Shijō-dōri, this place is difficult to find. Take a taxi or ask your hotel to call ahead for directions.

Les Champs d'Or, ✆ 255 2277. Kyoto residents in the know will tell you that this small French restaurant tucked away on a side street near the Nishiki market, is the best in Kyoto. Everything is impeccably presented, and set menus demonstrate careful thought. A robust lunch set here is priced at ¥3,800, making it one of the best deals in Kyoto. Dinner starts at ¥8,000. It is located fairly close to Dio Diva. Take a taxi or have your hotel call ahead for directions.

moderate

Le Zephyr, ✆ 752 8118, is a unique experience. Located on the first small street to the left as you walk east from Keihan Sanjō station, it offers fine French food in an informal atmosphere—eight chairs at a counter is all that you will find here. The prices are deceptive, as everything carries a surcharge. Although a set dinner is advertised at ¥2,800, the final bill will be more in the area of ¥5,000.

Natsuka, ✆ 255 2105, offers a slightly more refined setting for its French cuisine, with very polite service. It is located in Ponto-chō overlooking the Kamo River, between Sanjō and Shijō. A reasonable selection of wines by the half bottle makes this a good choice for solitary dinners. The dessert is worth saving room for—if the green tea cheesecake is available, order it. You won't get another chance.

Ashoka, ✆ 241 1318, is a good Indian restaurant, easy to find at the intersection of Teramachi and Shijō-dōri. Set meals start around ¥3,000, and you can also order à la carte from an extensive menu. The Indian chef performs his duties behind a plexi-glass case reminiscent of the Pope in his motorcade.

Hunan, ✆ 256 3515, is a good Chinese restaurant overlooking the Kamo River about halfway between Sanjō and Shijō on the east side. The shrimp and fried rice dishes are particularly tasty.

Gio Giono, ✆ 365 0202, is a perfect place for families, or for anybody coming into Kyoto station and looking somewhere nearby to eat. Large pizzas and decent pasta dishes are cooked up by Italian chefs.

inexpensive

The areas around Kyoto's several universities are scattered with cheap eating places serving decent food. The atmosphere in these restaurants tends to be studenty; the fare, Japanese-tinged western food. Two examples are:

Honrayado, ✆ 222 1574, near Dōshisha University just east of the Imperial Palace grounds, is very highly recommended. Its homemade bread is among the best in Japan, a delicious contrast to the usual white bread found in supermarkets. Lunch sets are extraordinarily good value. They usually feature some sort of stew served with salad and the terrific bread. Dinner is also good value.

Zac Baran, ✆ 751 9748, located near the Kyoto handicraft center, is a convenient place to stop in for a bite after visiting the Heian shrine. The theme here is jazz, and they play it loud. Good for light dinners in a hip atmosphere.

Speakeasy, ✆ 711 5277, is not located particularly near a University, but it also caters to a younger clientele. It's a great place for burger and fries, and the only place in Kyoto where you can get anything approximating an American-diner breakfast. It is located immediately west of the Shugaku-in stop on the Eizan train line. Look for a huge American flag.

Capricciosa, ✆ 221 7596. If you crave hearty portions of cheese and carbohydrates, this is the place for you. You will not find bigger portions of Italian food in Japan. There are several locations throughout Kyoto and Ōsaka. The number given here is for the most convenient one, located just east of Kawaramachi on the first street south of Sanjō.

Knuckles, ✆ 441 5849, on Kitaōji-dōri, 300 metres east of Senbon-dōri, is a cheap and popular foreign-run 'New York café', serving sandwiches, lasagne, cheesecake, Tex-Mex snacks, etc.

Performing Arts

Japanese performing arts are disappointingly represented in Kyoto. **Kabuki**, was born on the gravel banks of the Kamo River near Shijō bridge, but the only major performances in the city now are the *Kaomise* (*see* p.199) season at the Gion **Minami-za** theatre in December. (The same venue hosts visiting Japanese theatre groups for the rest of the year.)

Most weeks, there are *nō*, and sometimes *kyōgen*, performances at the **Kanze Kaikan** (over the moat, just southwest of the National Museum of Modern Art and Okazaki Park). Less frequent are those at **Kongō Nōgaku-dō** (a few yards north and west of the Yasaka Shrine).

In April–May and October–November, Kyoto's surviving schools of *geisha* perform their traditional dances (*odori*) in theatres in different parts of the city. Most famous is the **Miyako Odori** of the Gion *geisha*, which runs throughout April in the **Gion Kaburenjō** theatre (on Hanami-kōji, south of Shijō-dōri on the eastern side of the river). For dates and times of all the above, consult the tourist information centre's **Monthly Information** bulletin.

Next door to the Gion Kaburenjō theatre is **Yasaka Kaikan** which stages the twice-nightly **Gion Corner** show (*open Mar 1–Nov 29, exc. Aug 16; adm ¥2,800; shows at 7.40pm and 8.40pm. ☎ 075 561 1119*). This tourist 'show-case' is unfortunately the only place in Japan where you can see several traditional arts in a short time for a reasonable price. To a moronic English voice-over, a couple of bored-looking ladies in kimono go through the motions of a tea ceremony and listless flower arrangement. A leaden *kyōgen* farce is followed by a twitchy performance of *bunraku* puppets. Go if you like, but don't let it put you off a proper performance of the real thing.

Nightlife

Kyoto has its fair share of colleges, and college in Japan is a time (for some the only time) to let loose. Particularly lively districts are the northern part of Gion (the southern part is mostly exclusive *geisha* houses and other secret-looking places), and the area circumscribed by Kawaramachi (west), the Kamo River (east), Sanjō (north) and Shijō (south). Gion caters to a more adult crowd.

To actually step inside a random bar in Japan takes a little courage. You will see literally hundreds of signs for bars all over the areas described above; most, however, are small and usually cater to regulars. Some places can be extraordinarily friendly and you may find yourself jubilantly belting out Beatles tunes on the Karoke box with your new Japanese friends.

The two most prominent *gaijin* (foreigner) bars are the **Pig and Whistle** and **Bar Isn't It**. Drinks and eats are relatively inexpensive at both places. Bar Isn't It, down a side street two blocks south of Sanjō between Kawaramachi and the Takase river, is a noted pick-up joint: lots of *gaijin* males, lots of Japanese females.

The Pig and Whistle has an mix of even-keeled Japanese and foreigners. It attempts to recreate the atmosphere of a British pub—with darts and Guinness by the pint.

If you are looking for a dance club, **Metro** (✆ 752 4765) couldn't be easier to find. Take the Keihan Line to Marutamachi station and follow the signs for exit 2. The Metro is actually in the station building, up one flight of stairs as you exit. Events here vary so ring ahead, or check the listings in *Kansai Time Out*, a local English language magazine sold at Maruzen bookstore on the sixth floor.

Nara: the Ancient Capital

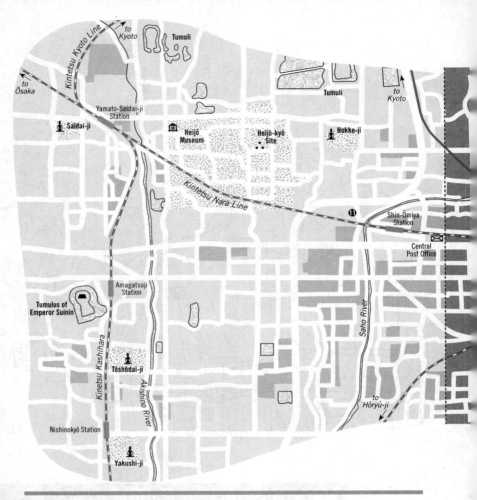

Key for Nara Hotels (for listings *see* pp.290–292)

1. Kikusuiro
2. Kankaso
3. Edo-san
4. Matsumae Ryokan
5. Ryokan Hakuko
6. Furuichi Ryokan
7. Seikan-so
8. Nara Hotel
9. The Nara Garden Hotel
10. Hotel Sunroute Nara
11. Nara Royal Hotel
12. Hotel Fujita Nara
13. Kotton Hyaku-Pasento

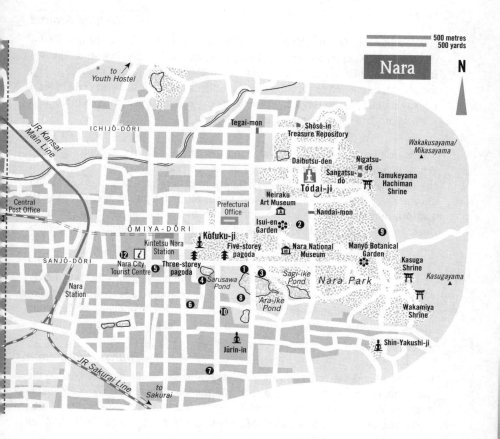

500 metres
500 yards

to
Youth Hostel

ICHIJŌ-DŌRI

Tegai-mon

Shōsō-in
Treasure Repository

Wakakusayama/
Mikasayama

JR Kansai
Main Line

Daibutsu-den

Nigatsu-
dō

Sangatsu-
dō

Tamukeyama
Hachiman
Shrine

Neiraku
Art Museum

Tōdai-ji

Central
Post Office

Prefectural
Office

Nandai-mon

ŌMIYA-DŌRI

Isui-en
Garden

❷

Kōfuku-ji

Kintetsu Nara
Station

Five-storey
pagoda

Nara National
Museum

Manyō Botanical
Garden

❾

Kasuga
Shrine

SANJŌ-DŌRI

Nara City
Tourist Centre

❺

Three-storey
pagoda

❹

Sarusawa
Pond

❸

Sagi-ike
Pond

Nara Park

Kasugayama

Nara
Station

❻

❽

Ara-ike
Pond

❶

❿

Wakamiya
Shrine

JR Sakurai Line

Jūrin-in

Shin-Yakushi-ji

to
Sakurai

❼

Nara is what many first-time visitors expect, and are disappointed to find lacking, in Kyoto: a garden city of parks, ponds, turtles and deer, where the pagodas and treasure houses still hold their own against the highways and advertising hoardings. If you can live without flash hotels and nightclubs, then Nara has almost everything Kyoto has, in milder, small-town form: a National Museum, cultivated gardens, an ancient temple, and five of the oldest and biggest Buddhist temples in the world. Historically, Nara's treasures are older and, in many cases, better preserved than those in the later capital. The town is infinitely more compact and negotiable, and you can achieve in a few hours on bike and foot what in Kyoto would take days on crammed trains and buses. It's smaller, of course, and there's less variety, but there's enough to fill three or four days of anyone's time. If concrete and traffic repel you, and if you're prepared to make a day trip into Kyoto to see the essential sights, you should seriously consider making Nara your base.

Getting Around

Nara's attractions fall, by and large, into two areas: Nara Park and the downtown district, convenient for stations and hotels; and west of the city, in a straggling line from the side of the old Heijō palace down to Tōshōdai-ji and Yakushi-ji. The former can be walked or cycled around; the sights in the west are all close to local railway stations. Only Hōryū-ji, which no visitor to Nara should miss, is more than a few kilometres from the main transport termini.

By train

There are two train stations in Nara, and this can be a source of confusion. The private **Kintetsu Nara station** is right in the centre of town, a few minutes from the information centre and temples. These trains are generally the fastest and cheapest way around; they connect with Ōsaka Namba, Kyoto and Nagoya. The **JR station**, though central, is a little to the south and west, and here you can catch direct trains to Kyoto and Hōryū-ji. Fares on the JR lines are usually higher, unless you've got a Japan Rail Pass in which case it's free.

By bus

You can also catch buses just outside the main exit of both stations that will deliver you to most of the main sight-seeing destinations. Relevant buses are noted in italics prior to the description for each location. A particularly convenient bus, departing from gate number 1 (*ichiban noriba*), loops around the central part of the city.

Tourist Information

Both the JR and Kintetsu Nara stations have information offices. Just outside the front gate of the JR station is the City Information Window (✆ 0742 22 9821, *open daily 9–5*); on the first floor of the Kintetsu station is the Nara City Tourist Information Office (✆ 0742 24 4858, *open daily for hotel enquiries until 6; all other tourist enquiries are 9–5*).

The Nara Tourist Centre (✆ 0742 22 3900) is on Sanjō-dōri, roughly equidistant from either the JR or Kintetsu stations. If you are looking for a place to sit down while you plan your day, this is it. It has a spacious lounge and, of course, an ample supply of brochures.

In front of Sarusawa Pond, there's a little office manned by the charming **Nara Student Guides** who will tour foreigners around the sights for nothing more than the price of lunch and admission tickets. Beware: the English-language map issued by the tourist centres in Nara is not to scale.

If you have a specific interest like tea ceremonies or martial arts, the Nara International Foundation (NIFS), ✆ 0742 27 2436, located on the sixth floor of the Kintetsu station building, has a good bulletin board and very helpful staff.

There is no Japan National Tourist Organization office in Nara, but they do publish a pamphlet called Walking Tour Courses in Nara, which you can obtain through any of their domestic or international locations.

History

The Imperial City of fairest Nara
Glows now at the height of beauty,
Like brilliant flowers in bloom!

Poem from the *Manyōshū* (Sheaf of 10,000 Leaves), 8th century

By the beginning of the 8th century the so-called 'permanent' capital at Fujiwara had become too small for the court's growing population of bureaucrats, so in 708 the decision was made to relocate in present-day Nara, 16km to the north. The peasant population was cleared, and 321 acres (now occupied by **Heijō-jō**, *see* p.280) were filled and levelled. Two imperial tombs were excavated and removed to allow this, but in 709 the court got cold feet about disturbing the ancestral remains, and restored them to their original positions.

The old Fujiwara palace was dismantled, and parts of it re-used. Timber was brought from Shiga to the north and Mie to the south; stones were carried from the area of present-day Kōbe and Ōsaka. Kilns were established all over the Yamato region to bake tiles and *onigawara* (protective gargoyles) for the roofs. The demand for furnishings, metal and woodwork supported a full-time workshop; in 764 it was commissioned to produce one million wooden pagodas as an offering of thanks for the defeat of a rebel lord.

Seven thousand civil servants were employed in the new palace, which served as the centre of government as well as the imperial residence. With its monumental, symmetrical layout, the new palace was unmistakably Chinese in design, but it already embodied a principle that can still be seen in Japanese architecture. While the public precincts, the great halls of state, were foreign in appearance, with painted vermilion pillars and curving tile roofs, the Emperor's own personal living and sleeping quarters employed the plain domestic style—unpainted wooden pillars and a roof of cypress shingles.

However, it was a religious building that immortalized Nara. Of the Heijō palace, nothing but a few museum pieces survive today, but Emperor Shōmu's great temple, Tōdai-ji, with its colossal bronze statue, still stands, in the same position, if not exactly the same form, as 1250 years ago. With universities, hospitals, orphanages, old people's homes, and dozens of monasteries and convents, Nara seemed destined to remain Japan's capital for centuries.

In the end, it was the temples and their ambitious monks who brought about its downfall. Shōmu was succeeded by his daughter, Empress Kōken, who later abdicated to enter a convent, where she fell under the influence of a monk named Dōkyō. Like Rasputin centuries later, Dōkyō won the Empress's trust through his powers as a healer; ribald rumours circulated concerning the nature of his relationship with his mistress. 'Don't sneer at monks for their flowing blouses,' went one song, 'for they have hammers in their trousers. When the bonze's hammer stands upright, he shines like a lord in all his might!'

Dōkyō persuaded the smitten Kōken to reascend the throne; after a power struggle, she succeeded, under the new name, of Shotoku. The mad monk's next suggestion was that the Empress abdicate once again, this time in his favour. A messenger was sent to an imperial shrine to put this proposition to the sun goddess. When he returned with a negative answer, Dōkyō had the man's Achilles' tendons cut. He would, no doubt, have tried again, but the Empress died unexpectedly, and Dōkyō was swiftly sent into exile where he died three years later. The Fujiwara family, shaken by this challenge to their power, moved the court away from Nara and its troublesome monks in 784. After Kōken/Shotoku, no woman was to ascend the throne for 861 years.

Central Nara

Sarusawa Ike (Sarusawa Pond)

This small semi-circular pond, 400m around, has been here for centuries and forms the centre of historical Nara. On a clear day, the two pagodas of Kōfuku-ji temple are reflected in its waters to the north. To the west, along busy Sanjō-dōri, is the modern JR station, and to the east Nara Park and the Kasuga Shrine. A dragon, a small one presumably, used to live in the pond until it was driven away by a shameful incident, involving an unnamed emperor. One of his concubines (her name was Uneme) drowned herself here after being rejected by him. The tree on which she's supposed to have hung her clothes is signposted in Japanese at the east end: Coat Hanging Willow.

Kōfuku-ji (Happiness-Bestowing Temple)

Unusually for early Buddhism, this was a private establishment, the ancestral temple of the mighty Fujiwara family, who dominated Japan as statesmen, emperors and empresses, and men of culture from the 7th to the 12th centuries. As they flourished, so did Kōfuku-ji, but after their eclipse in the late Heian period, it was consistently neglected until more or less the last half century. There are no original buildings: the oldest dates from 1426. But an outstanding collection of statuary, snatched countless times from burning halls, makes it an essential Nara stop.

History

The temple changed sites a couple of times as the emperors, and their Fujiwara ministers with them, moved around Kansai before settling in Nara. Kasuga Shrine, just up the road, had always been the Fujiwara shrine and in the 10th century the two were merged into one institution. Then in 1180 the monks made the mistake of taking sides against the Taira family in the epochal Heike wars. The entire compound, plus that of Tōdai-ji, was razed. This disaster had wonderful consequences: after the defeat of the Tairas, the temple was rebuilt and became a kind of factory of Buddhist art as craftsmen from all over Japan converged on Nara to study its ancient masterpieces and create a generation of new ones. The result was Kamakura period sculpture, one of the most exhilarating and accessible of all Japanese styles. Great sculptors like Kōkei and Unkei learned their trade during this period and established their studios close to Kōfuku-ji.

At the end of the Kamakura shogunate, the temple fell on hard times. In 1717 there was another ruinous fire, and in 1868 the Shinto zealots of the Meiji Restoration forced the separation of Kōfuku-ji and the Kasuga Shrine. Halls were requisitioned and converted into schools and offices. Not until 1958 did the government properly come to its senses with the endowment of the new Treasure House.

Touring Kōfuku-ji

Fifty-two steps lead from the pavement opposite the Sarusawa Pond up the embankment to the edge of the precincts. Once the large site was thick with buildings; more than just a temple, it was a municipal facility with a hospital, orphanage, old people's home, public bath house and university. All of these buildings have been lost and many were never replaced, including the Great Southern Gate. On your right is the **Gojū-no-tō** (Five-storey Pagoda), the second highest in Japan at just over 50m, rebuilt in 1426. The **Tōkon-dō** (East Gold Hall), just beyond it, is a striking building with proudly uptilted eaves. The pagoda was endowed by Empress Kōmyō, and this worship hall was built 11 years earlier by her husband, Emperor Shōmu; the two buildings were at one time surrounded by a wall, symbolizing marital union. The **Tōkon-dō** (*open 9–4.50; adm ¥200*) is full of National Treasures; its central image of Yakushi (15th century) is flanked by a Gakkō (God of the Moon) and Nikkō (Sun), which originally belonged to Yama-dera, a temple outside Nara. After the destruction of their own temple in 1180, the Kōfuku-ji monks marched over to Yama-dera and requisitioned these statues by force.

Other prominent buildings include the **Chūkon-dō** (Central Golden Hall), an uninteresting 'temporary' hall erected in 1852, and two octagonal pavilions, the **Hokuen-dō** (North Circular Hall, 1210) and **Nanen-dō** (South Circular Hall, 1789). Both contain valuable statues but the former is open only on 17 October, the latter at certain times during the spring. Enquire at the tourist information office for precise details.

Kokuhōkan (National Treasure Hall)

Open 9–5; adm ¥500.

This rather cramped concrete hall contains a higher percentage of masterpieces than almost any other collection; even the smallest book of Japanese art history will reproduce half a dozen of its sculptures.

Following the arrows as you enter, the first major piece is a metre-high head of the bronze **Yakushi**, stolen (along with his two attendants) from Yama-dera, and raised in the old Tōkon-dō. Being the heaviest statue, it could not be saved from a later fire: only the face, neck and one ear survived, hidden until 1937, under the new altar. It's one of the most perfect pieces of bronze sculpture in Japan, all the more fascinating for being viewed close up. The eyes have a far-seeing crispness which could only be realized in metal; the lips and nose are sharp but full, and the whole face seems to radiate intense concentration and sensual compassion.

The two **Guardian Kings** in the next case are among the most famous in Japan, small in size, but with magnificently powerful bodies, veins bulging in a rictus of rage. Adjacent to them is a case of exquisite Nara-period sculptures: four of the **Hachibushu** (Eight Supernatural Guardians of Buddha), including the beaked Karura (from the Indian deity Garuda), and Asura, a ferocious three-headed, three-armed demon, here transformed into a graceful youth and rendered almost realistic despite his fantastic appearance.

Contemporaneous, but in a very different vein, are the **Ten Great Disciples**, luminously soft figures of human saints whose realistic qualities were taken up by later sculptors of the

Kamakura period to produce characters in a nearby case: the **Six Patriarchs of the Hossō Sect**. Their lined faces, lumpy features and scowls of concentration convey the individuality of historical priests, and represented the closest that Japanese art had yet come to portraiture.

Tōdai-ji (Eastern Great Temple)

In Tōdai-ji, the two key threads of early Japanese history—the growth of Buddhism and the centralization of power under a supreme emperor—were knotted together in a single, brilliant building project. The famous Great Buddha may not be the loveliest bronze statue ever made, but it is certainly the largest; and, despite the usual run of fires and earthquakes, the hall in which it sits is still the world's biggest wooden structure beneath a single roof. Other temples are neater and better preserved; but everything you need to know about the Nara period and its history is encapsulated here.

History

Tōdai-ji came to life on 9 April, 752. On that day a sumptuous ceremony, attended by the highest ranking men in the land and a congregation of 10,000 monks, was held in the courtyard in front of the Great Buddha. At its climax, the Indian priest Bodhisena stood on top of a platform alongside the huge statue and painted in its eyes. Long cords trailed from his brush; their ends were held by Emperor Shōmu, 45th Emperor of Japan, and his Empress Kōmyō, who thus shared in the symbolic completion of the grand project. The emperor was a sick man; in reality, the temple and its statue were far from finished, but the ceremony had been brought forward so that Shōmu could witness the dedication of the temple which had absorbed so much of his money and energy, and which epitomized his political and religious ambitions.

The construction of Tōdai-ji marked a crucial moment in Japanese history, not just as an expression of artistic ambition and religious devotion, but as an astute piece of political strategy. The new temple was dedicated to the Kegon sect, one of half a dozen Buddhist variants which had filtered through to Japan since the 6th century; the choice was certainly no accident. Kegon's central deity was Roshana Nyōrai, the 'Cosmic Buddha', an ultimate and omnipresent being of whom all other deities, including the historical Buddha (Shaka), are manifestations. In the sutra on which Kegon based its teaching, Roshana is described seated on a lotus flower, the pose in which the bronze Great Buddha has been sculpted. The lotus has a thousand petals, each one representing a universe made up, in its turn, of myriad worlds. The petal 'universes' are each ruled by manifestations of Roshana, which manifest themselves in the 'worlds' as still smaller Buddhas.

To Emperor Shōmu, ruler of a young and still imperfectly centralized state, this complicated theological diagram had immediate parallels with the new political structure which he was keenly propagating: a central, universal ruler (Roshana and, by analogy, the emperor) ruling in his satellite territories through authorized representatives (Roshana's manifestations/the emperor's officers) over large numbers of lesser beings (the lesser Buddhas/common people). 'Of all the various laws,' Shōmu declared in an imperial prescript, 'the Great Word of Buddha is the most excellent for protecting the State.'

Shōmu, who had already been ordained as a Buddhist monk, was a deeply devout man and there is no doubting the genuine fervour and humility behind his grand scheme. But politically it represented a bold, almost arrogant, assertion of temporal power, a powerful symbolic act in the centralization of the Japanese state. Tōdai-ji was quickly established as *the* state temple, headquarters of a network that extended into every corner of the country. In each of the provinces, subsidiary local temples, called *kokubun-ji*, were set up as spiritual counterparts to the local government departments. The building project was both a symbol of state authority, and an example of it. By the 790s, when the temple complex was finally finished and fitted out, 50,000 carpenters, 370,000 metal workers and 2,180,000 labourers had been employed. The levels of taxation and forced labour demanded by this great undertaking brought hardship and starvation to many parts of the country, and exhausted Japan's meagre supplies of gold and copper.

The Tōdai-ji project raised another ticklish problem—the future role, in the Buddhist state, of the native Shinto religion. Although it never had the organizational and theological sophistication of Buddhism, Shinto was still the native religion of Japan, observed in various forms by many Japanese, from the peasants to the aristocracy; the Emperor himself, after all, claimed descent from the Sun Goddess. The problem was solved by an eminent Buddhist priest called Gyōgi (who is also credited with the invention of the potter's wheel). In 742, at the age of 72, the ingenious bonze travelled to the shrine of the Sun Goddess at Ise where, after seven days and nights in prayer, he received an oracle. The Goddess, speaking curiously in Chinese, declared herself well pleased with Shōmu's plans. Shortly afterwards the Emperor himself had a dream in which the Sun Goddess appeared as a fiery disc and explained that the Buddha and the Sun are the same.

Touring Tōdai-ji

The formal approach to the temple begins just to the east of the National Museum, and runs north through the heart of Nara Park, the most thickly touristed area of town: expect to be molested by giggling school parties and foraging deer in equal numbers. The precincts begin where the souvenir stalls end, at the **Nandai-mon**, the 18.8m high Great South Gate, rebuilt in 1199 after the original was levelled by a typhoon. Behind the protective bars are the two guardian kings, 8m tall, carved for the new gate by Unkei and Kaikei, two of the greatest Kamakura-period sculptors. Beyond the temple offices is the **Kagami-ike** (Mirror Pond) with a Shinto shrine on a small island; 500m to either side of here are the sites of the two seven-storey pagodas, each one 100m high, which were burned down by lightning and never replaced.

At the **Chū-mon** (Middle Gate) you pay an entrance fee (¥400) and enter the inner court-yard, divided from the outer grounds by a cloister-like roofed wall called the *kairo*. Large-scale Buddhist ceremonies are held here; in 1994 the temple hosted an international music festival with hundreds of musicians including Bob Dylan, Joni Mitchell and Jon Bon Jovi. As well as the usual water trough and tubs of smoking incense for ritual purification, a bronze octagonal lantern stands in the approach to the main hall. This is one of the few originals in Tōdai-ji, dating from Emperor Shōmu's time; the fine lattice work and airy scenes of floating *bosatsu* and heavenly musicians in flowing garments are characteristic of the supple, sensuous Nara style. The gate closes at different times throughout the year, but is always open between 8am and 4.30pm.

Daibutsu-den (Great Buddha Hall)

The double-hipped roof of the Great Hall, with its golden *shibi* (owls' tail finials) jutting up above the trees, is the symbol of Nara, visible from vantage points all over town. The current building dates from 1709—however imposing it appears now, in its original version it was even vaster: 88m along the front (as opposed to 57m today), but about the same depth (50m) and height (49m). The difference would have shown itself mainly in the length of the roof ridge (today's Daibutsu-den is narrow and rather squat compared to the original), and in the curving, Chinese-style gable over the main entrance, which the 8th-century building did not possess.

Inside, time, disaster and inept restoration have taken their toll on the **Daibutsu** (Great Buddha). These days he's a bloated, clumsy figure with chubby cheeks and rubbery lips who looks every ounce of his 400 tons. Cracks in his body, and different shades of metal (the head, for example, is much blacker than the torso) betray the hybrid form of the present statue. After a couple of decapitations and several near melt-downs, he's a bit like the knife which has had three new blades and two new handles. The giant lotus leaf petals on the left-hand side are original, as—apparently—are the Buddha's knees. But the point about this statue isn't its state of preservation so much as its size: 15m high (1.5m shorter than Emperor Shōmu's original), with a 5.3m face, a 2.4m ear, a metre-long eye and a nostril which a man can climb inside. The right hand is held up in the *mudra* (sacred hand gesture) signifying peace of mind; the left is held flat, indicating that all wishes will be granted, and five monks can stand together on this palm when the statue is being cleaned.

The construction of the statue was, for its time, an extraordinary technological achievement which cost many fortunes and not a few lives. Nothing this big had ever been attempted before. As well as mining the tons of tin and copper necessary for the alloy, the craftsmen also had to construct an immense mould. They built the statue in sections: first a mould was built for the Buddha's feet and legs, then a mound was raised around the cooling metal and the next few feet of statue were moulded and cast, and so on.

The disadvantage was that, until the covering mound was removed and the completed statue revealed, no one had any idea of how well the parts were forming a whole. Between 747 and 749 there were eight false starts, when the resulting Buddha turned out lopsided or unbalanced. The project seemed to be jinxed. Then, in 749, gold—the first ever to be mined in Japan—was discovered in a remote province. The Shinto gods, it was inferred, were smiling on the project, and at long last a satisfactory statue emerged to be gilded with the spoils of the new mine. A mystery disease killed many of the metal workers employed on the statue—modern evidence suggests they were poisoned by mercury used as an amalgam for the gold.

Roshana Nyōrai, the Cosmic Buddha represented by the great statue, is flanked by two *bosatsu*: Kannon, on his left, holding a mystic jewel; and Kokūzō, on his right, the *bosatsu* of wisdom and happiness. Behind this trio are two of the Shitennō, the Directional Guardians. The one on the west side with the brush and scroll is Komoku-ten, popularly considered the patron of writers; until recently, it was thought lucky for those engaged in literary employment to flick chewed up pieces of tissue paper into the deity's belly button, a practice now strongly discouraged.

At the rear of the Buddha's podium is a scale model of the original Daibutsu-den. One of the pillars to the east has a square hole in it of limited dimensions: anyone who can crawl through it is guaranteed a place in paradise.

Other Buildings

There's more to Tōdai-ji than just one hall: the smaller sub-temples are full of sculptures, infinitely finer than the fat monster in the Daibutsu-den.

The **Kaidan-in** (Ordination Hall, *open 8–4.30, adm ¥400*), due west of the Great Hall, was a crucial part of Tōdai-ji. Until it was built, the only authorities capable of investing new priests were in China—an obvious obstacle to the rapid Buddhification of the country sought by Emperor Shōmu. Accordingly, the famous monk Ganjin was invited from China to inject some continental rigour into Japanese Buddhism. Five disastrous attempts were made to cross the treacherous Japan Sea; by the time Ganjin arrived in 754, he had lost his sight as well as numerous disciples. But he brought with him earth from the sacred Chinese mountain Wu Tai Shan, and on this the ordination platform was built.

The present Kaidan-in dates from 1731 and contains a superb set of the **Shitennō** (Four Heavenly Kings), guardians of the four points of the compass. Their stern but astute faces and surprisingly dainty bodies still bear traces of the original pigments, particularly on Zōchō-ten, the staff-wielding guardian of the south.

On the opposite, east side of the Daibutsu-den, are several interesting buildings at the foot of the Kasuga Hills. Steps and a path lead up to a group of minor buildings closed to view apart from the **Shoro** belfry containing the temple's original 4m bell, its body 25cm thick.

Above and to the left of here is the **Kaisan-dō** (Founder's Hall), enshrining a statue of Priest Rōben, Tōdai-ji's first abbot, but the most interesting places are a little further on. The southernmost one is the **Tamuke-yama Hachiman-gū** (Mt Tamuke Hachiman Shrine) dedicated to the Shinto god of war, who gave his blessing to the construction of Tōdai-ji by means of an oracle. A little to the north is the **Sangatsu-dō** (Hall of the Third Month, *open 8–4.30, adm ¥400*), immediately recognizable for its elegant roof with its wave-like 'double-exposure'—the result of one structure being built on to an older one. The latter is the oldest building in Nara, predating the Daibutsu-den by 15 years. Inside, via the outer worship hall, is a dimly lit collection of priceless Buddhist statues.

The most ancient and remarkable of Tōdai-ji's great buildings is on the other side of its grounds, northwest of the Daibutsu-den. The **Shōsō-in** is a treasure house, built by Emperor Shōmu to house the thousands of priceless objects which found their way to Nara along the Silk Route (this stretched from the Mediterranean through the Near and Middle East, before passing into China, and trickling onward through Korea to Japan). Sealed for hundreds of years, and opened only on the rare orders of the emperor himself, it represents a time capsule of the treasures of 8th-century civilization: musical instruments, glass, mirrors, textiles from China, Persia and Southeast Asia. The building's distinctive design—it looks like a log cabin on stilts—seems to have contributed to the preservation of these objects. The old theory used to be that it was the walls of interlocking cypress logs that held the secret: swelling in damp weather and shrinking in dry conditions, they allowed just enough air to circulate in and around the treasures.

These days, the Shōsō-in's contents are housed in purpose-built concrete buildings. Once a year, a selection of them is displayed at the Nara National Museum. For this reason alone, late October and early November is the best time to visit Nara.

Nara Park

East of Kōfuku-ji and the Sarusawa Pond, a large *torii* gateway marks the entrance to the sacred territory of the Kasuga Shrine, a 213-acre forest parkland stretching over the lower slopes of Mt Mikasa. This is the home of the thousand or so deer who crop up all over Nara and add so much to its charm. They are sacred animals, messengers of the Shinto gods, and for centuries killing them was a capital offence. Extremely appealing on first acquaintance, they soon become irritating: they're spoilt rotten, and extremely cheeky. These days the emissaries of the divine are more likely to steal your lunch than bring tidings from heaven. During the October rutting season, the stags can become aggressive and unpredictable and are de-horned in a special ceremony; all the same you might want to steer clear of them at this time, and keep an eye on young children.

Nara National Museum (Kokuritsu Hakubutsukan)

Open 9–4.30; adm ¥430 (more for special exhibitions).

This small but richly endowed museum has more treasures than it can display at once: because of this, and for conservation purposes, exhibits are rotated, making it difficult to give a detailed commentary.

The **Main Gallery**, a Gallic-looking building opened in 1894, contains a variety of archaeological relics excavated from temple sites and burial mounds, and a showcase of pieces from the museum's finest collection: Buddhist sculpture. The statues are superb (many of them were compulsorily 'lent' by temples during the Meiji period), but their arrangement will be a little obscure to the uninitiated and those who don't read Japanese. Formerly, the statues were organized chronologically making it easy to stroll through and comprehend the development of style. This changed when the museum underwent renovations in 1998 and opened the New East Building. Now one room of the Main Gallery is dedicated to art made in Nara, another to Zen art, one to the art of Esoteric Buddhism, another to Korean and Chinese sculpture, and so on. To compound the problem for the non-Japanese speaking visitor there is scant information available in English unless you buy a book in the gift shop. An underground passage links the Main Gallery and the two modern Galleries (the East and West 'New Buildings'), both of which are primarily reserved for special exhibitions. In the underground passageway you will find excellent educational displays that demonstrate in detail the basic types and techniques of Buddhist art: the various kinds of statue, the pedestals on which they're mounted, and the different ways of carving, casting and constructing an image. You will also find flashy interactive video screens, which have information about the museum, and other historical sites in Nara as well. Unfortunately, all of this is exclusively in Japanese. For the special exhibitions, well-written English pamphlets are available. These exhibitions can be very well curated, though perhaps somewhat specific for the general tourist. Depending on your interest, they could be well worth the time and money. Every year, starting at the end of October, a special exhibition of the treasures from the Shōsō-in (*see* p.276) is held here.

Kasuga Taisha (Kasuga Grand Shrine)

East of the deer park, on the slopes of Mt Mikasa, is the Kasuga Shrine, founded by the Fujiwara family in 710. The four deities worshipped here, known collectively as the Kasuga Myōjin, were carried to Nara on the backs of deer: the animals which these days pinch tourists' ice-creams are their descendants. Rows of tall stone lanterns line the main approach to the shrine buildings, donated by businesses as well as by devout individuals. Off the path to the left is the pleasant **Manyō Botanical Garden**, a collection of flowers and herbs dedicated to the *Manyōshū*, an 8th-century poetry anthology, and said to contain every one of the three hundred plants mentioned in its verses.

The inner shrine begins at the **Nandai-mon** (Great South Gate), beyond which is a courtyard containing booths selling talismans. The **Chūō-mon** is the next gate. You can't pass or take photographs beyond here, but you can see through, past the **Haiden** (Oratory) to the four individual shrines of the Kasuga Myōjin: from left to right, Takemikazuchi, Futsunushi, Ame-no-Koyane (legendary forebear of the Fujiwara), and his wife, Himegami. Traditionally the halls here were rebuilt every 20 years, but the last time was in 1957, and after a gap of decades the buildings need a lick of paint here and there.

Left of the oratory is a **dance platform** where sacred performances are dedicated to the deities on festival days or on payment of a donation by a worshipper. The dances offered here are among the oldest in the country, and the **Hōmotsu-kan** (Treasure Hall, *open April–Oct 8.30–4.30, Nov–Mar 9–6*), a little further down the hill, contains masks and a pair of giant drums played on special occasions. The most impressive of these is the On-Matsuri, from 16–18 December, held at the small **Wakamiya Shrine**, south of the main shrine. Wakamiya means 'young prince': the deity worshipped at this festival, with *nō*, sumo and ancient dances, is the child of the married *kami* from the senior shrine.

Heijō (Castle of Peace)

Kintetsu line train to Saidai-ji station, then a 15-minute walk east to the museum (open 9–5) which is in the northwest corner of the site.

The site of the 8th-century Nara Imperial Palace and Heijō-kyō, the city that surrounded it, is today a bleak and lonely place of overgrown fields and semi-excavated avenues. The archaeologists began working in earnest in 1958, and only about one quarter of the site has been completed. Still, with a stroll around the site and a visit to the **Heijō Shiryōkan** (Museum), it's possible to get a feeling for the scale and magnificence of the first great city of Japan. Miraculously, given Japan's hunger for real estate, the site has remained more or less intact. A railway line crosses it, but the National Highway was expensively routed to swerve west just before the southern perimeter. The excavated areas can be visited: the raised concrete base was the **Daigoku-den** (Imperial Great Council Hall); lawns, bushes and gravel indicate the position of the main buildings, pillars and avenues respectively. The **museum** has models, aerial photos and sample artefacts showing the techniques of excavation and preservation, and some remarkably fresh-looking Nara-period coins, nails and even leaves.

Tōshōdai-ji (Temple of T'ang)

Kintetsu line train to Nishinokyō (change at Saidaiji) or buses 52, 97 or 98. Open 8.30–4.30; adm ¥300.

This magnificent and matchlessly well-preserved temple complex was founded in 759 by the Chinese priest Ganjin, who had a profound influence on Nara Buddhism.

In 733, in the first flush of enthusiasm for the Tōdai-ji building project, Emperor Shōmu dispatched envoys to China. Their task appeared relatively straightforward: to bring back a Buddhist master, a trophy holy man to go with the monumental temple which Shōmu was busy constructing. Almost nothing went according to plan. After ten years of searching, they finally struck lucky with a famous abbot called Chien Chen (Japanese pronunciation: Ganjin), then in his fifties, who accepted the commission and began preparations for the dangerous crossing to Japan. Ten years, six separate attempts and many disasters later, he arrived in Nara in 754. By this time, Shōmu had abdicated and Ganjin himself had become blind. He was immediately installed at Tōdai-ji with a brief to inject some Chinese discipline into the somewhat languid Nara monasteries.

In the end, Ganjin's zeal exceeded all expectations. He quit Tōdai-ji in disgust at its laxness, and with his surviving Chinese followers set up his own monastery here at Tōshōdai-ji, at a disdainful distance from the capital. Five of those original 8th-century buildings, and many smaller treasures, survive.

Touring Tōshōdai-ji

The finest of the halls is the **Kon-dō** (Main Hall) which can be seen through the **Nandai-mon** (Great South Gate), a 1960s reconstruction. Its magnificent tile roof has been rebuilt higher and heavier than it would once have been (there are plans to reinstate the lighter, flatter roof in future restorations), and the hall's imposingly weighty, stern form belies the subtlety of its construction. The seven bays of its long sides are narrower at the ends of the building than they are in the middle. This helps in supporting the roof (whose weight rests largely on the outer pillars), but also concentrates the eye on the centre bay and the statues which are visible through it.

At this early stage in Buddhist architecture, a temple's worship hall was itself out of bounds to lay worshippers. They prayed from the outside (the portico provided shelter), and the interior was reserved for the sculpted deities and their priests. The statues within have been toppled by earthquakes and battered by war, but they're still in remarkable condition. Carved by Chinese artists from Ganjin's entourage, they mark a fresh spirit in Nara sculpture, consistent with his newly rigorous approach to worship and discipline. Compared to the warm, humane sculptures carved 140 years earlier for Hōryū-ji, these are austere, mysterious, awe-inspiring figures. At their centre is the cosmic Buddha, **Roshana**, constructed out of dry lacquer on a wood and metal base, and surrounded by a halo of 1,000 lesser beings (864 of them survive). To the right is a very cross-looking **Yakushi**, God of Healing, and to the left an extraordinary **thousand-armed Kannon** with 953 of its eponymous limbs intact. A thick and mysterious fog once cloaked this hall for ten days, the story goes. When it had cleared, the monks re-entered to find this statue, carved and gilded by heavenly hands.

The **Kō-dō** (Lecture Hall), directly behind the Kon-dō, began life in 710 as a hall of the Heijō Imperial Palace, donated to Tōshōdai-ji by Empress Kōken in 759. The doors, brackets and Miroku statue inside are from the 12th and 13th centuries, however, and more than anything else the building looks like a Kamakura period hall. Among the temple's lesser buildings are a number of 12th and 13th century additions: the **Kaidan**, a three-tiered stone ordination platform, the **Shorō** (bell tower), the **Korō** (a drum tower also said to contain relics of the Buddha) and a long narrow building on the east side of the two main halls, containing priests' quarters and an altar. Behind this are two early 8th-century **treasure and sutra houses**, built in the same log cabin style as Tōdai-ji's Shōsō-in, and predating it.

The modern **Shin-Hōzō** (New Treasure House) apes this style in fire-proof concrete. As well as a set of illustrated scrolls describing the perilous adventures of Ganjin, and various wooden and dry-lacquer *bodhisattvas*, there's an 8th–9th-century **headless Buddha**, carved out of a single piece of nutmeg—more fascinating as a torso, one suspects, than it would ever have been as a perfect statue. In the absence of feet, hands or a face, attention is focused fully on the plump, muscular legs and torso and on the voluptuous, clinging drapery of the robe.

The temple's most famous statue is shown, unfortunately, for only one day a year, on the anniversary of Ganjin's death, 6 June. It's displayed in the **Miei-dō** in the northeast corner of the precincts: still clad in his original colours, blind eyes closed, the old sage himself sits in deep meditation on the verge of death. A quiet grove in the northeast contains his **grave**, beneath a stupa-topped mound.

Yakushi-ji

Kintetsu line train to Nishinokyō (change at Saidaiji) or buses 52 or 98. Both the station and the bus stop are closest to the back (north) entrance to the temple. Open 8.30–5; adm ¥500.

Modern reconstructions are a depressing feature of Japan's fire and earthquake-wracked temples and shrines, and the results are almost always disappointing. Yakushi-ji, though, is an inspirational exception. This 8th-century temple was almost completely destroyed by fire in 1528; sensitive modern restoration, based around the single surviving pagoda, has created a picture of how a big Nara temple would have looked at the height of its fortunes.

If you've entered from the north, make your way through the precincts to the humble **Nandai-mon** (Great South Gate), erected as a temporary replacement and still doing the job after 300 years. From here you can see the layout of the complex as the planners intended. Yakushi-ji was first built in Fujiwara-kyō, Japan's capital from 687 to 710. When the court moved to Nara in 710, the big monasteries went with it; the reconstruction of Yakushi-ji on its new site was complete by 730. It was the first temple to be built with two pagodas which stand, as they did then, on either side and slightly in front of the main hall.

The **Tō-tō** (East Pagoda), finished in 730, is the only survivor of the 1528 fire, and the only surviving structure of its period in Japan. Its western twin (**Sai-tō**) was rebuilt identically in 1984. Both show an unusual style, since the three true roofs each have beneath them a smaller lean-to roof which shelters the outer balcony. They look as if they have six floors, or rather as if a smaller and a larger three-storey pagoda have magically fused into one another. Critics are fond of describing the staccato effect of this interleaving as 'contrapuntal' or 'rhythmic'; it's suggested that the architecture of the pagoda may have been influenced by the growth of Japanese music which was taking wing at the same time.

The **Kon-do** (Main Hall)—a 1976 reconstruction—has a similarly complicated roof arrangement above its three great doors. Inside are three bronze statues, originally gilded, but glazed to an ebony lustre by the smoke and heat of the 1528 fire which they, but not the hall, survived. The central figure of the triad represents the eponymous Yakushi, Buddha of Healing, a solid and serene figure sitting on a large medicine chest. Much more striking are his attendants, Gakkō and Nikkō, deities of the Moon and Sun, on the left and right respectively; here again the temptation is to talk in terms of music. With muscular torsos but slender arms and feet, they have an almost feminine delicacy, sashaying their arms and inflecting their hips as if dancing to unheard music. The square slots in their forearms would once have been threaded with billowing scarves.

As interesting as the statues, and something of a puzzle to art historians, is the plinth/chest on which Yakushi sits and the mysterious reliefs visible around its rim. They're best examined from behind, through the window in the rear corridor. On the upper edge is a grapevine motif, held to be West Asian or even Greek in origin, and imported via India and China along the Silk Road. The ovals and squares are considered Persian, and the dragon, phoenix, tiger and tortoise on each of the four sides are T'ang Chinese. Most puzzling are the 12 hairy fanged barbarians peeping out from arched cave entrances. They resemble figures from Hindu temples, but there is nothing else like them in Japanese art.

Other Buildings

The **Kō-dō** (Lecture Hall), behind the Main Hall, dates from 1852 and is slated for replacement by a reconstruction of the original. Beyond the **East Pagoda** (the original one) is the **Tōin-dō**, a 13th-century hall containing a **Sho-Kannon**, a flawlessly cast, standing figure with a beautiful, almost arrogant expression. For a week or two in the New Year, and a bit longer in October–November, the modern **Daihōzō-den** (Great Treasure House) is open to visitors. Three objects stand out from its collection: an oil painting on hemp of the goddess Kichijo-ten as a plump, seductive looking court lady in multi-layered diaphanous robes; and two rare 8th-century paintings of Shinto deities, guardians of the temple whose shrine is over the road, just south of the Nandai-mon.

Southwest Nara

Hōryū-ji (Temple of Noble Law)

Buses 52, 60, 97 or 98 take about 50mins. All depart from the both the JR Nara and the Kintetsu-Nara train stations; alight at Hōryū-ji-mae bus stop (announced in English). The JR Kansai main line takes 12mins from JR Nara station to Hōryū-ji station, a couple of kilometres from the temple. Open summer 8–5, 19 Nov–11 Mar 8–4.30; adm ¥1000.

Hōryū-ji, 10km from Nara in the otherwise insignificant village of Ikaruga, is a landmark of Japanese history, a cradle of Buddhism founded 1400 years ago, containing many of its most important works of art as well as the oldest wooden buildings in the world. It's less accessible, and correspondingly less crowded, than the central Nara temples; but to the student of art or history, it must rank among the top three sites in Japan.

History

Hōryū-ji owes its existence to Prince Umayado, known to posterity as **Shōtoku Taishi** (572–622), a seminal figure of Japanese history who, although he never actually ruled as emperor, is credited with several of the most important reforms of the Asuka Period (538–645), the earliest of Japan's historical eras.

Shōtoku was deeply impressed and influenced by Chinese culture and by its religion, Buddhism, which he instituted as Japan's state faith. He dispatched the first ambassadors to China, adopted its calendar, established a fixed hierarchy of 12 court ranks, and in 604 promulgated the Seventeen Articles, Japan's first national constitution. 'A country does not have two lords, the people do not have two masters,' he declared. As a politician, Shōtoku's genius was to use Buddhism, with its conception of a universe ruled over by the single cosmic Buddha, Dainichi, to assert the power of a single emperor, and to dissolve the power of the clans which still divided Japan.

For all this, Shōtoku was deeply and sincerely devout, and the first great Japanese scholar of Buddhism. He studied the scriptures under a Korean master and wrote commentaries on the sutras which were used as teaching aids in Chinese seminaries. But his greatest legacy is Hōryū-ji. Despite being rebuilt after his death, its subtle spiritual atmosphere still embodies the innocence and delicacy of the earliest Japanese Buddhism.

In 601 Shōtoku had built a palace at Ikaruga, the birthplace of his favourite consort, and in 607 he founded a temple here, originally known as Wakakusa-dera or Ikaruga-dera. Its principal image was a statue of Yakushi Nyōrai by Tori Busshi, a sculptor who, like many of the craftsmen on the building project, came from the Korean kingdom of Paekche.

The years following the completion of the temple were sad ones for Shōtoku who died, soon after his mother and consort, in 622. Worse was to follow for his descendants. The heirs of Soga no Umako, Shōtoku's great adviser and statesman, fell out with the Prince's son Yamashiro, who had made a claim for the throne. When Yamashiro retired to Ikaruga it was taken (perhaps rightly) as a sign that he was plotting rebellion. The Soga family sent an army to storm the Ikaruga Palace. Outnumbered, Yamashiro, along with the last of Shōtoku's blood relatives, committed suicide in the palace grounds. In 670 the temple complex was struck by lightning and burned down.

Fearful that Shōtoku would seek ghostly revenge for the snuffing out of his line, succeeding generations of rulers rebuilt and expanded Hōryū-ji. A personal cult developed around Shōtoku, who was thought to have been reborn as a Buddha in the temple's statues. Until recently the Prince's image adorned the ¥10,000 note.

Hōryū-ji tip: many of the treasures of Hōryū-ji, Japan's finest, are displayed in the deepest murk, pointlessly obscured by crude bars and wire mesh. Remember to bring a torch (if you haven't got one of your own, borrow one from your lodgings: hotel rooms are required to have them by law.)

Sai-in (West Precinct)

From Hōryū-ji-mae bus stop, an avenue leads north to the **Nandai-mon** (Great South Gate), built in 1439, which frames the temple beyond it. The **Chū-mon** (Central Gate) gives onto the main compound and forms part of the **Kairō** (Corridor), actually a roofed wall, which encloses it. The **Chū-mon** dates from the early 8th century; its pillars swell in the middle, a technique know as *entasis*, used in Greek temples to eliminate the illusion of concavity, which may have reached China from Europe along the Silk Route. Unusually, only two bays provide ingress to visitors. Normally there would have been a third, reserved for members of the aristocracy. This arrangement is said to reflect an egalitarian streak in Shōtoku's thinking. In the outer bays are two **Ni-ō** (Guardian Kings), carved in 711; note the monstrous webbing under their muscular shoulders.

The inner courtyard is unusual in its layout too. Shōtoku's original temple was built on a north–south axis with the pagoda in front of the Main Hall as the worshipper approached them. Here they stand side by side.

Gojū-no-tō (Five-storey Pagoda)

This is the most fascinating structure in Hōryū-ji. Over a hundred feet tall, its five roofs diminish in size as they ascend in the following proportions—10:9:8:7:6. The roofs get steeper too, so that the entire building appears even more soaring than it is, as if about to lift gently off the ground. Like all the oldest pagodas, the primary purpose of this one is as a marker for relics of the Buddha. A chamber 3m below the ground contains plaques, a copper bowl, beads, pearls and a glass relic bottle inside two larger gold and bronze containers. Unfortunately, the excavation of 1949 revealed the relic jar to be empty.

The earliest pagodas were monuments, not buildings; it was only in later years that they were built with internal space and sanctuaries and images of their own. Hōryū-ji's marks a transitional period. There is no 'inside' to this pagoda, but instead four grottoes at ground level between the corners of the base. These contain remarkable tableaux of famous moments from Buddhist history, modelled out of clay with individual statuettes. Coarse mesh masks the dim interiors; this is the moment to switch on your torch.

The **south tableau** depicts the Paradise of Miroku, Buddha of the Future. The one to the **west** shows the disciples dividing up the historical Buddha's relics after his death, kneeling on either side of his coffin. More interesting is the **east tableau** in which Monju, a saintly disciple of the Buddha, and Yuima, a celebrated scholar, engage in learned debate. The latter is depicted as an old man who, rather than achieve Buddhahood, has opted to remain on earth to expound the sacred teachings. His frail limbs and slack features are poignantly and realistically modelled; on his knees rests a tripod desk from which he reads.

Finest of all is the **north tableau** which shows the moment of death of the historical Buddha, Shaka. This is a recurring image in Buddhist art but rarely has it been depicted with quite such passion and drama. The background represents the beetling cliffs and swirling clouds above Mt Sumeru, the centre of the earth in Buddhist cosmology. Dead Shaka himself, larger than life and still bearing traces of gold leaf, lies on a low bed; behind him *bodhisattvas* sit in calm attendance. But attention focuses on the human disciples kneeling in front. Their bony, elderly bodies are contorted with grief—heads thrown back, fists pummelling their chests, mouths frozen in screams of despair. The detail—from the disordered drapes of their robes and their pierced ears, to their bulging necks and tiny, individually shaped teeth—is perfect. Just one figure, to the left of the Buddha's head, remains impassive, withdrawn, it almost appears, into catatonic shock.

Kon-dō (Gold Hall)

The main hall of Hōryū-ji was rebuilt some time after the fire of 670, probably around 710, making it the oldest wooden building in the world. Wider, squatter, and more monumentally magnificent than the pagoda, it shares its steep roofs and smaller upper storey. The middle roof juts out as much as 14 feet, and supports, carved in the shape of lions and dragons, were added at a later date to prevent it sagging.

Several of the statues within date from the temple's original founding by Shōtoku Taishi, or just after his death, making the oldest nearly 1400 years old. They were commissioned by the temple's patrons and cast in bronze, probably by naturalized Korean craftsmen from the kingdom of Paekche. Historians differ on the artistic heritage of these figures. Certain details of the carving, particularly the dignified, rather stiff regularity of the folds and drapes, suggests an effort to reproduce in bronze the look of stone carvings of the Chinese Northern Wei Dynasty. Exotic details, like the elaborate open-work crowns and jewellery and the intricate honeysuckle borders, point to a Korean provenance. The situation isn't made any clearer by the reluctance on the part of some Japanese scholars to attribute their National Treasures to foreign, and especially Korean, genius.

The hall contains three separate groupings of statues, each topped by an elaborate canopy, plus the **Shitennō** (Four Guardian Kings) at each of the cardinal points. The left-hand statue is the least important, a statue of **Amida Nyōrai**, carved in the 13th century at a time when Amida was emerging as the pre-eminent Japanese deity. At the right-hand side is **Yakushi**, Buddha of Healing; on his back is a date (607) and an inscription, explaining that the statue was cast in memory of the late Emperor Yōmei by his son, Shōtoku, and his sister, later Empress Suiko.

The central space is occupied by a **Shaka Triad** (the historical Buddha, Shaka, flanked by two unidentified *bodhisattvas*) commissioned by Suiko as a prayer for Shōtoku's recovery from illness, but completed as a memorial the year after his death (623). Both are attributed to a sculptor called Tori Busshi and share obvious characteristics. They are composed, dignified, trustworthy figures: static but graceful, radiating calm and impersonal benevolence. Yakushi and Shaka hold their hands in identical *mudra* or symbolic gestures: the open right palm banishes fear while the extended fingers of the left grant wishes. Both sit cross-legged atop plinths which are completely covered by their flowing robes. The drapes are one of the most striking and characteristic elements of Tori's style. They fan out in a broad flat plane, almost, but not quite, symmetrical. The impression is of neatness and order—'rhythmical' is the word sometimes used to describe them. The figures flanking Shaka stand on lotus blossoms and hold in their left hands mystic jewels called *centamani*. Their head-dresses are ornate and unusual; they've been compared to Persian crowns worn by the Sasanian kings, and the headgear of Korean shamans. Behind each statue is a pointed halo with twining honeysuckle designs on the inner circle, and flickering flames on the outer edge, suggesting the power and passion which lie behind the serene faces of the deities. The seven miniature buddhas in the haloes of the principal figures represent their previous incarnations.

The hanging canopies are unique works of art in themselves, although they may incorporate later restorations and repairs. To their upper edges are attached beautiful miniature carvings of angelic musicians surrounded by haloes of blossoms, each painstakingly chiselled out of the thinnest wood. Below these are several wooden phoenixes, stylized in form (their combs come so far over their heads as to cover their eyes), but with realistically bony, bird-like feet.

The final set of statues represent the **Shitennō**, the directional Guardian Kings, familiar in other temples for their ferociously irate expressions and bellicose poses. On these Shitennō, however, attention focuses on the accoutrements of worldly rank, not physical prowess: the elaborate robes, clasped by a stylized knot, the rich cords encircling the ample bellies, the high-necked collars and minutely-detailed crowns. Stocky and pillar-like, standing on the backs of comically crude demons, they look more like dignified mandarins than burly warlords.

Some time after the rebuilding of the Kon-dō following the 670 fire, its inner walls were painted with elaborate frescoes of the Four Paradises acclaimed for centuries as 'some of the noblest examples of religious art in Asia'. As artists were copying the pictures in January 1949 a heater which they were using to warm themselves short-circuited during the night. The fire was put out before it could damage the structure of the building—but the delicate pigments were ruined forever. The present frescoes are reproductions. They depict: the Western Paradise of Amida (on the west wall), Yakushi (on the northwest), Miroku (northeast), and Shaka (east).

Other Buildings Around the West Precinct

The **Ko-dō**, built into the back wall of the West Precinct, was brought to Hōryū-ji from Kyoto in 990, and contains a 10th-century Yakushi triad. In front of it are two smaller structures: a **bell tower** with an 8th-century bell, and the **Kyōzo** or sutra repository.

Immediately to the east of the West Precinct are two long low buildings running north–south: dormitories for the temple's monks. The one closest to the West Precinct, the Higashi-muro, dates from the Kamakura period; its south end (entrance opposite a pond) is the **Shōryō-in** (Hall of the Prince's Soul), a temple to Shōtoku containing scroll paintings and statues of him and his doomed family. Even the Prince's horse is honoured, in a small shrine to the east.

Daihōzō-den (Great Treasure Hall)

The **Treasure Hall** (*open summer 8–5, 20 Nov–10 Mar 8–4*), a concrete fireproof struc-ture built to supplant the log-cabin original, contains enough masterpieces to fill a book all of its own. It consists of two separate buildings joined by a covered corridor. The first room contains archaeological finds from the original temple, Wakakusa-dera, and the second displays **images of Prince Shōtoku** himself at various stages of life. There's an appealing 13th-century statue of the two-year-old Prince, looking realistically childish despite his praying hands and earnest expression (he was a precocious boy who was born with the power of speech, and read Chinese while still a child). The most famous picture is of the adult Prince, with a thin moustache and youthful beard fuzz, flanked by his two sons. The father carries a wand of office and jewelled long-sword; the boys have miniature swords and dinky, Asuka-period bunches. This is the picture which was reproduced on the ¥10,000 note and gave rise to the expression 'a Shōtoku', meaning 'a tenner'.

The next room contains miniature, personal images of the kind that priests might carry in the sleeves of their robes; and the **Yumechigai (Dream-Changing) Kannon**, a small, smiley statue credited with the power of turning nightmares into sweet dreams. The final room of the first building displays the celebrated **Kudara Kannon**, a mysterious and intriguing statue, unique in Asian art. Little of its origins is known, but it seems to have turned up at Hōryū-ji only during the Edo period. Its traditional name indicates Korean manufacture ('Kudara' was the Japanese name for Paekche), but Japanese scholars dispute this; certainly nothing like it survives in Korea or China today.

It is a slim, tremendously tall statue (over 2m), both mild and imposing, with unnaturally long arms and legs. On its head and neck it wears a bronze crown and collar and it holds a long-necked vase or water jar in its left hand. The lacquer surface of the camphor wood, once colourfully painted, has become cracked and faded over time, adding to the aura of age and sanctity, although the date of its creation can only be estimated. In its flat, planar composition, the symmetry of its drapes and the long, elegant sleeves which flow to the ground in stylized curves, the Kannon resembles other statues of the Asuka period. But the relaxed set of the body, the dreamy, faraway expression and unmuscular, almost round-shouldered physique impart quite a different impression from, say, the Tori Busshi statues in the Kon-dō (this statue also used to stand there but, being wooden, it was moved out after the 1949 fire).

The second building of the museum contains drawings and scrolls, carved angelic musicians, a variety of statues of Buddhist deities from the 8th to 11th centuries, and two miniature Buddhist temples, its greatest treasures.

The **Tamamushi Zushi** (Jewel Beetle Altar) is named for its most striking feature, long since rotted to dust. When the seven-and-a-half-foot tall shrine was built in the 650s, the bronze open-work around the edge of the base covered the iridescent wings of 9000 *tamamushi*—the *Chrysochroa elegans* beetle. It contains a miniature statue, and the roof is a precise model of a tiled hip-and-gable roof, complete with owl's tail finials. The outer doors of the shrine bear painted *bodhisattvas*; the base panels are decorated with famous scenes from the scriptures. At the front, angels hover above two monks who make offerings to the relics of the Buddha; at the back, dragons and phoenixes flap about the legendary Mt Sumeru as it rises from the sea. The side panels are more celebrated: both depict the young Shaka (the historical Buddha) engaged in heroic self-sacrifice. In one he is shown calmly hanging up his robe on a tree, then plummeting through space down the cliff he has jumped off, and finally being eaten by the hungry tiger whom he has chosen to feed with his own body. The various figures are slim and youthful, with long delicate necks—even the guardian kings on the upper doors who usually have imposing, bulky physiques.

Tradition ascribes ownership of the Tamamushi Shrine to Shōtoku's aunt, the Empress Suiko, although no one knows for sure. The **Tachibana-zushi**, however, is named after its owner, Lady Tachibana, the mother of Emperor Shōmu's consort. It was built probably a century or so after the time of Shōtoku and enshrines a beautiful trinity of Amida and attendant *bodhisattvas*. They sit on lotus leaves which rise out of a piece of bronze realistically carved to look like the surface of a pond.

Tō-in (East Precinct)

The land to the east of the pagoda and Gold Hall was the site of Shōtoku's Ikaruga Palace, demolished by the Soga family after the bloody ructions which snuffed out his line. It was rebuilt as a temple a century later when the cult of Shōtoku started to take wing.

The two precincts are quite different in layout. You enter through the **Tōdai-mon** (Great East Gate) which marks the boundary between west and east, and the first building you see is the striking, octagonal **Yume-dono** (Dream Hall) standing on top of a thick stone base, with a dramatic flaming jewel mounted on the apex of its roof. The East Precinct has no Gold Hall or pagoda, the Yume-dono serving as a combination of the two. The name comes from an old story about Shōtoku: it's said that as he sat on this spot, pondering the Sanskrit scriptures, a mysterious old man would appear in his dreams and explain the meaning of the most difficult passages.

Within is a fine Nara-period dry lacquer statue of the priest Gyōshin, who supervised the construction of the Tō-in, and the **Kuze Kannon**, holiest of the Hōryū-ji masterpieces. It predates the Yume-dono, and is the statue most intimately associated with Shōtoku himself; tradition variously has it that he worshipped the statue during his lifetime, was the model for it, carved it himself, or was reborn as the deity after his death.

The statue is miraculously well preserved with almost all its gold leaf intact. It is only displayed to the public twice a year, from 11 April to 15 May, and then in the autumn from 22 October to 20 November. Until late in the 19th century, it was completely hidden from view; not even the temple's abbots had laid eyes on it for centuries. Then, in the 1880s, an American art historian named Ernest Fenellosa undertook a survey of Buddhist art works on behalf of the Meiji Government. Since the Restoration of the Emperor in 1868 and the promulgation of 'State' Shinto, Buddhism had been treated with, at best, indifference and frequently with official hostility. Fenellosa had no trouble obtaining letters which gave him access to any temples he wished. In 1884, against the wishes of the Hōryū-ji priests, the closed central shrine of the Yume-dono was opened and its contents removed. 'I shall never forget our feelings as the long disused key rattled in the dusty lock,' wrote Fenellosa. 'Within the shrine appeared a tall mass closely wrapped about in swaddling bands of cotton cloth, upon which the dust of ages had gathered. It was no light task to unwrap the contents, some 500 yards of cloth having been used, and our eyes and nostrils were in danger of being choked with the pungent dust. But at last the final folds of the covering fell away, and this marvellous statue, unique in the world, came forth to human sight for the first time in centuries.'

To Fenellosa, there was no question that the Kannon was of Korean manufacture. In style it has much in common with the serene stiffness of the Tori bronzes in the Kon-dō, but heightened and rendered more monumental and magnificent. The splayed drapes which jut out symmetrically on either side of the figure's skirts are particularly bold. The face is fleshy with traces of the 'archaic smile' of the Kon-dō's Shaka playing on the thick, almost negroid lips. In front of the chest, Kannon holds a flaming jewel in an unusual and complicated hand gesture. The filigree crown and halo teem with minute detail.

Chūgū-ji

Open 9–4.30; adm ¥400.

This small nunnery, east of the Yume-dono, was originally built several hundred metres away as the palace of Shōtoku's mother. When she died in 621 (one year before the Prince himself), he had it converted into a memorial nunnery which was moved and reconstructed on this site in the 13th century. The treasure hall, built in the 1950s over a shallow pond, contains Hōryū-ji's most beautiful and accessible work of art, usually referred to as **Miroku bosatsu**, Buddha of the Future (although there's disagreement as to the exact deity represented). It's very similar to the statue in Kyoto's Kōryū-ji temple: a slim, smiling youth, his right hand beneath his chin, his arm resting on his knee which is folded in the 'half-lotus' position. The neck, arms, fingers and naked torso (carved out of camphor wood, once gilded, now deeply tanned) are long and delicate; the face bears an expression of profound calm and benevolence. Despite the stylized proportions and the curious spherical buns on top of the head, there is something very human and realistic about the figure. It's an object of personal prayer and devotion, of sensuous, intuitive communion with the divine, in stark contrast with the monumental, ritualistic statues of the Western Precinct.

Also in this building is a reconstruction of fragments of a 7th-century tapestry, the **Tenjukoku Mandala**, embroidered by Shōtoku's consort and depicting the Prince in Paradise. In its time it must have been bold and impressive, but too little survives to form a picture of it today.

Shopping

Nara may not have the selection of craft stores that Kyoto has, and you will certainly not find the department stores and electronic stores of Tokyo, but it is a very manageable place to gift-shop. You will find everything you need either in the covered shopping arcade running south from Nara Kintetsu station, on Sanjō-dōri, or in Naramachi. The three areas run together, making it easy to casually wander about until you've had your fill.

Naramachi is an attraction in its own right and worth a stroll even if you have no intention of buying anything. Tiny shops selling everything from household goods, to food items, fine kimonos, pottery and antiques are interspersed with old wood-frame houses. Naramachi roughly begins south of Sanjō-dōri in the small streets just east of the covered arcade and extends south beyond Gango-ji.

(✆ 0742–) **Where to Stay**

Numbers refer to map, pp.268–269, which shows hotel locations.

Japanese-style

Nara has some fine *ryokans*, though none have quite the same renown as Tawaraya and Hiiragiya in Kyoto (*see* p. 257). Breakfast and dinner are included in the price of the room, as is service, so they may turn out to be a better deal then they initially seem.

expensive

① **Kikusuiro**, ✆ 23 2001, ✉ 26 0025, is a ten-minute walk from Kintetsu-Nara station and adjacent to Nara Park. The architecture is imposing and so are the staff at times; if some nose-sniffing at vulgar foreigners doesn't bother you, this place is highly recommended. Ask for a room facing the Ara Pond. Reservations are only accepted for parties of two or more (¥30,000).

② **Kankasō**, ✆ 26 1128, ✉ 26 1301, is friendlier and just as elegant as Kikusuiro. It is conveniently situated in the Park, just a stone's throw from Tōdai-ji and other principal sights (¥20,000–¥25,300).

moderate

③ At the rather unusual *ryokan*, **Edo-san**, ✆ 26 2662, ✉ 26 2663, you can enjoy the luxury of your own private cottage but, ironically, only if you're with someone else: reservations for solitary travellers are not accepted. The attractive cottages with their thatched roofs are set in the southern corner of the park. Excellent dinners with an emphasis on seafood are served in the cottages (*¥18,000*).

inexpensive

④ ⑤ Matsumae Ryokan, ✆ 22 3686, ✉ 26 3927, **Ryokan Hakuko**, ✆ 26 7891,
⑥ ✉ 26 7893, and **Furuichi Ryokan**, ✆ 22 2440, each offer reasonable rates for basic *ryokan* accommodation (breakfast is extra) and are conveniently located south of Sanjō-dōri. Hakuko is the easiest to find—look out for a sign in Roman letters on Sanjō-dōri just past the Nara Tourist Centre.

cheap

⑦ Seikan-sō, ✆ 22 2670, is in Higashikituji-chō, one of the southern sections of Nara. The reasonable price probably reflects its slightly remote location but, if you don't mind the extra walking, it is well worth a visit. Formerly the site of a geisha house, this old wooden inn has become very popular with foreigners. Book in advance and, if possible, ask them to fax you a map (*rooms from ¥4,000*).

temple accommodation

Many temples no longer offer accommodation, probably owing to the antics of renegade foreigners. If you are sincerely interested in temples that offer accommodation, consult the Nara City Tourist Centre.

Western-style

moderate

⑧ Nara Hotel, ✆ 26 3300, ✉ 22 5252, just squeezes into the moderate category and you may find that even the fancier *ryokans* listed above offer an equivalent deal with their two meals included. However, if you want to avoid *tatami* floors and common baths, this is the best Nara has to offer. It has big, Western-style rooms (plus a few Japanese) in an old tiled building, with restaurants and gardens, and a new modern wing. It is located 5 minutes by taxi from the Kintetsu-Nara station, on the southeastern edge of Nara Park (*¥14,000*).

⑨ The Nara Garden Hotel, ✆ 27 0555, ✉ 22 0255, is located in the heart of Nara Park and is priced along the same lines as the Nara Hotel. Good western and Japanese food is available in the restaurants.

⑩ Hotel Sunroute Nara, ✆ 22 5151, ✉ 27 0203, is conveniently set on the fringe of Naramachi (see 'Shopping', p.290). Although not spectacular, it is one of the more reasonably priced hotels in the centre of town (*¥8,000*).

⑪ The Nara Royal Hotel, ✆ 34 1131, ✉ 34 3231, is near Heijō, a ten-minute walk from the Kintetsu-Shinomiya train station (*¥8,000*). Although far from the centre of town, it has luxurious amenities such as a sauna and a heated pool.

⑫ **Hotel Fujita Nara**, ✆ 23 8111, 📠 22 0255, also has good modern facilities. It is set on the main road from JR Nara station to Nara Park. It has a number of restaurants, including the good but pricey) **Steakhouse Ginza** (*see* below).

inexpensive

⑬ **Kotton Hyaku-Pasento**, ✆ 22 7117, 📠 26 2771, a seven-minute walk from Kintetsu-Nara station, has single rooms starting at ¥7,000. If you reserve at the front desk in advance, breakfast will cost just ¥500.

(✆ *0742–*)   *Eating Out*

For all its art treasures and history, Nara has the nightlife of a small Japanese town—decent but modest restaurants, bars and *izakaya* (where you can drink and/or eat) which close early. If your hotel or inn is half-serious about food, you may find it most convenient to eat there.

Japanese

expensive

Like Kyoto, Nara is known for its *kaiseki ryōri* (*see* p. 30). **Onjaku**, ✆ 26 4762, offers a variety of beautiful *kaiseki* meals for lunch and dinner. Plate after immaculate plate of Japanese delights are presented in the refined atmosphere of its traditional-style rooms. Parties of five or more can call ahead and get a *bentō* (boxed) lunch for *¥5,000* per person. **Tsukihitei**, ✆ 26 4762 is tucked in the woods near Kasuga Taisha (*see* p.279) which makes for an enchanting dining atmosphere. Call in advance if you prefer a table and chairs (*¥15,000*).

Uma no Me, ✆ 23 7784, is a lovely restaurant perched above Ara Pond in Nara Park. The interior decorations change periodically as the restaurant features month-long exhibitions of individual artists and craftsmen. It comes highly recommended, particularly for the terrific set courses at lunch, a true bargain (*kaiseki* dinner *¥13,000*, lunch *¥3,500*).

moderate

Van Kio, ✆ 33 8942, is a good option for lunch if you are in the southwestern area of Nara, visiting Yakushi-ji (*see* p.282) or Tōshōdai-ji (*see* p.280). Exit at the South Gate of Yakushi-ji, follow the pedestrian path through the woods, past a shrine, and you will come to Van Kio. The main dish here is called *suien mushi.* Meat and vegetables are steamed in a ceramic dish and served with soup and a salad. Other interesting set courses are available for lunch and dinner, including several 'light lunches'.

Tokiwa, ✆ 22 2237, near Nara's two finest gardens, Isui-en and Yoshiki-en, serves seasonal dishes and has an elegant patio at the back with a view towards Wakakusa Hill. It is hard to believe that the crowd at Tōdai-ji is a stone's throw away. (*Open for lunch only.*) **Bekkan Kisuiro**, ✆ 23 2001, 📠 26 0025, serves what it calls a '*mini kaiseki*' and is a good option for those who don't want to go all the way with the elaborate formalities of the regular *kaiseki* feast. *Sukiyaki* and *shabu-shabu* are also on the menu (*prices start at ¥5,000*).

Yamazakiya, ✆ 27 3751, in the covered shopping arcade that runs south of Kintetsu-Nara station, has a varied menu and serves small and reasonably priced *kaiseki* starting around ¥3,800. It also offers c*hagayu,* a traditional Nara dish made of rice porridge cooked in tea.

inexpensive

Maguro, ✆ 23 3776, just a block away from the Kintetsu-Nara station, is a great deal for lunch or dinner. The name means 'tuna', and that is exactly what they serve, in various shapes and forms. Come here early for dinner or late for lunch as it gets crowded quickly.

Harishin, ✆ 22 2669, located in the southern part of Naramachi directly west of Gango-ji, offers very affordable *bentō* (lunch boxes). The contents of the boxes change with the season, but they are always excellent. If you reserve in advance Harishin now serves *kaiseki* dinners that are every bit as good as their bentos, and an excellent value starting at ¥5,000. Seating for dinner is available only from 6–9. Look for a small sign in Roman letters and a window display featuring a photograph of the meal you will be served.

Beni-e, ✆ 22 9439, is a *tempura* restaurant located just off the covered shopping arcade that runs south from Kintetsu Nara station. Lunch and dinner are both good value. It is located just south of Yamazakiya; look for a green sign with red and white Japanese lettering near a shoe store on the main drag. The restaurant itself is set back from the street.

Foreign

expensive

At **Mikasa,** ✆ 26 3300, in the Nara Hotel, the service and food are top-notch although the atmosphere is not exactly intimate. It is a comfortable place for a late lunch, and offers excellent set dinner menus with a French flavour.

Steak House Ginza, ✆ 23 8111, in the Hotel Fujita Nara on Sanjō-dōri, is in the western category because it serves steaks, but the steaks are cooked in a decidedly Japanese fashion. The food is delicious and prepared by an expert cook before your eyes. (*Sets start from ¥6,500.*)

moderate

Naramachi Trattoria Washio, ✆ 27 5675, offers reasonable pasta dishes in the heart of Naramachi. The menu is not extensive, but what you get will be pretty good. Set courses are also available.

Beni Bana, ✆ 26 7725, on Sanjō-dōri serves decent pizza and pasta and has menus in English. *Take away available.*

O-sho, ✆ 26 4827, on Sanjō-dōri, has basic greasy Chinese dishes—tasty, but they will take their toll on your health. *Take away available.*

Cous Cous, ✆ 23 9494, also on Sanjō-dōri just to the east of the covered arcade, has set meals with an interesting mixture of dishes; ask for the kangaroo (sets start at ¥*1,800*).

Nightlife

Nara is not the most obvious place to experience Japanese nightlife, but the following bars are recommended by local ex-pats. **The Bronx**, on Sanjō-dōri, is very easy to find, all the way up the hill right next to Sarusawa Pond. A cool, subdued atmosphere prevails.

Rumors is also on Sanjō-dōri next to the Yuraku Movie Theater. It aspires to be an English pub, but you will judge for youself whether it succeeds. It does have a good variety of beers, a limited kitchen, and loud music. **High Times** is a little out of town, close to Shin-Omiya station (one stop before Nara on the Kintetsu line), but has its own pool table. Ask your hotel to call for directions, as it is a little tricky to find.

The earnestly named **Kent Authentic Bar** is located in Naramachi, around the corner from Naramachi Trattoria Washio. It has a huge sign with an unmissably prominent fake coat of arms. If none of these bars suit your taste, you will find innumerable *izakaya* in which to drink and snack in Naramachi, or in one of the shopping arcades in the centre of town.

For dance clubs and the like, Ōsaka or the **Metro** (*see* p.268) in Kyoto are your best bets.

Osaka: Gateway to Kansai

Japan's second city (pronounced 'OR-saka', with the first syllable long, not 'O-SAR-ka') is one of the most important in the world, and many visitors, especially businesspeople, will find themselves spending time here. It's a lively, rowdy, ugly place famous for its fierce dialect, *Ōsaka-ben*, and for its inhabitants, known throughout Japan as cheerful, warmhearted, money-minded rogues, a world away from the cool Tokyoites or the refined denizens of Kyoto. There are a few interesting things to see here, but Kansai is too rich, and life too short, to spend much time here, especially when Kyoto and Nara are both less than 45 minutes away by train. If you decide to spend the night, bustling spots such as the Namba area offer much of the same neon and excitement as Tokyo, and provide a glimpse of modern Japan—so different from the vestiges of ancient Japan you are likely to see in Kyoto or Nara that you will wonder how it could have derived from the same culture.

Getting There

Shin-Ōsaka is a major station on the Tōkaidō **bullet train** (*shinkansen*) line, under 3hrs from Tokyo by the fastest service, but it is some way north of the city centre: take a taxi or the Midosuji subway line.

JR lines pass through Ōsaka station, in the north part of town. This station merges with Umeda, the terminus for private **Hankyū Line trains** from Kyoto. The comprehensive **Kintetsu rail network** converges on Namba station, a few kilometres south of Umeda. There is also the inexpensive **Keihan Line** from central Kyoto to Yodoyobashi in Ōsaka.

From **Kansai International Airport,** trains and buses connect to the city centre in 30–60mins. The JR Airport Express 'Haruka' train is free with a Japan Rail Pass or a JR West Rail Pass (¥2,980 otherwise) and stops at Shin-Ōsaka station (48mins) and Tennōji station (30mins) and continues on to Kyoto (75mins, ¥3,490). Those without the JR Pass may prefer to take Nankai Railway's Rapid Express train which stops at Namba station (29mins, ¥1,400). An airport bus to Ōsaka or Shin-Ōsaka stations takes just over an hour and costs ¥1,300.

From **Itami Airport,** a bus costs around ¥500, depending on where you are going. The bus makes seven stops, including Shin-Ōsaka, Umeda (Ōsaka) and Namba stations, and takes about 25–50 minutes. Schedules and fare information are available at the information counter in the airport.

Getting Around

Ōsaka's **subway** system (*see map on inside front cover*) is one of the easiest to use in Japan. There's plenty of labelling in Roman characters, and the stops are all announced in English. Even if all else fails, the official municipal guide book is reassuring. 'Take joy in getting lost,' it urges. 'Like one in hell who happens across a Buddhist monk, you can expect only helpfulness and kindness from Ōsakans who will guide you back to the promised land.' The most useful line is the red **Midosuji** (north–south) which connects Shin-Ōsaka, Umeda, Shinsaibashi and Namba. The **JR Loop line** circles the inner city and connects with the subway at various points.

Tourist Information

If you are unable to make use of the Japan National Tourist Organization's tourist information center in Kansai International Airport (located on the first floor arrival lobby, *open daily from 9–9*, ✆ 0724 56 6025), don't despair. You can always call the very helpful (English-speaking) operators at Japan Travel Phone, ✆ 0120 44 4800/✆ 0088 22 4800 (toll free). You can also collect maps and information from the Ōsaka Tourist Information Centre (*open daily 8–8*). There are two branches: one is located at the JR Shin-Ōsaka station on the east side of the main exit (✆ 06 6305 3311); the other at the Midosuji exit of JR Ōsaka station (✆ 06 6345 2189).

Ōsaka's single finest attraction is on Nakanoshima, a river island a few hundred metres south of Umeda station: the **Museum of Oriental Ceramics**, an outstanding collection of mostly Chinese and Korean pieces. These are ceramics raised to the level of high art and, even if you thought you weren't interested in pots, the wit and sensuousness of these will move you. Look out for the Tang Chinese dancer, with her elongated body and thin arms still bearing traces of gilt; and the towered pavilion, a metre tall, complete with miniature guards and slaves, which was buried with a dead nobleman. Especially appealing are the soothing, pale green celadons: one Chinese bottle, a National Treasure, is rendered diseased-looking by the bold application of brown iron splodges below the glaze.

Apart from this, conventional sightseeing is a bit limited. The **castle** is situated in a nice park, but the keep is a 1960s reconstruction, and the ancient temple of **Shitennō-ji** is a concrete job too. **Sumiyoshi Taisha** is one of the most famous shrines in Japan and offers a good opportunity to see what Japanese architecture was like prior to the advent of Buddhism (*see* 'Art and Architecture', pp.76–82). The current buildings date from 1810, however, and, set forlornly in the middle of a bustling city, the shrine lacks the mystique of Fushimi in Kyoto, or Meiji Jingu in Tokyo.

Ōsaka's great strength is its entertainments. The **National Bunraku Theatre** presents the best puppetry in the country. **Namba** is the teeming nightlife district of bars and restaurants alongside canals and beneath covered arcades; its focus is a bridge called **Dōtonburi-hashi**, which is as good a place as any to start an evening. Anyone who has seen the Ridley Scott film *Black Rain* will recognize these streets and their atmosphere. Look out for the Häagen Dazs café opposite the Kirin Plaza on the north side of the bridge. Décor includes a merry-go-round of porcelain, half-naked women, and big silver chairs that occasionally buck. The bridge itself is a spectacle, particularly on weekends when the Zoot-suited fledgling Mafiosos are out in droves, grabbing every woman who walks by and attempting to sweet talk them into either a date or a career in Japan's booming sex industry.

Ōsaka has hotels in every price range; even at busy times you should have no difficulties finding a room somewhere.

luxury–expensive

In the luxury category, there is the **Hankyū International Hotel**, ✆ 6377 2100, 📧 6377 3622, long regarded as Ōsaka's finestf hotel, but now challenged by the marginally cheaper **Ritz Carlton**, ✆ 6343 7000, 📧 6343 7001. Both are conveniently located near JR Ōsaka and Umeda stations. A little less pricey are the **Ōsaka Tōkyū Hotel**, ✆ 6373 2411, 📧 6376 0343, also near JR Ōsaka and Umeda stations, and the **New Ōtani**, ✆ 6941 1111, 📧 6941 9769, overlooking the castle.

moderate–inexpensive

Moderately priced are: the **Riverside Hotel**, ✆ 6928 3251, 📧 6298 3260, 10 minutes by taxi from the JR station; **Hotel California** ✆ 6243 0333, 📧 6243 0148, a model of Japanese kitsch, the **Rihga Grand Hotel**, ✆ 6202 1212, 📧 6227 5054, with its grand lobby, and the small **Hotel Ōsaka Castle**, ✆ 6942 2401, 📧 6946 9043.

Inexpensive accommodations tend far away from the city centre, and you may as well head up to Kyoto or Nara if your budget is tight. One exception is the **Ebisu so Ryokan**, ✆ 6643 4861, located near Den Den Town and the National Theatre.

Eating Out

Ōsaka has a daunting range of places to eat, from world-class European restaurants in the big hotels to pushcarts serving seafood and noodles all night. The best strategy is to pick an area and wander around. **Namba** and **Shinsaibashi** are young, noisy and 24-hour. The area round **Umeda station**, in the north, is quieter and more grown-up, and closes earlier. Finding English speakers is rarely a problem.

If you are in the Umeda, **Isaribi**, ✆ 6373 2969, is worth a visit. It is a classic *robota-yaki* (*see* p.31), where an incredible variety of foods are cooked before customers sporadically shouting out orders, acknowledged by the cook's answering shout. Excellent food in an authentic, if loud and smoky, Ōsaka atmosphere.

If you are in the Namba area a 200-year old *oden* establishment called **Tako-ume**, ✆ 6211 0321, will provide you with an unforgettable experience. *Oden* is basic, working man's food; a delicious simple stew of *tōfu*, cabbage, potatoes, and chicken. It's all served up in an old wooden shop at the far eastern end of Dotonbori-dōri by kind, elderly women. Try the house sauce (a mustard-miso mix), and don't shy away from ordering unconventional items such as whale's tongue.

If you are looking for sushi, some of the best—and cheapest—sushi restaurants in the world can be found in the area just south of Hankyū Department Store (next to Umeda station) and just east of Midosuji.

Japanese isn't much like any other language in the world, and no one seems to have much of a clue where it comes from, or how it arrived where it did. Linguists relate it to the Hungarian-Magyar and Finnish (Altaic) languages, and suggest that all three may have originated in Central Asia. Modern Japanese has similarities with Korean; Turkish speakers are said to find it a very easy language to learn.

Nobody else does. The technical difficulties posed by Japanese are enough to deter the most fanatical linguist. The language has multiple levels of politeness, depending on who is talking to whom, about what, and where. The written language possesses two phonetic systems (three if you include the Roman alphabet) and more than 50,000 *kanji* or Chinese-derived characters. 2,000 of these are necessary to read a daily newspaper; the knottiest of them consist of more than 30 individual strokes, which must be individually memorized, in the correct order. There are no short cuts: full literacy in Japanese requires years of patient study.

The good news is that short-term visitors don't need to worry. Without a doubt, the more Japanese you know, the more you will get out of Japan and the easier your travels will be. But with initiative, patience and some forward planning it is quite possible to have a full and rewarding holiday in the most out of the way places without any Japanese at all.

Communicating without Japanese

All Japanese study English for years at high school. Many of them are taught from standardized text books, by Japanese teachers who may never have travelled abroad themselves. Quite understandably, most of them have no confidence and are as embarrassed by their English as you would be by creaky schoolboy French or German. But, with patience and encouragement, simple questions and answers can be made understandable to most Japanese under 30.

The first trick is to choose a likely-looking candidate. University students are the best bet (since they are required to study English to a fairly high standard), and after them business-types (who might use English in their work). Don't start jabbering questions immediately.

Language

Try first to establish eye contact, with a smile and a nod of the head and then a polite, 'Excuse me...do you speak English?' Most Japanese, even bilingual ones, are constitutionally incapable of answering yes to this question (modesty forbids), but don't be put off. Phrase your questions simply and directly, avoiding complicated tenses or figures of speech. Remember that most Japanese find written English much easier to follow than the spoken form; and that your pronunciation of Japanese names may bear very little resemblance to their native form. Carry a notebook to write down words, simple questions and maps.

Japanese Phrases

The key to using and being understood is pronunciation, which is technically much simpler than in English. This, ironically, is the difficulty—Japanese has fewer sounds, and English-speakers often try to introduce diphthongs and stresses where there are none.

There are just five vowel sounds in Japanese, similar to those in Spanish and Italian. Pronouncing the following sentence, keeping the vowels short, gives you their approximate sound, in order:

Ah, we soon get old.

A I U E O

Avoid pursing your lips for the **U**.

A macron over the vowel ('ā', 'ū', 'ō' etc) doubles the length of the vowel. Macrons are used throughout this book with two exceptions. The two most famous Japanese cities— Tōkyō and Kyōto—are not macronized, and nor are words—like judo and shogun—which have effectively entered the English language.

Syllables are pronounced evenly and in full, with no syllable bearing more emphasis than any other. This is difficult for English-speakers to get used to, and causes a lot of confusion when they come to Japanese names. The famous city which suffered the first atom bomb attack, for instance, is usually pronounced by foreigners as 'huh-ROSH-uh-muh'. The correct pronunciation stresses each syllable equally—'Hee-Roh-Shee-Ma'— and a Japanese will genuinely not understand its English pronunciation. The same goes for Ōsaka: correct pronunciation—something like 'oar-sucker', with a lingering first syllable; incorrect pronunciation—'uh-SARK-uh'. Tokyo is 'talk-your', not 'toe-key-oh'.

The exception to the rule about emphasis is the 'u' sound which is often swallowed in the middle of, or at the end of words. Thus *arigatō gozaimasu* (thank you) and *sukiyaki* (meat stew) sound more like 'arigatō gozaimass' and 'ski-yacky'.

Useful Phrases

Greetings

hello, good day	*konnichiwa*
hello (on the telephone)	*moshi moshi*
good morning	*ohayō gozaimasu*
good evening	*kombanwa*
good night	*oyasumi nasai*
goodbye	*sayonara*, or to children and between young women *bai bai*.

Basic Phrases

excuse me	*sumimasen* (all purpose);
	shitsurei shimasu (on leaving or pushing past someone)

I'm sorry	*Gomen nasai*
please (meaning 'please go ahead', 'please help yourself', 'after you')	*dōzo*
thank you	*arigatō* (neutral), *dōmo* (casual), *dōmo arigatō gozaimasu* (formal)
thank you very very much	*dōmo arigatō (gozaimasu)*
don't mention it; it's nothing	*dō itashimashite*
how are you?	*ogenki desuka?*
I'm fine	*genki desu*
do you speak (English)?	*(Eigo) ga dekimasu ka?*
French	*Furansugo*
Japanese	*Nihongo*
I speak a little	*sukoshi dekimasu*
I don't speak (Japanese)	*(Nihongo) wa dekimasen*
say that again please	*mō ichido itte kudasai*
is there someone here who speaks English?	*Eigo ga dekiru hito wa irasshaimasu ka?*
really? (lit. '[is it] true?')	*hontō?*
what a pity	*zannen desu*
too bad/it can't be helped	*shikata ga nai* (informally *shō ga nai*)

At a Restaurant

menu	*menyū*
chopsticks	*o-hashi*
knife and fork	*naifu to fōkku*
water	*mizu*
coffee	*kōhī*
tea	*ocha* (green tea)
	kōcha (black tea)
how much is (coffee)?	*(kōhī) wa ikura desu ka?*
this	*kore*
that	*sore*
that (over there)	*are*
(I want) that one, please	*sore o kudasai* or *Sore onegai shimasu*
the menu, please	*menyū o kudasai* or *Menyū onegai shimasu*
the bill, please	*gokanjō o kudasai*

Transport

where is (the station)?	(*eki*) *wa doko desuka*
bus station	*basu tāminaru*
taxi rank	*takushī noriba*
hotel (western style)	*hoteru*
what platform is the train to Ōsaka?	*Ōsaka yuki densha wa nan ban sen desuka?*
what time is the train to Ōsaka?	*Ōsaka yuki densha wa nan ji desuka?*
platform number (eight)	(*hachi*) *ban sen*
ticket office	*kippu uriba*

Numbers

one	*ichi*
two	*ni*
three	*san*
four	*shi* or *yon*
five	*go*
six	*roku*
seven	*shichi* or *nana*
eight	*hachi*
nine	*kyū*
ten	*jū*
eleven	*jū-ichi*
twelve	*jū-ni*
twenty	*ni-jū*
thirty	*san-jū*
one hundred	*hyaku*
two hundred	*nihyaku*
three hundred	*sanbyaku*
six hundred	*roppyaku*
one thousand	*sen*
ten thousand	*man*
twenty four thousand, six hundred and seventy three	*ni-man-yon-sen-roppyaku-nana-jū-san*

basho	**Sumo** (q.v.) tournament
bentō	lunch boxes filled with a variety of foods
bosatsu	Bodhisattvas; divine beings who have achieved Nirvana but choose to defer it in order to help others (*see* pp.95–6)
bunraku	traditional Japanese puppet theatre (*see* pp.89–90)
daimyō	regional lords under the **shoguns** (q.v.)
donburi	a large bowl of rice with toppings, often pork or seafood (*see* p.25)
futsū	a local train, stopping at every station (*see* p.8), also *kakueki teisha*
gaijin	lit. 'outside person'; foreigner
gohan	rice
goshō	palace
guriin-sha	lit. 'green car'; first-class carriage in trains (*see* p.8)
hakubutsu-kan	museum, also *bijutsukan, shiryōkan*
hashi (or *bashi*)	bridge
jinja	Shinto shrine (*see* p.90)
kabuki	a form of traditional Japanese theatre (*see* pp.88–9)
kaiseki ryōri	Japanese *haute cuisine* consisting of exquisitely presented dishes of fresh natural ingredients (*see* p.30)
kami	Shinto deity (*see* p.91)
kamameshi	rice casserole, like paella (*see* p.26)
karesansui	a dry garden. Many Zen gardens are examples of this style.
keiretsu	loose but powerful agglomerations of financial, commercial and manufacturing power (*see* pp.98–100)
kimono	traditional Japanese garment (*see* p.40)
kōen	park
kyūkō	express train (*see* p.8)
kyōgen	traditional Japanese theatre (*see* p.86)
kūkyo	Imperial Palace
mama-san	women who run bars or clubs
manjū	small cakes filled with red bean paste
matsuri	festival
mikoshi	portable shrine, carried at festivals
mingei	Japanese folk crafts (*see* pp.40–42)
minshuku	Japanese-style inn, often cheaper than **ryokan** (q.v.) (*see* p.47)
mochi	cakes made from pounded rice, eaten at festivals and New Year

Glossary

nabemono	lit. 'things in a pot'; a kind of stew with vegetables, *tōfu* and sometimes meat (*see* p.29)
nomi-ya	drinking place (*see* p.31)
nō	traditional Japanese theatre (*see* p.86)
nyōrai	Buddhas (*see* p.95)
o-furo	traditional Japanese bath (*see* p. 14)

o-hashi	chopsticks (*see* p.32)
onigiri	a rice ball covered with crisp seaweed and filled with anything from pickled plums (*umeboshi*) to fish (*see* p.25)
oden	working man's stew of fish sausage, *tōfu* and vegetables (*see* p.29)
okonomiyaki	a cross between a pizza and a pancake (*see* p.26)
onsen	hot springs, spa (*see* p.14)
o-tera	Buddhist temple (*see* p.90)
o-tearai	toilet (*see* p.45)
ramen	Japanized Chinese egg noodles served in a variety of broths (*see* p.26)
robata-yaki	hearty country-side grill cooking, performed in front of the diners (*see* p.31)
ryokan	Japanese-style inn (*see* p.47)
sake (o-sake)	Japanese rice wine
sashimi	morsels of seafood dipped into a special sauce (*see* p.28)
sentō	Japanese-style public baths (*see* p.14)
seppuku	suicide by disembowelment
shinkansen	bullet train (*see* p.9)
shogun	originally a chief commander, *shogun* came to mean a line of hereditary military dictators who ruled in the name of the emperors
shōjin ryōri	delicate vegetarian cuisine (*see* p.30)
soba	buckwheat noodles (*see* p.26)
sumo	Japanese wrestling (*see* pp.43, and 83)
sushi	vinegared balls of rice with pieces of cooked or raw fish or vegetables pressed on top (*see* p.28)
tatami	thick, rectangular Japanese straw matting used as a floor-covering. Rooms are measured by the number of *tatami* mats they contain, which are usually of a uniform size
teishoku	set meals, usually at reasonable prices
tempura	vegetables and seafood dipped in a light batter and fried (*see* p.27)
tōfu	bean curd
tokonoma	traditional Japanese alcove which often contains simple ornaments
tonkatsu	deep-fried pork cutlets (*see* p.27)
torii	entrance gates to Shinto shrines, often painted vermilion
tokkyū	usually translated as a 'limited express' train, which makes stops at very few stations.
tsukemono	Japanese pickles
yūkata	light cotton summer **kimono** (q.v.), often provided in inns
udon	plump wheat flour noodles (*see* p.26)
ukiyo-e	Japanese woodblock prints (*see* p.39)
washi	Japanese paper made from the pulp of mulberry branches (*see* p.41)
yakitori	skewered, grilled chicken or vegetables dipped in sauce (*see* p.27)
yakimono	lit. 'baked things'; Japanese ceramics (*see* p.39)
zaibatsu	early collectives of financial, commercial and manufacturing power (*see* pp.98–100)

Forests have been levelled to produce the thousands of books in print on Japan. Most of them are rubbish, or simply wrong and boring. In particular, cast a sceptical eye on anything promising 'instant' Japanese, anything offering to reveal 'the real Japan', and anything by former foreign correspondents. Most of the following books can be found in a specialist oriental bookshop like the ones listed in Practical A–Z on p.15. Publishers may vary from country to country: in Japan, Tuttle, Kodansha and Weatherhill specialize in English language titles. In the following list, family names precede given names.

History

Barr, Pat: *The Deer Cry Pavilion* and *The Coming of the Barbarians* (Penguin). Witty, gossipy histories of the foreign communities in the late 19th century.

Cook, Haruko Taya and **Cook, Theodore F.**: *Japan at War: An Oral History* (New Press). Compellingly dramatic first person accounts by combatants and civilians.

Morris, Ivan: *The Nobility of Failure* (Secker & Warburg). Brilliantly indirect study of Japanese thinking through its many martyrs and suicides. *The World of the Shining Prince* is a study of the halcyon Heian period, through the medium of *The Tale of Genji*.

Sansom, Sir George: Japan: *A Short Cultural History* (Stanford University Press). First written in the 1930s and still the standard work—thorough and scholarly.

Seidensticker, Edward: *High City, Low City* and *Tokyo Rising* (Penguin/Tuttle). Heartfelt, elegiac, beautifully written accounts of Tokyo from the Meiji period to the 1980s.

Statler, Oliver: *Japanese Pilgrimage* and *Japanese Inn* (Tuttle). Part scholarship, part travelogue; superbly digestible accounts of Japanese history through the stories, respectively, of the Shikoku Pilgrimage and an old *ryokan*.

Storry, Richard: *A History of Modern Japan* (Penguin). Concise and readable.

Waley, Paul: *Tokyo: City of Stories* (Weatherhill). Anecdotal histories of all the main areas; brings fascinating life to the concrete and expressways.

Business, Politics and Economics

Rice, Jonathan: *Doing Business in Japan* (BBC Books). A sensible, unpretentious introduction.

Tasker, Peter: *Inside Japan* (Penguin). Accessible, if a bit out-of-date, introduction to contemporary society and economics by a securities analyst who writes like a journalist.

Van Wolferen, Karel: *The Enigma of Japanese Power* (Macmillan/Tuttle). Controversial but brilliant analysis of what makes Japanese society so different.

Literature

Bashō, Matsuo: *The Narrow Road to the Deep North* (Penguin Classics). Classic *haiku* travelogue by the 17th-century poet who was never happier than when he was completely miserable.

Further Reading

Birnbaum, Alfred: *Monkey Brain Sushi* (Kodansha). Short stories by young Japanese writers.

Collins, Clive: *Misunderstandings* (Marion Boyars). The best English fiction writer on Japan—sad, understated, unpatronizing short stories.

Endō, Shūsaku: *Silence* and *The Final Martyrs* (Peter Owen/Tuttle). The most accessible of contemporary Japanese novelists.

Keene, Donald (ed.): *Anthology of Japanese Literature* (Penguin Classics). Representative selections of all the greats up to the 19th century.

Mishima, Yukio: *Confessions of a Mask* and *The Sea of Fertility* (Penguin/Tuttle). The first and last works of the most famous (and infamous) of Japan's novelists who committed ritual suicide after an attempted military coup in 1970.

Murakami, Haruki: *A Wild Sheep Chase* (Penguin). Droll, melancholy, bizarre novel by the most successful living Japanese novelist.

Lady Murasaki: *The Tale of Genji* (Penguin Classics). One of the great works of world literature: a long, delicate, poignant tale of life in the 11th-century Heian court.

Ōe, Kenzaburo: The Silent Cry (Serpent's Tail). The best-known novel by the winner of the 1994 Nobel Prize for Literature, a painful and unflinching story of a man and his disabled son.

Tanizaki, Junichirō: *The Makioka Sisters* (Tuttle). Moving novel about struggling Japanese gentlefolk in pre-war Kōbe and Ōsaka.

Thwaite, Anthony: *Letter from Tokyo* (Hutchinson). Mild, elegant poems about Japanese life.

Specialized Guidebooks

Durston, Diane: *Old Kyoto* (Kodansha). Fascinating, illustrated guide.

Kennedy, Rick: *Good Tokyo Restaurants* (Kodansha). Lives up to its name.

Martin, John H.: *Nara: A Cultural Guide* (Tuttle). Solid but informative temple guide.

Moriyama, Tae: *Tokyo Adventures: Glimpses of the City in Bygone Eras* (Shufunotomo). Gossipy, garrulous guide to walks and days out in Tokyo, by a likeable old lady.

Mosher, Gouverneur: *Kyoto: A Contemplative Guide* (Tuttle). Written in 1964, and never updated, but still the best book about the ancient capital, full of charm and historical anecdote.

Travel, Journalism and Society

Barthes, Roland: *Empire of Signs* (Cape). Essays on Japan by the playful structuralist semiotician. Not everyone's *tasse de thé*, but stimulating nonetheless.

Buruma, Ian: *A Japanese Mirror* (Penguin). Subtle analysis of Japanese pop culture.

Carter, Angela: *Nothing Sacred* (Virago). The five essays on Japan by the late novelist are the best imaginative journalism on the country in English.

Hearn, Lafcadio: *Writings from Japan* (Penguin). Well-chosen introduction to the troubled 19th-century Japanophile from Matsue.

Popham, Peter: *Tokyo: The City at the End of the World* (Kodansha). Earthquakes, crazy architecture, religious cults, rabbit hutch existence—captures the excitement and weirdness of life in the biggest machine in the world.

Arts and Architecture

Nishi, Kazuo and **Hozumi, Kazuo:** *What is Japanese Architecture?* (Kodansha). Big, practical guide with lots of diagrams and illustrations.

O'Neill, P. G.: *A Guide to Nō* (Hinoki Shoten). Pocket guide to plays and terminology.

Visions of Japan (Victoria and Albert Museum). Based on a 1991 exhibition; less a book than an assemblage of photographs, essays and found objects bound in a cardboard folder.

Chapter headings and main references are in **bold** type; page numbers of maps are in *italics*.

Index

Tokyo: Orientation (see map opposite)

Roughly in the centre is the empty green blob of the Imperial Palace. Just to the east of here is a dense conglomeration of office buildings and department stores and hotels, centering around Tokyo station. Many railway lines converge here, but the most useful for tourists is the Yamanote line which girds the city in an irregular oval loop, intersected by ten criss-crossing subway lines. This is Tokyo's most important railway, and its 29 stations enclose and include most of the places you will want to see while you are here.

The Yamanote line isn't a perfect circle, but its most important stations can be approximately counted off as the points of a clock:

At 3 o'clock is Tokyo station, adjacent to the Imperial Palace and districts like Ginza (famous for cafés and department stores) and Yūrakuchō (location of the tourist information centre).

At 4 o'clock is Hamamatsucō, where the monorail departs to and from Haneda, the domestic airport.

At 6 o'clock is Shinagawa, a convenient station for trains to Yokohama and the cities immediately south of Tokyo.

At 8 and 9 o'clock are Shibuya and Harajuku, centres of night-time entertainment and youth culture, and disembarkation points for Yoyogi Park and the Meiji Shrine.

At 10 o'clock the mighty city-within-a-city, Shinjuku, is home to the febrile Kabukichō red-light district, and a dense concentration of skyscrapers. At 11 o'clock is Ikebukuro, a smaller and less interesting version of Shinjuku.

At about 2 o'clock is Ueno, a historic area with a museum-filled park.

Yamanote means 'High City'; the area bounded by the Yamanote line still corresponds more or less to the land settled by the Tokugawa shoguns and their feudal servants (see History, pp.51–68). The 'Low City' or shitamachi still exists, in the districts to the east of Tokyo station around the Sumida River; the most interesting and accessible area, Asakusa, is directly east of Ueno.